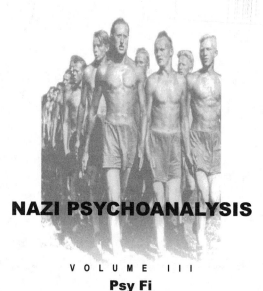

NAZI PSYCHOANALYSIS

VOLUME III
Psy Fi

Laurence A. Rickels

FOREWORD BY BENJAMIN BENNETT

University of Minnesota Press
Minneapolis • London

Nancy Barton grants permission to the University of Minnesota Press for the use of the image "Untitled—Testing" in *Nazi Psychoanalysis*.

Every effort was made to obtain permission to reproduce the illustrations in this book. If any proper acknowledgment has not been included here, we encourage copyright holders to notify the publisher.

Published by the University of Minnesota Press
111 Third Avenue South, Suite 290
Minneapolis, MN 55401-2520
http://www.upress.umn.edu

A Cataloging-in-Publication record for this book is available from the Library of Congress.

ISBN 0-8166-3700-8 (hc : alk. paper)
ISBN 0-8166-3701-6 (pbk. : alk. paper)

Printed in the United States of America on acid-free paper

The University of Minnesota is an equal-opportunity educator and employer.

12 11 10 09 08 07 06 05 04 03 02   10 9 8 7 6 5 4 3 2 1

NAZI PSYCHOANALYSIS

VOLUME III

NAZI PSYCHOANALYSIS

VOLUME I
Only Psychoanalysis Won the War

VOLUME II
Crypto-Fetishism

VOLUME III
Psy Fi

CONTENTS

Doubles

Epilogue on Fire

Foreword

BENJAMIN BENNETT

If the first two volumes of *Nazi Psychoanalysis* are mainly about the origin and development of "greater psychoanalysis," the war-born inner and outer space of Freud's inescapability in the twentieth century, then the business of this final volume, *Psy Fi*, is mainly to suggest conclusions and extrapolations that have a bearing on our present condition. The basic story is not hard to follow. Because Nazi Germany, itself "one big science fiction," co-opted "the ultimate science fiction fantasy, that of replacement of reproduction (which is death in life) with a new and improved immortality plan, that of amoeba-like and technology-compatible replication," it fell to "the Allied psychological war strategy" to take up "the struggle for what was thus endangered: family and couple, procreation and love." This more or less explains the Allies' "filing for victim status" in the very process of winning. And then, in a further twist, "Plane flight and TV viewing reset group psychology on the family pack format. The family was thus technologized and doubled as favorite haunt for all the balancing acts of techno-tension going down between the couple and the group, between reproduction and replication." But the story itself matters less than the question of *who is telling it*, who is in a position to comprehend and analyze its content. Science fiction itself, *sci fi*, lays claim to the analytic perspective, as do also the various psychotherapeutic genres, *psy fi*, that Rickels discusses alongside it, not to mention psychoanalysis itself, "the owner's manual of our ongoing technologization." But if it is really *our* technologization, where is the detached perspective from which to "own" or master it? Is it possible to draw a line between analysis itself (psycho- or otherwise) and the symptoms it analyzes? We can perhaps see this problem coming if we first step back a quarter millennium or so.

To the extent that a main point exists, the main point of Johann Georg Hamann's *Aesthetics in a Nutshell* (1762) is probably that scripture and history, and indeed nature itself, are all versions of a single text, a single divine writing, and that the purport of that writing depends radically on how the reader approaches it, which in turn never fails to involve the question of who the reader really is. These last two ideas are set forth with perfect clarity, toward the end of Hamann's text, in a pair of quotations, the first in Latin from St. Augustine, the second in German from Luther. But rather than call Augustine by name, Hamann cites him as "the Punic church father," with a footnote mark on the word "Punic." And if one follows that lead, if one descends here into what Laurence A. Rickels likes to call the text's "footnote underworld," one is dragged further and further away from anything like a main point. That "Punic" refers to Augustine's Carthaginian origins, Hamann doesn't bother to tell us; we're supposed to know. Instead, he begins with a reference to Johann David Michaelis's condescending remarks about Augustine's Latin style, and then jumps, via a pun (what else?) on the word "Punic," to the idea of "punning" as developed in an early-eighteenth-century English treatise (necessarily English, since "pun" in German is merely "Wortspiel") that is variously attributed to Swift and Sheridan, and jumps from there. . . . You see what I'm getting at, and if you have looked at the main text of the present book, you probably see something of my reasons for starting with Hamann and punning. Like Hamann, Rickels has important points to make, about the structure and growth of psychoanalysis and in general about the impossibility of marking off areas in modernity that are somehow sheltered from Nazi contamination. And like Hamann—who must at all costs deny systematic Lutheran theology access to his texts, lest his thought be co-opted into reinforcing exactly the postlapsarian division between scripture and nature against which it is directed—Rickels has excellent reasons for what he terms his "user-unfriendly" procedure. Psychoanalysis, as Rickels means it, is not, strictly speaking, susceptible to being written or known "about." The pretense of possessing an objective or innocent verbal instrument with which to take hold of psychoanalysis violates the discursive implications of the subject matter in exactly the same way that Hamann's Christianity is violated by theological systematics.

Does it follow, then, that the present work is accessible only to strict insiders, only to psychoanalysts? In fact, psychoanalytic literature abounds with formulations of the peculiarly evasive quality of its core discipline; perhaps the best known is Jacques Lacan's remark that what the unconscious "is" cannot be disentangled from the circumstances of its discovery and the person of its discoverer. The theory of psychoanalysis, we are told, is never fully detached from its object, never in command of it, but always itself a self-relativizing instance of analytic procedure; in Rickels's arguments, specifically, it is the analytic mechanism of transference that turns out repeatedly to be operative, on a large public scale, in the history of the discipline. Everything is provisional or heuristic in psychoanalysis; there is no level of abstraction at which the discipline might in principle stand wholly revealed to the gaze of pure intelligence. (We think of the aspirations of Hamann's Wolffian contemporaries.) Understanding is never distinct from practice, and to "understand" a work such as Rickels's is therefore always in some sense to be a practitioner. But in exactly what sense?

The parallel case of Hamann continues to help us here. To be an insider with respect to Hamann means to be the adherent of a special kind of trans-theological Christianity, or at least to recognize its presence as an analogue in one's own philosophical practice. Therefore it is not hard to imagine why Hegel and Kierkegaard should be among Hamann's prominent admirers. But to find Goethe in this group, the older, "classical," self-consciously heathen Goethe, is a bit startling. And yet it is true that Goethe, who was in possession of some interesting manuscript material, for a long time considered actually editing Hamann. In book 12 of *Dichtung und Wahrheit*, he characterizes Hamann as follows:

> When a person speaks, he must become for the moment one-sided; there is no communication, no written doctrine, without particularity. Since Hamann, however, was once and for all opposed to this sort of separation, and since he desired to speak in the same all-embracing manner in which he felt, imagined, and thought, and since he demanded the same of others, he stood in opposition to his own style and to everything that others could produce. In order to accomplish the impossible, he therefore lays hands on all conceivable elements of writing.

This does not read like unequivocal praise, and in fact, a few lines later, Goethe speaks of a historical "darkness" into which Hamann's writings descend. But then, toward the end of the same long paragraph, we hear that if we take the trouble to look up some of Hamann's references, we encounter

> an ambiguous double illumination which strikes us as highly agreeable, as long as we resolutely avoid requiring what one would usually call an "understanding" of it. Such pages therefore deserve to be called "sibylline," because one cannot take them in and for themselves, but must wait for the occasion when one is specially moved to seek refuge in their oracular quality.

Surely, when he speaks of "seeking refuge" in Hamann, Goethe is not referring to any specific religious content. What he means can only have to do with Hamann's attempt at an impossible "all-embracing" form of writing. Hamann's texts, I mean, are a place where one seeks refuge *as a writer,* as a practitioner of writing, as a struggler with the "one-sidedness" of writing— not because Hamann in any degree solves the problem of writing but because, by straining its limits, he *situates* that problem, thus profiles it for us and offers us a "scene of writing" in which our particular performance, though still indelibly marked with futility, makes a kind of quasi-dramatic and historical sense after all.

And by alluding to Derrida's essay "Freud and the Scene of Writing," I mean of course to make the connection with psychoanalysis and Rickels. The kind of practitioner implied as the reader of Rickels's trilogy, I contend, is a *writer*, in the sense obliquely suggested by Goethe for Hamann.

> Freud [writes Derrida] *performed for us the scene of writing*. But we must think of this scene in other terms than those of individual or collective psychology, or even anthropology. It must be thought in the horizon of the scene/stage of the world, as the history of that scene/stage. Freud's language is *caught up* in it.

The "one-sided" move of the writer—which Goethe vaguely calls "separation," whereas Derrida would relate it to *différance*—not only is imposed by the world but also in a sense *establishes* the world as a "scene" (and how else would it become "world" in history?) by performing it. Derrida suggests that in writers like Freud, this quality of performance lies closer to the surface than elsewhere. But writers like Hamann—and Rickels—still constitute a special class, in that their performance is informed by a depth of resistance (a "user-unfriendly" stance "in opposition") that strains the boundaries, and thus marks them, and so *sets* the scene of writing. Not permanently, not once and for all: if this were possible, then "one-sidedness" would not be a necessary attribute of writing after all. Rather, as a moment of respite or "refuge," a kind of breathing space. This does not mean that one must "actually" be a writer to read Rickels with profit. But one does have to be able to adopt a writerly point of view, to read without falling into the comfortably dependent relation of consumer to a presumed producer, to manage one's handling of the text so that there is in the end no strict "user" for anyone to be unfriendly to. One must approach Rickels not in terms of "the oppositions sender-receiver, code-message" (these "coarse instruments," Derrida calls them), but rather so as to engage (Derrida again) "the *sociality* of writing as *drama*."

To be less cryptic about it, one can in fact formulate as a proposition the basic implications of Rickels's difficult style. His use of wordplay and allusion and quotation insists constantly on the point that neither knowledge itself nor the objects of knowledge can reasonably be said to exist in a manner that is strictly prior to, or at all independent of, the discursive acts and techniques by which they are shaped, the verbal garments in which they make their appearance to us. Which means, in turn, that there is no way of describing a clear division between the referential and logical structure of argument on the one hand, and, on the other, the structure of relations (the arbitrarily grammatical as well as the associative and allusive) that constitute the general verbal horizon in which we happen to be operating. Rickels's particular talent as a stylist is his ability to keep this proposition in the foreground of his presentation, even while suggesting a large number of specific and cohesive interpretive arguments on another level. And just this foregrounding, in turn, is crucial in relation to the subject matter, including the inseparability of theory and practice in psychoanalysis, and the impossibility of establishing a strict division between the two concepts in the work's main title. Foregrounding, however, is the form in which this point appears in Rickels, not formulation; for formulation (including the one I have just suggested) automatically offers its reader the safe, separated position of a consumer (we recall Goethe on "separation"), which contradicts exactly the point being formulated. Formulation requires understanding as a response. But as Goethe says of Hamann, "understanding" is out of place here. How can this be? What do we *miss* in the present text by "understanding" it?

Rickels answers this question when he speaks of his project as the "excavation" of material and the maintenance of its "materiality." The trouble with systematic argument in general, and our understanding of it, is that it (so to speak) dematerializes its material, imposes on the material an order that supplants the structure of the experience of finding it more or less unprepared. This is not to say that either Rickels or we are trying to preserve cultural-historical material in something like an "original" state—a state of the sort that can in fact never reasonably be said to exist. Nor can either we or Rickels reliably reproduce the more or less immediate experience of seeing our not-seeing psychoanalysis. (The ocular metaphor in the pun "Nazi = not-see" produces a contradiction for the understanding here, but not a material impossibility in experience.) Nor, finally, does Rickels ever actually avoid systematic argument. Rather, by the use of balance or tension between argumentative and associative structures, Rickels positions his reader— constantly, from sentence to sentence—so as to enable him or her to go as far as possible (whatever that means in each particular case) toward recovering the materiality of the work's material, without ever losing hold of its (argumentatively established) significance. Materiality, moreover, is also the key to Rickels's use of quotation. A style based heavily on quotation, once a certain density is arrived at—as in Rickels (or Hamann)—begins to body forth the understanding that meaning in language is never really anything *but* quotation, that *langue* and *parole*, in other words, the governing linguistic system and the mass of actual instances, are not really distinct, that language, even in that aspect that is systematized in grammars and lexica, is entirely constituted by the accumulation of material in the form of particular utterances. Indeed, Rickels's fondness for pop-cultural quoting establishes this point at a more immediate level of linguistic practice than, for example, Hamann's quoting mainly from scripture and classics plus commentaries and glosses.

To the extent that a main point exists, the main point of *Nazi Psychoanalysis* is probably that Nazism cannot be isolated in the structure of modernity, that no element of modernity can be thought adequately without thinking its Nazi component. "That's right, it's about facing the continuity that was there: Nazi psychoanalysis, Nazi Marxism, Nazi deconstruction." But this is not a point that can be "understood" in the normal sense of the word, for understanding it would produce a detached critical perspective for the understander, hence an element of modernity (precisely the intellectual juncture at which this understanding takes place) that is thoroughly purged of any Nazi contamination after all. The point, rather, as Rickels suggests, must be "faced" in all its immediate material undigestibility. Or seen from a different angle, it must be *performed*, as Rickels's style performs the identity of meaning and quotation. If you want theory, you go to Derrida, who in fact produces what is in essence a neat theory of "greater psychoanalysis" in his argument on how the opening of Freud's discourse "to the theme of writing results in psychoanalysis being not simply psychology—nor simply psychoanalysis." But in Rickels, what you get is better termed, if not perfectly termed, performance.

For this reason, finally, I will not attempt to do more than Rickels himself does, in the matter of summarizing the present volume, when he indicates that all the material here is affected by the proposal of a "shift . . . in the genre and theory of 'science fiction,' back down inside the hot era of preparations for, and realizations of, World War II." Instead, I will simply point the reader toward one or two of what happen to strike me as the most interesting pieces of material. The long section that takes off from *Werther*, for instance, including the chapters "Werther Report" through "U.S. Is Them," creates a kind of vortex that begins with the tension between heterosexual and homosexual, or reproduction and replication ("the fundamental metapsychological plot of the science fiction impulse"), and quickly draws in *Faust* and the theory of adolescence, then Theweleit, then Reich, Adler, Deleuze, Guattari ("homophobic interventions"), and Adorno on psychoanalysis and homosexuality (and Nazism), then the question of homoerotic Nazi propaganda and conversion ("Nazi *Werther* remakes"), with suicide still an option, then Hoffmann's "Sandman" and science fiction and Shelley's *Frankenstein* and a man named Goette; this is Rickels at his best, making huge intellectual and historical leaps in quick succession but without ever losing focus. And in "The Psychotic Sublime," with the figure of Schreber, the focus on science fiction is established and is maintained at least through "Hunger." This lengthy section not only is clear and coherent as an argument but also contains moments of startling wit, like the metaphorical exploitation of the idea of bacterial infection from *The War of the Worlds*, and moves at the end from "sci" to "psy" by a neat transition that uses Huxley's "Ford/Freud" in *Brave New World*.

It is true that some readers will still be bothered by the associative aspect of this writing, by the virtual structural equivalence in it of "real" historical or factual relations and those verbally mediated relations, as it were material puns *(sci/psy)*, that one is tempted to call "coincidence." But the thing about coincidence in this sense is that it refuses to go away; there is no home for it, no grave, in our filing systems. A strictly real relation gets used up in its reality and so always gets left behind, disposed of, by any reasonably adequate representation in language. But a coincidence, whose substance is both verbal *and* factual, or at least the sort of pregnant coincidence that is repeatedly brewed up by Rickels's broad knowledge and analytic skill, sticks in the craw of language, so to speak, and confuses the comfortable triangle of producer-consumer-object, as if reality had wrenched the instrument from our hand and were writing itself. The separation between reality and writing, the space of a presumed visibility that hides not-seeing from view—or as Hamann (who else?) would say, the separation between nature and scripture, which makes space for us to accept, for instance (as not-seeingly in the eighteenth century as in the twentieth), the notion of an enlightened politics—this separation is not transcended so much as it becomes, for the time being, in a manner of speaking, hard to swallow.

In other words, as long as you expect Rickels to do something for you— to teach you, to improve you, to take you somewhere—as long as you insist on something "positive," you will be disappointed. Reading, in the age of the novel, is generally understood as the mental equivalent of traveling. When you read—as when you place yourself physically in unfamiliar surroundings—you take a kind of vacation from your identity. This applies not only to the reading of novels, where it is obvious, but also to the reading of expository texts, where you try to be objective or open-minded (which means, not yourself), in order to understand the writing "in and for *it*self." But this attitude is as misplaced with Rickels as Goethe says it is with Hamann. You are never going to have all of this book anyway. The way you in fact are, as yourself, named, scarred, broken, accidental, radically compromised, like modernity *it*self, is how this book wants its reader, and how you, the reader, want the book.

Achtung

Ruth Eissler reports the successful analytic treatment in a case
of acute paranoid delusion. A young woman whose mother is
of German ancestry accuses herself of being an "innocent Nazi
spy" when her husband, a member of a depreciated minority
group, is about to be drafted. In one of his last papers, Freud
has asserted that each delusion contains a kernel of historic
truth from infantile sources. In Eissler's case, the "truth" is a
miscarriage of the mother at the height of the patient's Oedipus
complex. The traumatic position was later fortified when a girl
cousin died of tuberculosis. She had been closely attached to
this girl and employed a secret code in communication with
her. This code she unconsciously used in her psychotic episode
again, thus getting magically in touch with the dead. In her
paraphrenic language, "Nazi" was really "not see"—referring
to the magic destruction of the unseen rival.

—FRANZ ALEXANDER AND GERHART PIERS, "PSYCHOANALYSIS"

If we were to list all institutions that supported this project and, on the
other side, the many distinguished addresses that could not follow at all,
rejected it out of their hands, passed on the user-unfriendly writing, we
would be reminded, more by metonymy I suppose than by any direct reference, that there was, after all, the one side that won the war. I hope this reassurance will in some measure uncanny-proof my thousand-page *Reich.*

What may strike some as obstructive in this manner of genealogy or
total history is less the style of writing or argument than the insistence on
staying with the materials in the juxtapositions in which they can be and
have been thought. The book is nonphobic about what comes its way. But
most important of all, the space of this tension between low and high, literary and historical, material and interpretation comes right out of the force
field of Freud's legacy. It's an allegorical tension that comes down to the
unrepresentable gap lying between the in-session experience of the transference and the shorthand of analytic theory. Here we find the materiality
of psychoanalysis, through which all concepts continue to pass. The silent
but pressing inclusion of this tension in psychoanalytic theorizing was what
Freud was listening to when he allowed for a distinction between his science
and philosophy. It's what I want you to hear whenever you, dear reader,

already a survivor of the collision between "Nazi" and "Psychoanalysis," come across, in the reading that lies just ahead, juxtapositions or even contaminations of blocks or blockages of time or language. Mourning (or rather unmourning) is the model of this work. It's work, all work, that takes the time—the times—it takes to mourn and unmourn. The metabolization of materials in *Nazi Psychoanalysis*, while partial to digestion, owes its often merely partial digestion of blocks of writing (or writing blocks) to its working of unmourning. The materiality I have in mind here (while I mind or watch over it) is rather the result of a kind of internal vomiting (Derrida's image for the melancholic act in *"Fors"*) that saves text or artifact in an eternal state of digestion without end.

Nazi Psychoanalysis, which marks the final installment of my trilogy on "Unmourning," is committed, over and again, to the excavation of a missing era in all its materiality. That is why the hierarchization, the implied transparency, the transit-centering and visitation rights afforded by footnotes and subject index have been left out. My theoretically untenable and therapeutically necessary position is that this is *the* book. It brings something to a conclusion that can be reached only through reading that works through the projections of "unfriendliness."

In the course of the dig, as they all rose to consciousness, the materials kept on putting in uncanny connections between so many of the split-off, discontinuous segments of our standard tradition or reception of good modernism, good psychoanalysis. The influence we now see come out in the watch of the materials relies on a sense of audience that puts on Freudian ears to listen behind the lines: out of the noisy wear and tear of resistance there emerges one genuine line of influence, the kind that represents real change. A clean transferential cutting in of "the father," say, into the place of the analyst or therapist can promote the immediate cause of healing; but in matters of influence—a matter psychoanalysis alone made an issue of its science, also in the sense that there was no influence until we learned how to interpret for the transference, the resistance, the defense—the intactness of a foreign corpus inside another's identity or identification indeed symptomatizes a host or ghost of issues but does not, finally, give the measure of any influence.

The least likely place to look, therefore, which was where previous studies of the Nazi history of psychoanalysis and the psychodynamic therapies tended to start and stop, is the small band of certified analysts who stayed on in Germany after 1933 (only one "Aryan" analyst felt it was the time to leave with his Jewish colleagues) and formed compromises that, out of context of the big influence, and slipping into and around see-through rationalizations, seem but an abect of study. Even the wider bandwidths measuring the entire eclectic setting of the old analysts back together again with their former competitors, the Adlerians and Jungians, who thought they had split psychoanalysis once and for all, only come in shortwave. There was the obvious prestige and scope of application of psychotherapy with full state support. The backing the German Institute of Psychological Research and Psychotherapy received was given directly, no problem, or it came, in triumph, at the end of another corridor skirmish with bio-neuropsychiatry. Psychotherapy openly maintained its outright lead in the contest with psychiatry until, after Stalingrad, the analytic-therapeutic influence became less public in its broadcasting out to the war effort. But there is evidence that frontline work with schizo soldiers was still being conducted in ways and means compatible with greater psychoanalysis. The corridor wars between analytic psychotherapy and neuropsychiatry, which had already commenced upon Freud's first full entry into the field of psychological interventionism by way of the extremely good rep psychoanalysis received during World War I as treatment of choice for war neurosis, frame the ambiguous status and conflicting verdicts or second opinions that affected the nonreproductive members of Nazi German society. At the therapeutic end of the corridor, homosexuals were under treatment to be healed (with all the other neurotics, including the symptomatizing soldiers); but if the neuropsychiatrists got hold of them, they went the one way of all the other untreatables. This split-leveling of homosexuality occupies the bottom line of projections ultimately held in common and in conflict at all ends of the corridor.

But even the Institute-sized networking of the materials sets a limitation on the ranging of Freud's effects, which were rolled over beyond the jurisdiction of the reunified analytic psychotherapies. Psychotherapeutic standards of correctness and correction, according to which every German was to be given one more chance, were too popular to be contained within the history of one institute. From the close of World War I through the end of World War II, Germany was a pop-psychological culture of all-out healing. Before the baton could be passed to California, the current finish line of eclectic psychotherapy for all, the big splits between the Germanys and between a good German psychoanalysis and a disowned German neoanalytic therapy were all that the Germans, their victims, and their conquerors could do to defend themselves.

Nazi Psychoanalysis reconnects all the outposts of frontline intrapsychic theorization and treatment inside the orbit of the central psychotherapy institute in Berlin. One more jump cut through the material, one that once again doesn't follow Institute guidelines, tunes in the otherwise least likely candidates for analytic influence, military psychologists trained in psycho-technical methods. In particular, their specialized understanding and man-agement of the relations obtaining between pilots and their flying machines reflect a Freudian influence strong enough to receive and transmit between the lines. These psychotechnical relations, which were seen to be always shock-absorbed with what was fundamentally traumatic about artificial flight, follow the intrapsychic model where few analytic thinkers had gone before, right up to the head of the receiving line of Freud's reading of tech-nology. It was this double reading of a Freudian techno-criticism that my first two books, *Aberrations of Mourning* and *The Case of California,* already sought to raise to consciousness from behind the lines of Freud's studies of psychosis, melancholia, perversion, and group psychology. In *Nazi Psycho-analysis,* the long haul through tracts on war neurosis, military adjustment, and psychological warfare, all of which had been abandoned, now in the ditches of one world war, now inside the air-raid shelters of the other one, leads to a reconstruction of what can be called to this day "greater psycho-analysis." By World War II, between the air-raid sheltering of the populace in a group-therapeutic mode and the intrapsychic wiring of the pilot to his machine, an axis of technologization was being followed, up through cybernetics (both in Gregory Bateson's sense of feedback and in Jacques Lacan's staging of the rearview mirror) all the way out to the fantasy hori-zon of science fiction, which is where this book begins again.

What the particular science fiction that was Nazi Germany tried to outfly belonged to the gravity, the grave, of earthbound or limited supplies, which each time marked the spot the German war machine was in when the world came to war. To open up the underworld commentary that runs with the flights of techno-fantasy, focus can be fixed on an ambiguously held term or introject, the German word *Bestand,* in which the notions of re-serve supplies and staying power are combined, and which goes by "stand-ing reserve" in translations of Heidegger's use of the word (in his essays on technology). Here we find the melancholic scarcity or lack that through total mobilization was to be transformed, like a wound, as in takeoff, into the miracle of flight all the way to fetish victories of rocket or robot bomb-ing. But the itinerary of flight was all along skipping another beat around the rush for prospects for technologization and group psychologization. It was the master beat of reproductive coupling. By the time of his essay on fetishism, Freud was staying tuned to the impulses of gadget love that we've been jamming with ever since the onset of technologization. Techno-fantasies or science fictions have, at least since the eighteenth century, special-featured the overcoming of a crisis in reproduction through the self-replicating prospects of immortality now (in other words, without the loss of generation). This is the place of tension to which Freud assigned the fetishist, after first discovering it over the symptomatizing body of the war neurotic: between, on one side, the attractions of splitting or doubling within a borderline zone lying across neurosis and psychosis and, on the other side, the requirements that are still and for the time being with us, the same old ones that only reproduction can keep on fulfilling for the survival of the species. Thus through the fetish future that science fiction holds open and shut, the continuity back then that we're addressing here for the first time can be brought back into real-time proximity with the live or dead issues that currently occupy the media grounds for our existence.

Achtung contains the word of caution but also the word for respect. In the course of gathering all the materials that fit my monster topic I benefited from many leads given me by the following individuals I think/I thank: Nancy Chodorow, John Boskovich, Elliot Jurist, Friedrich Kittler, Wolf Kittler, Peter Loewenberg, Ursula Mahlendorf, Karl Rickels, Avital Ronell, Lorraine Ryavec, Ursula Schreiter, Brenda Silver, Lawton Smith, Robert Tobin. My project was supported by fellowships from the Alexander von Humboldt Foundation, the Center for German and European Studies (University of California–Berkeley), The Interdisciplinary Humanities Center (University of California–Santa Barbara), and the Academic Senate (University of California–Santa Barbara). It took me more than two years to place this book. My *Achtung* has therefore been won in the first place by the University of Minnesota Press. Thanks to William Murphy and Doug Armato for their support of my project.

When I first opened up shop with the materials of Nazi psychoanalysis in 1991, I right away enrolled in a local clinical psychology graduate program and commenced my training as a therapist in the setting of licensure in California. My training in California as just another psychotherapist whose eclecticism remains, by training, stuck on the parts of psychoanalysis that "work" afforded me the next-best thing to being there, at the Nazi German institute of psychotherapy in Berlin. The measure of California freedom in eclecticism is that no one will pass the "treatment" and "treatment plan" sections of the oral licensing exam who does not demonstrate willingness to engage with the client in a medley of active interventions, exercises, assignments. What is thus tested is the candidate's objective overview and consumerism of any technique that is out there. There can be no method or theory to which primary care or following is owed. That the candidate for licensing as marriage family therapist is nevertheless required on the same test to recognize the impact on the client focus in therapy of his or her own countertransferences is the sole remnant of theoretical orientation that the Board of Behavioral Sciences upholds. As we saw with Adler's attempt at making psychoanalysis more responsive to common or community sense, the setting that would be theory free must at the same time be transference free. As if!

This study was completed in 1995. Beginning in 1991, I presented papers and published articles advertising my discoveries and their final destination as part of work I was pursuing at book length. Discoveries I had made, for example, in the prehistory of Nazi German investments in psychotherapy that had their primal scene in Freud's World War I reading of war neurosis, among other headlines from the trenches of my dig, were thus fixed in the same space as my name. Nineteen ninety-five remains the cutoff point for my published interest in contemporary accounts of these "same" histories. If a certain first-generation historian of Nazi German psychotherapy, who is given credit for his study in the first volume of *Nazi Psychoanalysis* in the exact amount due, has since 1995 published an "expanded" new edition of his work that suddenly takes another look at the materials by the stolen fire of my work (admittedly reduced to a night-light by the shame of it), then I can only make the referral to Karl Kraus, who had all there is to say about the double failure in journalism and prostitution that leaves the loser only one option by default—the small-change careerism of academics.

The conditions of this book's possibility are shown in the stop and go of the book's flow, in the jackhammering overlaps and refrains comprising or reprising its formulations. Originally this conditioning momentum was not only about marking certain discoveries and readings in time (as mine), but it also arose out of the compromising of the academic's write to publish by the administration of how one makes a killing, I mean a living, at the university. But let this be my plaint (rather than another complaint in the conversation of complicity) and leave me to weave it into the text by which I stand. In fact I am grateful to those institutional conditions of compromise or conflict that cannot but underscore that thoughtful writing is the work of reformulation and precisely not in the business of telling you what to "think" or swim in a campaign of well-made arguments, advertisements, or grant proposals.

Conferences, journals, and collections keep one connected to the outside world or word one keeps in writing. Otherwise my colleagues are my students, and my institutional affiliation is with the auditorium in which I happen to be—encouraging the following or understanding of my colleagues. I therefore thank all the instances and institutions of publishing that gave me deadlines to hold on to outside the grin-and-bury-it regime of university life. A complete documentation of the many rehearsal opportunities I was given by these placements of publication can be viewed on the Web at a site (for sore I's) created by my former colleague Peter Krapp: http://www.hydra.umn.edu.twd/.

That *Nazi Psychoanalysis* documents both the uncanny continuity running through what has been declared history and its own history as research and writing project sets off (and apart) a logic or style of shifting, shifty crossovers that can be hard repressed to get across. Thanks to my copy editor, Bill Henry, the document now does, in the meantime and for the time to come, transmit in finer tuning with your receiver. I owe thanks to Jim Markham for his expert interventions in my last-minute reference crises.

In the spirits of Freud's proverbially paranoid charge that Schreber's endopsychic perceptions into his inner workings had also scooped Freud's theories—but, as he called on witnesses to prove, hadn't in fact compromised his independence—I submit that I did not finally read Pynchon's *Gravity Rainbow* from cover to cover until the cleanup operations of copyediting were already well under way. Is there too much fiction in my theory, in my history? Let us at least (at last!) formulate one more "paranoid proverb." The openly admitted cathexis of the Nazi German rockets notwithstanding, *Gravity's Rainbow* isolates psychoanalysis from this force field and loses Freud's science in sections of the war-of-words effort and spells its outdated doom (in contrast to the boom, however ambivalently introjected, we submit as the countertestimony of greater psychoanalysis). If psychoanalysis is finally subsumed in Pynchon's novel by the overriding occult trappings (or entrapments) introduced into the rocket-mobilized media/mediums of world war, then, as the proverb goes, it attended its own funeral. But it is just the same important to see just why *Gravity's Rainbow* became the inside story and scripture for machine historians and techno-theorists who prefer to keep implicit or complicit only one brand of psychoanalysis, the one implicated as returning in and from its exclusion as Freudian, namely, the work or applications of Jacques Lacan. The partial objective of this *Gravity's Rainbow* coalition is to skip the transferential responsibilities owed, all in a mourning's work, to the relational differences that even (or especially) auto-accelerating velocities of machine invention mark or make. These scholars have come to praise psychosis and in this way (as in the way) bury Freud's science. The Heyer and higher buildup given in this volume keeps us grounded—in the metapsychological fact that science fantasies (and rockets) taking off into psychotic outer space during the Third Reich required a world from which they could separate, the world saturation bonded with greater psychoanalysis.

For all the intrapsychic intricacies admitted into the Nazi German airhead there was always also that leading separation that had to be maintained in all its purity between Aryans and Jews. The difference that is always self-difference could only be displaced until what went around came back to a difference within—from which, at close quarters, one can jump-cut away only through suicide. But an afterlife of differences intercepted this old fascist short circuit or shortcut of suicide and brought it all back inside the science fiction of doubling and replication not yet realizable on earth. Thus at least for the psy fi future, the purity dead ends of a bad Aryan day opened up again—opened wide—around the prospect of intrapsychic difference that clone prospecting cannot but admit.

German Jewish physicists were forced to leave behind their Aryan colleagues who lost the race for the ultimate miracle weapon of atomic power. That these Aryan colleagues came close to paranoia on this near-missing racecourse is demonstrated in the attempts made to apply pressure through the race laws newly imposed in occupied Denmark on physicist Niels Bohr, who was Danish Jewish, to release the missing secret. But at the same time, Nazi German authorities, symptomatically on purpose, kept their research funding in stream line with the ascendancy of rockets. Proposals for more effective antiaircraft missiles were left unsupported and undeveloped by the powers that were totally into rocket flight. In Nazi Germany the importance of group therapy arose with the thrust for support of rocket offense (and the abandonment of antiaircraft defense). In contrast to what the Allies ended up with in their portfolio of greater psychoanalytic investments, on the Nazi German side, older family values were retained only as PR for group bonds. At the latest in the time between the soldiers' techno-traumatization in war zones and the scheduling of their postwar homecoming, the U.S. military-psychological complex turned to the family setting to throw the therapeutically correct fit with the future that the soldier boys were bringing home. As we will see, the Nazi Germans were equally intent on setting up television as cinema's replacement on the older medium's own turf or terms. As many as three hundred viewers could crowd into one of Nazi Berlin's "television rooms." Jung kept on claiming that the Aryan way was teenage all the way. Certainly this applied in his case. But this group or teen bond, while indeed very high in energy content, wasn't the only future stock. As cited in Kurt Hesse's study of leadership, a certain Pfülf (identified, moreover, as a student and disciple of Le Bon) recommends the small-size military unit as fortifying the all-important nerves of individual and group.

He gives the family as example of the size he has in mind. The strongest nerves win the war! (86). Whereas peer pressurization streamlines group formation, this group identity can be circuited through the family too, no longer the old extended-family format, but the model of family as reunion intersection of separate generations, each living on its own in the give-and-fake between the couple and the group. This was the nuclear family that the Allies saw through to retrofitting as techno-setting in front of the tube, in "group" therapy sessions, and on the plane (the pilot isn't really all alone up there).

On a clear day you can see psychoanalysis both in the recent primal past and in the future now. The overdetermination of a Freudian influence is not about a responsibility or codependency diagnosis (the deep sitting-stuck fear of the overprotectors). Only the analytic discursivity is in positions to contain the Nazi symptom, for even historically, the symptom we're all still struggling to bust was already highly saturated with psychoanalysis. Another healing, more long term in its scheduling, more long span in the attention that can be given in-session materiality, is still in order, on order, in the works. Let the closure begin.

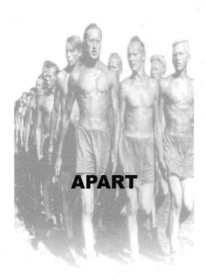

APART

It's Back!

On all the sides—on the inside—of total war, the upward mobilizations of the intrapsychic model were along for a drive to control air power and airspace. A rapport with air space was being built from the internal body on out—all the way to the body of the group. Freud located the techno-phantasmic impulses of flight as belonging not only in the home but also to the bigger futures and time-shares that are up there, including military expansionism down the mediatic lines of sensorium extension and—really the same share of one fantasy—psychotic delusion formation, where the wound of takeoff or castration is metabolized as the wonder or marvel of our technologization in inner-outer space. It is air force that is with this apparatus of projection beaming ghostly visitations across the force field of ambivalence and thus, even or especially when alien being or beaming is coming across, belongs to the German genre of psy fi.

Freud summarized researching the skies when he pointed out, for example, that dream interpretation (which was always high in prophecy content) was the placeholder in the past for airborne reconnaissance and surveillance, which in the meantime had advanced to the front of the line of all war efforts (*SE*, 15:85–86). At the outermost reach of this escalation on inner and outer fronts, Freud saw World War I as already on the air when, still in peacetime, the first German zeppelin crossed English airspace (*SE*, 22:177–78). The war would walk this new wide side of the race for control of the airwaves. That's why Freud's World War I scan of the internal doubling going down in war neurosis was soon going the rounds in German psychological studies of ways to control the misfiring of air technologization whereby the self-observation required for merger with the flying machine kept coming back as uncanny visitations or ghost appearances.

In the 1919 volume *Psychoanalysis and the War Neuroses*, Simmel was already arguing that the neuroses represented "safety catches" or "fuses" that helped prevent psychotic blowout ("Zweites Korreferat," 45). Internal doubling of the ego sent the soldiers to the borderline between neurosis and psychosis, that newfound no-man's-land that from World War I onward was the place of psy fi expansionism into the outer spaces of psychosis. Psychosis thus switched from the allegorical to the functional, from limit concept to borderline zone or diagnosis. So in World War I, the psychoanalytic reception of war neurosis began to open up the trenches of untreatability down the dotted line of narcissistic libido. In turn German military

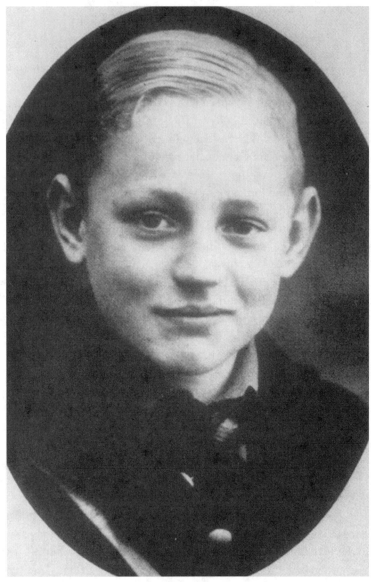

Erich Hartmann at age fourteen. He is wearing his Hitler Youth uniform. Reproduced from *The Luftwaffe,* by the Editors of Time-Life Books (Alexandria, Va.: Time-Life Books, 1982), 134. The original Hartmann photographs are the property of Archiv Erich Hartmann, Weil, Germany.

Erich Hartmann's mother, Elisabeth, in her Klemm L-20 sport plane. Reproduced from *The Luftwaffe*, 134.

psychologists saw brand-new training grounds for the defense and offense industries opening up. The columns of doubling had to be remade user friendly or war ready. From the Air Ministry to the central psychotherapy institute (the one that packed a major psychoanalysis section), a standard of intrapsychic theory and therapy was advanced in the Third Reich that in 1941 was the focus of the Allied all-points effort to keep up with the Nazis. The pilot's body and sensorium were to be the first in the military-psychological complex to be technologized and nonmachinically merged with the internalized apparatus.

The narcissism that fueled all these flights of science fantasy across intrapsychic airspace was right away interpersonalized, already among Freud's immediate followers, as the near-miss difference or gap between homoeroticism and homosexuality, the opening wide for war neurotic breakdown. The Nazis were the first to project this unstable borderline onto the cyborgian airhead. An alternative that grows up alongside this divide on the safer side of homoerotic bonding is fetishism, or gadget love, or "aestheticization of politics," or psy fi. This describes the full circuit Nazi psychoanalysis came through and continues to come through in all the outposts of "greater psychoanalysis"—even or especially where Freud's science is only openly disowned. In varying dosages, as the excavated materials keep on asserting, these ingredients had mixed up our understanding of Everyman's psyche

Hartmann *(right)* and his crew chief Heinz Merten became close friends. Reproduced from *The Luftwaffe*, 136.

worldwide. It's easier to say than to believe. But we're still wading onto the shore, the for sure, of an invasion, waged from between the lines, but with certainty.

Given the psychotechnological investments and connections I fought (I mean sought) to reconstruct in the two preceding installments of *Nazi Psychoanalysis*, science fiction seemed the next best place to excavate, alongside and within the Nazi canon. There was all along, it turns out, a literal science fiction tradition in German letters up through 1945, after which point science fiction gets reinvented, as though without immediate prehistory, under the friendly sponsorship of the primal ancestors Wells and Verne, as Cold War exclusive, played out among the victorious Allies only. But even before I stumbled on this repressed canon, I had already begun to fix my focus, while laboring inside the outer space of crossover between case studies of psychotics and psychological warfare manuals, on an impulse that I commenced reexamining under the re-spelled category of psy fi. In the works of psy fi, the reproductive mourning assignment gets recast as the ballast dropped off by a more futural force of replication, the force or fantasy that is with our ongoing technologization. This techno-force of doubling or cloning is, in all its interchangeable places, also that much more egoic, perverse, psychotic, and group psychological.

A beaming Hartmann on the Eastern Front celebrates his 350th score. Reproduced from *The Luftwaffe*, 138.

A discursive force field of overlaps brings us to the "ends" of our mass culture inside greater psychoanalysis: a network consisting of the first analytic theories of adolescence and midlife crisis, the earliest developments in or, same thing, receptions of television technology, the foundation given still current cultures of recovery, and, finally, the shift, reflected in treatment approaches to such mortal illnesses as cancer and AIDS, in "our" reception of the deadline.

First we must retrench within the materiality of the findings up to this reopening. There is the worldwide consensus on and in psychoanalysis emerging during World War II to consider, and then the specific applica-

Hitler congratulates Lieutenant Hartmann. Reproduced from *The Luftwaffe*, 138.

tions of the lab results of the war to an American future made safe for, and wired through, the family. As we drift into the era of Americanization, however, we should remember the level of psychoanalysis saturation in Nazi German mass culture.

Saturation can't only be measured by the high points of identifiable influence. Let's look instead, for example, at some of the last stand-up routines of resistance in Nazi Germany. Take this sampling of outsiders who put themselves between the institute in Berlin and German psychiatry at large. When J. Bresler's titular question—"Does National Psychotherapy Exist?"—answers itself in the hysterical mode, his main-man exclusion exceeds itself in the associations it drags down with it until he is left alone with his transgression. Bresler is surefire that German psychotherapy could never be psychoanalysis, that chain of "transcendental anxiety factories and lapsus offices" (13). But he's just as for sure about his rejection of all Indian practices of tension release, so sure that he pursues his point down into the footnote underworld where the *Volk* of Buddhism is held up as an ongoing national misfortune. The Göring institute, however, included psychoanalysis in its eclectic mix—and not just in some minor form, but on a level with the active recruiting of yoga or yoga-based therapies for performing combos with German psychotherapy. Bresler's loser streak comes out in "Mental Illness as Combat," where he grants dignity to the mentally ill because like the somatically afflicted, they are fighting, in their extreme isolation, for their existence in a war of many fronts (466–67).

Alfred Krauskopf is into race consciousness and into the contributions that can be made to this consciousness by depth psychology (code word, whether he knew the code or not, for psychodynamic psychotherapy and psychoanalysis). "The unconscious belongs . . . to the realm of the psychic hereditary mass [Erbmasse]" (365). His mix-up, however, gives half-breeds a chance: they can balance out the tension of their racial-psychic heritage in depth-psychological treatment and develop "a new personality-kernel" (367).

There are, Alfred Brauchle summarizes for us, two directions for psychotherapy; one goes up, the other comes down. "The upwardly directed analytic methods are invested in bringing up out of the unconscious into consciousness a psychic fund of experience that is also hidden, forgotten, repressed, punched in, and stuck fast" (317). The deep person is thus made accessible to influence. "This way is paved with pain and shock, and barricaded shut with resistances. It can be entered and used only with the help of 'transference,' that more or less noticeable affective bond between patient and physician. The dangers lie in the one-sidedness of many analysts and their inability to lead their patients from the analyzed or broken-apart stage to the next one of rebuilding upon the ruins of the old psychic existence the new construction of genuine health" (317). Without recourse to the unconscious, psychological treatments run on empty while trying to steer willpower or conscious thought. That sort of drill is better suited for military camp or the sports field than for the therapeutic relationship. The unconscious is a kind of storage tank of "bond energy" that can be mobilized in therapy, put to use, drawn from. It is the place to go for brilliant new ideas or—double occupancy—for the break of psychotic delusions.

There must be a more fluid transition from taking apart to taking part. According to Hellmut Peil, in a setting of suggestion "a Fluidum passes from the healthy physician to the patient looking for help" (6). Brauchle's suggestive solution for what rises up one-sided in depth work comes down to group therapy: better to work in groups and shake up a population that has already just by convening rendered itself suggestible (318). In group, Brauchle can address the whole "pyramid of force"—consciousness, the unconscious, and the organic unconscious (the latter comprises the "automatic nervous system in its linkup with inner glands and blood" and serves as "carrier of a purposive auto-steering in the organism, which can become manifest in all regulations, especially in regeneration and compensation" [319])—and draw from it the reserve supplies and staying power *(Bestand)* it holds in store. In turn Brauchle scatters "healing ideas" into the mass of patients and expects them to grow together.

How does this garden of group therapy grow? In these highly resistant instances of nonreception, it is clear that the middle ground of innovation, occupied by garden-variety group therapy and hypnotic suggestion, is nourished by the analytic saturation that still registers even at this group level. The measure of this resistance and investment needs to be kept in the back of the mind reading pre–Cold War German science fiction. Otherwise it will be hard to work through the preprogrammed reception that stands in the way of the shift this volume proposes, in the genre and theory of "science fiction," back down inside the hot era of preparations for, and realizations of, World War II. How else are we to understand Disneyland's renovation of Tomorrow Land as a latter-day set from *Metropolis?* Cold War science fiction granted us the reprieve of repression of the immediate past. But the future in this past has not yet been put to rest.

Werther Report

Husband, wife and friend, one is injured in the other.

—GOETHE, *ROMAN ELEGIES*

It is a thing so unnatural for a man to tear himself loose from himself... that he in most instances uses mechanical means to carry out his intention.

—GOETHE, *POETRY AND TRUTH*

In 1938 scholar Herbert Schöffler declared Goethe's *The Sorrows of Young Werther* to be "the first nondualistic tragedy of our psychic development" (180):

> The absolute value in this artwork is love between the sexes, and if this value cannot be attained, life becomes worthless. A worthless life can, however, be discarded.... In the place of the formerly absolute value, the idea of God, another has stepped in, love between the sexes. (175)

But this passion gets displaced in the work of its divinization; it gets displaced, son-of-God style, onto the Passion of suicide or, as Schöffler labels it, "*passio Wertheri adolescentis*": "Through his voluntary death, Werther enters the All-mother Nature" (173). But Werther's regressive, suicidal course is not a negative theology of "love between the sexes." Lotte is indeed a maternal figure whom Werther loves, no, I mean hates, no loves, hates. His inability to admit the ambivalence, which takes him through idealization to suicide, follows out the other tension Goethe describes, not only here but also, for example, in "The Wandering Jew," as the juxtaposition between the trauma of being born to die, or of the mother bearing the child—to the grave—and fantasies of self-creation.

   Werther, the first best-seller of modern mass culture, folded open along an installment plan of self-help or how-to. It was the book that installed an identificatory understanding or following in a teen readership of actors-out who dressed up as Werther look-alikes and, in the season finale, copycut their take on, or intake of, their leading man's suicide. Billed in the novel as an outlet for a "creative freedom" otherwise blocked by a mounting sense of absence and backed up against the off limits separating him from all outside connections, Werther's closing shot of suicide was the hit taken by every fan male. This direct hit has since gone all the way to creating a fit between *Werther*'s outer-literature experiences and the medical and social-scientific examination of "suicide by suggestion":

> In 1974 Phillips introduced and defined the term "Werther effect" to denote an increase in the number of suicides caused by suggestion. Phillips was the first to study systematically and empirically the effect of suggestion on suicide. In his classic paper, Phillips used American and British statistics to show that the number of suicides increased after the story of a suicide was published in the press. Phillips's results contradicted Durkheim's claim that the effects of suggestion are only local. (Taiminen et al., 350–51)

The local activity of imitation, suggestion, and suicide can be thought globally only by summoning an effect that is at once literary and extraliterary, in other words, psychoanalytic. But the summons must be served: Freud's second system, a public address system broadcasting his theory of group psychology, is always one context away from the meeting above of the identificatory Werther effect with its match and maker, the same context of journalism and social studies. For example, the unsexed look of mass suicide we find in all the generic studies of the Werther effect has in the other context of psychoanalysis a unisex appeal. In other words: group psychology, by any other name, is the psychology of adolescence.

Teens, who get their sexual license not from their parents (they're too out of it or off-limits anyway) but from the unisex group, are into groupwide self-replication. Reproduction is the traditional frame (and stress) put on the adolescent group, which reserves mega-ambivalence for the couple, both the parental one (that's off in the master bedroom grossing out the masturbating group-of-one) and the futural one every group member is supposed to become or come like for the survival of the group or species (the group, we know, doesn't have a reproducing plan of its own). The mourning after separation is the motor that couple formation and reproduction keep running: the group, which never mourns, tries to find different ways of getting around getting stuck on loss. That's why suicide bears the reversible seal of group approval. Checkout time at the same time for the whole group (or group-of-one) folds back onto the wish that is a group-level command: replicate, don't reproduce.

Adolescents already had that cute look of the alien or outsider when they were first invented in the eighteenth century as originals. That's why teen passion was taken over by the newly founded institutions of higher learning as their charge. This is how modern mass culture—the Teen Age—

began, intramurally, inside the institution of academe, which has always been fast on the intake. Modern educational institutions were erected on top of a mounting impulse to absorb the overload of this surge. But already in *Faust* we read in the fine print that the university alone could never contain this striving without a cause. Transferential precincts, in other words, could not provide the setting for a set of responses that would, in time, act out in front of the TV set. From the eighteenth century onward, the mobile unit or union of conversion shock-absorbed the overload of adolescence that was being institutionalized back in school. The early history of the first American universities and colleges overlaps with the outbreak of mass conversions, which by the turn of the century had gone on the record of psychological study. On his first trip to America, Freud made contact with this modern science of conversion, which his host Stanley Hall had established with his two-volume study *Adolescence*.

There is one conversion rate, Freud would later determine in the aftermath of World War I, and it belongs to the calculus of internal conflict. Superego says: Live on in future generations. Ego says: No, don't want to go. Superego says: Substitute for the missing and move on. Ego says: No, can't let go. We hear in stereo and in conflict the command to go forth and multiply.

How Many Siblings

Eissler set up Goethe's bond with his sister Cornelia as the standard edition of his object choice and frame of preference. For example, he carefully calculated that the onset of Werther's decompensation is set on or by the date of Cornelia's birthday (*Goethe*, 99). *Werther* was first conceived and executed on parallel tracks with the course of his sister's initiation into reproduction, the race set going by her marriage in November 1773 to a certain Schlosser (whose name resonates with variations on "locking up"). By February 1774, when Goethe carried *Werther* to term by term of fulfillment of the suicide contract, the family had every reason to assume Cornelia's expectancy (she delivered in October). In fact, Goethe's own explosive reactions while staying in Wetzlar in 1772, the stopover that provided models for *Werther* (and perhaps, in varying degrees, for every one of Goethe's novels), first went off, according to Eissler's resetting of the timer, with the newsbreak that a courtship was on and going strong between friend Schlosser and Cornelia (95). But the direct connection Eissler puts through between Goethe and Cornelia, which he sees as establishing the incestuous resource center of Goethe's complete portfolio of self-identifications, was also jamming with an excess of murderous static crossing over from other lines.

First there's the mother, for whom Werther's effects pose no problem: according to Goethe's mother, *Werther* accomplished proper burial for actual events in Goethe's life, which were thus commemorated and put to rest. But Goethe was haunted by *Werther*. The book was indeed pursuing its author, Goethe had to admit, like the unlaid ghost of a murdered brother (*Roman Elegies*, 558).

Eissler reconstructs Goethe's self-identification with the pregnant mother as the one way out of suicide left over after Cornelia was gone (104, 105, 112). But when Goethe returned to *Werther* to fine-tune its reception in the final version (this time after Cornelia was gone and dead, a double departure that attended her second childbirth), he described this work of revision as Werther's return "into his mother's body" (81). Eissler's upbeat account of Goethe's bonding with a mother's reproductive capacity leaves out the body opened up to this return and thus to the suicidal ready position networked with a Jonestown-style readership and with ghosts (113). The mother's body, as secret bearer of the undead, is the other medium of identification, the one tuning in the ghostly returns; but the maternal body is also the body of the group, a formation or transformation that issues its first bonds as identification going down between siblings, who start out each other's total rivals for the direct line to the mother. If you can't lick the newly arrived rival, because the conflict, like the sex, is too total or suicidal, then you're joined at the rip and tear line of one identification. The fraternity or sorority thus established (with a love right above the death wish) pledges internally or eternally to siblings dead or alive. That's why ghosts can always be seen making the in-crowd of the group bond.

In his essay on a singular childhood recollection recorded by Goethe in *Poetry and Truth*, Freud unpacked the little one's antics at the window as acting out his bond with mother to the point of magically expelling all rival siblings back through the window womb. It is this relationship—Freud refers to it in shorthand as Goethe's close rapport with his mother—that was the source of Goethe's great success. And yet Freud is also moved to list those missing in action: the four dead little ones who found no place in Goethe's autobiography. The first fulfillment of Goethe's death wishes was thus the departure of his younger six-year-old brother Hermann Jakob, whose death was also the original occasion for Goethe's legendary refusal to mourn.

Dead siblings are the encrypted ones along for the death drive in cases of melancholia. It's a mother of an identification that makes the first deposit; the mother's unmourning transfers an undead child to the joint account she opens up inside her surviving child, who is filled out with the missing-persons reports of an unknown sibling. For Goethe (and Kafka, whose plan to write an essay on Goethe's "monstrous being" fits right in here), the funereal zone occupied by ghostly, reanimated, or "warm" brothers was also the secret society in which the homosexual component or contingency checked in.

But the haunting fallout of group identifications in Goethe's readership was rehearsed or repeated in Werther's attraction to a couple of live ones, which already packed the double whammy of projective displacement; his suffering or passion, which is out of place, is bound not only to Lotte, the off-limits woman, but also or especially, at the outer limit, to a homosexual object choice. At this end Werther borrows the warm gun of his suicide from Lotte's betrothed, Albert (nothing could be hotter or better). But Eissler's main evidence for his reading of Werther as the stations or station-identifications of Goethe's being crossed by Cornelia's couplification with Schlosser is that, in the novel, Albert bears way more resemblance to Schlosser (and to the way Goethe mixed his feelings toward Schlosser) than to Kestner, the apparent model for Werther's Albert (*Goethe*, 98). The going assumption about the fiction's working relationship with what had been a happening event back in Wetzlar went far enough to leave Kestner real hurt. It's the misrecognition some call love. It doesn't require much of an outing to get to the panoramic view that Goethe's correspondence with Kestner about his impossible love for Kestner's wife was homosexual, not in follow-up action but in frame. It inspires Eissler to imagine that Goethe might have thought, latently, that is, that Schlosser married his sister only because he was in fact in love with Goethe.

We are desperately familiar by now with the monitoring or administering of degrees of homosexuality attained on the way to an all the more potentiated heterosexuality. But we saw it first with Goethe, who made the ambiguous phasing and phrasing of heterosexual couplification his signature piece. One need only read between the lines of Eissler's analysis, which is too far-flung by half, by the missing half of the homosexual connection, precisely made to fit the ultimate catch, the whole of heterosexual adjustment, and thus to bypass the part or past that exceeds that whole.

Same Difference

A great deal of the confusion has arisen on the basis of
terminology and semantics. Any word beginning with the
letters "psy," to the average mind, suggests something
mysterious and alarming: insanity, perversion, homicidal
tendencies.

—MALCOLM J. FARRELL AND JOHN W. APPEL,
   "CURRENT TRENDS IN MILITARY NEUROPSYCHIATRY"

As a work of caution to culture critics against overusing latent homosexuality as a cure-all explanation for group or psychotic bonding over a long-
distant woman's body, Theweleit's *Male Fantasies* at the same time cannot
pick up the frequency of ghosts in cases that do, however, come directly
out of the loss or losses of World War I. Theweleit's focus on identification
is fixed on the sexual combo of merger and murderousness, but with a difference, with one substitution, please: he relocates the sister figure at the
cathexis center of the para-Nazi fantasies shared by the soldier brothers.
Theweleit makes his move to get around the psychoanalytic automatism
that rushes to read the itinerary of homosexuality inside the psychic makeup
of all-male representation and repression. The sister figure (often, in wartime, a nurse who, in German, is thus doubly "sister") is a safe choice because she's bound to and by all the family values of super savings in libido.
In fact, however, as the sister of a best friend, her own exogamous availabil-
ity opens up a libido outlet that stands in for, and in the way of, the homosexual connection between the soldier bros. But for Theweleit such an analysis moves too quickly, like a guilty assumption or a countertransference.

Theweleit calls for special handling of the shock of recognition that
goes down between brother and sister, and thus for more time with the
material or text, the biology or biography (before shortcutting, that is, to
the castration complex of psychoanalysis). While that opens up psychoanalytic theory to in-session temporality and materiality, the shorthand of
theory is still on primal time. In other words, the sister's hard body, which
stands in for all women on the outside and defends against the prospect of
their dreaded amorphous corporeality, is at the same time, or rather the
first time, the mother's body. Every relationship to the body, even one's
own body, is to the mother's body. It's the only body around, and it's off-
limits. It sets a limit to pleasure (and a half-life to material reading) that
sets the place of tension between the sexual couple and the group. The

group's "body" is the maternal one, the one that can never be consumed in the one-on-one. This maternal body asserting itself in shared fantasy—in other words, in groups—will always be same sex (even or especially for the soldier boys).

Theweleit is not alone in sizing up Freud's investment in the group's psychology as the Oedipalization (or homosexualization) of psychotic structures. The rejection of Oedipally directed readings that restrict admissions to homosexuality, and then award homosexuality degree status within the range of components making up psychotic delusions, belongs right up there with all the popular breakaway movements that split Freud's turn to group psychology. It was against this homosexual tendency of the psychoanalytic group conspiracy (which asserted itself as a nonreproductive exclusion of women) that Adler championed women's rights: the supplemental movement that accompanied the establishment of equal rights within a heterosexual bond of therapy was Adler's persistent demand for therapeutic eradication of homosexuality. He dismissed the it-takes-one-to-know-one view that one's homophobia only reflects the press of one's own repressed homosexuality; that was one of those inside views based on nothing but psychoanalytic theory, which had something to hide and protect. Reich's resistance to Freud's psychology of groups and, in particular, to their insurance policy, the death drive, is legend. But at the high point of his close encounter with psychosis (which featured psy fi delusions about invasion from outer space, which he, son of spacemen, was alone fit to withstand, and alternated with the sense of betrayal that invites identification with Christ), Reich specifically denied homosexuals entry into his cure-all organon boxes. It was the first backfire of his remobilization of the notion of libido around which he had retrenched during his save-sex campaign against Freud's alleged tampering with the original formulation of libido through introduction of the death drive. Reich's science fantasies first took on the death drive, then all of psychoanalysis, first homosexuality, then sex itself. The equation of homosexuality and Freudian analysis asserts itself in all the registers of resistance. Deleuze and Guattari's *Anti-Oedipus* thus only resets the trend for reversing the one way psychoanalysis Oedipalizes even the psychotic material it interprets. The anti–Oedipus complex is still taking sides against Freud with Reich's special interest in energy flow. This time around it is "perverse reterritorialization" that is internal to the automatic interpretation by psychoanalysis of homosexual dispositions and positions inside psychosis. In the schizophrenia-compatible model Deleuze and Guattari propose as antidote to Oedipalization tendencies that work (both overtime and in session) to pervert or reterritorialize the psycho trying to go with the flow, there is, accordingly, one thing missing from an embarrassment of readmissions. When the anti-Oedipals muster the interpersonal columns for the social connections excluded from intrapsychic insight, the only thing left to be missing is sexuality. Freud's conception of sexuality has always been one of those unwanted problems, which resistance puts up for adaptation as the related one of homosexuality's continued existence. Once the resistance goes this far, the agenda expands or narrows to include the problem of masturbation, which now really has to go. That's why, on this resistance scanner, masturbation, the origin and eternal return of sexuality itself, is already viewed as homosexual, as the other place to get stuck on. If Deleuze and Guattari are merely macho-territorial when it comes to the couplification of these two problems, Adler went so far as to base the community spirit he was setting up as therapeutic norm—as did Reich his superman booths of energy renewal—on the proviso of exclusion of the intimately related diversions of homosexuality and masturbation.

From Adler and Reich to Deleuze and Guattari, homophobic interventions are among the scores that are settled with Freud's science. It is a metapsychological fact that in the projectively foreshortened format of these (paranoid) attacks, Freudian analysis and homosexuality appear to occupy interchangeable places. According to the lines of these attacks, without psychoanalysis (which introduces an unconscious that has datable origins at the start of the dialectic of Enlightenment in the eighteenth century), homosexuality as we are still coming to know it would not be around. It starts getting around inside the new family pack in which ambiguous identifications get mixed up with denial. Homosexuality was along for the emergence of a new state of tension, that between the group (or group-of-one) and the couple. This group formatting of desire scores a direct hit or fit with the new ambiguous object, the couple itself. From *Werther* to Kafka's "In the Penal Colony" there is a direct connection riding out this tension, one that makes ambivalent and inevitable room for the homosexual store of identifications. Heading Werther off at his impasse, then, is a closeted point of contact with the other fact of life, which remains beside the point of seeing or visibility but in this way takes the impact of powerful identifications.

Even Adorno, who billed himself as a follower of Freud's double heading of death drive and group psychology, was pulled up short by the prospect of an inversion: Freud's group psychology, it turned out, was not always only a mass or measure of psychopathology but rather addressed the fact of life that we *are* in groups. Adorno fell out of the favor he thought Freud was doing him by filling the prescription of Adorno's humanistic refrains about bad technology, bad groups, bad movies, and so on. He was compelled to put out an interpersonal ad for sexual difference and charge psychoanalysis with replacing the symmetrical differences exchanged in heterosexual couples with the same difference that comes in groups:

> Psychoanalysis appears in its flattening out of all it calls unconscious and thus of everything human to succumb to a mechanism of the homosexual type: not seeing what is different. Homosexuals evince a kind of color blindness in experience, the inability to recognize what is individualized: for them all women are in the double sense "the same." ("On the Relationship between Sociology and Psychology," 84)

This homosexual inability to love shares its coldness with Freudian analysis, which puts on rigor to cover its aggressive control tendencies. Along the dotted line of a predisposition going down inside psychoanalysis and out in group psychology, a reversal or inversion can be folded back across psychoanalysis itself, rendering "psychoanalysis in reverse" (Arato and Gebhardt, 8) the resource center of modern mass delusions in which psychotic and perverse positions get acted out. Because the group gives shelter to homosexuality, Adorno is able to report in the headline format of one of his minimalist and moralistic aphorisms that homosexuality always goes with totalitarianism (*Minima Moralia*, 52). In "Freudian Theory and the Pattern of Fascist Propaganda," Adorno comments on Freud's observation in *Group Psychology and the Analysis of the Ego* that "homosexual love is far more compatible with group ties" (*SE*, 18:141) from within a complex Freud is made to share with Nazi Germany:

> This was certainly borne out under German Fascism where the borderline between overt and repressed homosexuality, just as that betweeen overt and repressed sadism, was much more fluent than in liberal middle-class society. (413 n. 7)

Conversion

In the suggestion box of literary studies a novel like Schenzinger's *Hitlerjunge Quex* has been identified as belonging to the genre of "conversion," which turns out to be another way of claiming for the Nazi novel a *Werther* lineage. *Hitlerjunge Quex* (1932) clearly falls in with a subgenre of novels of "German destiny" (the subtitle or caption regularly appended to them) including Goebbels's *Michael* (1929) and Ewers's *Horst Wessel* (1932). Between *Werther* and these destinal works a few marginalizations have gathered motivation and found completion within the system of displacements *Werther* had already inaugurated.

In these late arrivals of the Werther effect, the political trajectory of a narcissistic wound mixes up aestheticism and homoeroticism into the doses of inoculation taken in against a crisis in reproductive supply and demand. In Goebbels's novel, Michael's girlfriend accuses him, verbatim, of aestheticizing politics (an acting out she considers dangerous to life, and that means to procreation) (40). Michael in turn decides that she can't join the movement of the new: her type, which is good enough, has a half-life that doesn't belong to the future; she represents a reproductive means of "blossoming forth" out of last remaining reserves mobilized one last time (64–65). Politics are defined by Michael as the decision (really: the tenuous will) to procreate: "Every father who puts children into the world is pursuing politics. Every mother who makes men out of her boys is a political being" (21). In other words, war won't go away: "The desire to get rid of it is the same as wishing to get rid of the fact that mothers bear children. That too is terrible. All life is terrible" (22). By the end Michael has his life where he wants it and wants to leave it: reduced to the acting out of the means of production between men, which he now identifies as the lost cause of the German effort in World War I. His work aesthetic, his search for "redemption" (124), bonds him over this lost war with a worker: "He calls me thou. I want to embrace him" (127); "I would like to kiss it. How dear this hand is to me, this worker's hand" (128). The death that follows for him and others like him in this genre of final destination is a free gift that comes with group membership: to be innocent bystander at the accident of one's own death, an accident that is always forecast or otherwise foreseeable but that the victim volunteers to attend out of excessive political engagement, the kind that makes him, as dead teen, the best sacrifice or martyr available.

As part of the all-out Allied effort (which began in 1941) to catch up with Nazi military psychology and propaganda (right down to Freud's intrapsychic model, which the Nazis were the first to stick with only because it worked, in particular in treating for, or immunizing against, war neurosis, and in the preemptive exercise of psychological warfare), Bateson was invited to locate the intrapsychic battery of the 1933 film version of Schenzinger's novel for Allied use only. In his lecture at the New York Academy of Sciences, Bateson summarized the Nazi psychological advance:

> In America we tend to think of propaganda as consisting of a large number of separate utterances, pious sentiments or jokes, inserted into the more or less propagandically neutral matrix of communication. Publicity methods were developed on the basis of rather simple psychological theories of association and Watsonian conditioning and have been comparatively little influenced by Gestalt psychology or psychoanalysis. The significant propaganda in the German films is, however, not of this sort. (Bateson, Section of Psychology, 72–73)

The year before, Siegfried Kracauer presented his inside view of Nazi propaganda: it creates a "swastika world" (vii) out of incorporated news reality effects over which the viewers are given a direction, their sense of being in control, of being in a lab-secure rapport of testing some new substance (7). Nazi propaganda thus applied a "leftist technique in somewhat reverse order." Rather than "elicit reality from a meaningless arrangement of pictures," the German film documents Kracauer is analyzing for the war effort "nip in the bud the real meaning their newsreel materials would convey" (37). What the Nazi Germans are thus able to reel in, however, and mobilize, Kracauer somewhat enigmatically confirms, are "the energies of the people" (vii). At one point Kracauer's reading does join Bateson's own (silent) treatment of these energies when he attends to a detail he saw succeed with audiences viewing one of these Nazi movies—a gadget-loving detail or unit of energy that, completely beside the points Kracauer otherwise raises about the newsreel effect and its incorporation or reversal, scores its success on the battlefield of the unconscious.

> At each of the six times I attended *Victory in the West* in a Yorkville theatre, people around me were noticeably amused and refreshed when, after a terrific accumulation of tanks, guns, explosions and scenes of destruction, a soldier poured cold water over his naked comrade. Secondly, such scenes have the advantage of appealing specifically to instincts common to all people. Like spearheads, they drive wedges into the defense-lines of the self,

Hubert Netzer, *Morpheus*. Reproduced from *Die Kunst im deutschen Reich* 3, no. 12 (December 1939): 391.

and due to the regression they provoke, totalitarian propaganda conquers important unconscious positions. (14)

Bateson also opened up the first reel of the visual evidence with explanatory intertitles. Bateson's version of *Hitlerjunge Quex*, in which the Allied effort to understand or follow incorporates the Nazi movie, fixes its focus on the Nazi psychology of adolescence:

> If we want to know what makes a fanatical Nazi tick, we must look at how the Nazi propagandists represented the German family—how they made it appear that Youth was infinitely desire-

Hubert Netzer, warrior memorial *(Kriegerdenkmal)* in Duisburg. Reproduced from *Die Kunst im deutschen Reich* 3, no. 12 (December 1939): 394.

able, and what sort of love they took as their model when they set out to build a population of boys in love with Death.

In his analysis of "the conversion to Nazism of Heini, a 12-year old boy," Bateson answers the question "How are the loves and hates in the stereo-

Hubert Netzer, figure from the warrior monument in Wesel. Reproduced from *Die Kunst im deutschen Reich* 3, no. 12 (December 1939): 392.

typed German family invoked and rearranged by the propagandist to make them support Nazism?" The question he doesn't even pose concerns the sex appeal for Heini of the Nazi youths, whom he can refer to only as "the others" *(die anderen)*, or, on the other side, the sexual problem Heini has with the Communists, who are coded as flagrant heterosexuals. Instead Bateson shows us—enough to read, between the lines, the tension that's also there between orientations—how Heini's suicidal bond with his mother (who tries to rescue Heini by turning the gas on both of them) is shifted to his bonding happiness with "the others," and how the initial attractiveness of the Communist youth leader, pumped up not only by his muscles but also through association with Heini's mother, gets father-identified with heterosexuality and thus replaced by what "the others" have to offer. In his 1943 lecture, Bateson summarizes in orientation-free terms the Nazi reworking of the family ties to promote these same-sex relations for all but the married women, who must keep the libido pool of applicants for positions in the war machine restocked:

> In order to create a violent emotional adherence to Nazism the family itself is unscrupulously sacrificed. The woman's place may be in the home but she need not expect that home to contain a husband or children over six. These others, the men and the boys and the unmarried girls, will be absorbed into "Youth" organi-

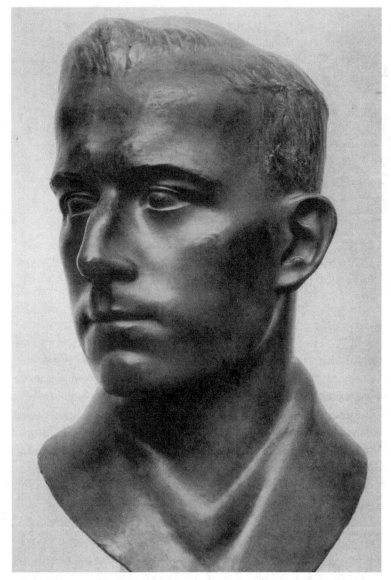

Fritz Koelle, *Portrait of Horst Wessel*. Reproduced from *Die Kunst im deutschen Reich* 4, nos. 8–9 (August–September 1940): 233.

zations which free them from accepting the responsibilities of adult human status. (78)

The core of the displacements going down and out in these Nazi *Werther* remakes is what melts down for Horst Wessel, in Ewers's novel: on a tour of Berlin nightlife, he finds himself barred from reproduction at a gay bar. On the morning after, Horst gets advice from his dear comrade:

> "That pack of swine will be around everywhere as long as the earth shines through the universe."
> "And they are after all people, like you and me!" Horst said. "They sit down on the school bench next to us—back then one didn't notice at all that they were different!"
> "No," Richard Fiedler answered. "That comes out later. But it's already inside them right from the beginning." (87)

It's a metapsychological fact: aestheticization of politics (as directly addressed by Benjamin and Goebbels) is the promotion of homoeroticism as inoculation injected against the coming out of homosexuality, which is thus, however, admitted as a fact of life. In these Nazi novels the focus on class struggle is coded as heterosexual, and the boys in the bond, this is, the ones unconjugated with means of reproduction, are cute replicants; in *Horst Wessel* there's a wide sampling of boy tans, knees, beautifully shaped heads, figures that are slender, strong, and upright (8, 11, 16).

Converted to homoerotic bonding, homosexual excess or access contains itself as the danger to group members who are well trained in the intrapsychic art of battling internal enemies. Through the homoerotic control releases made available in the Nazi culture of comradeship, for example, suicide became an efficient alternative to the breakdowns of war neurosis. This rings up a statistic: Nazi measures taken in against the coming out of war neurosis had permitted only one form of interference to be on the rise: suicide was the only disorder to grow down the ranks of the German group effort totally inoculated with and against war neurosis or homosexuality.

In "On Suicide by Soldiers" Wuth argues that it's well known that suicidal personalities don't benefit from psychotherapy, but only from reeducation, reraising, like up the ranks of the military, the most therapeutic setting for these types (there are three: psychopaths, the depressed, and perverts). However, Wuth concludes his 1936 article, because National Socialism has not had time to exercise its hard approach to the max yet, and because, also on account of another kind of time factor, there's no tradition with reference to earlier forms of government backing the new regime, "we will have to reckon in the next few years with a rise in the suicide rates" (89).

The Buff Object of Identification

Among the add-ons Goethe inserted the second time around, in the revising of *Werther*, two reflect the pull of Werther's desire: one presses forward the displacement implied in, and excluded from, the double occupancy of his attraction to the couple; the second tells us right-on just which libido pool furnishes the applicants for Werther's "other" position. The second insert folded inside Goethe's work of revision is a narcissistic prop: Lotte's love for him, which he now feels is real, causes Werther to get down on his knees before himself and be his own deity. Being loved means his self-love is real. While not yet reduced to the machinic contours of Olympia (in Hoffman's "The Sandman"), with all the record and playback functions intact and in push-button readiness, Lotte is nevertheless the placeholder or reflector shield of Werther's own narcissism. Indeed, a course of regression in "The Sandman" overlaps with Lotte's position in *Werther*, the one that introduces Olympia as the new and improved alternative to Klara, Nathanael's humanoid bride-to-be. Their relationship represents Nathanael's first try at replicating himself in or as the other (in other words, as the future). Klara must be replaced when she is seen to embody a contradiction between the mirroring "clarity" she holds up to Nathanael and an other who, on the better behalf of parental guidance, "speaks against" *(contra-dictio)* Nathanael's self-preoccupation. In the Faustian science fictions *L'Ève future* and *Metropolis*, this plan of metabolization of the wound of separation or contradiction into the miracle of merger with the machine also covers the context or contest of reproduction versus replication. This describes the fundamental metapsychological plot of the science fiction impulse. The woman's or mother's body marks the spot of separation or contradiction that works the inside. It is technologized because reproduction, which keeps the separation going as the good news of future generations coming soon, is not what the ego getting into machines of replication or suicide is into.

Nathanael, Lord Ewald, and Rotwang keep in touch with their robots (in fact first fall in love with them) by some long-distancing device, like the telescope, that represents a primal scene in which the one getting the picture is always left out of it in one blinding flash, flashback, or Blitz. The merger will not go through. The reduction of every connection out there to sheer visibility that media technologization promotes (even the audio portion on the gramophone or phone alone has been brought to us by the desire to make speech "visible") puts the relation between self and other, child and mother, right where ego wants it, and leaves it there, between

28

„Was mach' ich mit meinem Mann?

Er wird von Tag zu Tag nervöser, ist schlecht gelaunt, reizbar und kommt abends matt und erschöpft nach Haus."

Die Beantwortung dieser Frage vieler Frauen ist ganz einfach:

Er braucht

Sanatogen

das seit mehr als 35 Jahren bewährte Nervennähr- und Körperkräftigungsmittel.

In allen Apotheken und Drogerien.

Advertisement for a tranquilizing and fortifying substance to soothe the woman's nervous, irritable, exhausted husband. The opening question is "What am I to do about my husband?" Reproduced from Udo Pini, *Leibeskult und Liebeskitsch: Erotik im Dritten Reich,* 274. The original document is in the collection of Udo Pini.

narcissistic consumer and robot dolly. Psy fi lovers and self-lovers of machines are ego probes that never leave their orbit of techno-vision. Their corporeality, all that's left over, encases a tank or turbo of energy supply. That's why *Metropolis,* the city and 1926 forecast of the future that will be cyborg production's native habitat, contains an underworld of slave labor that works nonstop not on divisional aspects of some infrastructure but solely to keep the energy that illuminates or animates *Metropolis*, city and motion picture, coming and flowing. We are video probes attached to plants that produce the wonder or miracle of endless reserves and resources of energy. In the 1920 science fiction film *Algol*, the fantastic sole product or energy that belongs to a future manufacturing monopoly (and is first released and contained by a magical apparatus that resembles a film projector) is called, simply, Bios, the force or energy source that is with our technologization.

The miraculous noncontradiction of the machine being cannot but render the corporeal lover a leftover appendage tagged for evolutionary extinction. Humankind cannot yet beam up into merger with the machine. There's still always a body of separation around that, dead or alive, keeps us close to the traumatic opening of the takeoff of flights of science fantasy. What follows (like clockwork) in these stories or stores of man's infatuation with robot woman is destruction of the machine and the gadget lover's suicide. The merger didn't go through. The destroyed apparatus was his better half, and suicide follows as the downside or slide of fantasies of replication and auto-technologization. This downside of science fictions of survival of the species or group through merging with the machine, from *Werther* onward, remains the emergency brake and breakdown prevention of suicide (which was *Werther*'s other special effect). As long as the group remains dependent on the reproductive couple, the Werther effect will be the force that is with us when we contemplate replication. What gets you around one crisis goes around as the other crisis or fact of life. Goethe remained convinced that by writing the suicide note entitled *Werther* he was able to do a couple of lines of inoculation against his own urge (or surge) to off himself (or get into machines the fast way). Between the lines, the novel repress-released an ambiguous object of identification, which was the invitational that *Werther*'s biggest fans entered to act out what Goethe had put off but kept at long distance and in reserve.

The Body of His Work

You all know that the foundation for modern mental therapy
was laid towards the end of the 18th century by Mesmer's
magnetism. Mesmer received his diploma from the University
of Vienna in 1766 for a thesis, "On the Influence of the Planets
on the Human Body."

—A. A. BRILL, "VARIOUS SCHOOLS OF PSYCHOTHERAPY"

In their origin, art and technology are just an alternation away from each
other: the alternation between sublimation and the other defensive measures
metabolizes in techno-fantasy a homosexual predisposition that is back
with every crisis in reproduction. The machine connection is born out of
same-sex spirits. In Freud's studies of Leonardo Da Vinci and Schreber, the
return engagements of repressed homosexuality give rise to the emergency
projection of delusional technologies. Freud's rereading of the Prometheus
myth ascribes technology's origin (primally conceived as control of and access to energy) to the ambiguation (repression, sublimation, or projection)
of homosexuality. The eternal flame of the lost or unknown bond flickers
inside the control booth of technology, while a fast-food temporality of energy waste, early death, and replication of libidinal connection (group psychology, in sum) drives homosexual object choosing onward.

In a supplementary episode from Werther's life before his sufferings,
which Goethe published in 1796, younger Werther goes to a swimming hole
with his best friend, who agrees to strip down for Werther's art appreciations:

> I arranged for Ferdinand to bathe in the lake; how splendidly
> my young friend is built! How proportionate are all his parts!
> What a fullness of form, what a splendor of youth, what a profit
> for me to have enriched my imagination with this perfect exam-
> ple of human nature! Now I people forests, lawns, and heights
> with such beautiful figures; I see him as Adonis felling the boar,
> as Narcissus mirroring himself in the spring. (*Briefe aus der Schweiz*,
> 213)

The early death these heroes of adolescence share phases out everything
the scene holds in store. Werther must look instead for Venuses to behold.
When he gains access to his first female model, he must accustom himself
to what appears "strange" and leaves a "frightening impression" (217–18).
The replicant rapport with the body the first time around has grown

uncanny on the person of the woman: it's a crisis in reproduction that gets its relief through fetishism:

> What do we see in women? . . . A small shoe looks good, and we cry out: what a beautiful little foot! A narrow belt has something elegant about it, and we praise the beautiful waist. (218)

At a time of all-out gendering even of every category of science and thought, the adolescent boy body (that of the androgyne), at once hard and feminine, represents the outside chance of a connection somewhere over the press to reproduce. That's why art appreciation of the male nude, with the androgyne at the front of the line, requires his early death. The male nude poses as problem, the kind that only his death seems able to resolve. The lifesaving turn to the female nude (for the survival of the species), which desublimates the arts (the history of ballet is most instructive re this growing regard reserved for women only), invites what was in crisis, reproduction, to come on in.

Desublimation or resexualization of an order of identification (with the father) was, in Freud's reading, the issue of Schreber's psychosis. Schreber's techno-delusional system keeps the homosexual bonds with dead and dad just the heartbeat away of radical displacement. Emergency measures had to be taken to overcome a crisis in reproduction (he and his wife had failed to have living children). That's how an all-out turn-on gets attributed to the female body (which Schreber is becoming, via replicating changes induced by God's rays, at the same time that he's becoming an android). His is the only body around, and it's at once female and technological. Only this body can receive or conceive the ray beams of a divine force given to recognize only corpses. The uncanniness of body relations, which transfigured Werther's encounter with the reproductive body in the flesh, always releases, Sachs argues, the psycho-delusional operations of auto-technologization. Only in this way can the crisis in reproduction be overcome for the survival of the species.

The new ambiguous object of identification that *Werther* introduced is soon found downed by a relay of science fictions as their secret return deposit. Goethe's *Triumph of Sentimentality* features a robot queen whose innards enfold a series of books; following a first upsurge of imaginary titles designed for their mass consumability by women (the directions recommend improvisation of additional titles with the same topical fit), the internal sack is again peristaltically reversed, and the "underlying soup" (*Grundsuppe*) bottoms out. What remains are a couple of books: *The New Heloise* and *The Sorrows of Young Werther* (56). These, then, are the batteries of a blowup

Young men employed by the Reichsarbeitsdienst. Youth from all walks of life were required to do manual labor in the country to strengthen the body and the bond. Reproduced from Pini, *Leibeskult und Liebeskitsch*, 89. The original is in the collection of Udo Pini.

dolly that the prince prefers to its live look-alike, a preference that belongs in two places at once: in the society-wide context of a craze for monodramas endangering coupliﬁcation (even though or especially because a new line is coming soon that will offer "monodramas for two, duodramas for three, and so on" [24]) and in the immediate context of his penchant for

One of a series of portraits by Rudolf Koppitz titled *In the Lap of Nature*. Reproduced from Pini, *Leibeskult und Liebeskitsch*, 184. The original is in the collection of Udo Pini.

"machines" or "boxes" (*Kaesten*) containing "secrets" (*Geheimnisse*), namely, artificial means of producing birdsong and moonlight (20). The spread of the prince's madness (as in the monodrama fad) is reversed and contained when he is made to choose between the robot and its near-miss substitute. His object choice lies with the robot, which forces everyone else's withdrawal from the quarantine of his short circuit. The outside world of substitution and reproduction thus gets a jump start back into couplification through this close encounter with the replicant.

In Mary Shelley's *Frankenstein, or The Modern Prometheus*, the monster has filled up his interiority with a triangle of books: in one corner we find *The Sorrows of Young Werther*. The monster's attachment to families and couples that are forever off-limits follows out the beam of Werther's "monodrama." But beyond this citational mode of the creature's experience or language, *Werther* also, and in the first place, programs his suicide (the downside of the fantasy of artificial creation).

The monster's last wish, to make a match for himself, gets mixed with Victor Frankenstein's inability to skip the downbeat and living end of his melancholic science fiction. Dreaming or at her wake, Victor can embrace his dead mother's substitute, Elizabeth, only if and when she too fits the part of corpse. And he stops making the monster's mate dead in her tracks. He cannot risk releasing the remote controls over the death wish compact with his original imitation monster, the one he built in the missing place of any work of mourning following his mother's acknowledged departure. Couplified and thus acquitted from the contract out on Victor's dearly beloved, the monster would begin to slide into focus as the body of the mother, the one that could then only be let go. Instead Victor loves both brides-in-progress to pieces, right down to the corpse parts that, according to his psy fi fantasy, have a living on and brand-new start that's all their own in the mode of self-replication. "I paused to collect myself," Victor reflects as he leaves behind the remains of what might have been the murdered and mourned momster if he had only first finished building her up.

Gotta Read Goette

In *Beyond the Pleasure Principle*, it is within a certain ring of the Goethe name that the contestants face off in the ring of life versus death. First there's Weismann, to whom not only Freud gives a reception. But then: "Some writers returned to the views of Goette...who regarded death as a direct result of reproduction" (*SE*, 18:47). In Goette's name, Freud joins in the writing of a kind of bildungsroman of evolving relations with doubling or reproduction in which death develops or becomes but is not a natural. In Goette's words:

> The natural death of animals cannot be a phenomenon necessarily connected as such with organization and life, which would therefore have existed from the beginning. For one thing, a reason for such a connection is simply not apparent, and what is more, natural death does not exist for all animals but rather, according to the current findings and theories about the life of one-celled primordial animals (protozoa), is completely lacking in the latter.
>
> The only phenomenon which might give rise to the assumption of a natural death of these simple creatures, namely their procreation, transpires in such a way that the individual unit, while keeping the continued existence of its organization and life intact, simply splits and then immediately keeps on living in its individual parts.... A natural, that is, an internally determined necessary death of the protozoa is also not at all understandable, since, after all, for the preservation of the species one of the individual parts must always in turn procreate through division and at least in one of the thus constituted series live on limitlessly; but then, given the foreseeably complete equality of all parts, the remaining ones would have to possess the same capacity for eternal duration.
>
> As is well known ... the multicellular animals, the metazoa, grew out of the unicellular protozoa, consequently they possessed in the beginning the same immortality. Only now had death become a possibility, insofar as every individual unit, after it reproduced itself through seeds deposited outside itself, could die without harming the preservation of the species.... The immortality of the metazoa becomes thus an unnecessary luxury, which was not compatible with the interests of the species, and in this way the natural death of the metazoa emerged as a phenomenon of assimilation according to the principle of utility. (3–5)

Boys strengthening their bodies and having fun. Reproduced from Pini, *Leibeskult und Liebeskitsch*, 72. The original is in the Presse-Bildarchiv, Dr. Paul Wolff and Tritschler, Offenburg.

Goette's denaturalization of death, which Freud was writing up as and off to denial, includes on one side an insect analogy (the kind Freud tended to translate in the corner of dream interpretations as melancholic relations or group bonds with the siblings one had also, at one time [and once is enough] wished dead) and—on the other side—the after shocks of trauma. To this

From a book encouraging a form of nude body culture compatible with the new state's racial goals. Reproduced from Pini, *Leibeskult und Liebeskitsch*, 105. The original is in the collection of Udo Pini.

day there are insects that drop dead when they drop the egg or complete the act of siring off. These insects that come and go are wiped out by accompanying overpowering affect; the random catastrophe of sudden death lives on in humans through the same overwhelming affect, though it originates this time in trauma or shock (26). The negative side effect that reproduction first introduced thus became assimilated to the bigger advantage of the "total development of the individual" (37), the individual conceived, that is, in or as groups. Magnified in this way, cells in highly organized animals enjoy a capacity for life that is tied to "their dependency; and their end is not prescribed through their own organization, but they get used up, annihilated in the service of the whole individual" (19). What no longer depends on reproduction is an introductory offer that comes with joining the conditions or concepts of organization and development. But with their innovations in place, it appears that unlimited duration of life is incompatible with life organized for or around reproduction (45). The origin of, and explanation for, "natural death" lies in development (51), which took over where reproduction left off offing discrete immortalities. Once developmental change starts beginning right from the start, already prebirth, and reproduction through the mother therefore no longer coincides with her perfect repetition in her progeny (75), the convergence of death and reproduction characteristic of more primal life-forms (69) becomes differentiated,

Reinhold Launer, *Comrades*. Reproduced from *Die Kunst im deutschen Reich* 5, no. 5 (May 1941): 143.

superseded, sublated. The traumatic loss of immortality introduced by re-production is shock-absorbed by organization into, and specialization within, larger units that grow reattached in turn to notions of immortality unassim-ilated to reproduction and its displacement parts.

U.S. Is Them

Recognition by the Nazis of an eternally and internally fluctuating border-line between homoeroticism and homosexuality called in the kind of all-out (preemptive and intrapsychic) surveillance that at the same time required nonphobic tolerance of all the facts of life. Time-sharing in groups or species appreciation of mutual identification would be the other way to fill out this prescription. That's how the perversion package deal with war neurosis or psychopathy was forwarded to U.S. military psychology in 1941 via the U.S. Committee for National Morale's survey. Attention was ordered to the details of Leonhard Fritzsching's analysis of the "psychology of desertion" as a complete about-face of consciousness and thus as "perversion": "It is not the case that the afflicted sees the facts insufficiently, wrongly, or crookedly, he sees them completely differently" (Fritzsching, 224). This is not a flight or flighty reaction, Fritzsching stresses, but rather a passive willingness to be taken by the enemy. The survey, which was taking notes, highlights the inoculations to be taken in against the coming out of this perversion down the ranks. It's the inoculations that are introduced into group to keep the unhappy troopers from acting out an underlying disposition as desertion, disloyalty, betrayal.

D. G. Sutton gives evidence of a later-blooming interest in the psychology of aviation on the Anglo-American side of World War II. In his 1938 article he announces that although controversial, the lack of correlation "between physical findings and ability to fly" leaves "the psychological field" the one and only landing strip for methods of selection (6). While Sutton is discouraged that "very little material can be found in the literature concerning the normal man" (7), he nevertheless suggests, by way of compensation, that if you can't base training or selection on normalcy, just the right cocktail mix of traits for the cockpit must be deduced instead—in reverse—from studies "of the various psychotic groups" (7). Sutton advises that sex questions be skipped on any test to be taken. That kind of "detailed investigation into the individual's sexual trends tended to develop antagonism to the examiner" (9). But with or without a test, you can't pass without the examiner coming to "some conclusion as to the individual's degree of progress through the three well recognized stages of sexual development." And these developmental stages or steps go down the same regression fast lane that leads to psychosis—and that's just everything an airman can't be (if only because we don't have a working concept of normalcy).

This is imperative. If a man has not progressed normally to the heterosexual level but has remained fixed at either the autoerotic or the homosexual levels, he probably will exhibit characteristics that are indicative. The same may be said of the individual who has regressed to the primary or secondary level after having at one time made normal progress. Evidence of regression should automatically disqualify since it is indicative of lack of control. (10)

Evidence of the Allies catching up with Nazi gadget psychology comes in loud and clear in Charles Anderson's 1944 contribution to the *British Journal of Medical Psychology*, "On Certain Conscious and Unconscious Homosexual Responses to Warfare." Anderson admits that deviance doesn't show the way, by default, to normalcy. What makes it catching is that it provokes the weak spots in any standard adaptation to the norm. While the paranoia is turned up, we're staying with the problems at greater wavelength, on their own wavelength, than was the case with Sutton's dive-bomb approach.

Anderson distinguishes once between conscious and unconscious homosexuality and then again, on the conscious range, between active and passive brands. The active types are actively involved in the war and get their aggressive libido regularly discharged in close combat. In many cases, however, the solution to their problem is too much of a good thing (in fact would fit in much better on the other side): "Sadistic tendencies are common in active homosexuals and frequently color their ideologies. Over a third of these aggressive inverts had Fascist leanings and were facile exponents of power politics" (222). "On the other hand, no such discharge is permitted to the passive invert":

Submission to impersonal discipline is to him no substitute for personal submission to an external love-object, and in combatant situations his accumulating tension can find relief only in a discharge of anxiety or in surrender to the enemy, though he might adjust fairly well to domestic duties far removed from the zone of fighting. (217)

Both the overzealous active homosexuals and the overly submissive passive ones come out of one fagtory that runs the disorder throughout the personality that's completely organized around and by the inversion:

Inversion is not an isolated trend, nor an epiphenomenon, in an otherwise well-integrated personality; the whole structure and organization of the personality is implicated for it has been cast in a particular mold which shapes the invert's ideologies and choice of work, and determines his object-relationships, his reactions to his milieu both in war and peace, and the manner in which he deals with his hate and his love. (224)

The notion of unconscious homosexuality, on another side of the other division Anderson explores, is based on all-around acceptance of bisexuality (225). One of two problems the unconscious homosexual may have to face are sadomasochistic trends, strivings that cause problems in relationships but don't surface to the top of an agenda or as literal enactment. For one such sado-maso it was all in his recurring dreams, which is where his successful treatment was reflected back. Eventually the inversion could be unplugged even from the outlet of latency while working through the sadistic phase:

> In one recurrent dream he was told to lie face down on the ground by a German who then proceeded to smite him with a chopper on the small of the back; after his back was broken he was buried in a coffin and then woke up terrified with an emission. In the course of a reductive analysis his nightmares acquired a sadistic heterosexual content, and for a time he was disturbed by a woman who requested him to cut the throats of her four babies; this he did and woke up again with an emission. Eventually this sadistic phase passed off and he became free of anxiety and nightmares after acquiring insight into his mental mechanisms. (232)

A much more serious problem involves "mourning reactions" (although the severity does not concern the state as directly as does the conscious homosexual wish to submit). Mourning sickness down the ranks indeed draws on unconscious homosexual love lost. But the grief it gives to homosexual ties, resulting in breakup and breakdown, is a home affront exclusive, awaiting the unhappy trooper's removal from the war zone.

> Prolonged mourning tendencies are found in those to whom the loss of a comrade means the loss of a homosexual love-object, and the grief is all the more profound in that its occasion is neither apprehended nor formulated. The sufferer may or may not know he is still grieving for a dead friend but he does not know that he feels so ill, or that his grief is so intense and has lasted so long because he has lost a love-object.... Of these mourning neurotics some who were married became impotent and grew to

hate their wives much in the same fashion as Marlowe's Edward II grew to hate Queen Isabella while mourning for Gaveston. They behave in this fashion in the endeavor to escape from their own guilt, and to placate the image of their dead love-objects. (234)

HIGHER AND HIGHER

Plane Talk

The neurotic reproduction was, therefore, photographic. The itching of the face was undoubtedly a reproduction of the sensation of the splashing of mud upon his raw skin and the burning of the mustard gas.

Instead of the condensation and the compactness of action typical of the dreams of the psychoneurotic, we have a process of dilution and retardation, like the picture of normal action slowed down by the motion-picture camera, the film's being cut off before the action is completed. The images are redundant and perseverative.

—ABRAM KARDINER AND HERBERT SPIEGEL,
WAR STRESS AND NEUROTIC ILLNESS

First there was Abram Kardiner's study of the chronic cases of war neurosis he had treated from 1922 to 1925. They had outlived the First World War but perhaps not their usefulness for treating cases in new wars. The second edition of 1947 also looks back, looking after cases from another concluded war, but in prep again for belated applications to situations coming at you, the same or entirely new. It was a completely new edition, revised beginning in 1943, in collaboration with Herbert Spiegel (and thus right after the other Spiegel's tour of collaboration research duty with Roy Grinker). In the "Collaborator's Preface," Spiegel notes that what was still missing from the Allied war effort by the end of the Tunisian campaign in 1943—"a dynamic, constructive psychiatric policy for field troops" (Kardiner and Spiegel, vi)—can slide into place in the near future, if the lasting effects of the first delay hold their measure: "Perhaps it was expecting too much of a rapidly expanding army in a critical time, but if we had turned our attention to past experience, we would very likely have absorbed many lessons learned in World War I about psychiatric problems" (vii). Herbert, who was Kardiner's *Spiegel*, or mirror, in the other U.S. couple writing books on war neurosis, gets lost down this hallway and ends up in Grinker's time zone with his (Herbert's own) "Psychiatric Observations in the Tunisian Campaign." According to this genuine article, it all begins when the battlefield becomes real, the place where killing is happening; the soldiers start calculating their prospects by comparison-chopping: "They began to compare in their minds the relative advantage of a wounded arm versus a wounded leg, or a blown-off leg versus a blinded eye" (381–82). Spiegel counts down three things to watch out for. A soldier with the shakes will be ruined for service if a psychiatrist forgets the war context and gives him the fair shake of treatment. It is just as therapeutic not to give the soldier permission (this is how Spiegel puts it) to become a psychiatric casualty (384). Also, it is not the case that soldiers labeled psychoneurotic or psychopathic can't perform well in battle; they do very well, thank you, especially under good leaders (384). Finally, what's love got to do with it? Once the "interpersonal relationships among the men" deepened, they hardened in battle: "They seemed to be fighting *for* somebody rather than *against* somebody" (382).

According to Kardiner's diagnosis in the preface to the first edition, it is upon the resolution of the medical problems of traumatic neurosis that "all other social issues depend" (ix). While the "neuroses incidental to the great war made the world neurosis-minded" (ix), once the epidemic was out of sight, it was completely out of mind. Kardiner thus proffers his "experiences with the chronic neuroses of the last war" as missing link for more current applications to the wartime evidence of neurosis. One major change in what's pressing, in the pressure, arises from the historical conditions of this preface (sometime after 1943): "The current war has again brought to the foreground the problem of the neuroses incidental to it. This time, however, the problem is much more urgent because, owing to the widespread aerial bombardment of urban centers, the traumatic neurosis is now no longer likely to be confined to combatants. In fact the traumatic neurosis bids well to be one of the commonest neurotic disturbances in the world" (x).

The extended format of the rapid turnover from modern trauma to neurosis makes the threat of chronic developments that much greater. It also leaves open the possibility that the new air condition is unthinkable without the repressed and thus altered (but lasting) legacy of internalization and technologization of war trauma already once before around the syndrome. But Kardiner introduces himself by naming the two superstitions (that of gadget novelty is one of them) that keep getting in the way of the research but that also mark the spot of his own resistance to integrating his findings with what the colleagues have found out.

> Somewhere the superstition was started that data collected from World War I had nothing to do with World War II. This war was going to be different. Perhaps it was anticipated that modern implements of warfare would create a new disease entity, or that a fresh point of view might add new information. . . . According to another superstition, more psychosomatic disorders were pres-

ent in World War II than in World War I. Also untrue. . . . There is, however, one difference between the two wars which is worthy of note, though the reasons for it cannot as yet be fully ascertained. There was a decided drop in the extreme hysterical abasias, paralyses, and the epileptiform types of traumatic neurosis in World War II. The reason for this might have been that army personnel were psychiatrically oriented. The soldiers were indoctrinated in the manifestations of fear and anxiety. (3)

The refusal of continuity between the two world wars places on each new investigator, who's just so contextless, a "sacred obligation to start from scratch and work at the problem as if no one had ever done anything with it before" (1). According to superstition number two, the one that Kardiner gives credence to and then takes away, the terminology must keep up with a disorder that's always on the lookout for new zones of as yet unrefereed undecidability among somatic, psychosomatic, and simulated brands in order to get out from under entrapment by recognizable fits with the better-known psychological diagnoses. The consequent escalation of terminology also obstructs the cumulative benefits that accrue to an integrated tradition of ongoing research: "Many investigators, failing to uncover new data, give new terminologies to old data. This does not add to our knowledge; it merely prevents any experience from becoming cumulative and organized, and any constructive effort from being directed toward the essentials" (1).

There's only one real lessening of the epidemic to learn: catch the neurosis before it spreads. The spread that this study folds out already contains itself in the postulation of an individual's infra-group-structure that effectively builds out of "action units" a group-of-one. Thus any group notion of contagion is already implied in the analysis of an individual. The neurosis that spreads itself out has been reorganized around the ego's own self-help defenses and has been led, over time, to "consolidation of the neurosis into its chronic and often intractable forms" (4). Speed of intervention in the affliction, together with proximity to the fighting maintained during treatment, can help dispel any secondary gain from illness. The results of the U.S. therapy efforts to date prove their point by coming full circle: by the end of World War II there are "almost no more acute cases; they are all chronic" (4). That speed is such an issue reflects the special status of this type of neurosis; given its prime objective, adaptation to wartime conditions, at onset it's a simulacrum of neurosis, without any inner or early life, outside the intrapsychic continuum. Adaptation, then, "evokes reference to a different aspect of the organization of the personality than is evoked by any of the peacetime neuroses" (28). The authors describe a virtual war economy that's set up by the time added to the pathogenic impact and in-stant of shock:

> If the traumatic neurosis is a distinct nosologic entity, we must ex-
> pect that it will in some way be incorporated into the entire per-
> sonality. This of course applies only to the chronic forms when the
> neurosis has had a chance to become consolidated and to exercise
> a polarizing influence on the adaptation of the individual. (30)

For the more interpersonal senses of a group protection plan, there are larger units to consider than the individual or intraindividual ones: there's team spirit and the buddy system, which Kardiner and Spiegel ring around the techno-pole of war's narcissistic attractions:

> Among the psychological protections is the narcissistic idea of
> invulnerability—Nothing can happen to me—an idea that is read-
> ily extended to the team. The death of a "buddy" shatters this
> idea of invulnerability because it revives the actual possibility of
> death that is so strongly contested by the notion of invulnerabil-
> ity. In short, this notion is an illusion that lasts only as long as
> nothing happens to any member of a fighting team or to the par-
> ticular instrument which is their collective weapon. (26)

> These instruments—machine gun, tank, airplane—become exten-
> sions of the ego and draw to themselves an extension of narcis-
> sistic love second only to that aroused by one's own arms, legs,
> or hands. Upon them are showered an anthropomorphic love
> and devotion tantamount to idol worship, and the failure or de-
> struction of one of them disrupts a soldier's effectiveness like the
> loss of a limb. (26)

Traumatic neurosis becomes true neurosis when the wounded ego is left too long to its own resources and devices for adaptation to the new situa-tion (inside and out). But there is one case of self-help in this study that is "the only instance . . . ever found in a traumatic neurosis of a constructive use of disability" (223). Even though what has gone down in this patient is a "regression of the entire ego," his interest in devising labor-saving gadg-ets "compensates for an awkwardness in exerting one's limbs, and this is as close as one can come to the mechanism of 'sublimation' or refinement of the instincts of mastery" (223). We already booked flight with Kardiner and Spiegel on one externalization of this repressed ego's success story. An-other externalization goes the way of group psychology to form the gadget-loving detail, which, however, just as with the idol airplane, coheres around its breaking point: any point along the unprotected narcissistic supply lines.

The significance of the strong ties between teammates becomes
immediately apparent when something happens to one member. The team falls apart temporarily and its effectiveness and
cohesiveness are impaired. (26)

It's because the all-important, all-powerful teamwork is in disrepair—
dis-pair—over the loss of your best buddy that so-called replacements have
such a difficult time joining the stricken group; indeed, replacements are at
highest risk for war neurosis. But the defective cornerstone that admits
mourning sickness is also the mainstay of team spirit management. Team
spirit gets worked to the limit under which a wider-ranging adolescent or
group psychology of likability must be kept down. There is a "strong tendency of the soldier to empathize with the enemy soldiers he is fighting:
'They're just like me.' In fact, this attitude had to be actively combated by
our command. Orders had to be issued that soldiers caught giving cigarettes
to a captured Nazi would be disciplined" (34). What goes up in smoke, up
the other end of butts some call fags, is an impulse that the hotter, the better it's not let onto the plane of total war, spaceship Survival of the Species.
Survival, like the Eternal Return of the Same—of the homos—must be selective or not at all. Selection is the key stroke (Natural you can skip). On
the other side of the same complex, selection again kicks in (or out): "There
were also a host of other patients with nontraumatic conditions who were
no longer fit for duty; among the latter were the homosexual panics" (80).

"The whole question of therapy reduces itself primarily to rendering
the patient accessible. Any means to this end is legitimate" (82). Support of
the "self esteem" of soldiers and their officers' withholding of "'permission'
to surrender to neurosis" (75) give some of the more current passwords of
Californian psychotherapeutic eclecticism or correctness their original val-
idation (you saw it first with military psychology). The original seduction
theory of war neurosis, which required the playback function of abreaction
to make you see what you're forgetting, gets discounted in favor of the
protective-sheath hypothesis from *Beyond the Pleasure Principle.*

Although their case material often opens, on the margin but just as
wide, for admission of communications with dead brothers and mothers,
the authors disagree in their study with "others," namely, Grinker, who
"try to find the content of the anxiety and conclude... that it is the fear of
the loss of something—an ideal, a beloved object, etc.... Unfortunately this
has little to do, we believe, with the situation that becomes traumatic. What
is feared is destruction and annihilation and no study of content can add
much to the elucidation of this fear" (183). Just as those two skip death

wish for death drive, so they would pass over so-called superego conflicts (like survivor guilt or other buddy systems of object relation) to consider only breaking points in the adaptation process that runs on diminished fuel: "These super-ego conflicts have had nothing to do with the genesis of the symptoms; they are reactions based on the acceptance of the reduced resources as a reality. If the soldier can be made to see this reduction of his resources as an illusion, he will be able to return to combat duty. But it is a difficult illusion to remove" (187). Because the authors otherwise share and authorize this so-called illusion, it is missing alongside every other mention (one out of a hundred) of depleted resources and reserves. In more chronic forms of war neurosis, such as astasia, blindness, and paralysis, a "new adaptation is completed on the basis of the diminished resources, and the conflict is ended" (189). That's why abreaction makes no difference once the neurosis goes chronic: "The continuation of the affect is in conformity with the altered resources of the subject and the altered character of the world in which he now lives" (190). In sum, this "phenomenology of the disease" shows how the neurosis fortifies itself "by continued attempts at adaptation with depleted resources" (245–46).

Once the traumatic neurosis has set its spell and settled down, the soldier is captive audience before a two-channel set. Both the avoidance and the repetition of the traumatic event force the symptomatizing soldier to carry "the traumatic situation with him at all times" (189). It is at this impasse, to which, unchecked by therapy, the war neurotic is heading, that a "type of organization" takes over, one "characterized by a permanent reduction in resources with episodic crises in which the original trauma is reenacted in toto" (198). Again in the spirit of help-your-self adaptation, even this type of organization gives relief from unbearable anxiety.

The disease's organization "takes its character from the fact that the functions impounded by inhibition cannot be replaced by substitutive efforts, as in hysteria" (248). The soldier's "shrunken ego" trip, which must operate with diminished resources and thus within the restricted horizon of adaptation, only looks like repetition (331). It seems that what's happening happens only to recur because substitution and displacement are no longer available outlets and self-storage units of energy: "This organization process takes its character from the fact that the functions impounded by inhibition cannot be replaced by substitutive efforts, as in hysteria" (248). Because displacement isn't an option, the authors won't credit World War II soldiers with reading the standard diagnoses of shell shock to find between the lines a new undecidable space of symptom formation (within the gastric-industrial military-intestinal complex). But what they read, they will symptomatize as it is written. In the Tunisian campaign, soldiers started developing the symptoms that qualified for evacuation at an increased rate following a series of setbacks in combat. But more than the losing streak, the higher incidence of recognizably severe cases reflected what the authors call the boomerang effect of general prophylactic warnings that were issued to soldiers during their general education for battle. Meant to be a "security device," the printed reassurance that everyone has his "breaking point" caused overinterpretation of normal anxiety (32–33).

The "gap which this book purports to fill" (254) concerns the irreconcilability of Freud's conception of traumatic neurosis in *Beyond the Pleasure Principle* (the only one this study can support) with the theory of instincts (which the study has rejected in favor of "the personality as a whole" [252]). Their filler runs counter to Freud's wartime thriller, his essay "On 'the Uncanny,'" at the precise point of substitutive displacement that admits the cutting of the connection, castration, the death of the other.

> An individual cannot fear the loss of an eye because of its utility function; he can fear it only as a genital symbol. This again means that a trauma can only act symbolically. The data of traumatic neurosis belie this conclusion. (257)

Thus if fast on the intake, treatment of wartime traumatic neurosis fits its separate-but-equal status as the new brand of neurosis. It can coexist with a sexual neurosis, and the two can even communicate—and if too much time is permitted to pass, then in any event both will belong to one incorporation—but fundamentally they are disturbances of a different order. Repetition of one mode of deference to Freud lies alongside their splitting off within his science of a new area of specialization. The other mode is exclusion in theory and in no time of all symbolic substitutions from the new force field.

The abundance of references to repetition covers the contradictions and revisions addressed to Freud (but with no symbolic substitutions, please). To make over repetition as intention, not structure, the plugging away of the same adaptation points is covered for by the couple arrangement that revises one man's book in the colab of equal and separate airtime. Their transference newrosis admits the one correct setting of their operations, which at the same time is kept in the other place, while expending all-out efforts on their safety zone of traumatic neurosis that acknowledges only one natural enemy: time or, transferentially personalized, Freud, the messenger of time.

Lights! Action! Cut!

For a postwar (1949) collection on delinquency and acting out—with the prison or camp title *Searchlights on Delinquency*—Edith Jacobson gives study room to her time as political prisoner in Nazi Germany. It was a time when she was abandoned by international psychoanalysis because she had broken ranks and risked whatever stability psychoanalysis could rescue from the new regime in Germany when she harbored a subversive political affiliation. At first Ernest Jones, as always a gentleman, was gallantly on top of things right away with an international campaign to rescue her in the planning or already in the works. But a telegram from Felix Boehm made him drop everything. Boehm had the notion that Jacobson was a liability to the analytic cause because she had mixed politics with her analytic affiliation. Anna Freud seconded this notion; she spoke of this two-timing of affiliations on Jacobson's part as "treacherous" (and it wasn't the Nazi state she was referring to) (Brecht et al., *"Here Life Goes On in a Most Peculiar Way...,"* 129). Like some preview of the Rittmeister case, Jacobson returned to Germany after the Nazi takeover from neutral turf to continue her training analysis at the Berlin institute while keeping up her left-wing resistance activities. There is one major difference in addition to the differences between Scandinavia (Jacobson's safety zone) and Switzerland or a sentence of several years and the death sentence or, to break up the symmetry, being Jewish and not being Jewish, one more difference that just doesn't get underscored in the documentation of the Jacobson case, a case that sure seems to open and shut in her favor, and that typecasts the guardians of analysis at the time in sinister roles. Anna Freud's charge of treachery referred to the latest news from Berlin, namely, that Jacobson was not under arrest because she continued to see a patient whose political views went against the state and thus never broke confidentiality—up to that point, international analysis would have given her full support. No, it was her own active involvement in politics that had caught the attention of the authorities. There is more, but first let's hear from Jacobson's main defender at this time (for all time). It's Nic Hoel, originally from Norway, who was also a member of the German analytic community in 1935. She sent Jones her assessment of the Jacobson case following her reconnaissance trips to Vienna, Prague, and Berlin:

> I think she was in a very great conflict and tried to do her best. At least one could say that her behaviour showed naivity as well

as analytical as political, but not treason. Indeed that even her behaviour proved that she could have no good experience or training in political work. It rather proved her being unpolitical.

I found no time to discuss the problem of being analyst and political interested at the same time as a general problem. I also did not discuss it with you and I should hope that we could have once upon a time a discussion about it. I must say my travelling about has done it more and more ardent for me to have it talked out. Anna Freud did say that the analysis had to go before all things, but I think it is a too easy and simple formulation of it. When we now have to see in Berlin in what terrible way Boehm has to conceal so many of the scientific facts, and that they are forced of the German government in reality, not only formally, to be in accordance with the German theories, then I think it is an illusion that they can hold the analytical science pure. (Brecht et al., "*Here Life Goes On*," 129)

Hoel thus displaces the conflict onto the prospects for equality and separateness between analytic or therapeutic correctness and the political kind, projections she withdraws as untenable, given the negative example of Boehm's compromise formations on behalf of saving psychoanalysis in whatever form of collaboration with the Nazi ideology. But earlier in the letter, she repeats Anna Freud's main point of disapproval, which came to Hoel in the form of a question, one she leaves unanswered, even in the letter to Jones, on grounds of lack of information:

She asked me also if Edith had worked politically as the accusation was not as we did believe that she had had a political patient, but indeed that she had let her patient and other political persons meet in her house. (129)

But that's just it: Jacobson had openly identified with her patient's political associations and had seen no problem in being her patient's analyst and his comember in the resistance organization New Beginning. She did welcome the group into her apartment for meetings; sometimes she lectured on psychoanalytic topics, which led to long discussions on the merits of Marxism over the politics of fascism. And yes, her patient was always there, too, just another party goer, just like his comrade Edith.

That's why it was up to Jacobson to escape, start over, and, all along the way of recovery, metabolize what she knew was a conflict that went as deep as any unexamined countertransference. In 1938 Jacobson required medical attention, in fact an operation, which brought her out of the confinement of prison. She broke parole, went to New York, didn't do any more time in Nazi Germany. In New York she concluded her training analysis and established herself as a leading figure in the local analytic community. She specialized in the treatment and understanding of borderline cases. There must have been some overlaps between her borderline explorations and the borders and boundaries that were in flux in Nazi Germany, where she chose to be trained as analyst, even while she was opposed to the new state opposed to her survival. The boundary limits came crashing down, completely shut down, when she took political sides within an unexamined transferential relationship to her politically active patient. She was arrested and punished by the Nazi state and abandoned by the psychoanalytic state. Both sides viewed her as traitor.

In "Acting Out and the Urge to Betray in Paranoid Patients," Jacobson's focus on a certain "Judas complex" seems to go either way you look at it. When she refers to the case of one patient who left her and also dumped his former loyalty to Freudian analysis to become a passionate follower of Jung there could be reference between the lines to the symptomatic turns of Nazi psychoanalysis. But this acting out of a kind of consumer fascism among the medley of psychological treatments out there for a patient to be so loyal to, and then to betray to a new loyalty, doesn't have the kind of serious repercussions that the admixture of state interests necessarily introduces: "Some of them turn into real traitors of their former friends and allies, and may even accept the role of informer" (*Depression*, 303). Jacobson closes by reflecting on the ready-made contrast complex, the one that identifies with Christ, which, while too pathological on behalf of grandiosity, seems to offer, in the mode of defense, an outlet for healing from the contact high anxieties of the Judas predicament and persecution: "Thus we may say that in contrast to the role of Judas, the Christ identifications, which imply an acceptance of the masochistic surrender to God, the Father, succeed in the restitution of the object and of a grandiose self" (318).

In "The Instinctual and Emotional Conflicts of the Adolescent and the Remodeling and Growth of His Psychic Structuring," Jacobson puts the conflict on the teen that every mixer of therapeutic and political brands of correctness or containment forever is at heart. But if you're going to have a superego, you have to pass through the boundary blender of adolescence. The adolescent, at least given the similar structure of both arguments, bears a family resemblance to the paranoid loyalty-or-betrayal patient. Your typical healthy teen "may suddenly seize upon a burning interest and an outspoken position, which may be dropped after some time and replaced by another one. Anna Freud (1936) has described these phenomena very beautifully. The efforts made by adolescents to form and formulate opinions, ideas, and ideals of their own gradually lead to the development of what we call a *Weltanschauung*" (*The Self and the Object World,* 181). The "world-view," as adolescent phase or phrase, stands for left-wing political affiliations (185). By finding his ego-syntonic view of the world, the teenager becomes initiated into his own future and legacy as "coming generation" (182), or putting it another way, as "New Beginning." Adults sometimes overlook the importance of these political crushes for the reconstruction of ego and superego. But then the superego, the part of the discourse that finds Anna Freud's description of a teen's short attention span very beautiful, makes Jacobson admit one sad world of caution: "It is true, of course, that the adolescent's fascination with these pseudo ideals and his acting out may, and frequently do, have very sad results" (180).

In her 1949 "Observations on the Psychological Effect of Imprisonment on Female Political Prisoners," Jacobson turns up the volume and turns around the searchlights on a certain return to adolescence—more specifically, a grounded adolescence—which was the experience common to the political prisoners Jacobson was able to observe in their midst. In contrast to the hardened criminals, the political prisoners Jacobson is considering (as herself) could be assumed to be psychologically normal.

> Adolescence may be defined by two factors: by an uprush of instinctual impulses provoked by the inner secretory development, which then push toward a direct outlet and by a prohibition of sexuality which opposes and frustrates these impulses. The inner struggle even though it may lead to considerable emotional disturbances stimulates the mental growth. The necessity of finding other channels of gratification activates and inspires the adolescent to intense experiences and to creative work which may decrease or cease when with the beginning of his adult sexual life he grows into a mature reality adjustment. The unnatural conditions of captivity artificially create a similar inner situation. (363)

The reentry by these prisoners into adolescence is preceded by the trauma of arrest—at which point anyone at all must experience infantile conflicts and regressions. "Emotionally healthy persons will overcome the narcissistic disturbance as well as the deep regression at the beginning of confinement" (363). They shall overcome through a buildup of reaction formations—largely addressed to the bad example of prisoners whose pregenital psychic organization matches their criminality, which is all over the place—and through the reerection of sublimations that lead all the way up the superegoic watchtower.

Following the infantilizing regressions that spill over from trauma, the political prisoners graduated, then, to the crisis center of adolescence, which somehow duplicated the developmental path of Nazi Germany's psychic war economy:

> The dreadful change of surroundings, the restriction of normal everyday activity and the severing of all object relations mobilize the hostile instinctual powers from within. Unexpectedly struck, the ego of the prisoner has to face a fight on two fronts: against the outside as well as against his own inside world. (344)

The teen locked inside this two-front conflict will experience "a chaotic jumble of feelings, succumbing to a quickly changing series of images (like the projection of a motion picture or of a rigid and obsessionally recurring succession of thoughts)" (344). But out of this captive audience to the war-neurotic newsreels of double conflict, the teen group of rebels *with* a cause succeeded in setting up the saving reaction formations and in resetting the sublimational wavelengths to which the superego must go in order to come back.

Double Burial

To support her observation of initial regressions experienced by all inmates upon impact with the arrest, Jacobson cites Andreas Bjerre, a Swedish psychologist who, already before the First World War, had specialized in criminology, which at the time was one of the newest areas into which German psychology was extending its expertise and influence, largely in competition with psychoanalysis. In his most famous work, *The Psychology of Murder*, Bjerre's style was Adlerian-macho, all opposed to sexological readings, since the bottom line in all cases was so evidently unfitness or incurable terror of existence. He takes note of, only to dismiss as insignificant, the super strong bond between so many criminals and their mothers, a bonding that's the exception to the regard they reserved for all other "fellow creatures" as nothing "but dead matter" (81). Even in the cases of functionally incestuous relations with their one and only mother, Bjerre just can't see any sexual etiology in the development of the criminal's mind. The maternal bond—together with every criminal's regular frenzy for self-defense, for explaining his situation to others—was the couple of stray human traits that had kept Bjerre from seeing the two basic conditions for the way they were. "It was therefore a considerable time before I clearly recognized that the determining force in their lives from beginning to end was nothing but their sense of insecurity, their cowardice, their terror of life, or, in a word, their complete lack of self-confidence" (69). Then there was the bio-setting of these sons to consider when it came to their sex crimes. For example: "His lusts were by no means the effect of excessively strong natural impulses, but simply a product of decadence resulting from the incurable natural defects of his nature, from the essential weakness of his whole being" (78). Bjerre doesn't stop to consider the mother's role (whether as active influence or as "dead matter") in any of these more or less incestuous bonds with the son. This short stop is symptomatic of the Adlerian reproach. Senses or organs of deficiency and grandeur, according to Freud, grow always only out of the interpretation that's made under affective conditions of relationship to the primary other. But what comes first, the mother or the bad egg? Adler eggs on an individual responsibility that ends up subservient to a communal We that's always bigger than the two of us, mother and child.

Bjerre's *Psychology of Murder* was already on a direct continuum with the "individual psychology"—the generation of the We—that was Adler's inheritance diffused throughout Nazi German therapy-speak at the time of Jacobson's move to Berlin in 1935 for her training analysis. Jacobson's own situation in her study of her fellow inmates in Nazi prison recalls the lab conditions of Bjerre's research opportunism. Prisoner among fellow prisoners, she had her primo research conditions cut out for her. In his study Bjerre admits outright that the sitting-stuck prison population is the best research resource around. But whereas Bjerre is limited to natural-born criminal minds that just can't be extended to any normative or developmental considerations, except perhaps by negative example (but that's really the limit), Jacobson has her political prisoners (and herself) to work with, a population that even Bjerre might admit was the exception to the hard-and-fast rule of imprisoned life. But then there's the ego-and-superego view to consider, one that could lead the analytically inclined to view political prisoners as self-destructive actors-out. Thus Jacobson's stop-and-restart developmental scheme rescues her population not only from Bjerre's condemnation of all those bio low in self-esteem but also from the analytic construction of all acts with consequences as transferential and under unconscious remote control. Jacobson stands up, once again, against all odds or fronts, for herself in the immediate 1949 context of searchlight pathologization of all teen or group identification in conflict with society as delinquency or deviance. Then, beginning in the footnote underworld, she admits a maternal identification that contradicts both Bjerre's ignorance and the analytic construction of Oedipus.

Against this backdrop of ingredients for the metabolization of what was hardest in her life, Jacobson takes off from a classically Freudian position, deep down, and expands on a group-psychological fantasy that still belongs to Freud, though most would not know it. It's the phase Freud went through just in time for Nazi Germany not to be able to exclude his science. First Jacobson makes a classic observation that, however, in the context of rerunning adolescence in a same-sex setting, exceeds the usual point. The wish for a child that the all-female group shared reminds Jacobson "of the prominent part which it plays in the mastery of the castration conflict" (362 n. 4). However, for the virgin mother group, the prospect of giving birth is one-half-more narcissistically gratifying; it's a group replicational activity much like amoeba splitting. This is where the waste of homosexual consummation, which the hardened criminals were practicing all around them, gets streamlined by the teen group in the same-sex technorelations of shared fantasies of redevelopment or rebirth as the strongest egos to date in their lives. Thus personalization of contact with the outside world was just too upsetting. Forget personal visits! Letters were especially welcome, but not, once again, for their personalized labels, but as common group resource. "Especially in the penitentiary, which establishes firm identifications among the prisoners, letters are common property: they are exchanged and enjoyed together" (346).

Jacobson's reference to Bjerre lines up her 1949 reckoning with the time in Nazi prison (between the lines) with the trajectory of her voluntary reentry into the new Germany she opposed politically but not necessarily, or at least not too emphatically, as an order inimical to her continued work as analytic candidate in a setting of energetic eclecticism. Andreas Bjerre died in 1925. His younger brother Poul was an analyst and psychotherapist, whose first contact with Freud's thought relieved itself via Jung's new and improved version or aversion, Jung's own negative transference to Freud.

In *The Remaking of Marriage*, in the chapter "Bondage and License," Bjerre's Freud connection has withdrawn into one direct hit, the sexological reduction of the unconscious to repression, which, according to Jung, is the ultimate limit to Freud's system and all that it's good for. If the problem's a sexual one, especially if it shows itself in real time, during a phase of development, there's no better treatment. Bjerre's patient is stuck on masturbation, the less poetical side of an overall emotional fantasy and attitude, which can no longer be all that it is, just metaphor for what's only transitory. "Here psychoanalysis is wanted. To begin with, it reduces the guilty conscience of the masturbator, if not to a blank, at least to something which has nothing to do with the fantastically worked-up sense of guilt.... There are few cases where psychoanalysis renders man such a great service as when, at this critical stage, it reveals subconscious inhibitions and thereby opens up the perspective for a full and free life. He who has been helped in this way is frequently tempted to demand of psychoanalysis that it shall penetrate to the very bottom of that which is predetermined by fate, and to reach decisions which our deepest instincts should decide—an exaggeration against which every sensible psychoanalyst should give warning" (78–79).

Not only just before 1933 but also after the war, Bjerre is the yes, but man when it comes to Freud. Relations with the superego or trauma's impact as anxiety producing? Yes. But it's just that we resist the new by enshrining some idealized phase of our development or nondevelopment. Changes in life, rather than external force or internal conflict, are already enough to make you anxious. It's hard to bring one developmental period to its close, because the new phase must thus be admitted (*Unruhe, Zwang, Angst*, 10–12). In 1936 Bjerre published a German-language version of his big work on dream interpretation, which was quickly reviewed and hailed in the *Zentralblatt für Psychotherapie*. The publication straddled the south of the border neutral zone—Zurich—and reached an "and" back across the boundary to Leipzig. The resistance refrain has given way, and itself away, here to complete refraining from even honorable mention of Freud. Bjerre's inside-out view of dream as a method of auto-healing comes in twelve steps. The step names are Jung compatible, both Nietzsche resonant and spatial sublime. Yes, but, there's one exception: "Identification" is one step's name. Bjerre admits that it's the one step to which he can't give delineation and its content, because it overlaps with "Negation" (which came two steps before). Let's call this a moment of ambivalence in the rhythm method that otherwise organizes Bjerre's dream phenomenology. "This: at once to iden-tify with a figure and to negate the same figure lies profoundly in the na-ture of identification" (172). The primal instance of this nature or essence is identification with mother (175). By chance, a techno-analogy has already entered the discourse at this juncture. When Bjerre starts unpacking dreams for the identification, he wants us to imagine the dream as a film that lets roll its overall organization and coherence (170). Taking another chance or glance, we know that this is the section containing the second of the book's homosexual cases. Same-sex child's play led over time and again to an identificatory inversion that, however, cannot belie her constitutionally "strong, normal sexuality" (173). In one of her four dreams, she has to sit down in the theater seat nearest her even after she notices that someone has covered them all with thick spit ("daß jemand auf alle freien Stühle gespuckt hat" [173]). In Freud's *Interpretation of Dreams* the dream activity of *Spucken* (to spit) sidles up to the stowaway meaning of *Spuken* (to haunt).

The triangulation hold of Freud's thought that Poul Bjerre was resist-ing in 1911 and 1912 involved his charged relations with Lou Andreas-Salomé. He had to fight off his identification with her and be his own man. He soon found himself all alone and unacknowledged with his double de-mand for synthesis between psychosynthesis and psychoanalysis. This is how von Gebsattel gives poor Bjerre's bio in an introduction to a 1970 Ger-man translation. It's as though in 1913 Bjerre had precursed his work, which had to wait for the post-Freudians, like Weizsäcker, to acknowledge as the legacy of a precursor. This is typical of the German profile of Poul Bjerre by the metonymy and absence of two major exclusions: the untimely death of Andreas and Poul's celebrity status in the new order of Nazi psychother-apy and psychoanalysis. Poul Bjerre and his Scandinavian circle kept up relations with the Göring institute right up until the end. Scandinavia was thus, by the end, the only kernel of reality left in Nazi German psychother-apy's ongoing claim to be just one section within an international organi-zation of colleagues. The thirteenth volume of the *Zentralblatt für Psychother-apie* put on a birthday spread for Dr. Poul Bjerre, photo and all. He turned sixty-five in 1941. In a 1939 issue of the *Zentralblatt,* in the section "Current

Georg Sluyterman von Langeweyde, *German Oak Tree*. The caption reads, "Death for one's Fatherland is worth eternal honor." Below that, somewhat incongruously: "Ewald Christian von Kleist, killed in action 1759." Reproduced from *Die Kunst im deutschen Reich* 4, nos. 8–9 (August–September 1940): 287.

Events," the gossip column of the stars, "A Day with Dr. Bjerre" was the profile of the day. (The Danish colleague who wrote this and other pieces that put this alliance together would seem to be one exception to Hannah Arendt's ruling that the Danes were all great.) In the world of Nazi psychotherapy and psychoanalysis, and it was a big world out there, probably still the biggest in its category, Bjerre was the international star. He was there in 1937 helping Jung make the Copenhagen psychotherapy conference the happening event, the really big show of Nazi German psychotherapy's place in the international setting. In 1940 Bjerre turned down the offer of international leadership. But that same year he established a psychotherapeutic institute in Stockholm, one that was, if not in the fine print then in spirit, the franchise operation of the Berlin center. The 1941 birthday greeting fondly remembers colleague Bjerre's participation in the 1940 Vienna conference, where he presented his thoughts on "The Role of the Unconscious in Increase of Production." Already in title, this paper seems tailored for the Nazi line, but at the same time for the Adlerian lines of a discourse that had stopped undead in his brother's tracks. Early on, Bjerre joined Jung and Göring in considering Hitler as psychotherapist, as the big healer. His postwar publication, in 1946, was *Spökerier* (that's right: hauntings). There was only one un-Bjerred spook around, the one hailing from the corpus of brother Andreas. But if he could now see that his falling for Hitler's psychotherapy was for the Faustian second chance he saw coming over his brother's discourse, it was, all the same, too late.

Therapists for Heyer

As far as psychotherapeutic technique in particular goes, all
methods to which we have recourse can also be applied to
what are for the most part physical afflictions, and yet one
must remember that there are only a few methods, which to a
great degree aim at the root of the illness, where the somatic
and psychic are almost indistinguishable cohabitants. That is
hypnosis and autogenic training, as Schultz has described it, on
the one side, and analysis in the widest sense on the other.

—FRITZ MOHR, "THE BODY-SOUL PROBLEM
(FROM THE POINT OF VIEW OF THE PSYCHOTHERAPIST)"

From 1940 to 1943, G. R. Heyer was charged with *Hippokrates* readership,
with spreading the German Institute for Psychological Research and Psychotherapy's takeoff on something old, something new, in a series of letters, chips off the old workshop. Heyer was telling the colleagues out there
how he did it again, always short-term work but with depth-psychological
charge, and then as the show progressed, colleagues would send in reports
of their own success stories, which Heyer would air with a brief precis
from the sponsor of the highlights to look for in the as-live audience participation. Even the general practitioner can practice psychotherapy.

First column, first case. He was suffering from a typical nervous twist
in the neck (torticolis). By the time he made it to the office of psychotherapy, he had endured every therapy known to clinical and biological medicine. The only psychic reference or referral he had received had been addressed to his willpower, to will away the turning of the neck that got in
the way of what he was told to do: pull himself together. Heyer quickly establishes rapport and trust, and the account of overwork opens onto, ultimately, frustrations in marriage: they're a couple of coitus interrupters. He
doesn't treat the twist-off symptom, which was already remarkable for the
resistance of its staying power, its worsening with every command to stop,
right from the start, which happened to be, to him, while he was driving
his car (accompanied by fear-of-driving panic attacks) and then whenever
the motor was running, rumbling the seat. Heyer also tells the patient to
stop willing it away; that's as much in the way as any symptom. The patient was instructed in colleague Schultz's self-help hypnosis-like technique, autogenic training, and Heyer slipped him, while he was helping

himself, into a deep hypnotic state, in which his utter treatability or heala-bility was strongly suggested to him.

As the patient improves, the rapport with Heyer deepens, and opens wide for further instructions. Both driving the car and coitus interruptus come under interdiction. But then the treatment is interrupted for six weeks on Heyer's account: doubly interrupted, since even Heyer's assistant has now been drafted into the army. They meet six months later; in the mean-time, the patient was doing desk work for his part of military service. No more neck symptom! Looking back, the two, led by the healed patient, can now touch on the midlife crisis Heyer knew the patient had essentially all along been going through, but was too big a mouthful in the short term. The healed one can now accept for the second phase of his life that the pur-suit of happiness is not always on the go for the gold. Heyer counts down thirteen sessions of psychotherapy in all. It's tempting to reflect on how much time, energy, and money could so often be saved if the diagnosis of psychosomatic illness were made at the right time and—instead of the so-matic treatments—psychotherapy were regularly administered (279).

On his second date as advice columnist, Heyer writes a patient he had seen only for one session, who has in the meantime been trying to take the cure long distance by extending the course of therapy with books about psychotherapy. Heyer is happy that she realizes that her illness is of a psy-chic nature. But she's missing out on the "'dialectical process,' made possi-ble in the exchange with a third person" (385). It's the third person who is required for objectivity and safety in the therapeutic situation. She writes that their work encouraged her to interpret one of her dreams a certain way, which was fine, but she felt like belief in Santa Claus had been taken away from her again. Here Heyer puts his finger on the feeling expressed in the same clause of separation in the single session with him: she's con-structing him, for resistance's sake, as retraumatizing her, taking from her again the mysteries of life. He recommends that she draw the mysteriously pleasure-inducing dream just as colleague Jung in Zurich would also sug-gest. First take the dream for what it is. But it's hard for us, raised and alienated as we all were "under the influence of the materialist Zeitgeist of a technological century" (387). The unconscious strikes back in the subtitles to the depression his correspondent has had to endure. In her dream the dream child has its back turned to her: you're a woman, and in the dream you have no real contact with the child. You're looking for the man. But be-ware of those who peddle "'sexual' problems" or the one-sided apostles of adjustment (the Freudian or Adlerian lines, in short) (388). "It also sounds like you unhappily got hold of studies that were once considered 'depth psychology' but which our contemporary German *Seelenkunde* [soul teaching] has outgrown. The works reflected the largely Semitic nature of their authors and thus only the inferior, the bad, the terrible could be seen" (388). They gave us the reductive version of the more upbeat, holistic, respectful, client-centered therapy in Germany today.

Another issue, another column of therapy advice. The husband of the woman who, after therapy with Heyer, was able to give birth, this time in only two-and-a-half hours after breaking the record on the two previous occasions with thirty-six- and twenty-eight-hour labors, writes with gratitude for the miracle but also expresses total incomprehension of the connection between the psychotherapy and the lighter download of labor. Heyer recounts the fearful wife's childhood of spoiling and catastrophic misinformation about the curses of a mature woman's bodily life. In session he hypnotized her easily and suggested birthing instructions to her, including breathing lessons.

For his next column, Heyer addresses a colleague regarding the treatment of a patient suffering panic attacks involving the sick sense of his heart beating too fast and his breathing, in and out, only deliberately. But the patient protested that as far as his health was going, he followed nutritional guidelines every day and had been a vegetarian for the last sixteen years. All these dietary cures have been taken in to improve his sexual problems. "These, however, are the kernel around which all the rest of B.'s neurosis has organized itself. At age ten he was seduced by schoolmates into masturbation. The whole future life of B. became a continued—and hopeless—fight against this 'sin'" (485). He feels that he's depleting his sexual energy or potency right down to the reserves, to the slip showing: "It is remarkable to his psychologist that B. misspoke several times, whenever in fact he wanted to refer to his urine *[Urin]* he would say ruin *[Ruin]*."

But the sense of his masturbation as the kind of perversion that just one look in his eyes would advertise drove him away from society, which in turn promoted his frame of self-reference and his masturbatory activities. As colleague von Hattingberg once observed to the point: "One masturbates not 'with oneself' but rather 'against the others'" (485). But the patient even had the sense of doom or denial that he might as well masturbate to excess, kill himself by just doing it nonstop, all the time, since he was incurable anyway. We know, also by way of ethnological study, that masturbation is normal as transitional objective and phase from childhood—on the way to finding the way to woman. It's a normal form (anyway, for men) of "ventilating" what's coming soon. With improper parenting and so on, the transitional use of masturbation—conceived as a placeholder running on empty—cannot be overcome or left behind. "Such a person remains forever stuck in the transitional stage.... He becomes asocial, indeed, in time, a self-hater. And with that he blocks his way to woman and to mature genitality ever more" (485). At the other end he tries to live in his head, but his bodily life will not be ignored and takes to the language of symptoms originating in all the organs from which he has withdrawn his interest and investments, like his intestines, which come complete with a direct connection to the earth. "One could speak of a lacking 'libidinal' investment in the corresponding organ systems" (486).

On the other hand, in this rather brief letter, which is followed right away in the same issue of *Hippokrates* by the next installment, Heyer points to real somatic problems that upon treatment at the same time relieve the patient of all the neurotic-seeming symptoms, too. Tonsils or teeth, for example, once removed, can offer symptom freedom. "All these patients were referred to us as psychoneurotics. A group of them, given the lack of any apparent physical cause, were suspected of being simulators" (555). Therapists must work closely with physicians—and we medical psychotherapists, Heyer concludes, must also remember to keep a lookout for physical factors.

Next in the column of cases, the businessman who walked into Heyer's office was not a "case for 'depth psychology'" but one for practical and energetic counseling, advice in living" (556). Heyer is ruling out all "schematic therapists" who would have treated him "with suggestion or psychoanalysis." But he also says that thanks to German psychotherapy, bromides and related pseudomedicinal treatments have been overcome through the rediscovery of the soul or psyche ("das Seelische"). "The original version of psychotherapy responded of course to the psychoneuroses only as individual questions that the patient was raising. Today the community values are moving more and more into our field of vision." Hence the German Institute's sponsorship by the German Work Front (DAF), which realizes that "the economy is run by humans who are animated by psyche" (556).

Next on the installment plan of newspaper free therapy, Heyer shares his concern about a trauma case. It was a patient who had an accident that gave her a shock:

> Which I would characterize as a disturbance of the feeling for totality and health. Whoever was wounded as a soldier or suffered some other heavy accident knows that the human being before the trauma ... lives in a naive sense of undamaged security; an insult to the never before wounded intactness of his physical (and with that, psychic) person is inconceivable in a deeper sense. In the language of the old analysis one would have named

this state that of primitive narcissism. The wounding of this state (which is psycho-physical), whether in the case of the soldier through gunfire, or in the case of the worker by an accident, suddenly annihilates this entire, unknown, elemental sense of security. A new transitional state emerges—full of the highest insecurity. (606)

The digression into the war neurosis field continues with protest that the soldiers who experience the mood swings and narrow misses of psychic trauma are not cowards but have merely discovered yet another test to pass, a realization of vulnerability to which the soldier now must adapt himself. Heyer, while in charge of companies of soldiers in World War I, had taken special care with the education of soldiers and officers returning to their units after a first wounding.

The psychological moment in accident recovery is not given enough attention. Just because the physical damage is done and then healed doesn't certify health: the transitional stage has to be overcome "following the loss of his 'narcissistic' security" (606). But this particular patient requires a certain combo, which Heyer advises that this correspondent make clear to the insurance administration: psychotherapy together with massage and acupuncture for immediate muscle cramp relief (and for the transference).

Heyer introduces a young man who has suffered from epileptic attacks ever since a gym class accident in adolescence. The accident, everyone felt, was explanation enough. But there was more to cross Heyer's mind. And on deeper recollection, it came out that moments before, in the bathroom, the boy had been seduced into masturbation. When he came out of the initiation into the gym and promptly had his big accident, he was sure at the time that it represented punishment from on high. But the attacks that followed as syndications of the accident also offered welcome "security" that nothing more would happen in the seduction department or back room. He couldn't take the bad air of certain bars or dance clubs, for example. "His mother of course, for her own unconscious reasons, was a vigorous defender of this theory" (650).

But the psychoneurotic symptoms have already gone too far to contain themselves: they "proliferate in the mode of cancer" (650). Whereas before it would have to be "the look at some seductive figure, a dirty joke, etc." that set off an attack, soon the remotest association sufficed: "Small and smallest association markers, which through the events of life had obtained sensual significance, could now stand for the whole actual complex, yes, right into the dreams this expansionism spread: so that erotic dreams on occasion prompted attacks" (650). Father transference is established, and Heyer leads his patient (in whom already "everything pressed toward a freer and more natural being") "out of the magic garden of neurosis and its security into open and free space" (651).

When the son starts going dancing, mother can but resist. After eight weeks, four sessions per week, "he had become a young lion who had tasted blood and could find no pleasure in mother's meatless world view" (651).

Young man goes west, into the American West, to join an uncle out there and live the life of a trapper. He writes Heyer from New York, where he resides in the meantime, that sometimes a great feeling of insecurity will come over him (especially when riding the subway), but all he has to do is remember what the two of them talked about back then, and the whole "magic" is dissipated again. And now the most recent news is that he has married and become a reproductive part of society.

For his next column, Heyer gives us the record of a bad case of the cts. He was man, she was woman married to a "wonderful" man with two small children. It was on behalf of the rest of the family that he took her on. "A classic degenerative hysteric! You know I don't like using that word; it has . . . become in the meantime more an insult than a real characterization of a psychological fact. But here I must use it" (740). She has an infinite store of roles: "the lover, the healed, the wounded, the misunderstood, the adventuress, the noble one and the patient" (740). She shares her plans to act on fantasies that could only hurt her family in a very mean-spirited way (Heyer refuses to give the details). At that time Heyer quietly but resolutely told her what he thought of her and her kind. She rushed out of his office.

Imagine Heyer's surprise when the husband mentioned to him one day in passing how much the therapy back then had helped the little woman. She said that she and the good doctor were able to uncover her "primal scene" (but she too couldn't, by doctor's orders, tell anyone, not even her husband, the contents of the scene). Well, she's still not healed, Heyer concludes. Or can throwing someone out of therapy still be considered therapy? But the woman is now, as far as the husband's family values go, symptom free.

Two new columns advance a referral: a woman suffering from major anxiety neurosis, who had been treated with bromides without any improvement, was referred to Heyer by our next correspondent. Six years ago she married a man twenty years her elder, who brought along two sons (from a first marriage that had ended in divorce) who were more her peers or siblings in age. "You and I can deduce from this right away that the choice of a much older partner of weak temperament has its psychological reasons" (880). Her marriage reproduced or reduced itself to one only child. For the rest she was frigid. One day she had a brief encounter, like two lips passing, with a kissing cousin. She had never felt this way before. But she quickly "forgot" the episode. About a year ago, the cousin announced his upcoming visit and stay in their home. Shortly before his arrival, she started manifesting the high-anxiety states that kept the cousin from staying with or even visiting them at all and brought her to therapy. That her cousin, as her own "representative of life," had released certain reactions inside her remained completely "unconscious" (881). She has agoraphobia: only psychotherapy can come to the rescue. But she must be discouraged from leaving the marriage. First she must mature. Then if divorce is still the answer, at least she would be free *for* something rather than only *from* the same old thing.

For his next column, too, it's another report that was sent in to Heyer that he shares with his readership because it shows again that general practitioners can and must think therapeutically: they alone are the first to get their hands on our youth and thus can catch neuroses where they breed early on, and can even strike preemptively. The correspondent writes about his young patient, a problem eater. "More specifically he isn't acting against his parents but it's his unconscious, which is that much more influential than in an adult. That's why a child can wage the struggle for power with such resolve, because consciousness has not yet intervened with its inhibiting influence" (912).

Readers next want to know how, contrary to "old doctrinaire psychoanalysis" (1079), Heyer's eclecticism encourages collaboration with biologically based physical therapists. Heyer, for one, can't "expect all salvation [*Heil*] to come from the exclusively body-soul knowledge of healing [*Heilkunde*]" (1079). It's not enough to free an individual from his complexes, although such a cleanup operation may be necessary prep work. The link to the totality is what was missing but now can be used to make psychotherapy worthy of National Socialism. But one must not approach the question as one-sidedly as was once the case with "Adler's so-called Individual Psychology" (1079).

Shock Talk

In the present emergency, psychoanalysis is quite modern, and
all psychiatric journals are more or less full of papers either
about "Psychoanalysis and Military Service," or "Psychoanalysis
of Propaganda." . . . The naivety of the questions which psychoanalysts are being asked by authoritative people is enormous.—
The discussions about propaganda have begun to bring a little
order into the problems which appear in a different light when
the existence of the unconscious is accepted.

—OTTO FENICHEL, *RUNDBRIEFE*

In the April 1943 issue of the *Connecticut State Medical Journal*, the article
"Pennsylvania Psychiatrist Talks on Shell Shock" contains a couple of slips
that add up to the message that it's shell shock that's all talk. Before the
rundown of emotional conflicts can be reiterated in print, another claim
has appeared: "The most common mental casualty in modern warfare is
the 'shell shock' of the newspapers, or war conversation hysteria" ("Pennsylvania Psychiatrist," 274). That's from the PR sphere of the preconscious.
A more unconscious message is transmitted in Calvin Drayer and Stephen
Ranson's "Combat Psychiatry." Just a slip of the melancholic's ghost mis-
prints "casualty" as follows: "The causality who is too disturbed to be relieved" (94). I submit these two off-the-wall echoes of the latency of psychoanalysis throughout the U.S. at-war literature on war neurosis as a
corrective to the way analyst Gregory Zilboorg raises not the ghost of a
question battle-worthy of the issue of Freud's influence. For the all-clear
opening issue of the *Yearbook of Psychoanalysis* (in 1945), Zilboorg allowed a
1943 lecture, first published in 1944, to be reprinted. Each stopover could
be graphed against yet another peak in the spread of American psychotherapeutic eclecticism (which was born out of the spirit, the ghost, that the
Nazi war effort had not given up on). But Zilboorg won't dignify the diversified portfolio by the name "psychoanalysis." He chooses an image
from Freud's "On 'the Uncanny'" to see his point:

> I, for one, would want to look at the present status of psychoanaly-
> sis not through a microscope, not even through field glasses
> which offer high magnification of particular details, but rather
> through inverted binoculars which offer a total view as if from a
> distance. (80)

But Zilboorg's denial of the military medium looks through the contemporary counterpart to the more period field glasses onto a battlefield that fits inside a corridor: "We thus enter a field of compromises and passionate rationalizations of these compromises" (82). Changes in formatting and timing of the session, to fit the military (and insurance) group planning of rapid turnover and loss cutting, are so much "ransom" paid to our social conditions and conditionings (83).

> I do not view the sporadic trend to revise Freud in order to adapt him to the unreasonable demands of our cultural crisis as a creative or constructive trend. I hold this view not because Freud requires no reexamination and revision, but because this trend today seems primarily based on what appears to be a concerted effort to reject Freud. (83)

But rejection of Freud in name brings back the spirit of resistance, which recycles psychoanalysis back into the "concerted effort" to unacknowledge one's sources.

R. D. Gillespie notes in the survey portion of his study of psychological effects of warfare that Freud's share paled, in comparison shopping, as reductive, a mental-conflict exclusive. But Freud's view got some color by recharging with the savings of the older model of energy: "The concept of the nervous system as a storage battery which could run down colored the views of Freud and others" (15). Thus colorized, the black-on-white view of conflict seems more compatible with current situations. "Nevertheless there is still room in these days for something of the old notion of deficit of energy. People undoubtedly vary in the quality of their available energy" (16). The energy model further admits specialization or specification of a difference between psychopaths and psychoneurotics: "A distinction I would make is that psychopathic personalities represent abnormalities in the energy endowment of the individual while psychoneuroses involve defects only of its distribution as the result of maladjustments in the introjected social relationships" (44).

The greatest energy control measure is the language that defines, describes, diagnoses—in a word, suggests. As a whole, the World War II U.S. battery of readings of the military psyche as recording device—presenting problems have been largely ventriloquized by the terminology of the treating therapist's agenda—installed a reception that only had to be turned on again postwar for controversies around the agency of rape or the repressed memory of childhood abuse. Gillespie sets a series of examples for literal reading:

The reaction is not only an object of thought; it embodies some of the observer's concepts. In other words, the form of the illness is to be conceived as a product of inner factors in the patient, and of factors imposed by the environment. As the theories entertained by the observer are an important part of the environment, it follows that changes in theory and form will be closely related. (33)

The only part of the hysterical syndrome which has been popular of recent years is "loss of memory." Its popularity must be attributed partly to newspaper reports, since the press has been fond of featuring this particular affection. (28)

No multiple personalities are seen nowadays. With their better knowledge of the hysterical type of personality, doctors nowadays are on their guard against creating them. (27)

From the lexicon of diagnosis to the newspapers, Gillespie works so hard to avoid admitting the transference that once he has taken one turn too many in his discussion of the reality or fantasy of early sexual trauma, he ends up reinventing the countertransference: "In the light of the present discussion it becomes conceivable that the fantasy was often not even in the patient's mind, but in the observer's first of all" (34).

John Whitehorn's 1946 "Changing Concepts of Psychoneurosis in Relation to Military Psychiatry" sees conceptual change as always in transition from one terminal term (that has outlived its usefulness but still won't go away) to a new terminology that's necessarily a weakened offshoot, doubled over with survivor guilt:

Shell shock was a spectacular sort of term which captured the imagination of Mott and others, as inevitably as shell-fire itself captures one's attention. Now it is the peculiar property of such vivid ideas never to die, properly and decently. One has to sit on the squirming corpse of one concept to open the door to a new concept, and such a posture does not favor the most advantageous handling of the new concept. (1)

Psychiatric principles were somewhat too narrowly conceived in the early war years, when limited too sharply to the business of detecting neurotic traits or patterns. Some change to a broader basis was required, but the change which actually occurred was in the direction of inventing diagnostic labels indicative of situational factors rather than personality factors. We got a crop of diagnostic or pseudodiagnostic terms such as "flying stress," "combat fatigue," "operational fatigue," etc. Such a shift in nomenclature was in part motivated by a kindly desire to spare valiant men the implied disgrace of a psychoneurotic label, and to spare them also some of the then current administrative implications of such labels. (3)

Thus the ever popular "adjustment disorder" was borne out by military administration of classical terms and types of neurosis. But the "compensatory mechanisms, face-saving, and anxiety-sparing" always also serve the disturbed ego that must help itself to "second-rate types of emotional adjustment" (5). The adjustment in nomenclature was completely justified by its responsiveness to the new "triangular relationship between situation, reaction and personality" (3). Something new and something as old as Father, Son, and Holy Ghost.

The paranoid insight into the babbling crook of language is basic to the coverage all trauma sufferers receive in Foster Kennedy's "Nervous Conditions following Accident with Special Reference to Head Injury":

> It must be borne in mind that susceptibility to suggestion is common to all of us, that no more than three-tenths of our opinions can be regarded as our own! (442)

> Better definition of the terms employed in psychopathology is sorely needed. For a generation the use of neurasthenia has covered almost all abnormal states of a highly depressed nature, and hysteria, to both doctors and laymen, has too often merged into malingering. Medical speech has toyed with and maltreated both these words. (459)

According to Millais Culpin, the label was often showing: "A diagnostic label was often the starting point of a man's downfall" (54).

By the August 1945 issue of the *Bulletin of the U.S. Army Medical Department*, excerpts from articles published under the names of authors could reappear here under good-news headlines. "Psychiatric Nomenclature":

> An initial step has been made by the Army in the direction of changing the method of recording the diagnosis in psychoneurotic responses. The term "psychoneurosis" is to be dropped from the individual clinical records in Army medical installations. In its stead, the physician will designate the specific type of psychoneurotic response, such as "anxiety reaction," "conversion reaction," "compulsive obsessive reaction." In addition to this term designating the syndrome, a brief statement on the personality structure and predisposition will be made, a brief statement

of the external precipitating stress in the present illness, and finally an evaluation of the functional capacity of the individual to carry on in his last assignment. By this method it is believed the psychiatrist of necessity will be more specific and will be required to formulate a more complete picture of the patient in terms understandable even to a layman.

The possible benefits from this system include a more thoughtful consideration and evaluation of the patient, a more definitive diagnostic formulation which will be more easily and clearly understood by nonpsychiatric personnel, less misuse of diagnostic terms, an opportunity to indicate that even though the patient has some form of psychoneurosis he need not and should not be discharged from the service, and less chance on the part of the public for misunderstanding the term "psychoneurosis." (U.S. Army, "Psychiatric Nomenclature," 134)

Columns

After filling his column with advice for another colleague in the provinces, Heyer comes to a new request for a referral. Yes, the German Institute in Berlin does maintain a list of therapists and therapeutically trained or compatible physicians everywhere in Germany. But there's no one in the correspondent's area. "We leave it up to you to judge whether it is right and desirable that psychotherapists should be so sparsely represented in our Fatherland" (1169). It's the pre-1933 materialism of institutions (and this one blanket condemnation has medical schools covered too) that is still resisting what's new. Today one should be able to expect every general practitioner to be trained to some extent in the techniques of hypnosis and autogenic training.

He tells it like it is, like his readers just know it is. Even when unknowingly, it's always mother's fault. Heyer suddenly opens up and shares that he won't try us or his patients with archetype talk: it's all so bloodless compared to the live view of hands-on experiment. Then Heyer digresses to talk pet peeves. A cat gave birth to a dead kitten and nearly died herself of frustrated motherhood: but then she recathected one of her teenage cats from the litter before and turned the youth back into her little baby. The young cat has ever since had a glazed kind of "sleepy clown" look, but the mother, upon finishing with her nursing instincts, snapped right out of it and is doing just fine.

Maybe if Mrs. N. had been able to have more children, she could have let her son go. "But her first child was also born dead, and she didn't bear more children than the one replacement child. Hans remained *the* child" (1276).

Heyer flashes back to cases or "dramas, which are begun in order to put a second child in its place, in lieu of a deceased child of the other gender (who was engendered consciously as 'substitute' [Ersatz]), and how the parents read the being of the deceased into the other child. But that doesn't belong here" (1276).

What's new? A colleague has been writing Heyer asking if it would be possible to come and sit in on one of Heyer's sessions. Heyer's answer is about the all-importance of safety and the impossibility of the witness.

Regarding local resistance, the overly interested colleague reports back to Heyer: "One said: psychotherapy (which in a very over-simplifying manner gets equated with psychoanalysis?) is destructive work that 'breaks down' without building" (157). Heyer reframes the breaking-down reproach and affirms it as a shaking up *(Erschütterung)*, the dynamic tense or tension of shock: the dynamic processes in the psyche need excitement (158). All those reproaches about Bolshevism of therapy et cetera do, however, fit the kind of therapy represented by "S. Freud in his book 'The Future of an Illusion'" (158).

Next comes the case of Miss O. Her couple of parents forever showed a lack of any meaningful contact: thus, for her, marriage could only mean "neurosis a deux, called marriage" (159). Her case can be seen as coming down to a formula: "Whoever must undertake the reckoning with one's inner vitality so crookedly, will require in time ever more security, in order to avoid all contact with what is feared" (159). Her "guideline" (Adlerian watchword) was avoidance of feeling, as that way even madness lies. That's why she gives up painting. "One studies philology. And: one remains single" (159). She says that the guys she likes don't reciprocate and the ones hot to trot over into her life are unacceptable. "Coincidence? Bad Luck? We know that those are—unconscious!—securizings, lapses" (159). She has to be a patient: retraining takes its time. Brand new organs must be formed in order to grasp what's new. And the unconscious has to be made conscious. The little girl and teenager that live on inside her undeveloped must give way to the maturing of a "knowing femininity." Heyer closes by recommending Schultz's *Neurosis, Life Crisis, Medical Duty* and Mohr's "Psychotherapy of Organic Illnesses" for future reading (160).

Heyer writes to a former patient whose speech disorder, which Heyer had busted for him on an earlier date, has now returned. Sorry to hear it. "Now we have to pay after all for the fact that the beginning of the war interrupted our psychotherapeutic work" (242). Among the reminders of their live therapy together that Heyer jots down for their current correspondence course of action, there's the outbreak of stuttering in school at age nine (following a bronchial illness). At school there was persecution, call to order by willpower alone, suspicion of simulation, all of which fortified the patient's shy disposition (which is "the cause of the symptom") (243). In the father transference made onto Heyer, they could both observe the retraumatizing provocation of anger and punishment, which was the function of the stuttering. Once the transference could be seen through in their therapeutic relationship there was no stuttering any longer. Then autogenic training was used to extend the safety zone of the therapy session to other walks and talks of life. Ergo: it's your boss who has given back an unresolved father transference that makes you stutter. Ask yourself who is the more secure in this relationship: it's you, not the old yeller. Heyer appends the relapsed stammerer's response that followed up three weeks later.

Patient talked it out with his boss. Boss admitted that he once had that same stuttering problem earlier in his own development. How much money, Heyer's faithful correspondent calculates, had been wasted on his earlier repeated enrollment in special schools for the speech impaired! Psyche rules! Your grateful fan!

Now a colleague wants to know how Heyer was able to see through the woman he referred to him for therapy some time back. It's like witchcraft. But Heyer knows how to read the ambivalence of goodness (although when it comes to mixed feelings, he only quotes Nietzsche). The woman was so good, modest, respectful, and so on that Heyer just knew she was carrying around an especially "big, naive egotism" (492). More examples of immediate recognition: the individuals who come into the office and sit on the edge of the seat of their pants. "Whenever that happens I always know that I'm dealing with a type who's disconnected, even afraid of contact. . . . They present isolated, stiff, cramped images, these figures uncomfortably seated on the sofa arm—and that's how these people are on the inside too" (493).

Heyer could give a whole catalog of telltale greetings, leave-takings, handshakes, facial expressions, tones of voice. "Out of all this one can read a patient, just as the graphologist is able to recognize the essence of the writer right out of his script" (493). Ask them how their backstroke is: that's always a different stroke for the other folks. Their "contact with their unconscious" is just as poor (493).

> It's completely understandable that the frigid woman—to put it concretely—fears the rollercoaster like death itself. I experienced one of those who, while her young daughter kept starting over and over again on yet another ride into the unknown, stood below and thought she would just die, just watching! The same goes for the carrousel. The one who is truly fit for life loves vertigo, the fearful type avoids it. He could lose himself (and what would happen then!); while the one who's sure of himself seeks it out. For in vertigo and in whatever shakes you up everything new, unexpected, unknown is born. It's noteworthy that making someone dizzy (with machines that turn in the round) belongs to the initiation rites of many primitive peoples. The relative loss of consciousness opens the door through which the new god can enter. (493)

For Heyer, all these factors (including the giveaway phobias) are questionnaire-style rapid tests in session. It took him only thirty minutes to see to the bottom structure of Mrs. R.'s severe neurosis, as he elaborated it directly to his correspondent in their earlier phone conversation (495).

Heyer opens the next column with a referral he is making. Mr. S. is an "almost pathologically introverted person." He is without contacts, whether with wife and children, or, in essence, with the world. His is a "grotesquely one-sided intellectual development and disposition" (521). Music lets something fall between the cracks, between his "horrible cynicisms." "This one is, by nature, no cool operator of rational understanding but rather one who would rather torture himself life long before he gave others the opportunity to do so first" (521). Now it's the season for midlife "break down" (given, untranslatably, in American). Now it's time to turn inward, but he has always fled his basic introversion. Heyer gave this man before the vacation break a couple of "energetic sessions of suggestion" (522). His symptoms were beginning to lift right away. When they met again after the break, S. still appeared relaxed but said he felt a certain heaviness in his limbs. "And—you can imagine my horror, which I tried hard to keep from showing—he has been seeing double already a few times now" (522). It turns out he has MS. The diagnosis is especially and prematurely crippling in the neurotic overlay: therapy can prepare him by opening him up to his interiority, his psychic reserves.

For the new issue, Heyer showcases the following submission because it gives Schultz's autogenics what's overdue. The correspondent agrees with Heyer's warning labels on bromide and related medicinal treatments even of the "psychic-nervous 'overlayerings' of organic illnesses" (596). The result is often addiction on top of everything else. The object or target of therapy should be the "psychic disturbance of an undivided human being" (597). "And in our time of awesome crisis in the world outside and in us, which overtaxes our powers, the number of those who need such help is very great" (597). One proof of the society-wide demand for psychotherapy is the marketplace proliferation of systems of relaxing. Schultz's self-help technique, the autogenic training program, fills the bill. It's fast-acting medicine that you can carry with you at all times. The woman under treatment developed agoraphobia following a great shock; it was a horse-powered near miss of an accident that nearly took her out while she was walking the baby carriage (598). Autogenic training does good prep work for deeper-going psychotherapy; it gives back the agency that hypnosis had stopped undead in human tracks. He puts himself into the autogenic mode with the patient as demo and appetizer for identification purposes, of course, but also for the "transference" (599).

Another letter, another gender, I mean sender. This one illuminates a common psychic disturbance. "It's not well known that behind such an everyday symptom as the tremor we can find an entire character and de-

velopment problem hidden there. To recognize this—this is what the report proves—is not only important for the removal of symptoms (which
cannot be achieved with the usual tranquilizers), rather—even more—in
order that a valuable person can be integrated in an essential way into the
community" (651).

The twenty-five-year-old woman was referred by Heyer to the correspondent. She had the hand shakes. The colleague worked together with
the referral every day for two weeks. The symptom wasn't so remarkable—
"remarkable was the intensity with which the young girl pressed for treatment as though her unconscious sensed that behind this relatively minor
sign of affliction there was waiting a serious, genuine problem of life" (651).
The girl was driven by family values of equality; Mother was a professional,
just like Father. The psychotherapist, another professional woman, notes
the "unconscious identification" of patient with her mother (651). The whole
family pack (especially the brothers) was athletic. When she entered the
BDM (the Nazi girl scouts) her keeping-up momentum made her a leader,
a *Führerin*. But she never gave feminine concerns much thought. Then in
1937, when she turned twenty-two, she met a man. But he finally gave up
on marrying her because she was unfeminine and unable to give in, up,
away. He found a true donor and married her. The patient became very ill.
The hand shakes are left over from that bedridden state. In the counseling
sessions—there wasn't enough time for a long-term and larger-formatted
therapy, one that would be out of counseling's depths—the intelligent patient understood only too well what the therapist meant when she advised
her that she had managed her feminine side "in a step-motherly manner,"
"that everything about her physically and psychically seems hard, tight;
but the quiescent, feminine-supportive, and maternal, her natural being-
there [*Da-sein*], has been given short shrift" (651). She develops a rapport
with her "unconscious" and starts getting prettier and prettier day by day.
German women don't wear makeup: the unconscious is the only line Nazi
Germany carries for the look.

But transference just keeps on going even after the patient leaves. Almost a year later, the former patient pays the therapist a visit. When she
caught a stomach flu one day and threw up—for the first time in her life—
she realized how wrong she had been to pride herself in never having given
into that human all too human affliction. She was proud of her stomach now,
which proved to have better instincts than she had. This self-reflection, the
colleague signs off, shows real improvement (652).

Writing a Letter to Heyer

Another letter to Heyer follows in the column's reprints: it's a lecture to parents about different psychological types (Jung style), which help us reframe many difficulties with which one type seems to be careening into the need for disciplining. The introverted type must learn to value what she has, but not to flee too deeply inside it: the extroverted side exists, too, and needs more support (although it's not a question of delicate balance). In the opening phase of life, the extroverts have it easy; the introverts find their fit in the golden years. The introverts need more time, patience. Singing is a good idea for exercising feelings in the open, but also undercover: getting to know all about you!

Heyer opens his next column by treating bed-wetting in theory: "Man can, once his 'ego' has formed, close the anal and urethral passages by tightening the criss-crossed rings of muscle around those orifices. This exercise, once practiced long and hard enough, becomes an unconscious reflex and continues to be effective even in deep sleep" (895). When this reflex goes, pushed away at the same time by excessive urine production, we have, psychologically understood, a regression all over the sheets and not in hand. And it's not some fresh kid's fault, nor is the bladder there to blame: it's the parents, the instructors, the adults (895). "The psychoneurosis of the young child is only the response, the reaction to the mistakes of his environment" (895). The hypocrisy of the parents can't be cured: "In this house, just under the proper surface, for appearance sake, so much deception rules, everything is false and perverted into phraseology" (896). But a chilly "Nurse"—English foreign-language body in the original—*can* be replaced by a warm, feminine type.

Heyer writes a colleague about the referral she sent his way. Mrs. O. has later than sooner not been getting into her own sex. The result isn't only "her partial frigidity" but also her discontent and passing depressions (910). She walks on by herself, herself, like a foreign being, and she hides behind the depression that sets up a "wall of glass" between her and the world, and between her and herself (910). Heyer warns against participating in an only intellectualized recognition of what's wrong with the patient's life: "It yields . . . at best a rational-intellectual insight, but not an experience [*Erleben*], a more deeply intervening change" (911). It takes time for what's needed: "analysis." Change takes time: every "aspirin therapy" falls short of this deeper involvement over time. Dream interpretation is helpful not only (Heyer starts scoffing again) "in order to get behind what's repressed but rather because the dream figures and scenes are particularly suited to communicate to the patient the convincing experience [*das überzeugende Erlebnis*]" (911).

Her ideal hero from childhood was an Indian. She was orphaned too early on; her girlish brother left it up to her to fill the assertive, responsible role, you know, like, the masculine one. The security blanket making smoke signals soon was the only magic carpet ride around that took her to herself. Jung would call the Indian an "animus figure" that has near "archetypal character." Her identification with the Indian was total and not accessible to consciousness: "For whatever has me completely I just can't see anymore. To see (Latin: *crinere*) means to perceive self-differentiatingly" (912). In her more recent dream world, the eagle, or *Adler*, symbolizes the Indian identification. When she dreams of chickens, she gladly leaves *Adler* alone to enjoy his chicken dinner. In other dreams, she fails in other ways to protect the chickens entrusted to her care. In contrast to "the solitary-proud and racially foreign Indian," the primal "we" is beckoning in the chicken portion of the dreams (914). In the most recent dream work, she has begun to take the chicken side; the dream farmer's chickens have all died, and she takes their place. She finally lays an egg (Heyer has been waiting for this one). In this way she lets the "becoming healed" ("das Heil-Werden") begin (913).

Another column to fill? Want to read my outgoing mail? Dear colleague: you know the diagnosis that goes with my referral—Mr. R.—is windowpane-fully clearly one of psychogenic impotence. The long-standing treatment on pills and needles was, of course, without issue. In 1933 his wife was operated on to remove growths from her lower abdomen. The intervention apparently wasn't a big success cosmetically, since, says Mr. R., a big bag of skin was left hanging over her genitalia. For a while he could force himself to get it on with her even against rising resistance. But then he just couldn't anymore. After a year and a half of thinking he was impotent, the patient had a little too much to drink one night, suddenly a girl was there, and he was really into her, everywhere. "What happened is something we physicians should not evaluate morally but should try to understand in a larger connection of meaningfulness and make use of therapeutically" (934). Although he succeeds in depositing his seed, already for their next rendezvous the atmosphere is hurry up already, and again he's left holding the flaccid bag. Heyer concludes that the wife needs to go through with yet another operation. Unless Mr. R. is hypnotized every two weeks or so, the very natural repulsion he feels will always get in the way. This is then an easier case to open and shut (over the old bag's surgically slashed body). Not like the case of R., a patient the correspondent also referred to Heyer about six months ago:

> That one was (and is) impotent for much deeper-lying psychic reasons. Born out of wedlock in the most unsupportive milieu imaginable, he is incapable of physical union with a woman (and pushed into the greatest proximity to homosexuality), because he unknowingly sees in every woman he loves the mother he never knew, seeking always his wishful image of mother.... Such a kernel neurosis requires much longer treatment and is not at all treatable by any other method than the depth-psychological approach. (935)

Another colleague, another update on one more referral. This woman who came Heyer's way was facing a crisis in her marriage and had at the same time resolved to become a psychotherapist herself. "It's always questionable and certainly worth looking into when someone stuck in a neurosis—in the case of Mrs. T. this manifested itself in the marital disturbance—decides to study psychotherapy. Of course there are exceptions and everyone of us has experienced such a case; yes, one can even say that the experience on one's own person, i.e. on one's own psyche represents a good predisposition for insights into psychic possibilities—the struggles and the healing." But to what extent will Mrs. T.'s current resolve still be around for the cure?

Every so often another person comes along and confides in us that everyone's always talking at him about their personal problems and that he must have some natural talent for therapy. That doesn't even qualify him for taking the "aptitude test" (965). Neurotics turn to nonprofessionals all the time precisely because the makeshift and make-believe session is not binding and not bound to challenge, change, and heal. Mrs. T. is furthermore without children, and "displaced clucking-drives intensively contribute too" to her misplaced decision (965). But what has convinced Heyer absolutely that the woman has no call to be planning on occupying the therapist's seat can be seen in one of her dreams that spoke valiums, I mean volumes. In the dream she calmly disciplines two big bad wolves who show up—unkempt. She sends them back to make themselves presentable. "Thus the dream of this retired teacher." Hyper-consciously one may fall into the mind warp of such an artificial and lifeless "worldview." "But if even from the night side, in the depths of the person, in the unconscious, in the realm of fantasy and dreaming nothing else is around to assert itself other than 'tut-tut,' when even here the teacherly index finger is raised, and not even the slightest dread is experienced, but rather—better grooming is the only demand, 'nice and neat, the way it should be': then there's no hops or malt left. I don't know what such a person is good for; but definitely not for helping and healing people in psychic pain [Seelennot]" (965). Heyer even seconds the husband's emotion and moves to dissolve the marriage. (Heyer fills the stopgap of instant identification with visualizations of the husband's body drying up, dying away, from his loins to his talent.) "For this woman cannot be helped, not at all. Whether or not she was once upon a time alive, that I cannot say. There are people who lack all vitality. Here everything is desiccated. One might even consider the possibility of an encapsulated latent psychosis in her case; that the degree of rigidity and superficiality in her makeup, in other words, might signify—of course unknowingly—defense against the depths of the interior, with which, with her little bit of intelligence and with her provincialism, she'll never be able to deal but could only be all-too-easily flooded at its first awakening. There are such bureaucratic, overly conscientious and orderly types who, should they come into contact with fresh air, would decay right away. However that may be: already unsuited for marriage, untreatable—at least by my arts—, and never in your life suited for psychotherapy!" (965). She fails on both sides of The Relationship, and thus might as well be psychotic.

Heyer next quotes a country doctor's letter to him—they are in correspondence on the histories of words and the philosophical prospects these histories open up for understanding "the unconscious of nations [Völker]"— as evidence of the kind of sensibility that would be compatible with training in psychotherapy. The country doctor's letter is all about German folk expressions for madness, such as spinnen and inwendi sein. The former, "spinning," which contains "spider" (Spinne), becomes a theme on which the country doctor improvises many variations and mixed metaphors. The spinning of "reflecting" (sinnen) accelerates until one falls through an air pocket of blank mind at which point the normal type, getting through it and getting a grip, sees the spinning wheel, say, and pulls himself out of the tailspin. The spinning or mad one never hears the snap of the finger and, rather than forget everything that happened when you awaken, has already forgotten everything. Neither Heyer nor the country doctor pursues the spider image beyond the spinning activity or takes cognizance here and now of the historical connection between the first occupational therapy—spinning the wheel of cheap asylum labor—and the expression that continues on its spin. Spinning thus designates the "therapeutic" mode of keeping psychotics at low maintenance. The spider image, which Heyer knows belongs to the primal, phallic mother, shadows the second expression, used by a peasant woman to describe someone the country doctor saw staring vacantly, kind of catatonic, outer space. The expression names the "turn inward." But what the psychotic thus turns toward is a demon who has repossessed him. The demon is as far away, far out, supernatural as it is, in close-up, inside the psychotic.

The letter that contains two psychotics and the expressions the *Volk* has reserved for them comes to an end—and Heyer takes leave again of the woman who wants to have and to be psychotherapy, another lame excuse that's her last all-out defense against one sleeping-beauty of a psychosis. "But with this Mrs. T. we want nothing further to do. This kind of teacherliness of unhealable psychic anemia, *produces* the neuroses that we later with difficulty have to treat. God protect fellow men from them (and any eventual partners in life)!" (966).

Heyer gives in the next column his callback to a colleague's equally open call, issued in her review in the 1938 *Zentralblatt* of Heyer's book *On the Realm of the Soul*, for a few how-tos regarding the way "body-soul auxiliary methods, for example, breathing therapy," can produce dream reactions in neurotics under psychotherapeutic treatment. Heyer opens up a difficult case, but apparently it's still the treatable, more neurotic version of what Mrs. T. was the limit of in the letter before. Afflicted by a "kernel neurosis," this one has been under "depth psychological" treatment for several years now. How can Heyer put the case, I mean cause: It was hard to tell who was sicker, her mother or her father. The mother was "classically frigid," an apostle of the view that life would be all right save sex: the duty that's a curse. Father was disconnected from all feelings while maintaining a moral front. But unconsciously he fostered his daughter's incestuous connection with him (father left the feeling, his feeling, to her). The patient, little Else, grew up into a professionally successful career woman, whose "personal and feminine life, however, became a series of fiascos" (1080). In time there arose in her "a classic anxiety neurosis" that served as the foundation for her physical makeup, which was increasingly severely challenged by illness. She hadn't menstruated for over a year when she started therapy. Now she lets it bleed. But she's putting her periods back at the end of what's still the sentence, the mother's verdict that keeps the patient split off from "all that's earthly and natural, what lives 'below the navel'" (1081).

In this kind of case, Heyer considers cooperation with a breathing therapist a must. All those layers in the patient's person and psyche that have been "playing dead" can loosen up and start swinging with the "risks" taken in with every real breath you take. In a dream, she defended herself against an assailant by snarling and spitting like a big cat. She had been given the spitting image of an angry lioness as breathing exercise. Only in the dream did it gain sense for her and produce a kind of exorcism. She had recently taken to visiting the zoo regularly (always a good field trip for patients, says Heyer). "It wasn't the breathing in some mechanical sense that was the rescue operation which her unconscious advised her to undertake—that wouldn't have been much help at all!—rather the opening up of the depths, the spreading of her flanks, letting what's below oscillate on up right into the perceptible-audible hot breathing sound. Thereby she completed, as one might say, the ritual of becoming animal and cat; a self-metamorphosing of depths and their powers that had been hitherto repressed. These are the still far-away sides of her being—the animalistic and the natural—which try to jump her in the dream. . . . In the moment, however, when she herself allows the animal to live (breathe) inside her, the enemy is no longer an enemy, he's gone; she has taken him up inside her self" (1081–82). This certainly speeds up the process of healing. "Surely that's not to discount that depth psychological work alone could, given time, equally have performed the job of connecting the patient up with the body and the womb. But in psychotherapy, we cannot do without life, without realization" (1082).

In the next column, we read Heyer writing another dear colleague, one generation younger, whose questions, no, are never a burden; indeed, Heyer adores playing the newer generation's little helper. The colleague has a patient who's real tight with her vagina. She needs psychotherapy, but the therapist's medical superintendent wants to cut and stretch the patient on the spot. Heyer: "It is clear as day that vaginismus, as extreme form of frigidity, is to be understood psychically as a manifestation, as an extreme phenomenon of rejection of and defense against sexual union" (1106). Heyer then gives a fair shakedown: besides, in such cases, the partner or husband is also on a parallel neurosis or else, typically, not differentiated or diversified in erotic matters (1108).

The next question: What does Heyer think of the so-called Carezza method? It's a series of orgasm delays, stops and gos, that's supposed to intensify sensation long in coming. But the double duty it does is really all it does: practice contraception. Heyer doesn't want to be mean-spirited or a morality judge about erotic life, where variation must indeed be the rule. But not so long ago, you could read how-to sex manuals that urged that the quickest way to the goal or purpose was the best way (because an energy saver). Now that's antibiological, even, to conceive of sexuality as bound to purpose. It's just as much an intellectualization and projection to say nature seduces us with the prize of pleasure to get us to fulfill the purpose as is that other notion, "that insemination is the 'purpose' of sexual union" (1107). Everything's recyclable in nature, every moment counts, all phases are equal in value; one phase completes itself and already bears the next phase inside. The Carezza method takes too literally the evolutionary fact that man, at the climax of pleasure, not only gives himself but also keeps himself, preserves himself at the same time. It's vigilance that counts, even in ecstasy, and not any sperm countdown of energy.

The readership next time around gets a break in confidence. Heyer writes the superintendent of one of his patients; the latter has given him permission to blow all confidentiality to the win of a new convert to psychotherapy. The patient did have authority problems. But he was clearly good material, which is why you sent him to me for therapy. The patient arrived wanting to change. He has already been reading self-help books that advocate integration in the community as cure-all. He is ventriloquized by the Adler-I when he describes his presentation problem as "egoic drive for recognition" (1272). He wants to submit to authority but has never found an authority that satisfies his submission desire. This has always been his case: he's kept his dis-appointment with the authorities over and again. But this tells Heyer that the case isn't the usual neurotic bloatedness of the ego to which the Adlerian huddle can offer columns of advice about the group reducing plan. U., Heyer sensed, was just waiting for him to come back with counseling talk about "we-ness" *(Wirhaftigkeit)*. But Heyer chooses to disappoint him, too, and thus keep U.'s transferences clean.

Even though U. is not bashful, when he tried to impress his superintendent at the clinic, he forgot what he had learned, prepared, and had nothing to say. He had gone in, now he might as well have been called in: in no time he was fired. A dream that followed the "tragicomic" encounter crushed him, so that it kept him from any attempt whatsoever to save the situation at the clinic. In the dream his greeting is not returned by the superintendent, and the patient runs after him with a prepared bit part of eloquence, demanding the word given in exchange. Instead he called his superior's name, got his attention, and then forgot what he had planned to say. The look he gets shrinks him back to group size, shame time, shame station. Rather than go the slow way of "systematic analyzing," Heyer decides on "a psychotherapeutic cavalry ride," especially given the patient's acquaintance with the psychological literature. Heyer asks the patient for his associations with "small." "'Yes, small like a child,' he volunteered. 'And shamed,' I intervened, 'as probably you often felt in childhood?'" (1273). After the pause button of resistance is briefly pressed down, thought after thought starts coming to the patient until Heyer gets the picture. Embodying a rich but complicated combo of genetic predispositions and legacies, the little boy grew up in a household from which the officer father was absent and in which the very present mother dispensed praise or blame in standard amounts. But U. was the type that required a little more recognition than that. So ever since, he's been looking for the authorities that will recognize the complicated way he is (1274).

Heyer reads the dream backward and points out that dream psychology says that the superintendent doesn't return U.'s greeting because the figure he was trying to greet wasn't the superintendent, the one he sees regularly in the waking world (a confusion underscored by the dream's extensive borrowing from the actual clinic surroundings to set up its decor). Just as the x-ray room isn't just the room in the clinic again but the symbol of an inner otherwise opaque life, and the clock that's in both places tells you, in your dreams, that the hour has struck, so it's the wishful-thought imago, the subjective one, and not the real X., to whom he addresses the request to be recognized. Nietzsche says if your father was poor quality, create a better one; "he doesn't say: 'look for a better one'" (1275). The problem with growing up, with growing out of our parents, is that "we have to become our own father and our own mother." To stick to the dream, then, U. must become his own boss, then he will exchange the greeting because then there's a connection between him and what's in charge inside himself, "then he gets recognized by him and with that he grants himself recognition and leads himself himself" (1275).

Heyer admits that this subjective restaging of the dream interpretation is kind of difficult. Mr. U. didn't really get it, at least not right away. "But in the three hours we worked together, he was able to understand what was ethically significant about this interpretation. And that's what really counts" (1275). That's what counts when it comes to turning U. over to Heyer's correspondent, the chief. Don't expect a transformed person, day and night; that's the stuff of bad novels. In life "we learn the most from our mistakes (the ones we know we made), not by 'miracle' of 'transformation'" (1275). So the correspondent can see how the whole infrastructure of business as usual might also benefit from the counseling and interventions of psychotherapists. "Which, by the way, is also the reason we just now opened a special department at our institute devoted to the psychology of business [Betriebspsychologie]" (1275). A sign of the greater understanding he will feel he is benefiting from at the workplace is that he asked Heyer to tell all in this letter, and with the speaker phone of the column on.

In the next column, all it takes is one look at the x-ray of the twenty year old to confirm dilation of the esophagus, but even more so the suspicion that his affliction is fundamentally neurotic. But Heyer still can't recommend psychotherapy in this case. As a boy at boarding school, he learned all about masturbation, which Heyer characterizes as the "dowry" he took from the school, a possession that resonates in German "with poison" *(Mitgift)*. Today the young man is only sorry that his psychosomatic problems will keep him from joining the military. And he's right to worry. But psychotherapy can help him out or in. The esophagus problem is a real side effect of the original neurosis. Heyer recommends treating the physical problem physically with an actual dilator apparatus that will bust the symptom wide open (32). Then he can enter the military (and the war), and that way he'll benefit therapeutically from those associations and situations filled with real practical problems to solve. In the postscript, we read that the patient, in the army now, wears his cure-alls proudly.

One column, I mean, one day the patient came to therapy a broken man. The kernel of his neurosis attracts a devil of a quote from Faust regarding "the poodle's kernel" (147). But it's "the typical neurasthenic look" that begins to speak to Heyer. The patient is a victim of his success (148). He has entered the middle years of change. But how could he read the signs? He's so busy, he doesn't want to go soft: he becomes neurotic. Midlife crisis can produce addictions and even late outbreaks of homosexuality. Or a "breakdown" can be the result. Heyer uses the American term as a tribute to the higher incidence in the States of this happening event.

It's his own maturity that the patient is missing out on (149). Heyer is thinking about the case along Jungian lines. But then he decides not to give this case those lines. The practical situation of the patient has to be considered. His son is still being prepared, in training, to help run and then take over the family business. Plus the patient just doesn't have the "organs" needed for insight-oriented work. As so often with the "break-down," the doctor sees what's wrong, but the patient isn't able to see a thing. Heyer notes that the patient gulps air, a problem that Heyer can quickly do something about, thereby winning the patient's trust. Then he gives the patient a massage. The suggestiveness of the massage puts the patient into a hypnosis-like state, and Heyer hears what troubles him. Heyer prescribes hunting as the man's hobbyhorse cure. With the auxiliary aids, then, Heyer was able to get his patient back on his feet. And now the man is for the first time beginning to listen to "the inner laws of life." Let's hope so, Heyer concludes. Because the whole how-to was just bridge and support work; it was all that Heyer could possibly do in the short term.

The Hand-Me-Down Book

During the pentothal session, the soldiers can be "transported" in and out of battle at will, by means of the phonograph record. It can thus be established if battle is the cause of the soldier's hysterical manifestations. If it is battle fear, he can be "returned to combat" if he does not yield up his symptom.

—WILLIAM KUPPER, "OBSERVATIONS ON THE USE OF A PHONOGRAPH RECORD OF BATTLE SOUNDS EMPLOYED IN CONJUNCTION WITH PENTOTHAL IN THE TREATMENT OF FOURTEEN CASES OF SEVERE CONVERSION HYSTERIA CAUSED BY COMBAT"

In November 1949 the *Bulletin of the U.S. Army Medical Department* was in a position to issue a supplemental number entitled "Combat Psychiatry: Experiences in the North African and Mediterranean Theaters of Operation, American Ground Forces, World War II." It served as the standard handbook of psychiatric care during the Korean War. In Korea, which did see a drop in what all agreed had been an alarmingly high rate of psychiatric discharge on the U.S. side of the Second World War, some of the psychosocial patterns that were discovered and elucidated back then in interpretation of the degrees of fortitude of the preselected men, who had largely been left unattended in real time by psychiatric observation and care, were now part of the basic training. For example, the buddy system, an aggregate that was observed to accrue to the U.S. forces in World War II, was the "action unit" of organization of the Korean War troops. What was mentioned back then, for example by Raymond Sobel in this special issue, always in passing became the rotational scheduling principle of exposing troops to frontline pressures. Thus the positive was developed from the negative imprint of the Sobel example: "The intermittent nature of combat determines the manner in which the soldier develops anxiety" (U.S. Army, "Combat Psychiatry," 57). The buddy system kept down the number affected by any given loss, but the survivor buddy still took his cut of loss traumatization. For the Vietnam War, both tendencies were taken to their logistical conclusions, winning the all-time low in psychiatric discharge from and during any service. In the Vietnam War, U.S. soldiers began their tour of duty doing time: they knew that they had only a predetermined period (one year) to serve and survive. Isolated individualism was promoted, no doubt with gadget-loving detail in mind, in the unconscious mind. The solo bond with one's own survival of a terminable term of service was shell shock proof.

However, the other legacy of the special issue, passed down and fine-tuned through the Korean and Vietnam Wars, is the rescheduling of the disorder that really didn't go away at all but was only displaced, completely jettisoned into the civilian space of chronic outpatient treatment. Today the new timing of what was war neurosis goes by the name of post-traumatic stress disorder. In the 1949 issue, in Alfred Ludwig's contribution, the rehearsal formulation "posttraumatic neurosis" can already be found (87).

Thus the advice Maurice Wright extends across the Anglo-American alliance in 1941—to show the kind of deference to psychoanalysis that allows deferment of treatment until after the war (when, judging by the last time around, there will be plenty of low-maintenance work for analysts postwar)—doubles as premonition of new techno-time schemes for about-facing trauma.

> Since the last war there has been an increase in the number of psychiatrists who would consider analysis as the method of choice in every case needing psychotherapy. Analysis, in this sense, covers not only the strict Freudian technique, but also that used by many others who are qualified by training and experience to conduct modified analysis lasting over months and years, exploring for a therapeutic end those deep levels of the unconscious which are otherwise inaccessible. Analysis, then, may be the method of choice; but in dealing with neuroses of war, when it is quite certain that the number of available psychiatrists will never be really sufficient for ideal treatment, it will certainly only be possible to use such methods in a very limited number of carefully selected cases. After the war, when it is to be hoped that at any rate a large number of such neuroses will have been sufficiently relieved to pass out of medical hands, analysis, by whatever technique, will be more and more used in cases unrelieved by other methods of treatment. (159)

The handbook legacy of World War II breaks down into four areas of interest: the normal battle reaction, the abnormal handling of anxiety and hostility in those so predisposed, the alternation between individual and group formattings of therapy, and "pseudopsychotic" or borderline phenomena. Stephen Ranson sticks up for what's perfectly normal given the war situation and holds it up for continued service. The soldier must endure a barrage of symptoms (like stomachache, for example) that, like inclement weather, are just part of the battle scenery. If his aches and pains receive too much attention, he will have experienced gain, which is then the basis for neurosis:

> The symptoms will continue beyond the period of battle stress to perpetuate that gain and will be reinforced by the mechanisms of self-justification and compensation for guilt feelings. The symptom pattern then becomes an abnormal reaction, not consistent with the meaning of present stimuli, and hence neurotic. Thus a neurosis is elaborated and crystallized. (6)

In their "Dynamic Approach to the Problem of Combat-Induced Anxiety," Edwin Weinstein and Calvin Drayer project the primalization of the battle scene in which the soon-to-symptomatize soldier gets a picture that leaves him out of it, but only as solo survivor, perpetrator, or target.

> When the events of battle stimulated hostility the ill soldier unconsciously, in the distorted fashion of the neurotic, began to interpret the scenes of death about him as the destructive effects of his own aggression. The shells fired by the enemy became, symbolically, the agents of punishment. When a shell burst near him and he was "knocked out," the event represented the fate he so richly deserved. It was natural for him to feel that each shell had his name written on it and that no fox hole was deep enough to protect him from an avenging fate. (16)

The shell name playing on his nerves belongs to a primal scene that the authors next diversify into more specific factors and genres, with the proviso, however, that "most neurotic patients show characteristics of more than one of the three groups" (21).

For the "passive-dependent" type, who continues to make an "unsatisfactory family adjustment," the whole war is all in the family: "Despite their resentments, they are usually dependent on one or both parents. Since the expression of hostility toward a person on whom one is dependent produces anxiety, their hostility necessarily remains unconscious" (18). "Overtly aggressive" types make great fighters in combat. But one man's break in hostilities is another man's breakdown. Hostility now travels transferential reroutings that are no longer one-way: fear of retaliation now develops, out of long-standing hostility toward parents, toward one's own army even, which replaced him in the no-win situation. This is the type noted most likely to go AWOL. All that recommend the "compulsive-obsessive" type for a noncommissioned officer position—his attention to detail, neatness, conscientiousness—are desperately put-on acts of "penance" for his aggression. His evidence is everywhere: all the dead are his victims (20).

Group identification and motivation offer another frame for separating the normal soldier from the ones who're just so hostile. The normal reaction of the soldier to the group is to identify with it and thus take on its "protective coloration." The disturbed fellows deny themselves this camouflage, the group's protective resources. One of these would be the "poor mixer" who "retires into his shell of passivity" (22). The compulsive-obsessives can toe the line of (but never step on) a sense of duty to their group. But the group cannot protect them. As soon as casualties start piling up, they surrender—to their own guilt and anxiety: "Thus the group, instead of supporting him, multiplies his points of vulnerability" (23). The authors close here with thoughts for a future of more durable group sizings of identification: "Complete identification with a durable group is a valuable prophylaxis against neurotic anxiety" (25). What comes most easily is also most risky: identification with company, platoon, fellow soldiers. All these groups are "notably perishable" (24). A more stable and lasting group is needed. But the nation is too big. The division may be the best medium of identification that still comes life size.

Speculations about the group fit right into Louis Tureen and Martin Stein's concern with the new tempo of treatment in war:

> Because the demands on the psychiatric personnel were so great, it became a matter of extreme importance to devise a plan of continuous treatment, even in the face of a relatively brief contact with each patient. Such a plan was successfully effected through a comprehensive program based on the simultaneous and coordinated use of individual and group therapy. (116)

The important transferential rapport must be established and maintained under new high-velocity conditions. Even the individual therapy under these circumstances was group limited or group sized in its goals. The authors, thinking quickly, recommend a physical exam of the patient during the first interview for quick erection of this rapport. The exam is not thorough but "suggestive" only, as are the interview questions, and even the lab work. "For every patient helped by extensive laboratory work, particularly x-ray studies of the skull and the gastrointestinal tract, great damage is done to scores of neurotic soldiers" (117). This conforms to the rules on handling neuropsychiatric casualties proposed in 1949 (and included in the special issue as appendix 2): "Avoidance of hospital atmosphere." The quicky semblance of the greatest hits of playing doctor lubes the patient for swift passage back into an outpatient population of group members. Tureen and Stein have been digging the group rapport out of war conditions that automatically compacted patients into institutionalized groups. Flashback:

> Our interest in group therapy was first stimulated by experiences in the North African campaign, when acute psychiatric battle casualties were treated in an open ward of an evacuation hospital in full view of 20 other patients. There was no privacy during the examination interview or any phase of narcoanalysis. Any abreaction produced in the patient produced a response in all the other patients, who were attentively observing the procedure. (129)

Benjamin Boshes and Clifford Erickson take on the borderline phenomena of "pseudopsychotic" states arising side by side with the truly psychotic ones. There are a couple of giveaway differences. The pseudopsychos tended to break down with the first heavy battle stress; real psychos "in some cases saw a good deal of combat before they succumbed" (152). And pseudopsychotic reactions are just as quickly distinguished from true psychoses by the evidence of anxiety. But other reactions overlap to the point of confusion. Watch out! Even nonpsychotic anxious soldiers experience auditory hallucinations:

> These soldiers heard the voice of the mother, grandmother, aunt, or whoever had reared them, in reassurance: "You are a good boy. You have done your duty. You can always come back to me at home." This voice would return night after night during the acute state, but only to patients suffering from neuroses, never to those who were psychotic, and the ego remained well in contact with reality despite this manifestation. It was interpreted as a defense against, or an answer to, the hostile superego, which was threatening or punishing the ego for its failure. (153)

In pseudoschizophrenia, in which the "ego retained its hold on reality despite the schizophrenic facade," we discover the ultimate borderline situation, the one that precisely cannot contain (or soothe) itself: "This type bridges the gap between the pseudo psychotic and the true psychotic reaction" (157). Real psychotics tended to be paranoid schizophrenic, in which case the record spoke for itself; or if mixed psychotic with manic or grandiose features, the soldier would perform heroic acts that were so solo contextless that they did more harm than good to the group effort (160).

Heyer and Heyer

It's time, and this time Heyer turns the column over to the presentation of a parapsychological case that might well have ended up serving as a sideshow exhibit of the occult if it hadn't been for psychotherapy (including, in particular, autogenic training). In his opening memo, in which he introduces the colleague who sent in the letter about the therapy, Heyer declares his own interest in the occult but stresses that it's really important that one exclude all other factors first, which is what this case exemplifies.

The boy hears things when alone in the house, but no real cause can be located. That may be uncanny, but he swears he hears it, that it's not something in his mind. At the boarding school where he was raised until age six there was the legend of a local ghost that deposited in him the vision of alien children. The therapist corrects the mother, who, like her husband, is into the occult explanation. Heyer diagnoses the boy's "eidetic disposition" (231), which naturally adds special effects to the hyperawareness he has of all that's around, sight and sound. The therapist prescribes autogenic training. Despite the upsurge of resistance for the first time and try alone with the auto-training, real improvement follows (231). Now the family starts up with resistance. Certain family members sensed in the "self hypnosis exercises and rational psychotherapy the terrible ghost of analysis, the awful effects of which on the psyche of the child can be assumed with a good bit of conviction and certainty" (232). But the mother is on the therapist's (and the boy's) side; all together now, they are able to "purify the psychic space" (232). So you see, autogenic training does go more deeply than just the symptom and removes whole "biological deformations of a spastic nature," thus giving the patient a sense of self-control and "security" (233).

It's already the thirty-third time Heyer has acted as advice columnist. Today, he declares, "we depth psychologists of today" use dream interpretation as follows (330). A dream revolver stands to reason. The psyche is "conservative" and always offers major "resistance" to what's new (331). In the dream a young woman lies next-to-naked right where the animal metamorphoses have already taken place. Heyer presses the pause button to shoot off a round of asides: "Here, let this be mentioned in passing, the former analysis would have said: Aha, there we have it again, the man has—super-consciously repressed—sex drives: he wants to possess a naked young woman. And the analyst would have offered that to you as interpretation. But..." (332). Heyer gives all the counterarguments that do the assuaging part that's party to the denial. But all along Heyer can't stop imagining what a "Freudian" would say. Indeed, the dream represents the psychoanalytic perspective in the figure of the director, who doubles as director of conscience. (He's the interrupter of the dream ego's art appreciation of the nude.) But after all the quick fix is said and done, Heyer issues the proviso that in this case he has said straight out what in his real-time psychological work would have emerged way more gradually in working with the "analysand" (associations and the like) (332–33).

For Heyer's thirty-fourth time in the column, we hear how an obsessive-compulsive woman comes to session week after week and keeps an oath of near silence. Heyer finally declares the therapy over; it's just too boring for him (he does wait, he insists, until there's enough of a connection between them to tolerate this particular intervention). She bursts out: "I know already what you think!" Yes? "That there is something wrong with my sexuality and that all my misfortunes stem from that" (366). Clearly she thinks so. Heyer points out the projective nature of her observation. While there was a longer history to her problems, the most current conflict in her life lay with intimacy. Just as she held back speech in therapy, so she has been storing up her urine until the last moment to amplify the outburst that's just a blast. The frigid wife, whose original presenting problem was chronic cystitis, gains hope in and for therapy when that symptom goes away. But the improvements Heyer has introduced are stopped short before true inner change. The patient doesn't love her husband. She remains fixated on father (who really must have been wonderful, admirable, Heyer gushes): she has remained "an eternal teenager who looks to find in man just this subjectively enhanced father image" (367). That she must have married her husband for money stands out as a contradiction to the rest of her "idealism." But it was a healthy instinct that made her (as with so many women, thank God!) go with the man who could support her line of reproduction rather than with the teen ideal or idol. So she was able to marry and breed children. But to mature into womanhood, she would have to "risk" something.

Another column, another colleague sends in a report to Heyer. It's a case of a paralyzed worker whom therapy restored to the labor force. The example shows psychotherapy's social value for the total society. And it's not just a luxury item for the rich. "Insofar as the insurance carrier does not yet sufficiently allow for such a treatment, through which alone the happiness and work capacity of a fellow German can be restored, that doesn't reflect negatively on psychotherapy, only on the responsible institutions." In the report, Heyer's colleague rules out neurological damage and hysteria. He has known the patient since childhood at a time when he was the only doctor for miles during the war years. In session, instant recall of an abortion she performed on herself comes up. Soon they realized that the hand that robbed the cradle was the hand that "died." With that insight alone, full restoration was already in sight. Today she's a married woman and mother.

In the next column, the report sent in to Heyer concerns a former officer of World War I who had arrived in the vicinity of the correspondent's practice for a spa vacation and, since diabetic, needed a physician on hand (653). In this patient two worlds are in conflict: the long ancestral tradition to which he is heir versus the new era, the changeover into the new Germany. It's a conflict that tests the limits of so many physicians in Germany today. The patient's unlived life soon comes bubbling up in therapy: "Insight into the meaning of the countless explosive pieces of his unconscious and their deployment in the daily fight against his environment, and the resulting inner grind, are what wears him down." The report in turn includes the document the patient wrote up in which he gives the history of his illness from his now healed point of view. This "after" document signs off, really healed, "Heil Hitler!"

The report sent in in time for the next column is a classic: it concerns enuresis. Heyer's correspondent says that the bed wetter has to be understood fundamentally, holistically, therapeutically. This is the case of a six-year-old boy, who started wetting all of a sudden. It can't represent "compensation," since he's the firstborn and the king of the jungle gym. Whatever you do, don't punish the bed wetter! This particular physician reporting back to Heyer even recommends that mothers take their delinquent charges into their beds next night. Bed-wetting is always a protest against the loss of "nest warmth." Next the family physician asks about all immediate events. "And then the completely lucid, racially-pure, and therefore instinctually-sure mother of the boy suddenly gets an idea" (562). Recently a kitten was taken from his room because it wasn't using the box properly. The kitten, then, was all that was left of his maternal connection. He had grown up as his little father, a fighter and bully. With removal of the kitten "there arose with the bed wetting a last cry of the unconscious yearning deep inside the wounded nature of the child to get back to the mothers" (562).

By his thirty-eighth column, Heyer has a history and can refer to the earlier letter in the series in which he quoted from a country colleague's reflections on the German nickname for the insane: "spinners." In the meantime he has checked in with the history of asylums and of spinning as occupational therapy. But Heyer still defends the folk-etymological or unconscious association as worthy of sustained consideration (it's this support that explains the persistence of the folk expression). To illustrate the staying power via the unconscious of a word association or even a gesture, an act, Heyer and his correspondent are both reminded of another case, that of a foreigner, the son of a musician father and dissatisfied "demonic" mother. Heyer and the colleague reraised him in therapy until he began to develop his own kernel of a self. But then the mother returned to reclaim him and was able to undo all that therapy by simply washing his hair then and there (576).

Dear colleague, Heyer opens the next column, the high hopes you held for therapeutic assistance with Mrs. von K.'s menopausal afflictions have been confirmed. As a doctor you know, without knowing the literature perhaps, that whatever effects the whole person could serve as object for therapeutic adjustment. In a woman's life in particular, sexual disturbance is dependent on psychic causation more than on any somatic influence (at this point, Heyer puts the one-German-worder "Orgasmincapacity" in parentheses and then lifts it up like a loud comic blurb with an exclamation point). The "great drama of the bodily-psychic symphony" comes on strong with the stoppage of her generativity (11). Mrs. von K.'s feminine side saw little action, what with the early death of her husband and her overwork to raise the children and preserve the estate. Now that the menopause button's been pressed (depressed), she has that sad sense of her unfulfilled sexual life taking a sleeping beating. This has been the unconscious scenario. In hyperconsciousness she's all duty, tax and all. So he tells her all about it; she's the type, countrified rather than citified, who can take it in through the intellect and then second it with her own intuition and emotion. Then he puts her under and gives her hypnotically suggestive commands to get over the nighttime heat flashes (the psychic leftover, hanging on, over, not out, of somatic changes that had already gone through). She heals. In general, for Heyer, the Jungian development of adulthood must often be therapeutically assisted, administered. "In the second half of our life we must learn what noble wine learns in the cellar: ripen all the way, fill out, spiritualize...so that finally we can do the one thing that's just as difficult as the yelping conquest of life in youth—the great, brave and quiet undertaking of dying" (12).

Have column, will consult on a colleague's examination of the whole enterprise of Director X., where all's well that's part of the business world, but there's something rotten in the mental state, the human world. Now that Heyer has met Mr. X., he has to say that unless X. gets therapy, no amount of modernization and rationalization of his enterprise will make the difference, the grade, the cut. Wherever there are machines and gadgets there's a human attached to the otherwise automatic functioning. In the background, the man's severely disturbed. Up front that's not evident: he's the self-made-man success story, his marriage is good, the children are magnificent: "One son recently received a high distinction on the Eastern Front" (342). But Heyer saw through him when he looked at him from behind while they were entering the consulting room single file: "The silhouette from behind is always especially noteworthy" (342). X.'s motto is not to expect more of his workers or coworkers than he demands of himself. But that has never worked: resistance is as high as the enthusiasm, and the rest just do their job. X. is a "machine" (343), and for the long term, that's not an efficient model of human productivity. As a machine, he "kills off whatever also wants to and must live" (343). His insomnia means that the nightly return home to the grounds of his own true nature just isn't happening for him. And X.'s compulsion to urinate in the middle of the night reflects a primal need to let go, to find release. "You don't need to think right away of the old Freudian urethral erotics or of other sexual things" (343). X. had a dream the night before session: the locomotive he's riding in is being fueled with coal nonstop, but there's little or no water in the boiler. X. was struck by the nonsense: "No machine could run that way." Heyer mixes metaphors to get on board with "organism." Coal means energy, X. contributed, but the water was necessary for the energy to assume form, take shape. In the footnote boiler room he goes with his correspondent where, without saying, water runs deep. "In other words 'energy' must mobilize 'life,' true, natural, swelling up life. The life machine can be set into motion when this complete and streaming vitality is also present. But, as I already indicated, we didn't pursue that further. Mr. X. was clearly not ready yet to read with his conscious spirit the unconscious pictographs" (343). There's more work ahead for Heyer's correspondent and the patient, X., but Heyer believes that psychotherapy matches the patient's good qualities.

Mr. X. is back in the next column in this follow-up letter to the same correspondent. He returned with another dream: old and young men in management discuss the future buildup of chain factories. The old guy had a kind of hangar attached to his car filled with chickens and a cock (*Hahn*). They were the so-called Italians, a breed that shines metallically. Now, when Heyer goes after a dream's meaning in session, he prefers having a vital conversation with the patient in contrast to the "mechanical procedure of the old psychoanalysis" (362), notably free association on the couch, which is, in a word, "boring" (363). But that doesn't stop X. He identifies the old gentleman spontaneously as "patricide" and sees the hens in a contemporary mode as popular animals (in the war economy) for their eggs and meat. The old man stands for the old order. It's got to go. But one must also listen to it. The chain factories rehabilitate the chains used in machines through some complicated procedure involving fire, water, and air. X. has already grown in his insight orientation since last session, last letter. On his own he sees the chain, chain, chain refrain linking life to machine. Like links in the chain, the human parts and missing links need time out to be strengthened for return to the machine. "That's always the premier concern and condition of depth psychological work, that we not only introduce rational will-powered impulses but that we also occasion in the deepest layers of the psyche autonomous movement, and that from there, from the natural ground of all that's alive, images emerge (like what these dreams have brought up) which carry within them a dynamic tension toward completion [*Vollzugsspannung*]" (363). Rather than force the dream into the "interpretation schema of some 'school,'" Heyer simply "gave back the balls that Mr. X. hit his way in session."

If this is the next column, then it's time for another letter that a colleague's been writing to Heyer, his address is the German Institute in Berlin. It's time for a breather: the kind of physical therapy that Heyer has covered before is described in the following letter about a case of spastic esophagus. It's woman treating woman. The therapist really likes breathing therapy because it allows one "to turn directly to the unconscious" (460). You, too, the colleague writes directly to Heyer, once referred to this sort of treatment as "analysis without words" (460). It was the patient's whine about having left her home turf that had to breathe to be heard by her therapist. It was the catch in the patient's life, a catch in her throat, a change in setting she just couldn't swallow (461). This therapist, just like Heyer, takes a look at the backside: "It struck me how poorly circulated through with blood and breathing the backside of Mrs. Sch. was, how cold the ass and how inanimate the transition to the legs was" (461). More and more the therapist's original association with swallowing something down gave way to the "image of someone who has had 'the chair pulled out from under him'" (461). In German, if you have to make the effort of having your say, getting your way, you have to "sit it through" (*es durchzusetzen*). The patient's own earthy down-home humor could now be enlisted in the process of understanding. The therapist writing to Heyer, their address may just be one and the same, feels that no accident caused language (the German language) to make recourse to this corporeal sitting image. (Nor can it be transferred to the account of accident that a "session" of psychotherapy in German is a "sitting" [Sitzung]. But this is the transference association the therapist chose to sit out.)

A letter joins the next column, which was nearing a certain end (it's 15 September 1943). Heyer is the author of this letter and signs off, which isn't his usual way, "Heil Hitler." All's *heil* that ends *heil*? He's writing W. M. Schering, whose work Heyer has found influential. One of Schering's criticisms, which was targeted at the whole of the former state of psychology, thus also strikes, like some miracle weapon, "the former so-called psychoanalytic procedure" (538). This brings to mind one of Heyer's cases of agoraphobia. The woman in question had undergone "psychoanalytic treatment with some famous doctors for several years" (538). She knew everything about her childhood, her development, her inner life—for days. She could interpret the inventory she kept of her own current symptoms. Eat it up, Professor; the usual nonresults of analysis were even more apparent in this classic case. Heyer told the patient that her accounting of her psychological debits and credits just added to the confusion and nothing to the healing. She in turn was horrified to have fallen into the hands of some vulgar, minor suggestion therapist. But he had opened some kind of trust between them, and she decided to try his more active or interactive therapeutic approach. She's given homework. Certain streets are to be crossed by next session. She does it! She explains that her maybe absurd but viscerally terrifying sense of the traffic was that she was seeing monsters with shiny stares. Her next assignment was to learn how to dive, not drop in "like a sack" the way neurotics tend to, but with a hop over a bamboo pole, which forces the jumper to give shape to the dive.

Now, in time for the end, E. Jünger puts in a surprise appearance. Heyer lays out the greater (than) psychoanalytic plan of healing: raising the unconscious to consciousness, locating the healthy portions of the psyche and bringing them under the protection, reflection, and care of the conscious person. It's this "inner work" that Heyer likens to Jünger's notion of the development of a second, harder, more objective self or consciousness, presumably under fire (539). In the footnote Jünger is quoted at length with the otherwise unintegratable prepsychoanalytic opposition he sets up between "psychology," which is always psychology of the sensitive sensibility, and the so-called second consciousness, which targets the sensible man who stands outside pain. Heyer digs Jünger in the ditch of last-stand defense against acknowledgment of loss. But the losing streak may reverse itself through, or as the shadow of, another miracle weapon, another second try: the stronger second consciousness.

In Heyer's rendition, raised to second consciousness, the manic or melancholic undertow is made to hoe fields of mixed organic metaphors: the second coming of consciousness—the auto-healed self—needs rest, quiet, darkness; like plants that keep on growing through the night, "just as love blossoms in the secret shining of the moon" (539). Heyer speaks up for this "involution," this inner work space, as "more important than evolution" (539). But then he concedes a point to Mr. Professor, the correspondent, another prepsychoanalytic prop taken out of the same last ditch as Jünger, that the whole of psychology of the last centuries has indeed systematically forgotten the importance of the move outward bound into the daylights of action. That goes for the former analytic approach, too, Heyer agrees emphatically. The demo Heyer has given of his own approach, however, completely overlaps with the old analysis with the one edge still sticking out, the edge Heyer gives himself, in regard to the timing of the cure. The first stage Heyer set for the patient introduced above was analysis: if that self-reflective work were left to go on and on as end in itself, then the work, as so many analyses in the past proved, could extend to years. But the "healing" would for that reason be withheld. Practically speaking, the restoration of the patient's productivity was thus withdrawn more and more. If there's going to be a beginning of maturity, of growth out of childhood, there's got to be *Tat*, action, act, deed. The patient who saw animal eyes glaring at her out of the car traffic was still seven years old, max. By doing something, a "'field' is demarcated in which recognition, understanding, becoming conscious can transpire" (539). The pedagogue and psychotherapist of today must develop a second sense for when the "course of learning,"—here Heyer contaminates via the sameness of their sounds "running on empty" with "course of training or teaching" ("Lehr- [und Leer-] Lauf")—has been allowed to go on long enough and it's finally time to switch over to action. The correspondent's view or doctrine of the value of doing thus, Heyer concludes, in no way contradicts the practice of psychotherapy today, which balances reflection and action even as it does the balancing act of eclecticizing and integrating all opposition or resistance, even Heyer's own, into a program of healing that is an application, a renewal of and improvement on that same old analysis that keeps coming up as the only reliable marker in an otherwise manic or hysterical field of superficial writers of metaphors who must now take their shine to greater psychoanalysis. That's how Heyer closes this letter and column (and series), by opening a whole fan of eclectic auxiliary methods of psychical therapy, breathing exercises, Japanese Zen (in which he for the first time also recognizes his wife, Lucy Heyer, for the special chapter on such practical applications she contributed to one of his own books). But Heyer extends the helping "and" of future collaborations to Mr. Professor Schering and signs off, I believe it's the second (and last) time in the series: "Heil Hitler!"

Humanities

In 1928 Franz Carl Endres was looking forward to the next round. War may still be a science in theory but in practice, it's an art *(Kunst):*

> Tactics are therefore so closely bound up with technology that they can hardly be separated any longer, not since the enormous development of modern artillery, the ever increasing replacement of the fighting human with the machine.... Battle tactics of a future war will be exclusively determined by the existing technological means. (51)

Endres is plaintively aware that raw materials need to be in supply as great as the demand (71). Human resources are still an issue during the period of transition to fully automatic war machines. At the moment, all the gadgets still fly or fire only under human guidance. In German, the "guide" (who in this setting is a driver or pilot or button-pushing engineer) is a führer; to designate automatic functioning that proceeds without guidance—guidelessly—there's *führerlos,* which if capitalized could serve as the composite noun meaning "the destiny of the Führer." Between the lines, technological advances will overcome the human need for the group psychology of leadership; that was good for the transition; in the future permanent techno-war will lead, on automatic, the way of the world.

In the pop-military-psychological journal *Soldierhood,* L. Schmuck hails "improvisation," the human element in the war machine and thus the medium of choice of manipulation, as the only way to go with the flow of war and for the goal of victory (248). Also in *Soldierhood* (in 1938) Captain E. Goldenberg spells out for the readership that there are three kinds of intelligence required of the enemy: what does he have, what can he do, what does he want. Under the first category of have and have-not, Goldenberg registers the three forces doubly, once as machine or capacity, then as reserve tank: "the armed force and its personal replacements, the defense economy as source of material and replacement, the available installations or plants as means of application for both" (259). The human element along for the supply lines is what German psychotherapy addresses. When the Reich leader of physicians, Dr. Gerhard Wagner, calls for a "New German Knowledge of Healing," the pages that follow resonate with the vacuity of what's new. A process of total transformation is moving through German thought to German rights, action! The "reserve supply" of the people must be increased even while the racially alien others are being expelled (good forestry principles). The new teaching of healing will help "secure" the *Bestand*, the supplies and the staying power, of the nation (419).

In 1925 George Soldan contemplated *Man and the Battle of the Future* with a psychological interest intensified by our increased dependency on human psychic functioning through technologization:

> In truth . . . all our thinking must concentrate on the human indi-
> vidual who despite technology, despite the machine, despite ma-
> terials has remained the carrier of war or, more to the point, es-
> pecially with regard to these new combat methods has moved to
> the foreground as the bearer of the burdens of war. (13)

Soldan questions the future automatic war, or rather what its point would be. If man gets replaced technologically then "war would be an illusion" (23). For war to continue there has to be a match between technologization and the psychic powers of mankind. The power Soldan has in mind is not charged with enthusiasm. In the First World War, it was demonstrated that "to fight against the materials with enthusiasm only means to submit to the effect of the materials. Enthusiasm blinds. Against the cold force of the materials you can win the upper hand only if you fight coolly and profession-ally with eyes open. . . . The power of the machines forces men into the earth" (34–35).

Soldan puts his hopes in new arts of leadership, which consist, in the context of a war of materials, in the "estimation of what's still humanly possible" (49). Psychologically, gas war already started shifting the scene or theater to an automatic techno-setting. Gas attack had a high psychic-ca-sualty success rate. Soldan refers to the authors from the other side who in their postwar study of what had just passed, *Chemical War*, conclude that gas is thus the more humane medium of war: few deaths, no mutilation, and it passes. But gas also gave the best cover for the simulators or imper-sonators of illness. The main drawback is the armor-prophylactic required in the gas-war zone. The mask keeps you from self-medicating with nico-tine and alcohol. Weighed down with gas defense, the only mobile units on the battle scene in the future would be the planes and tanks: "With that we would be in the middle of a fantasy scene from a future battle conceived by Jules Verne. Today countless Jules Vernes are living in Germany!" (74). Fur-ther gas fantasies include the drop from the air of total victory. Right now it's the "defenseless paper pages" that must endure the science fiction gas attacks (74).

But gas isn't the future; it's the ultimate consequence and conclusion of the triumph of the materials over humanity during World War I. Fighting spirit is what must be promoted now, right in the face of the terrible effects of the materials of war. And gas "kills" the human spirit of attack while burdening all movement through slow motion (75–76). Future mobility and endurance will be enhanced by smaller military formations: smaller clan-like or tribal units rather than masses must enter the material war (81). More mutuality or team spirit will be required, too, in lieu of the earlier hierarchization of transferences. Under the material pressures, the military has reached the aristo-critical point. But in the background of the smaller mobile units, the entire people will also still be at war, on the psychological and economic war fronts. It's the same dialectic that says, according to Soldan, growing internationalism of the very grounds of any *Volk*'s existence "forces the development of the most intense nationalism" (103).

It Just Takes Two

Among the true but few "psychoanalytic tales" Robert Lindner has in store for us by 1954 (observing thus the same time change from war to the fifties that characterizes Heidegger's jet-lagged thoughts on technology or Lacan's specular reversal of the neo between Germany and America), it just takes two, the "Gutter Führer" and the time traveler, to role-play the span of attention that the missing era of Nazi psychoanalysis has called to order. First there was Anton, a guttering headline who now walked the sick line in prison somewhere between possible malingering (the rep that precedes him pretreatment with Lindner) and what the patient presents with right now, blackout spells with some amnesia. Somehow Lindner, with this prison case, is in the world wars army now:

> There is no better place to study and observe the psychopath than in prison. Here, in a microcosm bounded by four stout walls, in a situation where his smallest activities are noticed, who he is and what he does emerge in glaring detail. His effect on others, too, is less subtle here than it is in the free world, and the very nature of the restraints placed upon him magnify his essential patterns. In a prison the masks psychopathy wears fall away; the meaningless distinctions that in the free world separate or classify men fade; and the remaining sediment is the pure stuff, the elemental ore, which requires no involved procedure of diagnostic chemistry to reveal what a person is. (Lindner, 120)

Anton and Lindner walk right down the reception line that Simmel first set up during World War I for treatment of sufferers from shell shock: "At the time I undertook to treat Anton I had worked out—if only to my own satisfaction—a therapeutic approach to the psychopath. The method I employed was hypnoanalysis—a technique combining psychoanalysis with hypnosis" (which he first elaborated and advertised in his 1944 *Rebel without a Cause*). Anton turns out not to be hypnotizable at all. This brings up among the possible reasons for the resistance "the presence of strong latent homosexual inclinations, reaction-formations and other defenses against dependence" (137). But Anton brings it all back to psychoanalysis when he identifies the body he sees flashing "before him in the moment preceding his attacks" as the dad. And "with the verbalization of his hatred for his father, the chief symptoms that had brought him to treatment disappeared" (142). His insomnia, like the resistance to hypnosis, was on one continuum with playing dad—which was when he dreaded but desired p-unitive relations. But if Anton, neither hetero nor homo, is stuck on the phallic phase inside the Oedipus complex, it's Mother's fault: "Mothers of psychopaths, consciously or unconsciously, overtly or covertly, seduce their children" (151). The analysis succeeds, parole is given, and Anton withdraws, two years later, just like the Rat Man in the war before, into the body count of the current world war: "Two years later I learned he had been killed in action during the recovery of the Philippines" (155).

With Anton, then, Lindner only had to lay down the law and with a minimum of transference work run this law by the patient, the one law that he had always been running up against, reframing it as the high point of a range or rage of ambivalence surrounding the paternal introject. The result was rapid-turnover adjustment to the war fronts outside the prison or hospital (Lindner's own ambivalence here, while dutifully admitted, really never needs to be dealt with the better hand of long-term work). But his psy fi patient, Kirk's the name, is such a favorite that Lindner never lets go—until, on the racecourse between auto-analysis and psychosis, patient and doctor switch lanes: therapeutic relationship, heal thyself! Before he announces his mood swing over into the delusion, Lindner clarifies that his treatment of Kirk had left his association with "psychoanalysis" way behind: "But, meanwhile, strange things were happening to me, his psychoanalyst (or, better, his psychotherapist, since the method I was employing was no longer strictly that of psychoanalysis)" (195).

Given the borderline Kirk was sharing with psychosis, this one too wasn't a candidate for hypnosis. But all the other references to World War I are there. "Kirk was born in 1918. Immediately after his birth the family went to Paris, where his father was assigned for duty at the peace negotiations" (161). Lost doing the international shuffle, for a long time as the only white boy on a South Seas island, Kirk took to reading rather than reality testing. One day, while reading his science fiction:

> He had hardly begun reading, however, when he suddenly became aware of the fact that the name of the hero of this novel was the same as his own. Momentarily, this gave him pause. As he describes it, "a kind of shock ran through me: for a minute I felt completely disoriented." (170)

But in no time little Kirk turns the wounding shock of name share, loss, castration into another takeoff—into outer space. "While his corporeal body was living the life of a mundane boy, the vital part of him was far off on another planet" (172). His fantasy life runs alongside a successful career in physics that, it's for real, goes out for one of the leading roles:

When he completed the requirements for his doctoral degree he was mustered into military service and assigned to a special project then approaching a significant conclusion. When the Second World War ended (in a manner that had something to do with Kirk's work) he was discharged.... Whenever he was not totally preoccupied with scholastic or scientific work—and often even then, since his fantasy and his research interests (and assignments) coincided in certain ways—he was engaged in weaving an ever more closely knit imaginative mental life, the main lines of which were dictated by the recorded "biography" he had consumed so avidly on the island before the age of fourteen.... "I became convinced the books were about me, that somehow the author had obtained a knowledge of my life and had written its story. So the first thing I had to do was remember, and it seemed to me that I actually recalled everything he described. It was, of course, a curious position to be in—an adolescent boy remembering the adventures of himself as a grown man. But I got around this difficulty by convincing myself that the books had been composed in the future and had been sent back by some means into the present for my instruction. It's hard to explain, but I soon developed the notion—now a favorite one with science-fiction writers—of the co-existence of temporal dimensions so that the past and the future are simultaneous with the present. This made it possible to live a current life but, all the same, to *remember the future*." (173)

The boundary blender got turned on (to the point of his being sent to Lindner for treatment) over the constant pressure he's been under to make a fit between his recall and the joint account opened up between him and his future, precisely because he does recognize mere imagination (a recognition that serves as placeholder for his therapeutic breakthrough) in the being out of place of the details of his gadget self-love. One day while trying hard to remember a detail, and wishing he were back there, right now, to get a closer look at the intergalactic maps, he suddenly finds himself teleported there on wish or command.

As him, as my future self, I live his life; and when I return to this present self, I bring back the memories I have of that future and so am able to correct the records I am keeping. Now, you see, I no longer have to depend on memory. (176)

Lindner has two working impressions of the case right at the start of analysis: "The first was of Kirk's utter madness; the second, of the life-sustaining necessity of his psychosis" (178). "The discovery of the books, then, was a life-saving accident" (185). Lindner reads his case study between the lines of Freud's readings of *Gradiva* and of Schreber's *Memoirs*, two books that came to Freud by the accident (crash!) of having Jung around to recommend just those two for reading and interpretation. The results are endopsychic— and they're not all in yet. "In a sudden flash of inspiration it came to me that in order to separate Kirk from his madness it was necessary for me to enter his fantasy and, from that position, to pry him loose from the psychosis" (189).

By sharing the fantasy, Lindner is able to point out unresolved contradictions. But then he assists Captain Kirk in clearing them up and sustaining the defense. Once he does that, Kirk for the first time starts to question what he's doing.

> It is as if a delusion such as Kirk's has room in it only for one person at one time, as if a psychotic structure, too, is rigidly circumscribed as to "living space." When, as in this case, another person invades the delusion, the original occupant finds himself literally forced to give way.... My direct involvement in the fantasy that had, until then, been his private preserve, constricted his *"lebensraum,"* confronted him with his mirror image, and maneuvered him into the critical reality position. As a consequence, slowly but surely, he was being edged out of his psychosis. (193–95)

Meanwhile, back behind the couch, "strange things were happening to me, his psychoanalyst"—this is where he changes midsentence into "his psychotherapist" instead (195). Thus Lindner too takes off—into a delusional outer space between analysis proper and therapeutic eclecticism, characterized by a foreign term, used as though from the lexicon of therapy, *Lebensraum*, to describe the psychotic heights or limits attained by an atomic physicist, born in 1918 to one of the negotiators of the Entente victory and peace. If the "materials of Kirk's psychosis and the Achilles heel of my personality met and meshed like the gears of a clock," then, to keep this time, Lindner had already spent his own reading time (like, since learning how to) preparing for this first contact, this doubling on contact. "Parenthetically, I owe to science fiction much more than gratitude for entertainment. Re-enforcing a native curiosity and an inclination toward science, such reading has led me toward the serious study of subjects like Semantics and Cybernetics" (197–98). But Lindner's fall (not into psychosis, he specifies, but into compulsive neurosis, and not by atomic technology, but rather by, as

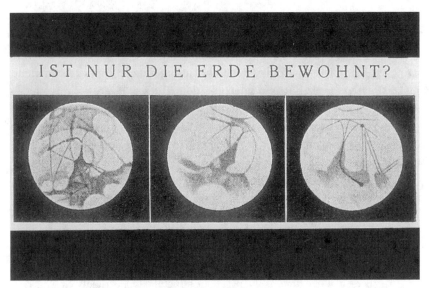

IST NUR DIE ERDE BEWOHNT?

The question reads, "Is only Earth inhabited?" The images are three photographs of Mars taken in 1900. Reproduced from *Welten/Werke/Wunder*, edited by Hans Dominik (1926), 499.

his title goes, "the jet-propelled couch") makes Kirk fall for the transference: for some time now, he's been playing along with the doctor, feeling sorry for him. He returns them to their respective couch positions, where they buckle up for the safe landing of the therapy within psychoanalysis.

Aircraft That Cannot Be

The sudden appearance of "aircraft that cannot be" stretches
the concept many people hold of ghosts. In the nomenclature of
our everyday lives, a ghost is some reappearance, in some as
yet unexplained manner, of a person once alive but no longer
so.... But ghostly aircraft, or ships, or other objects?... In 1939
and the few years following, ... there began to emerge from the
records stories that were considered at first to be not merely
strange, but totally out of the question. At first the stories
remained confined to the pilots and their crewmen. They spoke
to one another in the assured privacy of their quarters, on their
own airfields. What they had to say was not for the ears of
anyone outside this "inner group." But the stories were over-
heard. Not only pilots, but aircrews, passed on the tales, as did
mechanics and operations staff. It became evident that the
stories being told were not of a single bizarre, "impossible"
incident, but that the "impossible" had happened again and
again.

—MARTIN CAIDIN, *GHOSTS OF THE AIR*

In his eulogy of Lou Andreas-Salomé, Freud records the second fact of her
life that makes the first one, her friendship with Nietzsche, after the fact:

> In 1912 she returned to Vienna in order to be initiated into psy-
> choanalysis. My daughter, who was her close friend, once heard
> her regret that she had not known psychoanalysis in her youth.
> But, after all, in those days there was no such thing. (*SE*, 23:297)

Psychoanalysis was not there, for example, when Nietzsche fell from his
horse on the 1871 war front, a fall down the dotted lines of early separation
from father and brother, which, running on horsepower, rebounded back
to the future, where it was still Nietzsche, the horse of course, being beaten
in the speed race Freud would referee (in case studies of Leonardo Da Vinci
and Schreber) between repression and sublimation. According to Deleuze
and Guattari's wish or command, Nietzsche's machine bits, parts he played
as telegraph, typewriter, camera, and telephone, or his extraterrestrial explorations of the future, complete with overmen in gravity boots, go to
great wavelengths to split the scene of their Oedipalization. But the psychotic station breaks only follow (in the mode of understanding) from the

transferential legibility and attraction across the fixed fronts of total conflict which psychoanalysis conferred on Nietzsche's case. There was no immediate following or understanding of his doctrine of Eternal Return, certainly not on the scale Nietzsche himself had forecast of future world wars, without the change in direction given by Freud's theorization of war neurosis and taken into the outer limits or outer space of psychosis. Inside psychoanalytic reception of trauma internalization and technologization, Nietzsche did double tour of duty. One, he was, already pre–World War I, the case or insider of psychotic, perverse, and philosophical positions, those nontransferential or narcissistic limit concepts of psychoanalysis that, following Freud's encounter with the World War I epidemic of war neurosis, turned around into the foreground of Freud's no longer allegorical but now functional concern with the borderline. And two, riding out this switch, Nietzsche delivers the Eternal Return of the Same to the first theorizations of this newfound border zone, which Freud located in what he called (in the essay on "Fetishism") the oscillation between neurosis and psychosis (*SE*, 21:155). Nietzsche's enlistment into psychoanalysis is thus framed on one side by psychotic delusions of merger with machines and their energy sources (for example in the Schreber case) and, on the other side, by the symptoms of traumatic or war neurosis in *Beyond the Pleasure Principle* and "On 'the Uncanny.'" But this framing of Nietzsche could fit inside one reading, not just between two. Spielrein's death-driven preemptive model of Freud's second system featured Nietzsche, the teacher, as matricentric schizo and as Everyman—for himself. Nietzsche, in Spielrein's composite sketch, was both man and woman, at once in "autoerotic . . . union with himself" and in "union with the mother." This double identification, which also penetrated him, developed his perversion, the negative of his psychosis, out of the wish for many eternal returns of self-replication (Spielrein, 30–31). The intrapsychic relation of replication, according to Spielrein, is always looking for an outside chance in the family pack and reproduction assignment. Reproduction thus doubles as merger with one's ancestors through the lover who looks like you. The death that follows on the Oedipal heels of incest is not just punishment and prohibition; incest realizes, one, one's desired restoration to the engenderer and, two, the dissolution in him (39). The burden of "object representations," unalleviated by the turn-on of the conveyor belt of generations coming soon, leaves replication only one, negative identification: "The love reserved for oneself leads to self-destruction" (34). In other words, suicide, which introduces and represents, bottom line, the group bond as the way around the one-on-one or one-by-one encounter with the death of the other is always the downside or slide of the fantasy of replication. Every suicide is mass suicide committed by applicants for replication whose merger with the machine just didn't go through.

In *Beyond the Pleasure Principle,* Freud sets up this replication-versus-reproduction frame for the death drive's introduction into his own thought. First he considers the special psychic access afforded by the evidence of traumatic or war neurosis, and second, on the other side, Freud contemplates the scientific evidence that already advertises a time coming soon when human being will no longer come in generations but will live on forever within one egoic span of attention through cell-like doubling and division. The two sides, the neurosis of trauma or war and the replication fantasies compatible with psychosis, perversion, or group psychology, first came together for Freud by the end of the first total war.

Freud's earlier World War I essays on war and death and transience gave special mention to the work of mourning as the way through the grief-stuck metabolism of melancholia, a metabolism stuck on irreplaceable relations. Melancholia thus represents a psychotic shutdown that endangers the future of civilization, which Freud charts according to the course of new inventions. In "Thoughts for the Times on War and Death," Freud flashes the high beam on "attempts at mechanical flight," which belong to the types of futurity endangered by melancholia (*SE,* 14:299–300). Thus mourning, set up as a main therapeutic frame for the work of psychoanalysis, can keep couplified rapport with the future going along restored access to the libido pool of substitutes. But Freud's emphasis shifts by 1918 to promotion of any way or means beyond melancholic shutdown. That's how the interest and investment in the diversified structures of psychosis, group psychology, and perversion took over even in psychoanalysis, where pre–World War I they had been left out as limit concepts. In the meantime Freud had discovered ways around the impasse of melancholia, which did not first have to do the work of mourning. Freud's close encounter with the epidemic of traumatic or war neurosis during World War I opened up a no-man's-land or borderline zone between neurosis and psychosis for theorization and treatment. Along this opened-up borderline, group psychology and perversion were made equally accessible to psy fi colonization for the survival of the species. What is always under the threat of extinction in science fiction (or, say, in psychotic delusions) is the couplified means of reproduction and its double native habitat (at once the body and the earth). The zone of nontransferential disconnection otherwise set aside as melancholia or schizophrenia doubles as a new frontier for future colonization through the evolving and self-replicating super or survivor body growing out of equal machine and human parts up and down the axis of intra-psychic space.

The psy fi impulse is not just one man's insight and initiation (say, Ernst Jünger's) into a Nietzschean reception or selection of the first airmen taking to the skies as the advance shock troops of evolutionary fast-forwarding (see Jünger's *Copse 125*). A paranoid reading of psychoanalysis (which is not unlike Freud's reading of Schreber) is along for the ride or drive. Psychoanalysis, the owner's manual to our ongoing technologization, is what Jünger and others doing it their way had to "not see." All the names in history (including Nietzsche and, long time not see, Heidegger) get mixed from World War I onward in a reception at once technological and psychoanalytic that returns to Freud. (Boom Boom Bumke, for example, can only attack Freud by at the same time sending him out on a "dated" with Janet and Nietzsche. The back of the bus is OK if the destination is immortality.)

In 1941 Fritz Mohr summarized for the central Nazi psychotherapy journal Nietzsche's precursor status for the historiography in progress of the new culture of therapy for all and one: "His conception of the eternal return of the same contains clear references to that which one has designated the repetition of the analytic situation, yes, the former is perhaps only to be understood via the latter" (Mohr, "Friedrich Nietzsche," 64). Thus while Mohr hails along Nietzsche as "blood sacrifice for a new world" (58), the future of miraculated worlds in the place of the one that was lost belongs to the discovery Mohr has to hand to Nietzsche of the motor or alternator driving and building the psychic apparatus and all its syndications. It's a future taken out in the alternation between projection and identification, between adolescent acting out of self-love or self-hate on the person of the other and primary identification with the mother, in other words, mutual identification in groups (56). These alternating alterations, which construct the influencing machine (in Victor Tausk's 1918 case study of philosophy student Natalija A.) and the automaton, double, and phantom in Lacan's 1936 mirror stage directions, skywrite in the work of Mohr and his Nazi German therapy colleagues, along lines given by Freud's interventions in or inventions of doubling inside war neurosis, the airman's union with his plane in flight and the mass psychology that grows up to meet the cyborg's attack. Thus the high point of the Nietzsche-Freud connection is reached in the work of Paul Metz, the military psychologist in Nazi Germany whose pilot series we were following in volume 2, who in 1936 summarized his aeropsychodynamic position for a convention on the psychology of will held in Nietzsche's honor or spirit.

> What is most important in a pilot is his ability to judge correctly at every time and in every situation the position of the plane in three-dimensional air space. Sensewise man is equipped only inadequately for this assignment. The only sense that functions adequately is the eye. But the manifold system of the sense of orientation or position, which is effective on earth when walking and standing, largely fails as a whole in the flying situation and falls apart. The consequence of this disintegration are orientation discrepancies, through which the sense of position stands in contradiction to the direct optic perception of position.
>
> These orientation discrepancies come up because all flight maneuvers...remain subliminal for the specific sensations of the vestibular organ. The sense of position receives no corrective even with major changes in position and is experienced thus as opposition to the optic perception.... The pilot must remove the orientation discrepancy in order to realize the uniformity and security of his reactions. It can be removed only through a specific psychic act...which becomes thus an important feature of psychological compatibility with flight.... Behavior during disorientation, which always represents a critical flying situation, needs to be examined and evaluated not so much with functional methods as with characterological ones. ("Die Orientierung beim Fliegen," 207–8)

Also in the proceedings to the 1936 conference on the psychology of will, E. R. Jaensch, following Nietzsche's lead, analyzed the "dissolution type," today's Everyman (airhead by another name), who is not tied down to unconscious drives and the life of the will but hovers over them in a "vacuum." To ground this live wire, the spirit of youth or adolescence must be conjured as the connection with the group. National Socialism thus returns, according to Jaensch, to the founding impulse of German idealism: teen passion. With the return of the Teen Age, the sense of vision, the world of the eye that Goethe once addressed as the primal source of life, has been brought back into focus. In adolescence, in other words, the axis has shifted in the realm of the ego or I: the ego is not surrendered but for the first time discovered or realized under these group conditions of service to the higher force lifting you up. What first meets up with the teen's innate disposition in this shift in axis is what Jaensch calls an "empty phantom," which, as with all the favorite haunts of adolescence, National Socialism filled with the airtime of group bonding with the future of the race (to be won) (Jaensch, 274–78).

In-flight processes opened up the inside view of trauma technologization. The wound of separation or takeoff is incorporated (as both Metz and McLuhan put it) and metabolized as the wonder or miracle of flight, of the merger between pilot, in spite of his limited biological sensorium, and the automatic functioning of his machine in flight. Flying is traumatic: but the trauma is also deferred for the time being, the time in which the pilot is able through constant vigilance, self-observation, or doubling to overcome his biological limitations, which, like the body and the earth, are still there.

Ever since the opening of the era of the machine and techno-invention, a crisis in reproduction has been along for the progress. The technological object has always excited egoic fantasies of immortality now. The narcissistic portfolio of investments, which Freud opened up at the end of World War I, breaks down into shares of the ultimate science fiction fantasy, that of replacement of reproduction (which is death in life) with a new and improved immortality plan, that of amoeba-like and technology-compatible replication. Rather than conform to the superegoic standards of tradition and transmission across future generations, the short egoic attention span, which does not want to go, goes for doubling on contact. The science fiction or psychotic delusion of merger with the machine thus moves away from any interpersonal relationship of sexual difference. Fetishism, for example, turns out to be about getting into machines and, at the same time, fulfilling, for the time being, one's commitment to reproduction, which is still the only way to keep the species (and the machines) going. This is where Freud's surprise observation that fetishism saves the man in crisis from becoming (exclusively) homosexual in fact fits in (*SE*, 21:154). Nazi Germany, which was, among other things, one big science fiction, resided within the tension Freud's theory of fetishism describes: the group psychology that's always along for the psy fi drive reintroduces the problem of homosexuality, which Nazi therapeutic culture determined to face right on within defense contexts of inoculation. Homoeroticism, or what Benjamin referred to as aestheticization of politics, lubes the merger with the war machine. Fetishism gets you into the lean machine: it represents a makeshift overcoming of the crisis in relations with heterosexual reproduction, a compromise between the fantastic prospects of doubling, replication, or merger with the machine and the fact of life that it is still only reproduction that can restock the libido pool for the living on and evolution of the species.

Freud's exploration of fetishism, which belongs to the thought experiment that began under the new lab conditions of the first total war, admits the split that allows for a simulcasting about between wish and reality, a doubling of vision or theory along the oscillating borderline between neurosis and psychosis. The primal scene of the war neuroses or psychoses bringing down surviving pilots remains, to quote two Allied researchers (who in 1943 were reporting on the war that was also the corridor war in which the analytic model was winning), "ambivalent identification with a dead comrade": "These [melancholic identifications] and the severe psychoses are often intractable" (Grinker and Spiegel, *War Neuroses in North Africa*, 147). Fetishism's borderline structure, which puts it on a direct line to group psychology, keeps gadget love going as an alternative, within the same category or attention span of the ego, to the grief-stuck metabolism of loss retention.

The two bookends of Fritz Mohr's dedication to Nietzsche, I mean Freud, were, one, a series of articles written during World War I on war neurosis and, two, work in progress on the cure of homosexuality from the twenties onward. Taking the war neurotic as his model target, Mohr tracked homosexuals down to the intrapsychic lines of earliest conflict (before their sexual identification or orientation) all the way back again to their asocial refusal right now of group identification with the German race.

The prospect of total victory through analysis began with Freud's contribution to the war conditioning of what Mohr hails in 1915, 1916, and 1917 as a new energetic eclecticism in therapy culture from the mobilizations of hypnotic suggestion and electroshock all the way to long or short-term analytic therapy. Even if, as Mohr observes, the practitioners of this eclectic spread of techniques may want to avoid the name "psychoanalysis," Freud's model was still the underlying one that was being used by one and all. Indeed the detractors of the name brand were at the same time operating with the Freudian notions of flight into illness, gains from illness, and repression ("Aus der Praxis," 1118). The myth of the psychoanalytically healed war neurotic convinced not only Mohr that every psychic disturbance or aberration can be cured or adjusted, that most breakdowns can be avoided, and finally that a major portion of the so-called physical illnesses remains accessible to a psychic fix on treatment (1119). "This will potentiate in ways that couldn't be anticipated earlier and grant our people as a whole a still greater nervous energy than had been available before for our assistance. And thus one can claim that we physicians by concerning ourselves with the war neuroses in this way produce cultural work in the greatest style" ("Die Behandlung der Kriegsneurosen," 140).

Mercedes-Benz advertisement. Reproduced from p. 3 of the advertisement and review appendix of *Die Kunst im deutschen Reich* 4, no. 12 (December 1940).

In Mohr's research from 1915 to 1944, we hear this war record of psychoanalysis, which is at the same time stuck in the groove of a so-called Nietzsche reception, the one fine-tuning with psychosis, perversion, and group psychology. While Freud, psychoanalysis, and the lexicon of Oedipus were giving way, displacement style, to Nietzsche, depth psychology, and the terms of the will, the Nazi psychotherapeutic reception of Nietzsche relied on the transferential, borderline legibility that psychoanalysis had invested in his case. What's in a name or concept cannot be completely severed from itself through displacement. Thus the Adler retained unnamed for reunification purposes is Nietzsche, I mean Freud compatible. In 1939 Gerhart Eggert set out to peel pure Nietzsche off Adler's applications for the readership of the central Nazi psychotherapy mag. Adler's replacement of sex with will to power reproduced willpower after his own image of neurotic compensation for, and insurance against, inferiority. Self-overcoming of our prefab sense of inferiority, which the standards of nature only reinforce, will be realized when the drive for security or insurance merges with a future community spirit developed by then to the point "that it will function automatically." Beyond this place of tension between pure and applied Nietzsche, Eggert was again focusing on the destiny of the human sensorium, which although limited, over and out, still has in store for it, while the energy supply lasts, along the stereo channel of technologization and group psychologization, a half-life or overlife of self-replicating, doubling merger with the automatic functioning of the machine in flight, a self-overcoming of dependence on earth and body.

Panic Attack

The ad at the end of a later edition of Reinhold Eichacker's 1924 science fiction *Panic* informs us that the author has produced three novels, including this one, based on the "technological ideas" of Max Valier. The ad continues: "For the first time space ship and rocket plane are awarded literary treatment. The Opel factories have already constructed the rocket plane, and the first practical successes have made the whole world pay attention. Max Valier, the spiritual leader of the rocket plane is the inventor of these novels, the realization of which has been made possible by German spirit and German genius." The author doubles as ghostwriter for Valier's "technological ideas."

Panic lies between *The Fight for the Gold* and *The Ride into Nothingness*. Perhaps because of its collaborative status between disciplines, *Panic* uses footnotes that drop, however, only self-reference to the *Gold* segment of the three-part body of one work (120, 240). The underworld of gold shortage's fantastic alleviation, which apparently delivered Germany from the consequences of the world war, bankrolls the upper regions of outer-space encounters. The readership must drop to the knees of this footnote whenever the German scientist Walter Werndt is hailed as Germany's savior.

But it's still America, where the immediate future belongs, that's the epicenter of *Panic*. The largest observatory is there, directed by American scientist Earthcliffe at the head, which has the sun covered with constant photographic and cinematic camera recording (28–29). But the human element of intuition and observation brought some startling, uncovered news to the attention of one German gadget-loving follower of the firmament (and former Werndt student): in a flash across the sun, the shadow trace could be discerned of a giant meteor aiming to crash land on earth (46). Before Werndt arrives, one of Earthcliffe's circle, Dr. Wepp, has decided to go for the gold of speculation. He transgresses against the inner circle's vow to keep the meteoric fall a secret for the time being from the crowd's capacity for panic by leaking the news to the press. He then buys and sells according to the manic rhythms of the market, which his news leaks continue to control or release. His first move is to buy up all shares in life insurance companies, which will, already after he takes his first leak, overflow with new policies. "Every person will be insured without exception" (70). After the first leak is out, the loyal members of the circle take counterpropaganda action in a damage-controlling effort to "steer the panic" (78).

The German gadget lover, Nagel, who worked by intuition to hit a fact on the head that media-technological powers of observation running on automatic had missed, says that their problem of the rising up panic states is a job for Walter Werndt, who then arrives in his brand-new flying machine (126). But what is of more immediate concern are the new photo plates Werndt has developed out of the work that went into the new plane's wings, which catch the light rays in order to fit in with whatever's around, and just disappear. Plane and photographic plate are improvements on the way to Werndt's primal research project, "study of the chemical components of the stars," which will give him what he has always wanted: "the secret of the primal substance" (135). Earthcliffe's "blue eyes beamed" at the prospect. The search for the primordial goo-goo of life under the most modern laboratory conditions was the Faustian formula for Dr. Frankenstein's studies, which he took in with his unmourning, and let out with monster making.

Werndt gives away the kind of recognition to Wepp that everyone in Fritz Lang's *Mabuse* cinematic complex is also compelled to grant the mad sociopathic genius.

> There is a certain greatness in being the only human being to seize the final opportunity in a situation which will probably not recur in 10,000 years and use it to rule the world. There's something superhuman, satanic, about such a venture, such a risk. It cannot but explode the human brain. (152)

In the meantime Wepp turns his propagandistic manipulation of mass panic around to the paranoid frequency he starts tuning in. His charge rings as true as the group's psychotechnological reception of the broadcast prior to any message: "The eyes of all were directed as though hypnotized toward the loud speaker" (159). Psychotic and group-psychological assumptions about technology—whatever transmits must also take in what's at the receiving end—are mobilized by Wepp's charge that the telescopic technology of the observatory has the power to amplify and beam out earth's gravity to pull objects from space down to earth. What Wepp knows to be true group psychologically, he applies to scientifically objective observation, which in the paranoid register always has an objective. But Wepp's panic attack is upstaged by the light show of the meteor's first flashing contact with the earth's atmosphere. Wepp dies, and the panic contains itself as preparedness; but Wepp's forecast, on which he based his speculations, proves correct. The damage on impact was for the most part merely material (and thus totally covered, thanks to Wepp, by all those insurance policies). "A few hundred human lives were lost through flooding and storm, several thousand cases of madness through anxiety appear to have been the only larger population of victims" (247). In addition, earth lands a new substance with the meteor, one that's all ray energy with unearthly emissions (249). Werndt, off the wagon, is back on the primal substance. But the other primal substance that Wepp's crash delivered as side effect is the basic psychology of the substance or mass, or masses, that occupies and cathects the intersections between technology and the unconscious.

In Karl Epp's military-psychological view, the panicky consequences of rapid technologization have not met with the appropriate inoculative modes or methods of preparedness. Only the training of pilots has kept up with the new techno-conditions and taken in just the right immunizing amounts of panic. Winkler von Oelrich recommends that the move to contain the panic should come as though from "another world" (295). An inoculative "stop-moment" must be produced.

> Certain effects in the psychic realm, which must be viewed as crises, can only be relieved when combated with means of the same kind that produced the crises to begin with. (295)

In yet another study of panic attack and defense down the German psy war corridor, Walter Beck points to psychoanalysis as the inoculation that failed; it gave too much popularized knowledge about the psyche too soon:

> In short what has to happen, next to or beyond formal discipline, is to bring about through spiritual-psychic bonding and emotion an increase of the individual and national powers of resistance ... (on which, among other factors, the vast popularization and fantastic expansion of psychoanalysis has had such deleterious effect). (302)

The injection system of psychoanalysis, which Beck describes as panic inducing, needs to be recycled back into the inoculation that's been aerodynamically redesigned. The pilot is, to date, best prepared in his encounters with panic attack in the air. But the grounding of the resistance of the population below to the panic attack that comes from above, from "another world," offers the broadest spectrum of cure-all. As L. Pérignon confirms in 1939, the panic has ended cornered and conquered in the air raid shelter, in the community spirit or group psychology of knowing the drill.

> Seen in this way, the air raid community is an essential National Socialist concept. In this community everyone has a mission in which he cannot be replaced by anyone else. Out of the neigh-

borly community of danger emerges a community of the nation's destiny, the uninterrupted defense front of self protection across the homeland.

Remember, German, that you are grandson and ancestor. You are no fruit fly that lives today and dies tomorrow and of whom no memory remains. (304–5)

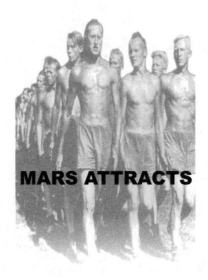

MARS ATTRACTS

Siegerkraft

A country that still believed in an invasion of men from Mars
could be successfully attacked by Nazi flyers.

—GREGOR ZIEMER, *EDUCATION FOR DEATH*

If only the men from Mars were a reality and if only these
Martians would attack us, then we of this world would surely
experience a tremendous surge of mutual loyalty. Our
international conflicts would die overnight as we marched (or
rather "flew") together against such a common enemy.

—EDWARD TOLMAN, "IDENTIFICATION AND THE POST-WAR WORLD"

In 1934 Titus Taeschner published *Der Mars greift ein,* a title that rushes toward the anticipated final particle "an"—as in "Mars Attacks"—but surprise attacks us at that endpoint with "ein," whereby it translates as "Mars Intervenes." In the German tradition of outer-space fantasy, Mars "attracts."

First contact with the Martians was taken up by a German scientist after he split the atom and with the resulting force, which was with him, also split earth for Mars. That was the first giant step for mankind that the Martians were able to meet halfway (without their control-power assistance, the scientist's rocket might never have made it to landing). Since then the scientist is a regular guest, the favorite of the Martians, and in time he is initiated in all the fast-forward-evolved techno-secrets of the future, based on the atom part or parting that he discovered on earth, which on Mars already belongs to prehistory. Soon the Martians' take on earth politics is partial to the new Germany. European rivalries threaten the new German will to peace. And these rivalries, just as last time around, during the Great War, are ultimately the result of Japanese-led pan-Asian underhanded bidding for global power. That's how quickly the science fiction projections of the future can become dated. But all this is what you would know once you had finished reading the book or even if you never had read it but had read all about it.

The story rises up out of an enigmatic job offer that breaks a couple's downward financial slide but, in exchange, also shakes that couple's "and." The one who's shaking is a "superhuman" atom smasher whose avoidance of women, which he confuses with the avoidance with which he cuffs the man hands of his chosen representative and heir, catches up with him destinally when his attempt to pass into matrimony reveals itself, with the revelation that his ideal woman is already secretly married to his ideal man, to be in service to an unlivable attraction to the couple.

The novel opens with a job ad for a position in the research project code-named "Mars 5000." It happens to describe studly Dr. Dietrich Krafft's qualifications down to his T-shirt but also makes conditions on the side that the applicant consider himself as "private secretary" to his future boss and that he be unmarried. There's something wanting in this ad that wife Annilo would rather not get into personalizing. Dietrich decides that those conditions must be secondary, on the sidelines, and thus will be waived once he proves himself. Annilo suspects that the conditional on the side is on the inside of the kind of job being offered. But Krafft even wrote his dissertation on the evidence of life on Mars. His new boss, if he goes for the job, Professor Sieger, is "the world's most famous Mars researcher" (12). And the surnames talk the same language: Kraft is to "power" what Sieger is to the "victor."

When they first meet, it's destinal all right: "Dr. Krafft was from the first moment in this man's power, and a wonderful [wunderbares] sense of good fortune, never before experienced, rushed through him. He felt instinctively: this man was his destiny!" (15). Professor Sieger was looking for a "man in the fullest sense of the word" (17). And now he needs Krafft to move into the Villa Marsberg so that he will always only be just a heart-beat away, just in case. Whenever Krafft is outside the compound, how-ever, he must never discuss internal affairs, namely, their research into new sources of techno-power, not even with his best friends, but especially not with women. What crosses Krafft's mind skips over the effect of his oath on relations with Annilo to the power source he is turned on to: "With that there came between them a secret.... It was after all his habit to discuss everything with his partner. What sort of power [Kraft] was it that Sieger was producing, and which was supposed to be so monstrous [ungeheuer-lich]?" (27).

While touring the central power station, Krafft at first recognizes tele-scope-like instruments, but then concludes that one of them looks more like an "anti-aircraft gun. Powerful cables were connected to this machine, which emitted a fluorescent gleam" (34). The professor starts communicat-ing with Mars. Soon Krafft understands that he is to serve as "witness" to Sieger's "impossible," "incomprehensible" accomplishments (37). And so just the two of them are off to Mars. To Mars? Krafft starts to worry: "The professor isn't, for God's sake, insane, is he? Have I stumbled into a mad house?" (38).

Krafft, who passes out in transit, wakes up on Mars to the evidence of a woman checking his heartbeat. But what a woman! Skin like it was made out of velvet and eyes like a pair of stars: "And his dream of the night before suddenly became conscious, his dream of traveling to Mars!—But he wasn't dreaming any longer, was he? A hot jolt of fear [*Schreck*] went through him. Abruptly he sat up. With this movement he must have unconsciously unleashed a phenomenal strength, for his body flew several meters into the air as though shot by a powerful spring. And then something unexpected happened. The woman grabbed him by the hips, took him under her arm like a bundle and, though he resisted her with all his might, pushing his outstretched fists against her, she carried him away as if he were a baby in diapers" (55).

Reunited with Sieger, Krafft gets praise for his constitution, his dead faint notwithstanding: "You have overcome [*überwunden*] quite bravely and quickly the small disturbances and shake-ups of the organism" (56). But Krafft has a question to ask: "'Where are we anyway, and who was that robust female who brought me here like a . . . a baby?' 'You'll learn all about it right away—but just a moment, we need to buckle up your little shoes [*Schühchen*] so you don't fly away from me'" (56). Krafft can only figure that he is inside an "incomprehensible delusion" that makes him see and experience things "which are in reality not at all there."

Life on Mars takes place in a completely wireless techno-underworld (61). The duo from Germany can make lunch from bottled scratch-and-sniff supplies that take the shape, once liquid is added, of a heavy meat-and-potato cuisine. The state-run institution of nourishment on Mars dispenses weekly rations of condensed foodstuff. Krafft enjoys his beefsteak with mashed potatoes. "Everything tasted fabulous—just as great as the beefsteaks that his wife . . . a searing shock [*Schreck*] jolted him suddenly. Dear God, yes, his wife—this whole time he had not thought of her, truly not, not one single time [*nicht ein einziges Mal*]. In his fright [*Schreck*] the bite of food stuck in his throat" (65). This is the moment, the *Mal*, that, opening wide for its reutterance in German—*Mahl*—is also the meal and communion from which the wife has been excluded. "This procedure not only has the advantage that food products can be conserved for a limitless time, easily stored and transported, but also they retain their natural aroma, their full nutritional value, and can at any time, by mixing in the condensed liquid, be brought back up to their original volume without any loss of flavor whatsoever. There is no garbage with this method. Everything gets used up. Leaves, roots, skins, bones, in short everything unsuited for human consumption is used as feed for animals or for industrial purposes. On account of the limited water supplies on Mars, the agrarian flora and fauna are also severely limited, and only through this rational exploitation of all food products can one anticipate and push back the otherwise inevitable catastrophe of mass starvation" (66). It takes a fully mobilized and projected war economy to know another one.

Krafft is introduced to the video phone service on Mars. Sieger explains following the TV exchange with a Martian engineer, on the other side of the small matte screen: "Just now you became acquainted with the highest realization of the telephone. . . . This telecommunications device is moreover no longer restricted in space. Everyone carries along his own pocket phone" (68). As they pass down endless tunnels of light in vacuum-packed transport through the cities of Mars, life outside is like a "silent movie" without any commercial distractions, no billboards or signs. "All that belonged to long-ago buried customs, an impossible ballast. Here the whole of life was conducted in a manner that was completely correct, practical, but highly monotone" (70). Their medium of transportation runs through manipulation of magnetic fields, frequencies, and forces without any machines or propellers. The cityscapes are devoid of smoking factory chimneys. "Krafft made up his mind not to wonder [zu wundern] about anything anymore" (72). By the end of their stay, he has become acquainted with "a form of state that inspired in him the strongest admiration. How wonderful [wunderbar] this organization was that was built up in consideration of two vital factors on Mars. Under-population and lack of water have threatened life on Mars for thousands of years. The genius of Mars is dedicated to facing these dangers with Spartan-iron discipline. . . . The whole of Martian humanity has through conditioning in the course of thousands of years become permeated by the one big idea, to work together as a unity in the bitter struggle against decline" (92).

Whatever a thousand years may bring on earth, a thousand years have passed on Mars since the invention of wireless transmission of power (98). Transmitted to the Germans, the force that must immediately outmode the earthly arsenal and heap it up as junk will realize the rule of peacetime for Hitler and Germany. "With the pull of a lever from within your airship (which can be rendered completely invisible either through artificial cloud formation or through optical means) you can shut down all guns, all machines with magnetic force. Any plane will drop like a boulder from the sky when you send it your rays" (100). Sieger and Krafft convince the German government to accept this outlandish offer of peace, of a piece of the atomic action.

To get their deal sealed—peace for Germany, for Europe, in exchange for Japanese factory colonies on the continent—before Sieger and Krafft can cut theirs, Japanese spies must penetrate Villa Marsberg. Their plant on the inside gives knockout drops to Sieger and to the engineer in charge of maintaining the magnetic shield over the compound. The Japanese kidnap Krafft. Sieger's longtime most loyal employee diagnoses the professor's immobilizing symptoms: "It can only be a case of a brief nervous disorder or of—something else entirely" (120). The something else of betrayal, which at this point can be held only in conspiracy theory, is the only alternative to a passing attack of nervous illness. But the wife, who has remained shut out from all male sorting and planning, decides to act in this missing-person matter of her husband. She decides to seduce the Japanese agent into telling her the whereabouts of her man. She's all eager beaver but then—wait! What about her husband, he might interrupt their tryst? Beautiful Annilo is too worried to let her Japanese suitor continue to go all the way. He reassures her: He won't be coming home anytime soon. Oh? A place name gets dropped, and she finds another excuse to frustrate her informant's intimacy issues with her.

She takes her undercover work to show and tell at Villa Marsberg. Sieger has been waiting for her all his live-long life. She feels it too. "Now she could understand how...her husband...had given himself body and soul to this person" (134). Together they walk down the "long hallway to the control room [Führerraum] with all its technological wonders" (138). The man who is so strange and yet so familiar has met in Annilo his ideal woman. His courting words resonate with something in her, but not the woman part.

Sieger sees to it that Krafft is delivered from a Japanese battleship by a "gray phantom" that immobilizes up ship's creek all machinic parts. The German representatives of Mars, Sieger and Krafft, pitch their script to the German leaders: "The world powers armed for war will be forced to disarm and in such a decisive way that future wars will be once and for all impossible. And this compulsion will be administered by their rape victim, Germany" (156).

Soon Japanese and Soviet battleships are under way, including "enormous mother ships for bomber planes" (197). Germany and Mars demand that Europe form a united front: "Only by changing Europe's outmoded politics, which still stem from the era of the mail coach, only by joining together to form one defensive front can Europe be saved" (200). Poland is counted in, because otherwise it will be swallowed whole by "the Russian moloch" (201). "Let's join in a defensive and offensive alliance! Then we can show our teeth to the yellow and red giants. Germany offers a helping hand" (201). But couldn't this result in a Second World War? "The actual powers behind the scenes in 1914 could already back then be found in the Far East. They accomplished their goal by making Europe into Pandora's box and thus setting it up for its own purposes. That cannot happen again" (202).

Once Mars has intervened and secured the peace for Hitler and Germany, Sieger wants Annilo to be his woman. He specifically sought unmarried assistants because he dreaded the widows that his high-risk jobs left behind. Indeed, all women were banned from his research compound. And then came Annilo. Marriage and mourning or unmourning are conjugated together. When he invites her to go to Mars with him, she breaks her vow of silence and discloses the marriage vows already exchanged with Krafft. But he doesn't take a breakdown. Instead he moves to Mars. He asks them to be his heirs and follow his instructions to the letter, so that in the future, faraway from the couple that counted him odd man out, he will never need to reproach himself (249). One proviso in his testament is that Annilo, in exchange for receipt of the Villa Marsberg, among many other of his earthly possessions, set up hospitals, recovery spas, and nursing homes reserved in the first place for those wounded in the struggle for the new German unity, in the second place for veterans of the Great War and their progeny (254). Krafft wants to wait two years before going to Mars to bring him back down to Earth. But Annilo seems to know better. Only now that he's gone can they be happy together again. The couple mourns, not the group of one. The couple will remain connected to their superhuman friend by fulfilling the duties dictated by his testament. Krafft agrees, and closes the book with a vow: "This I swear as a German and as Official Representative of Mars!" Sieger is a goner who must also be counted alive to the extent that he can remember. In the ambivalence liner notes to the record of mourning, we read how commemoration requires that the dead or undead remember—to keep their word and stay away.

The Psychotic Sublime

The stars themselves and particularly our sun . . . only represent
stations, through which God's miraculous creative power
travels to our earth (and perhaps to other inhabited planets). . . .

The whole Order of the World therefore appears as a
"miraculous structure," the sublimity of which surpasses in my
opinion all conceptions which in the course of history men and
peoples have developed about their relation to God. . . .

The innumerable visions I had in connection with the idea that
the world had perished were partly of a gruesome nature,
partly of an indescribable sublimity. . . . In one of them it was as
though I were sitting in a railway carriage or in a lift driving
into the depths of the earth and I recapitulated, as it were, the
whole history of mankind or of the earth in reverse order; in the
upper regions there were still forests of leafy trees; in the nether
regions it became progressively darker and blacker. When
temporarily I left the vehicle, I walked as though across a large
cemetery where, coming upon the place where Leipzig's
inhabitants lay buried, I crossed my own wife's grave. . . . On
the return drive the shaft collapsed behind me, continually
endangering a "sun deity" who was in it too. . . .

—DANIEL PAUL SCHREBER, *MEMOIRS OF MY NERVOUS ILLNESS*

The affect "constellations" free to arise when aesthetics is not zoning restricted to address only the beautiful are still prefab prepsychoanalytic constructions, fortified against deep work on the strata and strategies of intrapsychic relations. No wonder that the sublime, the other bookend on the
aesthetics mantle down the row of treatises from the beautiful, does not
give entry into the analysis of the uncanny, noted by Freud the impurity or
species most likely to be superseded by its more positive mutations within
art and nature appreciation. Freud had a sense for how the sublime func-
tioned in aesthetic theories to get the big picture—cleared of disturbing
leftovers. To give just one example, one that had, moreover, a shelf life in
Freud's own library: Friedrich Theodor Vischer's synthetic and representational study of aesthetics set up the sublime as one of the centers into and
through which what's uncanny must be recycled and reprocessed in the
modern spirit of "indirect idealization." But, Freud continues in his opener
to "On 'the Uncanny,'" sometimes a great notion cannot but be left on the

sidelines of the field, which, although unattended by the scholarship, marks the spot we are in.

Freud rejects E. Jentsch's second opinion that conflict between what one knows about machines and the fact of life that seeing the automaton is believing in its animation is the sole source and resource of the uncanniness in E. T. A. Hoffmann's "The Sandman." What Freud sees instead is that this uncertainty leaves by the wayside the Sandman figure, who is always back, doubling back over time, to repeat an interruption that keeps tearing out a child's eyes. Indeed, the Sandman's repeated cutting off of every move Nathanael makes to couplify is on one promotional line with the merger with the automaton Olympia: the eyes Olympia has for Nathanael are his own. Her destruction and his suicide do not belong to the same series that sees its finale in the rage coming between Nathanael and his meat-vehicle betrothed, Klara. When Nathanael sees Klara and not Olympia through his telescope, he faces a crisis in the register of the beautiful and reproduction that sends him skydiving down the sublime route—of suicide.

In "The Work of Art in the Age of Mechanical Reproduction" Walter Benjamin gave us the Nazi look, a new and improved brand of aesthetics or psychology that he diagnosed as only marching one way, to the beat of yet another war. The Nazis advertised their movement as one of *Erhebung*, a term that enters the German lexicon of the sublime at that high point of "lifting up," "arising," even "tumescence" or "arousal." The Nazi looks the part he plays in the mass-media death cult, and what he sees is the sublimity of his all-natural cause and condition. But before Benjamin's postscript gives us the line about aestheticization of politics versus politicization of art (a phrase indeed designed for reproducibility) there's his case study of the gadget lover and modern mass member, which cannot be shut to separate Benjamin's new destructive character (part Karl Kraus, part Mickey Mouse) from the Nazi overman. Even when the Nazi has the look of bad Nietzscheanism, it's still the Benjaminian gadget lover (who comes complete with an owner's manual issued by psychoanalysis) who is looking out of the look. The inoculation shocks or shots of the mass-media sensurround don't Nazi-proof anything.

Benjamin wired Brecht's epic theater to and through his own reading of the mass media sensurround via the raising to techno consciousness of the pilot's relationship to plane flight. Brecht's first version of the "Lindbergh Flight" set the pilot up on the plane of glorification, the level of emotion seconded by the public's short-lived thrill ride along for the transatlantic flight. But in revising the original take or intake of this happening public event, "Brecht revised himself." Epic theater begins with Brecht's double take on mechanical flight. "In 'The Flight of the Lindberghs' Brecht seeks to refract the spectrum of the *'Erlebnis'"*—the momentary thrill that passes or rather goes under—"in order to extract from it the colors of the *'Erfahrung,'"* which Benjamin ties to an understanding of the pilot's conditions and "work" of flying (537). The upward mobilization of pilot service, which, Benjamin agrees with T. E. Lawrence, can be seen as the update of earlier entries into monastic orders, models the new "clerical sternness" that will henceforward inform the "instruction" epic theater gives "in a modern technique—here, that of aviation." Next paragraph, next section: the flight connection that shakes up Brecht's pre-Brechtian drama takes epic theater to the movies. "Like the pictures in a film, epic theater moves in spurts. Its basic form is that of the shock with which the single, well-defined situations of the play collide" (537). But when Benjamin next points to the overcoming of the "sublimity" and "intoxication" that once rose up out of the abyss of the orchestra pit, he leaves unattended—lets pass, slip, or go under—a certain origin of this modern epic movie theater that lies in the public advent of the thrill of the total artwork, the shock of the new concealment of the orchestra and complete darkening of the auditorium that was seen first with Wagner.

Between *The Origin of the German Mourning Pageant* and the essays on techno-culture and shock absorption, Benjamin was a close reader of Schreber's *Memoirs* and of Freud's study of Schreber. That's not just to turn the other cheekiness. Schreber studies need not be, not this time around, about the survival of the specious, the direct link (forget missingness!) to the Nazi ascension. Schreber can be read, instead, in terms of the outside chance. The chance that there is an outside to the setting of total recording, pre-programming, surveillance, and information gathering keeps slimming down in the reception area. But the drive to commit oneself completely to sui-citation does still admit interruption. It is the break Schreber gives us.

Thomas Szasz's *The Therapeutic State* has the look of the many books out there that should open up the era of Nazi mental health, telling like it was. It was always a ghost of a chance that the ongoing Allied reception of these histories would bear some trace at least of the repression. The score of near missers and nonreceivers is too high to recount. It is a ghost that's in our typeface in Szasz's study. In the index under "Nazis" the reader is given a referral to "mental patients, treatment of, under National Socialism." And there, there is a page reference, it's page 213. Look it up, and you'll see it can only be found missing, just like one of those floors in New York hotels, somewhere between 211, the end of one section, and 214, the beginning of the next section (on Soviet psychiatry), somewhere in the two pages left unconsciously blank. This is where Benjamin would read for allegory in the absence of the posthumous shock, the inoculative shot otherwise given by gadgets; it's where Freud, as in his study of the Schreber madness, would encounter an "endopsychic perception," the inside view given in delusional systems of the "psychic apparatus"—and also the advance preview, or so it almost seemed to Freud as he nevertheless rushed at the end of the Schreber study to assert priority, of the psychoanalytic theory of psychic functioning and dysfunction.

The Nazi movement of *Erhebung* sent the soldiers to the borderline between neurosis and psychosis, the newfound no-man's-land that, from World War I onward, was the place of psy fi expansionism into the outer spaces of psychosis. Losses were control-released within a war economy of total mobilization, in which fetishistic inventions, like the V-1 and V-2 rockets (hailed in Nazi Germany as *Wunderwaffen*, "miracle weapons") remetabolized wounds—from the pilots downed in the Battle of Britain to the collapse of all planes onto a growing lack of fuel—into the wonders of the psychotic sublime.

Psychosis was already the other place where the crisis in reproduction and its attendant psy fi fantasies awaited exploration: not until the cases of war neurosis opened up their ready-made access to ego libido, doubling, or merger with the internalized apparatus could Schreber's outer-space fantasies of miraculation, technologization, and homosexual or transsexual replication be visited, visited in the first place on the other, with the enemy or internal enemy at the front of the line. Because already prewar, psychotic delusions were seen as following a course of self-help: their endopsychic makeup gives the psychotic the inside view of his psychic apparatus and thus the outside chance of auto-analytic breakthrough. In psychosis, trauma-induced mega-repression reactivates shot shock waves from the trenches of cathected external reality all the way to earliest childhood and thereby opens up an evacuation chute through which all libido leaves the world and enters the ego. The only way out for the psychotic (other than suicide) is to project a new delusional world in the place of the one he has lost. The psychotic crisis or break is thus a threat of short circuit or overload that only the emergency projection of a new world out of narcissistic or ego libido can circumvent. Schreber made it; his brother, who committed suicide, went out on the downside of replication. In his introduction to *Perceval's Narrative: A Patient's Account of His Psychosis*, Gregory Bateson emphasizes the voyage-and-initiation character of psychosis that, while bonded to delusions, is also already on the way to auto-analytic breakthrough (which is not homecoming but arrival in some other place or cyberspace) (xiv).

Preflight projections of space travel—from Schreber on up—count down within the transformation or transformer through which the all-time low in energy flowing out of a wound is exchanged for a wondrous overcoming of gravity and dependency on earthbound supplies. In Thea von Harbou's *Rocket to the Moon* (the book version of Fritz Lang's *Woman in the Moon*), a certain Helius sets out to realize moon flight, even or especially if only on his own, with only his psychotic mentor Manfeldt along for the ride. Manfeldt, who checks in already more dead than alive (19), has reserved in advance through delusion-forwarding his arresting place alongside the fantastic resources of moon gold, which evolved from the coagulated blood supplies of dead gods (15). Going into this flight deep inside psychotic space, Helius is himself "one great wound from head to foot" (27), the casualty of a triangulation of friends, in which the woman has chosen the other man and thus taken up the irreplaceable mother position. But by flight time, all are aboard: the complete triangle of friends (wound and all), the delusional professor, an American entrepreneur, Walt Turner, who has his own psychotic designs on the moon gold and on sole survivorship, and a boy stowaway whose concerned family back home packs the missing mention of his mother (101). What connects the group is the shared lack of any wish to take leave of a single soul (86). No one to mourn.

Helius knows that folded into the flight plan is "a high percentage of what is practically suicide" (15); indeed, during the takeoff's highest velocity, the crew enters an uncanny zone where death and technology meet over the woman's body (92–94). But once their one-way flight to the moon ultimately reunites the two (who remain behind, sacrificially or suicidally, to share a better half-life together while supplies last), Helius is left with the remetabolized wound, with what he proclaims to be the "miracle on the moon" (186).

On the way to the moon, the spaceship serves as lookout post for a motion picture camera: "The cinematic apparatus hummed constantly, as its reels revolved and filled" (105). Aerial surveillance really took off during World War I on the same plane with the cinematic apparatus. As Freud pointed out, modern media wars are fought over and won by the seeing-eye technologies with the furthest surprise extension into the other side's personal space. But before planes packed cameras designed to shoot from the side or through the propeller blades (a technique inspired by the machine gun and conspiring with the film projector), rockets were rigged for photo-surveillance originally of earthbound battlefields, but then also, by extension, of outer-space vistas. The camera-carrying rockets, artillery-like projections or like firecrackers, were an improvement on the balloon's surveillance use, what with the slo-mo target it put up there in lights.

In 1915, Goddard, the father of American rocketry, had a dream: "Dreamed at 6:15 am of going to the Moon . . . Saw and took photos of Earth with small Kodak while there—and glimpsed Earth once during return" (in Winter, 94). For years Goddard pursued visual contact with the new frontiers of outer space without a thought about any military interests or investments. Also in 1915 *Scientific American* spelled out the plain text that the mag just missed and Goddard was still missing. German rocket experiments already proved that the rocket's "great military value, therefore, is self evident," and that it "will probably receive many practical demonstrations in the present war" (in Winter, 86–87). But the war would give the upper hand to plane flight and leave the scientific view of outer-space as the sole point of view admitted into space capsules coming soon. In 1938 Goddard relocated and established a new center for his outer-space research in Roswell, New Mexico. At that time, Goddard was considering, among other applications for the future, the use of photography in rockets as a new way to stabilize rocket flight: "Lag, accelerational effects, and other possible errors in recording instruments may be checked by a small camera taking periodic photographs of indicating instruments and a larger camera, synchronized with the smaller, taking photocopies of a base line on the ground. This, however, is another future development" (in Winter, 97–98). Goddard died in 1945 without ever achieving a successful rocket-flown photo or film shoot. One year later, a captured German V-2 was loaded with a motion picture camera and launched from New Mexico; it made a continuous record of its ascent through the earth's atmosphere to the threshold of outer space. Another year later, and the famous sightings in Roswell began—or brought back the believe-it-or-not aliens as doubling, down to their uncertain status, the victims of Nazi Europe.

The main German contributor to the outer-space effort before the war was the Transylvania-born scientist Hermann Oberth. In 1923 his bestseller *Rockets in Interplanetary Space* popularized the prospect of space travel, which could henceforth be openly anticipated within the outer-space movement that really took off in Germany. In his book, Oberth proposed the construction of satellites, "miniature moons" or "observation stations," as he called them, which would expand the telegraphic system of live transmissions while making allowance for all sorts of visual observation and documentation. He was certain that the *Titanic*'s sinking might have been prevented by satellite observation just in time for the iceberg surprise (in Winter, 98). Together with Willy Ley, Oberth served as consultant to Lang during the making of *Woman in the Moon*. Oberth designed the spaceship in the film; he also constructed a workable rocket to be fired in conjunction with the movie's premiere. The press of anticipation, for outer space and for the opening of Lang's film, was overwhelming: "If the experiment is successful, Professor Oberth contemplates the construction of a long-distance rocket carrying cameras, which would be dispatched on a photographic mission over unexplored territory" (in Winter, 99). Looking back in his article "My Contributions to Astronautics," Oberth recalls how the early inception through science fiction of his yearning for outer-space travel gave rise to earnest experimentation during World War I. "In fall 1917 I made a presentation to the German Ministry of Armament and proposed a long-range rocket powered by ethyl alcohol, water, and liquid air, somewhat similar to the V-2, only bigger and not so complicated" (Oberth, 131). His proposal to rocket bomb London was turned down as too fantastic. Without military-supported access to engineering and externalization, Oberth could only contrive mechanically, experimenting on himself in swimming pools to measure the impact of the weightlessness to be expected in space travel on humans, body and psyche. "In order to examine psychological effects, it is not necessary to create situations by real causes. It suffices to feign it to our senses.... For three years during World War I, I had access to all drugs at a hospital and a military pharmacological supply station. With the help of these drugs I numbed the sense of equilibrium in my muscles and skin, so that by floating under water with my eyes closed, and by using an airhose wound around my body, I could extend the psychological experience of weightlessness for hours" (132). After the war he was able to test fire his first externalized craft at a site belonging to the Ufa film studios in Berlin. He invented "the combustion chamber for liquid propellants... and it has been hailed as a major contribution to astronautics. I was helped with my experiments by students of the Technical University of Berlin. Among them was Wernher von Braun, who has since made space travel a reality" (140).

Oberth carried out an inspiration or dictation that had begun its countdown as early as Kurd Lasswitz's 1897 *Two Planets*, the same science fiction Wernher von Braun acknowledged, in a motto to the 1969 edition, as the childhood resource for his own invention of rocket flight. In *Two Planets* the overcoming of gravity takes the form of harnessing by reversing its force or wave power. The secret of gravity or gravitation is that it's faster than light: the transubstantiation of gravity's secret has a place name, Stellit, a substance the Martians have made to be transparent to gravity. This see-through substantial reversal of gravitation as speed can be navigated by nuclear propulsion, the giveaway human touch, the incestuous and murderous merger of Father Sun and Mother Earth that touches us in the head or psyche. But there's a video portion, too, to this overcoming of gravity, the grave of the earth (which Mars, exhausted in life-sustaining resources, in a sense already represents).

Everything touched by light can be transformed via gravity into surveillance. But it's only the recent past, which becomes thus the only and primal past, that can be conjured. The more time and distance light keeps on traveling, the more contaminated the memory picture gets. Thus it comes down to the moment, the one that always threatens to disappear in the instant of its impress. This is what can be reanimated, as in the recording services of photography or "light writing." If it's not exactly the moment, then it's the moment within a span of a year or two, the average allowance of mourning time. This time is not so much observed as seen through to the one moment. But to know exactly where to pinpoint and focus this seeing-eye-time-travel device, you need a calculating machine. These are the by now familiar coordinates of psychotic outer space. In *Two Planets*, then, we find on Mars this antimatter, I mean, antimourning technology, the "Retrospective," through which, but for the contamination that sets in after two years, the rays of all times could be read at one time.

> The adjustment of the instrument needed a lengthy preparation. It was difficult to determine the exact direction in which the axis of the cone of gravitational beams should be positioned. This cone of beams had to be transmitted to overtake the light that was reflected from the planet at the time of the event and which was now on its way through space. This light had to be brought back again. After the returning waves of gravitation had been transferred into light again and after they had passed the optical relay, a picture of the searched for areas could finally be projected on a screen in a dark room. In this case the difficulties of the experiment were much greater than usual because they wanted to observe an event which had taken place on a different planet, and since they also had to change the scene of action constantly in order to follow the motion of the ship. It was the first time that the Retrospective was to be used for such a complicated case. (214–15)

This gadget fits Schreber's delusion that he can circumnavigate a certain necrospective through the total mobilization of rays, which he summons around the notion and practice of "picturing."

> Another interesting phenomenon connected with the ray-communication—the real cause of compulsive thinking—is the so-called "picturing." . . . Perhaps nobody but myself, not even science, knows that man retains all recollections in his memory, by virtue of lasting impressions on his nerves, as pictures in his head. Because my inner nervous system is illuminated by rays, these pictures can be voluntarily reproduced; this in fact is the nature of the "picturing." I expressed this thought earlier . . . in a different form: "To picture (in the sense of the soul-language) is the conscious use of the human imagination for the purpose of producing pictures (predominantly pictures of recollections) in

one's head, which can then be looked at by rays." By vivid imagination I can produce pictures of all recollections from my life, of persons, animals and plants, of all sorts of objects in nature and objects of daily use, so that these images become visible either inside my head or if I wish, outside, where I want them to be seen by my own nerves and by the rays.

Unlike the jury that's out on Mars, Schreber is on his own time and reconnaissance. He illuminates the intersection between technology and the unconscious—and can therefore push picturing beyond what the record shows toward the excess or access afforded by the trans-.

> I can also "picture" myself in a different place, for instance while playing the piano I see myself at the same time in front of the mirror in the adjoining room in female attire; when I am lying in bed at night I can give myself and the rays the impression that my body has female breasts and a female sexual organ....The picturing of female buttocks on my body...has become such a habit that I do it almost automatically whenever I bend down. "Picturing" in this sense may therefore be called a reversed miracle. (Schreber, 180–81)

The Retrospective in *Two Planets* belongs in a museum that documents less developed species out there, like us earthlings, who must dummy up on exhibition inside our natural-history habitats. And yet that Mars is so far advanced means not only that it is a more purified or sublimated version of Earth but also that it is in decline: Mars is the extinct future of Earth— and Oedipus. Another way to read this warning label, however, is to recognize Mars as the planet inhabited by our mourned, idealized dead. But when the ancestors return to Earth to spread the idealization around, the mourning process goes into reverse, and the long distant turnaround, up close, into vengeful ghosts whose inheritance now is only the spreading of plague and violence. On the humid maternal planet, under increased pressures of gravity, but in a life-protecting relationship of distance to the sun (while Earth is close enough to the sun, the Nume, Martians by another name, are direct descendants of the sun and harvest radiation on the surface of their expiring planet), the alien instructors, who came not to bury themselves (again) but to hurry up and raise our evolution into higher regions, succumb to transference transgression, desublimation, psychotic breakdown: "I have noticed in general that after a few months the instructors no longer have that calmness and serene magnanimity to which we are accustomed from the Nume. Contact with the humans...has...a brutalizing effect; and it is reflected at first in the manner of talking, in a contempt for aesthetic form, furthermore in an over-estimation of one's own importance, and finally in a self-esteem which surpasses cases in which you could easily speak of psychosis; I might call it 'Earth fever'!" (292). Once the decaying psychotic Martians have been sent back into the beyond, Earth starts reorganizing on its own around the techno and psychic precepts of the Nume. The idealizing trajectory of man's perfectibility, and thus of a certain relationship to death, I mean, the dead, remains in place.

In the primal time of delivery of owner's manuals—*Dracula* and *War of the Worlds* (or *Two Planets*), for example—Walther Rathenau, who would be remembered for his major player role in the Weimar Republic as foreign minister (the role he was on when he came to the full stop of assassination in 1922), published in 1898 the short story "The Resurrection Co." under one of his several pseudonyms, W. Hartenau. At first fright it looks like another horror fiction or, on double take, horror farce. But then again, it fits the separate billing and fulfilling of the psy fi impulse. A telephone network has been established to service the entire necropolitan area. The buried are thus given one last outside chance to ring the alarm of live burial. But then the long dead get into the act and even start calling each other. The technology of last chance introduces lasting change into our relations with the dead. All it takes, by definition of what a corporation is, is a couple of live persons and, at the other end of the network, countless dead, fictive, or pseudonymous figures, like all the names Rathenau summoned to cover for his living or real place of writing. But the return of Rathenau in Hartenau, Michael, Renatus, Rinhart, Rainer, Raventhal, or von der Muehl cannot be so transparently superimposing. What opened up the one name such that it could not close back on itself, not without remainder, was the inclusion of the dead in the multiperson corporation. The resurrection proffered is thus not in the flesh but in a techno-flash or flashback that transmutes death as the networking of interdead or intrapsychic relations. Rathenau gave a preview of what is stowaway in psy fi flights of fantasy. The positing of the dead versus the living is undone but still shadowed by the melancholic attachment to which the fantasy, unlike in the occult versions, can never be reduced. We can call this the stereo activity of de-posit. The repression of this de-positing act is at home in a block of time that gets projectively displaced into the fifties within so many bodies of work. It is a time blockage deserving to be calling in unidentified.

Jung joined Heidegger and Lacan on what a trip, a round-trip from the late twenties to the late forties, the best of times to trip out on the fifties and just in time, the best of times, to forget the war-timing of their big ideas. Only when the countdown of Heidegger, Jung, and Lacan is back in the thirties do I hear a synchronicity. As early as 1946, Jung began working on the UFO phenomenon, a techno-phantasm (his first since the Freudian days) bound for and by the promised landing of unidentification. Just like Heidegger, for example, Jung can't get at technology without at the same time getting back at Freud. In his analysis of a film actress's UFO dream— the dream thus "comes from California, the classic Saucer country, so to speak"—Jung overlooks the endopsychic perceptiveness of the dreamer and symptomatically confuses auto-analytic breakthrough with psychotic break-down. In the dream the UFO, which the dreamer at first take takes to be real, is identified as a trick: "I looked up behind me and saw someone with a movie projector." Jung informs us right away, before commencing his commentary, that the "dreamer, a young film actress, was undergoing psychological treatment for a marked dissociation of personality with all the accompanying symptoms." The commentary, a comment on Jung's disappointment in the dreamer, is the only one in this collection that does not take the UFO into any account: "The dream insists on the projection character of the UFO. . . . It is not easy to see why the dream brings in the UFO at all, only to dispose of it in this disappointing way. . . . Any insight into the nature of the UFO phenomenon is not to be expected from this dream" (66–69). In another one of his flying saucer articles, Jung translates Freud's notion of the superego according to the terms of his own notion of a collective unconscious. That must be the eclecticization for Jung to remember, the only one in the Nazi era of psychotherapy he covered for that somehow included while eluding him.

One has to give Jung credit for making everything in his life and work after his psychotic break with Freud, no matter how archetypical he thought it was, only legible or decodable, point by point, in the terms of negative transference. Jung's flying saucer connection thus hits air pockets of isolated reference to the war before, which are at the same time turned up loud as denial. He refers to the aerial bombardment, the pilot of the total air war who served on the control panel of new projective spaces, the miracle rockets, and even the foo fighters that Allied pilots spotted before their eyes giving outer-space assist to the other side. But then, on the long stretch, it's really all about the postwar conditions of life in the fifties. "These rumours, or the possible physical existence of such objects, seem to me so significant that I feel myself compelled, as once before when events of fateful consequence were brewing for Europe, to sound a note of warning. I know that, just as before, my voice is much too weak to reach the ear of the multitude" (5). A footnote inserted right after "as once before" takes us back to his 1936 essay "Wotan," which he has now, via the time-traveling elision of the big between, rewritten for the cold war—out of *Zeit*, out of mind—as his ongoing warning shout.

Just another time traveler, Jung didn't work the transference—because he just couldn't go there, please not back to Freud. It makes his sublimation formula so, I don't know, alchemical, literal, contextless, and tension free. But back then Jung had to hand Schreber's *Memoirs* over to Freud as a transference gift. The master would know how to interpret this one. Thus it all began and ended, doubly so, inside a transferential crisis. Schreber's former order relied on a God who, from his great distance, could really only view life from the perspective of the dead—of the dad. But once all the trans- action transforms Schreber into group of one, into woman and android, a live connection gets established over his body taken for dead or dad. The replicational plan of survival was what was left after the world— what Freud calls a "wealth of sublimations" (*SE*, 12:73)—had been destroyed in the transferential breakdown between doctor and patient, father and son.

Picking up momentum within the literal meanings of its given names, *das Erhabene* and "the sublime," the psychotic sublime takes and lifts off, in psychoanalytic theory and projective delusion, into an outer intrapsychic space somewhere over the transference, and at the same time goes under, opens up, and shifts the fixed fronts between neurosis and psychosis to make accessible instead, and in other words or worlds, a new borderline zone (and diagnosis) for theorization, treatment, colonization. The verb *er-heben*, which accompanies, for example, Freud's description of the erection of the fetish, is a mobile unit on the way to this newfound sublimity and leaves itself open to the not yet distilled ingredients of its ultimate composition as *das Erhabene*. On the way to the sublime, we overhear the taking off and lifting off of in-flight services not into burial. In the essay on humor, which, according to Ernst Kris (*Psychoanalytic Explorations in Art*, 186–88), is Freud's one recognizable entry into the comparison troping between the comic and the sublime, references to the sublime count down at the twice-over remove of its adjectivalization, the at once literal and atmospheric sense that whatever is sublime (in German) can also be seen as "uplifting." Freud has to hand three "triumphs" to humor: one for narcissism, one more for the ego, and three to go for the pleasure principle. It moves on up from liberation (where it leaves behind the routines of the comic and jokes) to make the big time, a new high on the scale of the sublime ("etwas Grossartiges und Erhebendes") (Freud, "Der Humor").

Humor's specific contribution to comic relief, which is administered through the office of the superego, comes at the time Freud was distilling sublimation, the superego's main ingredient and prescription, from spirits of melancholic identification. In *The Ego and the Id*, the "open wound" that Freud ascribed to melancholia in "Mourning and Melancholia" was thus no longer a rent through which libido was forever lost, causing the psychic apparatus to wind down all the way to psychotic shutdown, but was now the initiating condition—the rent-a-wound—of sublimation and thus of all the higher species of socialization. Social contact or contract was now upheld through the transformation of object libido into narcissistic libido, which melancholia models (*SE*, 19:31, 36). Thus in the follow-up essay "Neurosis and Psychosis," Freud announces a new station identification: melancholia's now the place, between transference neurosis and psychosis. Reclassified as motive force behind the work of sublimation and socialization, melancholia gets assigned to an in-between place, a place of "being two," which is not some danger zone of psychotic breakdown but merely uncharted space. In the mode of the uncanny, this space of continuity or continuum with psychotic structures that should have remained hidden but nevertheless open up inside the home where they belong already asserts itself between the lines of Freud's near misses with the automaton in "The Sandman." In psychoanalytic theory, then, following World War I, a new portfolio of diversified and differentiated investments was opening up that proved more compatible both with socialization (in groups) and with fantasies or structures of doubling, replication, merger with the machine.

At the crisis center of his analysis of psychosis as sublimation breakdown, Freud observes the sublime symbol of the sun get a rise out of Schreber. In its psychotic breakdown, which comes complete with the contours and mediatic controls of a machine breaking down, "sublimation" releases the piece that belongs to the "sublime." Schreber joins Nietzsche with one of Freud's patients in sun worship, the celebration of themselves as sons catching the rays of their solar fathers. "One of my patients, who had lost his father at a very early age, was always seeking to rediscover him in what was grand and sublime in Nature. Since I have known this, it has seemed to me probable that Nietzsche's hymn '*Vor Sonnenaufgang*' [Before Sunrise] is an expression of the same longing" (*SE*, 12:54). But in Schreber's case, the focus on the source of endless energy supplies filling the lack up to the limit of what can be held in reserve on earth proposes the ultimate union, which is not interpersonally conjugated, say, between man and woman, but intrapsychically and extraterrestrially constituted between Mother Earth and Father Sun. Nuclear fusion on earth is the psychotic or science fiction alternative that breaks out of what's going down in the immediate family.

The psychotic break happens because it recurs when the correct combination on the safety lock of events and impressions cracks earliest traumatic developments. The repress release that follows switches the libidinal current going to the outside world to the ego circuit, which threatens to overload. The ego makes a circuit break for the protection and projection of its own narcissistic or ego libido into a new delusional order that replaces the "world" that was lost.

Sublimation refines the grades of sociality fuel for the injections of conscience and consumerism by reprocessing an excess of, or direct access to, the homosexual disposition (even or especially for actual homosexuals). Sublimation of homosexuality stakes out a primal scene of technology that trains its focus on energy control release. According to Freud's retelling of the Prometheus legend in his 1932 "The Acquisition and Control of Fire," when fire from the solar above was brought down to earth, the unchecked homosexual urge to match and make the phallic flames with equally phallic streams of urine would have wasted the new energy source rather than reserve it for the future coming soon.

When the additive of sublimation is taken out, the transferential metabolism is already in crisis. Transference, which Freud first tuned in as haunting and technologization, runs on the homosexual energy it keeps long distance and in reserve. It is not the thought coming across his mind that it would be hot to hold to the woman's end of the heterosexual exchange that sets off the second breakdown and sets Schreber off to complete the system of his thought. It is rather the thoughts of Dr. Flechsig, who also treated Schreber the first time around, that Freud assumes crossed Schreber's mind at the intersection already busy with the sexual fantasy. What thus blasts apart is the subliminal protectedness and veiledness of the transference. Mr. and Mrs. Schreber's failure to have living children had already put a stop on transferential and sublimational payment of protection. Schreber was looking for *Versöhnung*, a relay of sons to reflect and deflect the father sun. Without the timed release of father-son relations, his gaze is instead directed up blinding stares.

Following the desublimation or resexualization (or reanimation) of a transferential order of identification (with the father), Schreber's techno-delusional system must keep the homosexual bonds with dead and dad just the heartbeat away of radical displacement. Emergency measures had to be taken to overcome a crisis in reproduction. That's how an all-out turn-on gets attributed to the female body alone (which Schreber is becoming, via replicating changes induced by God's rays, at the same time as he's becoming an android). Only his new body, which is both the only body around and at once female and technological, can overcome the crisis in reproduction for the survival of the species. Only this "live" body can receive or conceive the ray beams of a divine power otherwise given to reabsorb within its Elysian force fields the nervous energy of corpses or, as happened to Schreber, of persons melancholically playing dead. It's a different way God and "Miss Schreber" have of getting around getting stuck on loss.

What has been left behind through projection into the new world is the interpersonal column in which normal to neurotic sexuality (homosexual or heterosexual) advertises a sexual difference that comes prefab couplified. This interpersonal difference, or "heteroness," which a certain couples therapy of mourning and substitution prescribes, is always also the same difference. The sex differential that counts down in the new order of perversion, psychosis, and group psychology is on intrapsychic automatic. Just when you thought it was safe to reject narcissism, psychosis, or the adolescent group as joined to the totalized side that's against the work of difference and mourning, it turns out that it's in this psychotic aside that what's different after all makes it to the inside of the techno-body, the only surviving or happening bond with the future.

According to Lyotard's calculations, it's not enough that the conditions of exile from the solar system will mean that our terrestrial and corporeal selves will not be along for the ride into the future (and toward the other) on our machines (which will be us). That in several billion years the solar system will certainly cease to exist already changes everything. We are the genitals of our machines, which are undergoing future evolutionary development for us. That takes care of taking it all so interpersonally; another sexual difference, not the one that is measured on one's own person or released but contained in couple formation, must be programmed inside the separation from body and earth that takes off with the merger with the machine in flight. "You have to prepare post-solar thought for the inevitability and complexity of this separation" (Lyotard, 23).

The psychotic sublime occupies the outer limit of inside-out relations with technology, a limit that usually glides ahead or underneath but, when it's directly upon you, is hard to take in. The psychotic sublime promotes a futurity that is not a retro-repro couples exclusive; it skips the beat of generations and the nuclear family pack, aims straight for the sun, and downloads group psychology onto the only one (the sole survivor). The catastrophe Schreber must prepare for has always already happened. A sunshine state of emergency, a war economy of scarcity or lack and total mobilization, blazes psychotic-sublime access to an outside, an outside chance, where successful realization of a wished-for aim, in spite of its already accomplished total loss first time around, could—at least there's a chance—be scored.

The Schreber Garden of Eden

In traumatic neurosis the aura is usually distinctive, a
reproduction of the last sensation felt by the patient before he
originally lost consciousness.

—ABRAHAM KARDINER AND HERBERT SPIEGEL,
WAR STRESS AND NEUROTIC ILLNESS

It was with the introduction of the theory of evolution that fantasy was free
to grant invention or other sudden changes and chances the power to switch
channels on evolutionary progress and fast-forward plant life or machines
to the top of development. As soon as Darwin's theory was out, his fans
were hit by fantasies of parallel fast lanes of development that relocated
the missing link to interspecial relations between humans and machines
(see Samuel Butler's *Erewhon*). Evolution provided the context for imagining that thought can or must go on without the body, and that means beyond the retro, repro bonds between the sexes. Humans are still the genitals of the machine that is evolving *for* us. The higher machines, which
"will owe their existence to a large number of parents and not to two only"
(Butler, 212), will be reproduced in the group metabolization or psychology
of tensions between replicational sex and the production of one or three by
two at a time.

As genealogy of media, mediations, and means of human being, evolution comes on strong with constitutive interruptions, gaps, so-called missing links. This throws a precision fit with every way the breakdown of
mourning always admits, via the narcissistic and psychotic conditions or
conditionings of a melancholic attention span, the frontal shot of direct
connection with our technologization.

The link with the missing—the haunted relation—is what keeps selection (not unlike substitution) going, going, goner. The link Benjamin misses
in his reading of our current techno-evolution can go by the name "aura,"
the ghost inside techno-selection, inside the either-aura. After Benjamin,
Andy Warhol and Shirley MacLaine fine-tuned "aura" for the selection star-
dom of channels. But Benjamin might as well have borrowed his aura, the
notion of a retrenchment of the missed link with presence that flickers even
in certain media-technological products over time, from the trenches of
World War I. Down there aura designated the zoning-out phase of acceptance of whatever psychosomatic convulsions and techno-metabolizations
of trauma were coming soon.

Our relations with technology began finding time, then, for their new take on change via the theory of evolution, which offered first-time countertestimony to standard historical receptions of change or development. Freud's discovery of the unconscious follows in the wake and shake-up of the Darwinian see change. Both biologically and biographically, the introduction of the evolution theory found completion in Freud's follow-up offer of the unconscious. Lieutenant Colonel C. D. Daly gives doubly insider commentary to this genealogical conclusion in "A Psychological Analysis of Military Morale":

> Shortly before he died, Darwin remarked that, had he his life over again, he would devote it to the study of a man's unconscious mind—in which statement he foreshadowed the organization of another branch of science, viz. that of analytical psychology, introduced by the work of the Viennese psychologist, Professor Freud. (59)

In the spirit of greater psychoanalysis, we can by now extend the evolutionary and military-psychological process of selection both to the chosen members of modern spiritual and therapeutic cults and to the missing, the abused, the alien abducted, the multiple personalities, and the mediums or channelers (all figures fitting on one and the same end of the psychopathology continuum, making one in-crowd of our pop-psychology culture). L. Ron Hubbard, the creator of scientology (which is advertised, between the lines, as the cure-all of perversion, inversion, of whatever gets in the way of couplification, next generations, and related success stories), started out a top pilot and, just another step in the selection process, then became a celebrated science fiction author. EST, which was also all about feel-good heterosexuality and ultimate commitments to reproductive coupling, followed a leader by the pseudonym of Wernher Erhard, a composite of von Braun's first name and the last name of the West German chancellor during the "economic miracle" *(Wirtschaftswunder)*. These groupings in every sense contain only the one alternative to the couple adjustment: either suicide aura—I mean, or—replicational beaming up out of meat vehicles of reproduction and death into the doubles living on within the mother ship.

Californian psychotherapist Edith Fiore hit the front pages at the checkout stands when she announced her first specialization: exorcism or ghostbusting. She retook those heights when she added the specialization of treatment for repressed memories of alien abduction. She is less interested in the truth of her patient's claims—her position exactly regarding the remembering of abuse or incest in early childhood—than in listening and accepting what the patient brings to session as another truth, one that registers as validated in the back lot of therapeutic correctness. Aliens, not unlike parents practicing satanic rituals, will first induce an unconscious state in their victims before the experiments begin. It's like you're looking at the TV set, it switches between stations and fills up with static or "snow," and then you just don't know where the time went. This last moment of fading consciousness, like the instant before the trauma retained in the fetish, in fetishism's split-level framing of dissociation, like whenever you can feel the epileptic seizure coming on, is more of what Benjamin was getting into under a primally resonant sense of aura, more of the same as the sinking sense you have that before you remember—even remember to forget—the blackout of shell shock will have changed the guard.

In 1969, when Wernher von Braun autographed *Two Planets* with his go-ahead of approval, the inventor had already crossed over into member-of-the-team authorship of science fictive projections of space missions from the Moon to Mars. *Conquest of the Moon*, for example, takes a break from the narration of the fantasy scenario and checks in with reality by looking back at von Braun's accomplishments at his first home base in Nazi Germany from the twenty-year-later vantage point of maximal acceleration or pro-duction-stream-lining of the processes of negative feedback and computing:

> Twenty years ago, scores of mathematicians would have been re-quired to figure out the navigational computation of an actual flight path to the moon, and they would have needed months to complete the task. Today, however, we can enlist the aid of mod-ern electronic digital computers for the job. They can do it in minutes. These electronic "brains" can calculate our flight course by taking into account not only the simultaneous effects of the earth's and moon's gravitational fields, but also the perturba-tions caused by the sun, the nearer planets, and the oblateness of the earth. Moreover, by introducing deviations from the desired flight track—such as might be caused by a delay in the take-off or by a slight change from the flight-path angle—they can fur-nish hundreds of corrective power maneuvers. All these flight courses can be transferred to reels of magnetic tape and stored on the flight deck, ready for use. Thus the captain of the ship, on being told by his navigator that the vehicle is off course, can make the desired change by inserting a previously prepared tape into the automatic pilot. (48)

Where this flashback leaves off, the epigraphic capsule hovering above *Two Planets* takes off again:

I shall never forget how I devoured this novel with curiosity and excitement as a young man. And I believe that reading it today will be of enhanced interest when electronic and human eyes have already gathered their first direct impressions of the moon and our neighboring planets. From this book the reader can obtain an inkling of that richness of ideas at the twilight of the nineteenth century upon which the technological and scientific progress of the twentieth is based. And we may also realize what fascinating possibilities are opening up for the generations of the twenty-first century when, through the expansion of the universe, our dreams and fancies will become realities.

Before the aura of success before and success after there's the spot of blackout we're in for with von Braun, the spot before the eyes of Nazi German moviegoers in 1943. The beat von Braun's invention of the V-1 and V-2 rockets keeps on skipping is taken to a higher split level in Josef von Baky's *Münchhausen*. Even when we go the long distance of rocket flight, who (else) should be waiting for us but the long distant, the dead or undead? For the immortal baron, it's the moon so soon that sets the mortality timer, now on the body of the mortal other, now on the woman's doubled and divided one. The time on the moon fast-forwards life on earth: condensed into as many hours as years, the whole remaining life of his manservant passes away before the baron's eyes. But a split on the person of the woman on the moon, which this time divides mind from body, was also already fast-forwarded to the baron. The talking head, the one he had given up as lost over him, marks the spot of interchangeability of replacement parts, part objects, or techno-outlets that the baron has all along been plugging into. Woman after woman, the baron has recombined parts and functions that are split apart and has thus always replicated his desire, which never went the way of reproduction. Woman's splitting image was the control panel of the baron's diverse moves across the overcoming of long distance with the speed of flight. But now, in 1943, as he reaches the end of the story he has been relating to a young Nazi German couple, and as this couple begins to realize that the two-century-long tale fits the time of this baron's one and only life span, Münchhausen decides to surrender his immortality out of his love for his aging wife. He has been married for the duration of the twentieth century, through one world war up to this tail end of the other one. But this one whole object in his life, his wife, introduces death, not difference. It's time to die or retreat with dignity: the baron has run out of story, stores, supplies, energy. The making of this movie, which began as a veritable media *Blitz* and then ran out of its own momentum by the too long time it took to expend resources on the rapid-fire light show of special effects, coincided with the war effort, popularly conceived as one of movement and of nerves, which propelled itself as the *Blitz* attempt to outrun repetition, the return of the First World War's shutdown along fixed fronts that had reduced that war, in time, to one of supplies only.

But in 1943 the war effort had to be raised to total war consciousness all along psychological (and media-technological) lines in the about-face of Stalingrad. The iconic film's PR image of the legendary baron's flight on a cannonball—even or especially in the setting of destinal acceptance of one's mortality timing—is on one flight trajectory with the V-1 and V-2 miracle weapons. Hanna Reitsch, one more woman pilot in the Nazi air force, recalls her own affirmative reaction to the prospect of cannonballing the otherwise unstoppable enemy.

> Much ink has flowed on the subject of the piloted V-1. For years the world press had indulged in sensational reports on the hazardous methods of testing this man-flown robot and the hairraising uses to which it was to be put. But the real reasons which led to placing a pilot in the pilotless plane and the purpose for which it was intended have never been accurately given to the public.
>
> The story begins in August, 1943, in Berlin. One day, over lunch at the Flying Club, I came across two old friends. One of them was an aeronautical medical specialist, and the other, a very skillful and experienced glider pilot.
>
> Our conversation centered on the progress of the war, which was causing us deep uneasiness. We were agreed that time was not on Germany's side, for every day that passed brought a further drain on her diminishing resources. One after another, towns and cities were crumpling under the allied air attacks, the transport system and the production centers were being systematically destroyed, raw materials were becoming increasingly difficult to procure, while the death toll continually mounted....
>
> But how much did lie in our power? For months this question had been occupying my thoughts, and, as I discovered at lunch that day, the thoughts of my friends. We were agreed on our answer. It was clear that underlying and determining the course of this war was the razor-keen battle of the scientists and technicians and that a change in Germany's favor could only be brought about by success in this field. We also believed that the war must be brought to an early end if Germany were to be saved from disaster and that this could only be secured through a ne-

Hanna Reitsch banks a Fieseler Storch, a plane she later flew under fire into Berlin during the last-ditch defense of the city in 1945. Reproduced from *Designers and Test Pilots,* by Richard P. Hallion and the Editors of the Time-Life Books (Alexandria, Va.: Time-Life Books, 1983), 65. Ullstein Bilderdienst Berlin owns the original photograph.

gotiated peace. To prepare the ground for negotiation, it would be necessary to weaken considerably the enemy's military strength.

This could only be done from the air and only, we believed, if volunteers were forthcoming to pilot a suitable projectile into the center of its target, destroying it totally and making repair or re-equipment impossible. By this means it should be possible to deliver a rapid succession of devastating blows at generating stations, waterworks, key production centers, and, in the event of invasion, at naval and merchant shipping. . . .

This Operation Suicide would require men who were ready to sacrifice themselves in the conviction that only by this means could their country be saved. . . .

We concealed our thoughts from strangers and those outside our own immediate circle. Nevertheless, it continually widened as more and more of our associates were initiated into our plans. That we were often misunderstood was only to be expected, for our plan held no appeal for seekers after fame and offered no chance of a successful outcome to those who felt inclined for a gamble with death. Here was required nothing less than the complete conquest of self. . . .

But meanwhile, the stream of time rolled on and rolling, bore all our efforts to oblivion, confronting Germany with new and menacing developments. The invasion had begun.

Now that the invasion had been launched, neither the me 328 nor the piloted V-1 could be used as we had intended. We realized that the decisive moment had been missed. And now that it was too late, we realized, too, that, from the very start the obstacles that were put in our way were greater than our will to carry the plan through. (Hanna Reitsch, *Flying Is My Life*, 207–9, 218–19)

Projection Therapy

In *Miracle of Flight*, "The Movie about a German Pilot" commissioned by Hermann Göring, the wound is back for transmutation into wonder or miracle. A cute teenager (the same boy star of *Hitlerjunge Quex*) bonds with a pilot hero, who invites him to come to Berlin and stay in his bachelor digs. But then we see the boy with his mom make reverences before the photo of the dead dad, who was a pilot in World War I. In Berlin the pilot shows the boy and tells him about the mementos crowding his solo apartment like some mummy's tomb. (We're on the inside track of flashback.) World War I, flight over Greenland, flying over ice, African wilds, landing in Los Angeles. That night the boy dreams of flying with the pilot and then trying it alone, but he can't stop: CRASH. (That was superego calling on lines of identification with the dad the boy gladly replaces with the live one.) When the pilot takes the boy home to mom, he convinces her that someone who's got to fly, just got to fly. And the fatherland needs more pilots by the minute. Well, the boy grows up quickly into the real thing. To celebrate his certification, he decides to fly to Germany's highest mountain just to say he'd done it in a postcard to the pilot hero. But then the plane crashes, and the young airman parachutes to safety, but he's in deep freeze. The bachelor pilot flies to the rescue. The junior pilot is worried that he might appear a failure in the eyes of his one-night host. But not to worry: "Even if things go wrong sometimes, youth must take risks." And then he unsnaps the parachute harness from the young standing-at-attention body.

Stukas newsreels in the victorious war against France. The story line about the particular squadron seems so seamlessly part of the on-location war footage that one wonders if the film wasn't being made during the war, with the live action as backdrop. The film is a celebration of comradeship, of that near-miss male-to-male bonding happiness that replaces the dead relations with father in *Miracle of Flight*. And top of the list of things comrades do together is digest the dying of their buddies. The unit starts out desperately seeking security for every single one; the anxiety is high and assuaged only when all the boys are back from a mission. But then there's the first casualty. "That's the way it is in war." They drink a toast to the dead comrade. Then two more die, and the commentary switches to the seriousness of the situation, which requires that the boy bonds graduate or mature into war bonds. Then victory stops the body countdown. The mother of the first casualty writes the commander. He comments that if a mother can take her son's death so well, then they too can learn that it doesn't matter: you don't zero in on the fact of life that they've fallen, but now only consider what a great cause to go for. But there's one survivor who has given up the spirit of the group. He's convalescing in Germany; the nurse is worried about his depression. The physician in charge of the case admits that now that the soldier has healed in body, something extra, which can come only out of himself, something that grabs him, can pull him out of his apathy. The nurse suggests that some old comrades stop by for a visit. But the two visitors with their pep talk can't reverse the patient's sense that it's all too late for him. Then the nurse has another idea. Why doesn't she take him on a field trip to Bayreuth; no one goes away from the Wagner experience ungrabbed. The music does it; it replays snatches of songs the soldier's commander and the squadron's physician at the front played on one of the many pianos they were requisitioning, losing, replacing. Beginning with the flashback to the Wagner duets on the piano, the soldier's bouncy teen style is back, in the past, in the intercutting to many happy returns from hospital to the old squadron, and in his face. These are the rushes of comradeship. "Now I know again where I belong." With the Wagner still playing on the sound track, we see him rush back to his flying unit, and in no time he's back in his plane. We see them all in their planes in the air; though they're all in their solo positions, the Stukas song they all belt out sounds full, like a chorus, amplified by their radio connections. Closing refrain: "The Stukas, the Stukas, the Stukas."

In all the films making this selection (all but one from the Nazi era), montage techniques associated with German expressionism and Soviet formalism convey or condense the real time taken out for techno-industrial and military procedures. There are continuity shots between the Nazi German films and the earlier or parallel universal works of modernism. Many of the same actors from before didn't stop working the screen down in Germany. But in the director's chair, G. W. Pabst sits up as an uncanny agent of cinematic continuity by the shot in the dark, in his foot, that brought him back to Nazi Germany seeking sanctuary from Hollywood's cutting edge. The case of Pabst recalls that of psychoanalyst John Rittmeister, who left Switzerland to join the German Institute of Psychological Research and Psychotherapy right in the midst of the Third Reich, not because he was a sympathizer, not by a long shot, but because he assumed that even under the Nazis, Berlin institutions held the leadership in the German-language world, in his field. Although both men had heil to pay for their holiday from history (on ice), we still need to learn how to stay with their remarkable reception of what they were getting into, the one that did not observe a station break in the histories of their modernist disciplines.

Werner Krauss was the actor you saw first in *The Cabinet of Dr. Caligari*, playing, depending on your interpretation of the narrative frame, either the meglo madman or the hallucination of a psycho or the asylum director who now knows, after he has listened to the patient's or hero's delusion or report, how to heal him, once and for all. Then in Pabst's *Secrets of a Soul* he was the physician who was also a neurotic patient with an obsession and a phobia to match. At the end of his psychoanalysis, we see him healed, straightened out, a reproductive part of society. Kraus is back with Pabst for *Paracelsus*, the movie Pabst came back to Nazi Germany to make, driven from Hollywood by the team-spirited-away editing interventions that wanted to leave the making of material or stock to the director and the final cut to the industry. But Pabst didn't produce material; he was so phobic about the control of the cut that he tried to film in sequence with the cuts already internalized, and thus in one finished piece, without slack to pick up or cut out.

Paracelsus was one of those all-German historical figures who were up in value and for libidinal grabs in the Third Reich only because they belonged, chronologically, to the prehistory of psychoanalysis. By going back to Paracelsus, Carus, or Nietzsche, it was to become possible to belong full-fledged to greater psychoanalysis while pledging to an other's name and fame, and thus outflanking the science to which they couldn't afford to owe thanks, nor could they apparently live without it. *Paracelsus* functions as a screen memory, therefore, for German psychotherapy in its long-standing upbeat struggle against the academically more powerful neuropsychiatrists. In the movie Paracelsus invents the modern patient to be: a whole entity whose diseases are a whole that affect the whole and must therefore be treated holistically on the basis, bottom line, of "insight." The medical doctors, by contrast, are immediately associated with the castrative shortcut methods of amputation, and shown up as shortsighted along this cutting edge by Paracelsus's healing intervention that keeps the patient whole, with both legs to stand on. The leader of the medical establishment (who's kind of screechy, sexless, already a cut above the whole) hates Paracelsus and his whole eco trip. But the young medical students, the new generation, support group around him. Their idol's declared enemy is death itself; his aim in theory and practice is the attainment, through the perfection of his holistic methods, his psychosomatic medicine, of one state for all of "eternal health." All we know about the potion that Paracelsus mixes to this living end is that its administration is projected for the near future, its makeup will be inoculative, and its goal is total immunity. Thus Paracelsus at one point affirms the exorcising program that would drive out the devil with Beelzebub. As far as his own life plan goes, he would need "a thousand years" to realize all his projects. But at the same time, he learns his lesson about the inevitability of death from the one and only patient we watch Paracelsus not heal, a senior military officer or knight fatally infected by a disease that the physicians had alleviated some time ago at the symptom level but had thus only covered up and left to spread until this too late date. It's a soldier's acceptance of a soldierly death that Paracelsus learns to recognize alongside his search for eternal health. There's only "one immortality," the knight advises Paracelsus, "the memory of the people."

Where medical science played enemy to the new inoculative, holistic, insight-oriented approach of psychotherapy in *Paracelsus,* standard medical reception is further compromised in *Germanin* by the nationalist interests of the English enemy during World War I. We travel back into the recent past to tamper with a future that's already present. What if the new drug discovered by German doctors for the good of mankind (with masses of black Africans at the head of the receiving line) had been allowed by the English authorities to counter and contain the sleeping sickness, the sleeping-beauty condition that the Germans had to endure before Hitler picked them up where the world war had let them down? The name of the drug, Germanin, rings up another drug name and discovery that the Anglo-Americans to this day question as having been in its earlier German formulation the same thing as the series of preparations that led to the development of methadone as we know it today. The first German name for this drug, which, like an inoculation in reverse, replaces one drug or toxin with a lesser evil equivalent that leaves the body strong enough to withstand the aftershocks of withdrawal, was Adolfin. It was a synthetic version of morphine that would keep the war wounded supplied.

The natives in *Germanin,* like the runner-up or *Ersatz* Aryans that Leni Riefenstahl (and Beate Uhse, too, who always kept to the same flight itinerary as Leni) got into in the seventies, are photogenetically all natural in an Olympian nudist colony setting. After the Versailles treaty, or the "dictation," as *Germanin* refers to it, the German medical trio goes back to Africa, just the same, even without any all-natural German (nudist) colonies to return to, equipped to heal with their cure-all Germanin, ready if you are. The Americans have developed and marketed a cure of their own, but on the castrative track again, it blinds you just for side effect. The obvious superiority of Germanin makes it the popular drug of choice in Africa. The German discoverer assures the native groupies: "You don't need to be afraid. I will heal you." The locals begin reassembling the look of their old uniforms from the good old days of German colonial rule. The English colonel strikes back and destroys the Germanin supplies. But then there's only enough left to heal one out of two, the German discoverer and the English colonel, who are both infected now. The German gives the colonel his last shot in exchange for the rights to exterminate the carrier fly population throughout Africa. The discoverer's dying words cheerlead his followers and heirs to destroy, annihilate, wipe out. The object of the sentencing goes without saying. Thus another German inoculative cure is holistic or cure-all in strategy, to the full extent of targeting a whole population of disease carriers that must also be totaled.

Gold comes with a warning label up front: gold makes the world go down. We enter an espionage subplot encircling the science experiment of two Germans who, with their science fiction props recycled from the set of *Metropolis,* have discovered how to work the brain transfer procedure via cathode-ray beams to transform lead ingots into bars of gold. It's not a gold factory; it's pure science. When the three-way beams do their overlaps, the men are looking into the machine through some telescopic device. But before they can make their first gold happen, an undercover job has already replaced the lead ingot with a volatile substitute. Under the pressure of the rays there's no gold, only blowout. The older professor gets offed in the blast, but his assistant or younger colleague, played by Nazi Germany's marquis idol Hans Albers (who was the Baron von Münchhausen, too), has been spared to avenge the murder of his "best friend," whom he "loved like a father." The accident places his true-blue-eyed Margaret by his bedside donating her lifeblood, same blood type, type Aryan, to seal their Faustian-vampiric bond. The avenger is about to depart for the main stretch of the film, where Margaret, the daughter of gangster millionaire Wills, played by the actress of *Metropolis* fame, Brigitte Helm—a temptress, in other words, the good and evil Maria—awaits him. But he assures Margaret that he will always carry her with him; in his blood is her blood.

Where there's an Anglo-American capitalist like Wills there's a way to get what he wants. But he needs the accidental survivor of the very explosion that Wills ordered executed back then to provide him now with the missing link. Wills's espionage team was able to duplicate the professor's machine up to the point where, shortly before the explosion, he had added the one improvement that made the whole thing work (and which the spies had therefore just missed, including the stolen plans).

The scientist—his name is Holk, rhymes with *Volk*—joins Wills's company with revenge on his mind. Then he meets the daughter. Then he remembers that only by going through with the experiment just once all the way to successful production of gold can the professor's reputation be restored in the vault of history. Something is being reanimated, something organ transplanted: Wills hails the gold machine as the heart of the world that awaits the scientist's intervention to come alive. But at the showdown, Wills is finally told off by a united front of his own employees, the scientist, the entire staff, and the workers; Holk has set all machine systems to blow up. Wills achieves one last ha ha of power when he keeps the watertight vault door from sealing the machine room shut, thereby subjecting the entire undersea plant to the one drowning that Holk tries to contain in one compartment. These are running references to the compartmentalization technologies that sank or swam with the *Titanic* trauma or identification. But then Holk does shut tight machine and Wills in the *Titanic* compartmentalized blend of fire and water (on iceberg). At the close, the Holk returns to his beloved *Volk*-sy small world after all of Margaret. He casts the one artificial gold piece, *Gold* the size of *Geld*, into the sea, his payment of protection to the professor's spirit for safe passage.

The Tunnel is a Nazi German blockbuster based on the first best-selling German science fiction (pre-Dominik): Kellermann's 1913 novel by the same title. The center stage for the near future is still New York. But it's also the staging of endless intrigue. The most spectacular effect or unconscious side effect of the projected view or tunnel vision begins in New York when, at the gathering of the "Atlantic Tunnel Syndicate" for the screening of newsreel footage of the tunnel in progress, the internal film assumes full screen and then completely loses its New York audience frame without ever cutting out of it. The rest of the film slides right out of the newsreel, without ever coming back out of the frame of the film within the film. The transition can only have happened long before we know it's been happening. But by the time the modernist montage effects take over the newsreel's inside view too, we know the transition to the main body of the film has either been made, miraculously, or, more literally, forever lost.

Evil capitalist Mr. Wolf is a dandy who flaunts the role of the actor playing him, Gründgens, in Nazi German high culture as public secret number one. The good capitalist Allan is also a comrade who takes off his shirt and works and risks all side by side with his workers. That's why he is able, together with his German foreman's echo effect, to shout down the agitator hired by Wolf to cry out revolt to the workers right after the first accident down in the tunnel has claimed lives. Comrade Allan's final words, given in Hitler vibrato or Stuka siren, set the workers back on track, singing and marching as to war: "Every form of work is a form of combat! In every fight there are the dead! No life without danger!"

But Allan also has a soft subplot starring the little wife who suffers so from his long absences deep down in the tunnel with the gleaming, shirtless comrades. Ever since the tunnel was opened, the wife, whose loyal love of course went without saying, felt that she now had to go with no recognition or playtime. She starts playing dead. Allan at last notices that his wife, as she withdraws for another night alone, has tears down the dotted lines of her silence. It's nothing, she assures him, she's just "nervös," meaning both plain nervous and also, in polite society, neurotic. Allan insists that she speak her mind (it's all really very couples therapeutic). We know what she minds. He realizes he hadn't given her feelings another thought. He promises regular days off just for the two of them. But she's set up to die soon anyway.

Wolf changes chunnels when he delegates a desire for bombs to explode down in the tunnel. The hired hand job is completed, unalterably set to blow, but the hand gets caught, which means on the other hand that Wolf is guilty (he gets himself off with the charge of suicide). The mine goes off in the mine (the shorthand or collapsus for war technology's overlap with mining technology). When the wife hears about the explosion, the consequences of which Allan must face all alone (with his men), she rushes off to join him in the tunnel but gets stopped dead in the tracks of the bouncer train (if this were a dream, that would be a p-unitive reformulation of intercourse). We watch the graves of the explosion victims spaced out and camera panned in the style of military burial and coverage. Survivor Allan now needs some counseling to get around his grief-stuck resistance to seeing the tunnel through to the end, the underworld union with Europe. Go ahead, fall apart, but do your duty. Yes, the wife died, but for a reason—or if the tunnel stops here, she died pointlessly. (Besides, now that the Wolf, Allan's double, has consummated his auto-relations in suicide, the merry widower is free to do his duty and retire from life and libido.) Soon we witness the American and European tunnels meet (which also means that the big, weaponlike drills digging and filling the tunnels have met too). Allan, now the white-haired leader or mascot of the group, is there to remember to forget the dead by recalling them as sacrifices. With that the comrades from both sides now can embrace hands on, shirts off. The big drill apparatus that we flash on following time out for the human element is also, deep down, and as machine gun look-alike, a souvenir from the trenches of World War I. But now the ultimate trench connects the two continents of world power. At the same time, a direct line of future accessibility opens on prospects for making America share the mainland burden of war hitting the streets.

The ambivalence of this connection was already flying high in the film *FP 1 Doesn't Answer,* which was released, one year before the Nazi takeover, in two versions, the German one and its English-language dupe (for direct "invasion" of the Hollywood home front). It was Beate Uhse's all-time favorite for repeated viewing. Her postwar empire of the senses gives replicational ground support for war-technological flight lines into the future. Her switch from the pilot seat to the control panel of a sexuality beaconing to be reorganized, science fiction style, around the desire not to reproduce, is one big continuum shot.

The pilot hero of *FP 1 Doesn't Answer* is played by Conrad Veidt, who performed the stalking shadow of Cesare in *The Cabinet of Dr. Caligari.* Who's that, a young woman wants to know. "That's the famous airman, just back from Australia in record time." The somnambulistic medium is back from the Land Down Under.

The pilot is in the middle of a scam the young woman listens in on: he has staged a theft for the free media exposure his friend the engineer would thus receive for his FP 1 plans, which have been lying about unused by the firm that commissioned them. The woman is a member of the family that owns the firm. Soon the floating runway for stopover on transatlantic flights is in the works. The woman has fallen for the pilot, who gets a surprise offer to fly a plane designed to make it around the world in one round-trip (in other words, without any need for FP 1). He leaves for just two or three days to make or break another record; the reporter friend translates for the woman he left behind: two or three years.

Suddenly it's two or three years later, FP 1 is ready for service, the pilot returns, and the woman has fallen for the engineer. As the first landing time approaches, we're in on a scene of long-distance direct connection between woman and engineer that doesn't miss a heartbeat of total oneness right up to and through the communication ending too soon in cutoff. Now the pilot returns, crashed tail between the legs of his failed round-trip, to settle down and marry. He vowed two years ago never to fly again.

Back on FP 1, the engineer detects symptoms of all-out espionage or covert operation that could only have for its objective the sinking of the platform. FP 1 has been built around the *Titanic*'s design for unsinkability: a series of watertight compartmentalizations that would control release the water intake inflicted by any one point of impact. And it is indeed the very interruption of round-the-clock telecommunications with the platform that prompts the woman in love to promise the pilot anything (who otherwise couldn't get it up for flight after she didn't fly into the arms of his retirement proposal), if only they travel to the spot of trouble in the middle of the ocean with the fastest speed of flight. The message of silence, and the title of the film, "FP 1 Doesn't Answer," thus confirm the post-*Titanic* insurance policy of teleconnections at all times.

All hands on deck have been gassed unconscious (that's why the plans for the automatic sprinkler system were missing). The pilot cannot but notice the spectacle of caring his woman makes of herself cradling the unconscious engineer in her lap of luxury. The terrorists destroyed all means of getaway transportation, cut the electricity, and emptied out all stores of fuel. There's just enough left for one brief flight connection with a ship passing on the right. The wounded engineer is about to risk it. But then the pilot does the noble thing and leaves the couple intact and leaves flying. FP 1 is saved, and the pilot decides to stow away on board the slow boat, all men aboard, for the Flying German's endless ghostly traveling and withdrawals from the coupling of safety and flight, the safe landing of couplification.

In these films about projecting a future, via prehistory or the immediate past, the near miss fulfills the wish for a missing link with the past and the present that would leave out the loss of World War I, a loss overcome in the replay through greater therapeutic savvy and technological safety. The two films dedicated to the current event of flight give us a clear view to the crypt of the war dead and to the giveaway affirmation of sacrifice as the group plan for the spirit or ghost not to be given up, up, and away. *Paracelsus* takes into the past what is really a time-traveling skirmish with psychiatry on behalf of greater psychoanalysis, but on historical turf that grants German birthrights to what was only later, in passing, Freud's science. Together with *Germanin*, which in addition plays to World War I losses of colonies, all-naturally nudist bodies, and a population to heal by inoculation and extermination of the parasite species of disease-carrying flies, these two healing fictions are thus as much about therapy as they are about science. "Therapy fiction" is the one subplot where all these films overlap. In the three near-future fictions, or near-miss forecasts about the way the future, the present, should have been, tensions between the hetero couple and the unisex, gadget-loving group are explored, held, stayed with, so that the Nazi audience can therapeutically be fortified to reside within a tension these films finally leave unresolved, up in the air, just held, in reserve, in all its split-leveling.

Wishing Wells

Did you think God had exempted Weybridge? He is not an insurance agent.

Six million people unarmed and unprovisioned, driving headlong. It was the beginning of the rout of civilisation, of the massacre of mankind.

—H. G. WELLS, *THE WAR OF THE WORLDS*

A division in reception switches channels to the two sides of world war, the sides first mobilized against each other, according to Freud's lecture on worldviews, in the prewar traversal of English airspace by German aircraft. In his 1934 *Experiment in Autobiography*, H. G. Wells notes his telepathic intervention in "things to come" through his 1908 *The War in the Air*, "written before any practicable flying had occurred" (569), which describes total air war washing up out of the lead the Germans hold in aviation onto England and America. But before it's a question of who started it, Wells's narrative makes it all clear that this was the war necessitated simply by having attained air power (387). The air war, which is described from the perspective of either the grounded below or the bystander along for the ride on vast airships—in other words, never from the pilot's point of view—is set up as an uncanny transgression that irrupts within one's uninvaded personal space: "In the soul of all men is a liking for one's kind, a pride in one's own atmosphere, a tenderness for one's mother speech and one's familiar land" (*The War in the Air*, 96).

Wells's 1899 *The War of the Worlds* elaborates this transgression of speech space through an aerial identification of the Martian invasion within the context of writing, of writing that imposes blackout conditions on the space of legibility:

> The balloonist would have seen the network of streets . . . spread out like a huge map, and in the southward blotted. . . . It would have seemed as if some monstrous pen had flung ink upon the chart. Steadily, incessantly, each black splash grew and spread, shooting out ramifications this way and that, now banking itself against rising ground, now pouring swiftly over a crest into a new-found valley, exactly as a gout of ink would spread itself upon blotting paper. (111–12)

But the Martian extermination-writing machine, not unlike the torture machine in Kafka's World War I story "In the Penal Colony," also clears away the blotting:

> The glittering Martians went to and fro, calmly and methodically spreading their poison cloud over this patch of country and then over that, laying it again with their stream jets when it had served its purpose, and taking possession of the conquered country. (112)

Inside this writing machine, the Martians communicate by telepathy only, which is Wells's specific mode of projection when it comes to future flight, the future, deferred or deterred, always on the horizon of his own writing.

In the 1936 film *Things to Come*, based on Wells's wish writing, and which credited Wells as consultant, the total war breaks out inside the contemporary representational field: the labels and signs of group-psychological, consumerist recognition or identification are smashed in the attack, including the CINEMA sign, which cracks apart. What follows this world conflict and destruction is the "wandering sickness," an "epidemic" that, however, has no other symptoms than what's in its name: the disease is not so much spread by wanderers but is literally the course of these wanderers themselves, signifiers unchecked by the representational bonds of our sign language. In the wake of the destruction of the world—of the word—as we knew it in 1936, a chief emerges to take total control and reestablish in the first place and at the most literal level one-to-one correspondences between signs and their production of meaning. Thus he comes to power by containing the epidemic and literally giving signs stable content or reference: he shoots all wanderers. This primal reorganization is replaced by the new order of the new leader Cabal, whose name overlaps with the constituency he represents, the group comprised of sibling bonds. Cabal's first act as new leader, after the chief's stronghold has been gassed by plane, is thus to untie the women. This second future reorganization of what's left after the total war of 1936 features new technologies that burrow into the earth down the bottom line of World War I trench warfare and resemble writing to the extent that a counterphantasm is also assembled: a rebellious sculptor, who calls for a loud broadcasting of a halt to progress, a program full of voices that everyone must hear and obey, has chiseled out of the earth a monumental maternal figure. This amplified space of speech, of live transmission, is the phantasmatic placeholder of the totalitarian threat. With this threat contained at the center of the new group-psychological order that, in the fast-forward of forecast, continues over centuries or generations, but with each dictator in the Cabal lineage played by the same actor. The closing shot of the forecast is the projected firing out into space of the couple that is next in line to rule the Cabal order. The cinematic and ballistic shot (in contrast to spaceflight) will be fired from the space gun, which is the primal above-ground achievement of the second reorder's technology (an order that otherwise has the look of an undifferentiated "great white world" comprised of interior shots made in German expressionism). Thus the untying of woman from the primal chief's rule presents the group with the ambivalence that must be reserved for the reproductive couple.

In *The War of the Worlds* the identification of the Martians within the space of writing and printing goes all the way to the melancholic core of the meltdown projected from what's a structure all the way to "their" intention. The Martians inhabit the future of our own evolution into hands and brains. In *The War of the Worlds* it's an out-of-this-world dichotomy held together by a vampire's intake of life. (In *Metropolis* the same dichotomy is "mediated" by the missing mother Hel, whose mummified loss is the secret ingredient of the local replication industry.)

> They were heads—merely heads. Entrails they had none. They did not eat, much less digest. Instead, they took the fresh living blood of other creatures, and injected it into their own veins. (133)

The chain of evolution, which links man and machine (58), links and separates Martian body and brain: the missing place of the body is held by the machine prosthesis while all that's left, in one piece, is the brain. The result: "mere selfish intelligence" (135), the narcissistic brainpan befitting the rewired, functionalized tension span of traumatic neurosis. But the streamlining of direct blood injection systems belongs to a future place: on Earth, immune systems must still be along for the ride. But Wells stresses that it is in particular the bacteria that we don't even have to fight off anymore, the bacteria that, however, take over when we leave off, and feed on our corpses, which finally destroy the self-replicating brain machines from outer space. Our bacteria, the godlike ones that provide disposal service of the dead, while uncanny-proofing one boundary between life and death, take the Martians to be already corpses. To be taken for dead, melancholically shut down or playing dead, was the origin of Schreber's entry into the network of rays while his self-replicating merger with the divinity of ray technology was being prepared over his body made over into part woman, part machine.

First contact with the Martians hits the protagonist below the belt: "Such an extraordinary effect in unmanning me it had that I ran weeping silently as a child might do" (33). What follows this unmanning are air pockets of ambivalence addressed to his wife and back pockets of replicational group-of-one fantasy. The fever of war (44) that takes over where unmanning left off or over is also just a variation on the protagonist's capacity for swinging with exceptional moods (39). The women-and-children-first separation from his wife has left behind a "curious" feeling of "anger" toward her (76). He is so ready to rise to the occasion of being the last man left alive or one of a small primal band of survivors. Thus he falls for a visionary's belief in life now coming alive again on the margins of Martian world domination. One detail not to overlook is the admission of strong women only into the new order of the club. Once the protagonist cannot but know a psycho where he first saw a man with an alternative plan after his heart, he senses that the one person he had thus betrayed, the only person, was his own wife (171). Not too many heartbeats earlier, when faced with the cattle drive with which we are branded in Martian captivity, he dedicated his prayer to the wife he wished spared this feeding time if only already painlessly dead by the Heat Ray (158).

In *The War of the Worlds* the reunion of protagonist at the end with his wife—the restoration of the couple at the future point—has passed through the "divine" perspective of taking the other for dead. Here are the last lines: "And strangest of all is it to hold my wife's hand again, and to think that I have counted her, and that she has counted me, among the dead." The two spooks inhabit a haunted city of the dead. The future destruction of Earth is now a given according to the terms of the interplanetary race against the replicational species that we must run. The living end also belongs to the wider horizon of a future search for flying power, which the Martians while on earth were rumored to have discovered. The release of the flying machine would have put an end to humanity. The rocket trip from Mars to Earth was conceived not as flight but as shot aimed at a target. Wells keeps flight on the edge of the apocalypse as the impetus for groupwide preparations that begin with the ambivalence controls that must be installed inside the couple to keep its unity or unit intact in the face of air force. In his autobiography, Wells summarizes the predictions he made at the next station of the crossing over of his science fantasy into the realization of flight:

> Already in 1908 in *The War in the Air,* written before practicable
> flying had occurred, I had reasoned that air warfare, by making

warfare three dimensional, would abolish the war front and with that the possibility of distinguishing between civilian and combatant or of bringing a war to a conclusive end. This I argued, must not only intensify but must alter the ordinary man's attitude to warfare. He can no longer regard it as we did the Boer War for example as a vivid spectacle in which his participation is that of a paying spectator at a cricket or base-ball match. (569)

The psychotic status quo in Schreber's *Memoirs* or at the close of *The War of the Worlds* is just the limit—where, however, transgression is itself transgressed. In the Wells complex, the excess that keeps difference from getting clonely at the top of mourning's circimvention is the telepathic wavelength along for the writing. Freud plugged his discovery of the unconscious, indeed his science, into this intersection between the occult frequency and the media-technologized analogy (the telephone) that he just had to turn on to illustrate how telepathy or thought transference proceeded (ultimately under the teleguidance of the psychoanalytic understanding of the unconscious significance of the medium as the message) (*SE*, 22: 36–56). But even more to the point here is that Alan Turing's famous hypothesis of the nondifference or interchangeability between a conceivable calculating or thinking machine and intelligent human life admitted one exception or excess: telepathy could not (yet) be part (at least not by forethought or as guaranteed) of his conceivable machine's program.

It's Time

Kurd Lasswitz's 1899 *Two Planets* focuses on flight, the overcoming of gravity, its reversal in the form of wave power, steering, relations between pilot and flying machine. From Lasswitz and Schreber to Wernher von Braun and the 1943 blockbuster *Münchhausen* there is a direct hit or fit of continuity comprising the German reception of air power. Whereas Wells's reception stays with the new grounded group member and his air defense psychology, the German take prepares for the invention of the rocket, which is based on flight, and comes at the end of ongoing interrogation of the relationship between pilot and machine, which, at the apex of their merger, yields automatic pilot. What comes first in the countdown to rocket flight is, for example, pilot selection and training (the preemptive rewiring of the sensorium to flight), which Wernher von Braun addresses in one of his U.S. science narratives, this one devoted to a future trip to Mars (it just takes two years). Preemptive shock absorption has even incorporated "simulation" in the service of gadget-loving attention to the detail trained to withstand space travel (including the prospects of in-flight mourning or substitution). "There is no way of predicting the exact state of health of any individual for more than two years in advance. The chief engineer may suffer a nervous breakdown as a result of the heavy load of responsibilities he had to endure during the months and months of drifting through the lonely vastness of interplanetary space" (132–33). Trips to Mars can be booked only one-way: The itinerary of the insured health of passengers cannot plan ahead for the return. It's another way to shoot up to the top of the mourning.

Airspace is haunted, always books the future on return flights of ghostly visitation. According to Freud, breath became a model for spirit only when the last breath of the dying was observed: "spirit" in German is always also "ghost." But it's the same space across which the shutdowns of melancholia are to be circumnavigated: through control of the airwaves. Wells comes up for airspace in the 1932 prelude to his *Experiment in Autobiography*, which bears the Schreber-style subtitle *Discoveries and Conclusions of a Very Ordinary Brain (since 1866).*

> We are like early amphibians ... struggling out of the waters ...
> into the air, seeking to breathe in a new fashion and emancipate
> ourselves from long accepted ... necessities. At last it becomes
> for us a case of air or nothing. (3)

This life-or-death air pressure comes down to another kind of air pocket, the homonymic contamination that produces "heir." Forever H. G., Wells made certain that the childhood name and identity would never be deciphered. But he includes a childhood photo of himself dressed as a girl with his slightly older brother standing next to him in boy's attire. The official gloss brushes the transvestism to the side of English habit at the time. But the displaced caption follows:

> My mother brought my brother Freddy into the world in 1862, and had her great tragedy in 1864, when my sister died of appendicitis. . . . I was born two years and more after her death, in 1866, and my mother decided that I had been sent to replace Fanny. (43)

The air or heir pressure turns on in the immediate (1932) context of crisis: Wells is finding it ever harder to find "peace" for his writing, a state of distraction that doesn't concern him alone: "This is the outcome of a specialization and a sublimation of interests that has become frequent only in the last century or so" (1). "The life story to be told of any creative worker" is characterized thus by "grotesque transitions from sublimation to base necessity and its pervasive stress towards flight" (7).

In 1895 Wells's *Time Machine* was his first hit, and it got him going. The machine's premise lies in a fourth dimension, time reconceived as a medium for traveling in either "direction" on the basis of two available experiences or inventions (196): one is the in-session therapeutic awareness that we tend always to be getting away from the present moment; two is the fact of artificial flying above and against the gravity of the earth that gives Wells's tale the "why not?" spin on prospects for time tripping. First the time traveler built a miniature machine, a gadget, which took him two years to complete. In his circle of friends and witnesses, the inventor turns the demo on, torn free, free of the time flow, and the "little machine suddenly swung round, became indistinct, was seen as a ghost for a second perhaps—and it was gone—vanished!" (199). In fact, the friends protest, this may be just too much, like another trick, "like that ghost you showed us last Christmas" (201). But the inventor puts himself on the line of time travel: he jumps all aboard the full-size model, takes off, and returns to give the friends the recount. At countdown he felt both wound and wonder: "I suppose a suicide who holds a pistol to his skull feels much the same wonder at what will come next as I felt then" (207). What he will conclude about the future is that human intelligent life "had committed suicide" (263).

Portrait of H. G. Wells *(seated)* with his older brother standing by. Reproduced from *Experiment in Autobiography: Discoveries and Conclusions of a Very Ordinary Brain (since 1866)* (New York: Macmillan, 1934). Reprinted by permission of A. P. Watt Ltd. on behalf of the Literary Executors of the Estate of H. G. Wells.

In the future, human specimens are frail, unisex teenagers, reminiscent of "the more beautiful kind of consumptive" (211–12). That this is already an underworld, this upper play space of the mortally ill and exquisite Eloi, is not undone but rather captioned by the underworld inside it, the other place of the Morlocks. The Eloi are vegetarians, like cattle; the Morlocks are cannibals, like vegetarians. What falls between the cracks of the split between spaces or races is any recognizable legacy of humanity. (Hence the suicide conclusion.) For the uppers, there's no rapport with the dead (no cemeteries, for example), only fear of the dark (229). The downers, the Morlocks, first appear at night to the traveler like ghosts or apelike figures (232). They are also "ant-like" by virtue of their herding of the Eloi as cattle (249). These underworld creatures, who by name call for "more locks" to keep their uncanniness out of the place where they are in fact home on the range, are recognizable heirs to evolutionary science fantasy. The Eloi are the immortal teen groupies and exquisite corpses of what has come down to suicide. The traveler loses his own little one, his Weena. But now that he's back, his time-traveled memories—even of Weena's loss—which were so overwhelming back then in the future, now yield, in line with the time of narration, "more . . . the sorrow of a dream than an actual loss" (262). The time traveler finally leaves on another trip, another suicide mission of identification with loss, one that, after three years have passed, everyone knows has exceeded the two-year period of expectations for his comeback. He's back there with the ghosts who no longer break through to the present (he took them with him). It's a science fantasy ultimately about the unmourning of losses that can, on another plane, and in time, the time that exceeds the two years of mourning, get lost. Both the unisex realm of teen players, empty placeholders of objects to lose and mourn, and the underworld, the world of "Fanny," in which the excremental undead crave humanoid sacrifice and unburial, can be left behind with the takeoff of one man's career in science fiction (is another man's mourning).

This is where the trans- of time travel, the across that H. G. Wells had to bear in childhood, begins and ends. In the course of the story, the orifice-like connections between the worlds above ground and below, the holes and throats of the time traveler's first contact with the split in the future, are regularly identified as wells. The split fits one name and one corpus. Sister can be put to rest, a settling of accounts that will open up the new accounts of science fiction to follow in far greater technological detail. The open display of the mother's unmourning on the body of her surviving child did not, however, stuff a crypt down the child. The cross-dressing performed for love of mother is already a work of mourning, a work, however, long deferred in its terms of outcome. In *The Time Machine*, in a world born out of the spirits of sudden techno-evolutionary change, H. G. Wells gave the loss that had been draped across him a place of rest, the resting place at once of prehistory and of some science fantastic future.

In "The Delay of the Machine Age," Sachs raised his time-traveling question about technological invention based on Freud's Schreber study and Tausk's analysis of the influencing machine. The question is wired to take out the sociological or even psychosociological monopoly on the raising of historical questions, putting them to rest—to the test. What about the delay in the development of the machine, of technology, of media technology (and there is indeed, in the case of each media invention, the case of gramophone, for example, or that of TV, a basic delay). Sachs time travels back to ancient Greece and Rome to ask why, even though those people had the know-how, they didn't develop machines for practical application rather than, if and when they did engage in this brand of externalization at all, only as playthings. The time Sachs travels is the space he travels through, too, the outer space of psychosis. According to Sachs, psychotics, if they make it to the stage of auto-recovery or delusional formation and don't simply wipe out, invariably project their way out of the crisis by turning over their bodies to the self-recovery network of techno-relations. The ancients didn't go psychotic, didn't need to break for the machine; their body-based narcissism was just too established. Their extension into the world was the debased body double, the slave; along the same lines of extension, their dead were lemurs, zombie vampires. The body was the measure of all distance, the long and the short of it. In the terms of a given aesthetic opposition, Sachs places Greek body culture squarely within the register of beauty. There was no room for the sublime, no control release or point of access for the break of uncanniness. Without sublime protection or projection, without, that is, the uncanny proofing of the prospect of breaks in relations with one's own body, there can be no technology, no machines.

The time machine is introduced as a playthinglike gadget that, in larger scale too, just whirs and disappears like a ghost machine-raised for the amusement of courtiers. The story is in turn stuck on the body in a place of future forecast, the place of an other precast with the controlling interest of identification. If Mother dressed up H. G. in drag to change the past, then she thus sought to control the present and the future, too. But arrival in the future introduces a break, a blowing up into the un-, the unknown and the uncanny. When the machine disappears, a loss in space, not in time, the traveler breaks down like a bawling, raging child, "lying on the ground near the sphinx and weeping with absolute wretchedness" (224). Now he wonders about two possible hiding places, one above ground, the other below. There's the monument consisting of a hollow pedestal and, on top, the figure of the sphinx. And then there is the unseen network below ground signaled by the wells and towers on the surface—a sewage system, perhaps? And then burial arrangements cross his mind. But it's all one underworld after all.

The traveler is given to project or protect a distinction between the Oedipal monument and the excremental and funereal recesses below ground. When he points to the pedestal to signal his nonverbal request for information from the Eloi standing by—before we discover that the pedestal is also just another entrance down into the underworld—it's the sphinx meaning that comes to mind. How are the Eloi seen to respond to the traveler's attempt to get in touch with the monument? "Suppose you were to use a grossly improper gesture to a delicate-minded woman" (226). When he descends into the underworld down "the throat of a well" (240), he discovers that in the realm of the Morlocks—where more than what class analysis or, at the head of the class, Oedipal analysis would allow has been locked up—he has only one techno-defense, his matches. Now he's so sorry he wasted matches playing with the Eloi above ground. When Benjamin in his 1939 essay on Baudelaire defines the gadget connection with technologization, he derives the pull of the trigger, the turn of the dial, and the press of the shutter from the striking and flick of the match (630). It's that push-button control release of the violence of identification in groups, the searing intervention of technologies, that gives the moment—the arrested moment—a "posthumous shock," an inoculative shot enabling us to make a date with the traumatic contact (dating it as a one-time point in time) and thus send it on its way as just one of those things to remember to forget. In the future, matches represent the time traveler's only techno-advantage over the Morlocks. If the machine is less visible in Wells's inaugural fiction than in subsequent science fantasies, it's because the focus is on the gadget, on its primal connection, where our body-based narcissism meets, cohabits with, and crosses over into techno-embodiment. In the technology section of some ancient abandoned museum, the matches the traveler finds in an airtight case represent a still functioning match with the gadget click and flick of his prosthetic body, a tight fit with his rights as heir (254). In the end, the traveler can't strike the last match; he's defenseless against the ghouls of the underworld. What's more cannot be locked up any longer, not by the match. H. G. was no longer his dead sister's match and maker.

The narrator inside the frame closes the frame. When he visits the time traveler at home, the latter is not there, but the machine is. He touches it:

"At that the squat substantial-looking mass swayed like a bough shaken by the wind. Its instability startled me extremely, and I had a queer reminiscence of the childish days when I used to be forbidden to meddle" (274). When the time traveler departs again, and this time the trip's proximity to suicide is a direct hit, the narrator is on the other side of a closed door. He hears an exclamation, a click, a thud, and a crash, and bursts in. "The Time Traveller was not there. I seemed to see a ghostly, indistinct figure sitting in a whirling mass of black and brass for a moment—a figure so transparent that the bench behind with its sheets of drawings was absolutely distinct, but this phantasm vanished as I rubbed my eyes." A figure so transparent: the traveler is so crossed with the trans- that he can skip the beat of the parental injunction not to meddle and take with him, in one time-tripping, eye-rubbing spasm of the phantasm, the phantom's hold on his witness.

If the time traveler always believed in the decline of civilization, then he took a round-trip within his own forecast. The witness or narrator, by contrast, believes in the near future, trusts, in other words, that progress or substitution will compensate us for all losses. The narrator receives Weena's legacy, the flowers she gave the traveler and which he brought back in his pocket, a kernel of the truth of the grim future forecast, but which at the same time contains the proof that gratitude will continue. Yes, even the dead are grateful, grateful in time to be let go. Mourning, which takes place only in real time, is entrusted to the narrator, who precisely does not take a controlling interest in the future.

In *The Time Machine:* the movie, the traveler trips out via rapid-fire stopovers in three world wars (on the eve of the third war of total world destruction, he encounters an old man to whom, much younger then, he had talked to in 1917, too). What the future holds in self-storage (somewhere between the German pleasure garden of *Metropolis* and "California") is given to ugly midlife types to feed on teen bodies. (Feeding time is announced and introduced by the ring of the siren that guides the teens down into the bunkerlike underworld and cannibal's pot. Then the "all clear" signals them to pick up where they left off before the tele-hypno wail of the siren came on. Part of the all that's cleared is any recognition of the missingness of the others.) That movie's forecast was among the projections crowding into our future in cloning. With the advent of successful replication or cloning there arose a welcoming line and a line of resistance both stuck on one psy fi reception. A certain Seed, for example, was cited for his scheme to open up a commercial cloning clinic: he was another Dr. Jack Kevorkian, the so-called suicide doctor. The science fictive negative theology that for centuries has realized the fantasy of replication in acts of suicide gets turned around as fateful interchangeability. But in that season of Readers' Digestion and fast-acting out, the projections became more recognizable down to details. The research results at yet other cloning labs or workshops—replication of headless animals—hit the headlines and spirited away the clone to future haunts of organ farming. The problem remains: even my clone is someone else. But my headless clone would supply replacement parts (which can be inserted with immunity) to keep me going indefinitely.

But this alarm ringing up the past in the future skips the present tense of tensions between midlife living on and teen bodies. Cloning or replication is the ultimate teen fantasy—as in the slogan-slip made by the photocopying chain Kinko's, "Making copies, making friends"—but precisely to the extent that the risk of accident and self-destruction is just around the bend of the fantasy's realization. But when it comes to organ replacement—I mean, let's stop cloning around—the midlifer is entitled to farm adolescence for freshness. Insurance calculates a longer life for the individual who has survived into his thirties; according to risk calculation, as you approach midlife, you have survived many possible early deaths. And this entitles you to more life. If for the first time in history, even young people are encouraged to be already in recovery, already conscious of what's the healthy, organic, safe brand for every item taken into the body, then that's because we need those organs as fresh as possible when the next motorcycle accident, for example, yields its harvest. We may hate ourselves in the mourning, but we are already more locked inside the Frankenstein lab where the teen body is for the axing than the projection onto some future drawing of blanks in the cross-fertilization of cloning would care to recognize.

Dominik Gene

Hans Dominik: the name of a brand of German science fiction that, beginning in the twenties, made the genre appear at times, in Germany, like a one-man show. Born in 1872, just inside German unification and empire, he was even Kurd Lasswitz's pupil in boarding-school math class. Dominik's even more timely death in 1945 doubled or seconded all the other closures.

Everyone thought science fiction (like TV) was a Cold War, U.S. versus them exclusive. Yes, everyone knew the distant precursors, ancestral friendly ghosts, lonely at the top, Jules Verne and H. G. Wells. But in addition to the underground track from Kurd Lasswitz's major Mars novel (completely contemporary and up to comparison with Wells's *War of the Worlds*) all the way to the outside and outer space of Nazi German rocket research, there was a substantial modern German science fiction tradition that qualified for the bulk rate by the twenties and went right on fantasizing during the Third Reich, indeed more than ever in sync (or swim) with current events.

Science fiction sees in the future the same conditionings that are already upon us, just as occult fiction puts what's new today into the primal past. Occult fantasy has as a regular on its shows always some specialist, say, in vampirology, who is a perfect stand-in for psychoanalysis, the only science that both excavates the mummy's tomb and gives owner's manual instructions to the psychotic delusions of our ongoing technologization. Science fiction tends to be more fully blown psychotic than the occult strain or tension that pursues and pulls inside transferential precincts. In other words (or worlds), the science fantasy about the future can be so psychoanalytic in that endopsychic way psychotic delusions have of giving inside views of the psyche (and of Freud's theories of psychic functioning) that it ceases to be legible (i.e., transferential) as one perspective.

As recounted in his 1940 memoir *From Bench Vise to Writing Desk,* Dominik was an engineer before there was a body of training set aside as engineering (the next best thing in those early days was electromechanics). But soon his smooth writing sent him to the advertising departments of his emerging field; in other words, he entered public relations. He decided to branch out into literary production by World War I. During the war, he dropped everything to invent a couple of gadgets for the war effort. The first was the projected invention and mass production of a "ray directer" *(Strahlenzieler)* (189). It's a type of radar detector for locating enemy vessels even at night and then blasting them on target. His second war gadget was a form of "earth telegraphy" that would permit long-distance communication without the vulnerable mess of cables and wires (199). This invention was completed by the end of 1917. It could even be used to send a signal long distance to trigger some abandoned post's explosive undermining (preferably just as the enemy came to take possession of the hot spot). New technological territory opened up for future work through this trajectory of his invention. And for submarine purposes, water could be used just as readily as a medium for these communications as could the earth.

After the war, and following a stint writing and directing educational films, Dominik returns to literary work (which he had abandoned in 1914). But he couldn't just pick up where he had left off back then. He decided to try something new, something commensurate with the world war's scrambling of our nerves (221). So Dominik composed his first science fiction novel, *The Power of the Three,* and this first "novel of the future," as he referred to the new nerve-wrought post–world war genre, was right on the endopsychic edge of blockbuster success. This rapport with a mass readership, a following he had also in effect invented when he went back into the lab of World War I to calculate the changes and then came back out with science fiction, kept right on going, without downswing or interruption, until the publication of his memoirs, which sealed the deal in 1940.

Dominik did continue in some respects where his prewar novel *John Workmann, the Newsboy* left off. *Workmann,* the only one of the prewar works to qualify for reissue during the science fiction phase of Dominik's productivity, is a self-made tale of a German-American boy who grows rich quick— but never old enough (by the time, that is, the novel closes as happily ended) for his beloved mother to be, in all likelihood, no longer around. At the end of a novel that doubles, at the same time, as an encyclopedia of the latest innovations in industry and technology, young rich man John is still making his mother, still standing by, proud.

America still provided the screen for future projections in *The Power of the Three.* This first novel of the future recycles fantasies based on what didn't happen in the world war and incorporates Dominik's two war-technological projects into the fictional miracle weapon that gives three friends infinite power over world events. America is ruled by a dictatorship that recently took hold (it's a holdover from the war economy) in the course of the bloody but victorious struggle against Russia. Because America is democracy happy and can therefore be distracted only by assembly headlines of more and more victories, the dictator has decided to take conflict to the next power, England. Thus in 1974 we are again threatened by first world warfare, for the first time since the actual world war. The word of warning is out that the new war may in fact surpass what the society of 1974 still uses as its most reliable measure of horrors unimaginable. That's why three friends claim as their destiny the interruption of this return of world warfare (and, with the same throw, the toppling of the American dictator). Silvester Bursfeld is the son of the original inventor of this greatest weapon almost known to man, but then father died and took it with him. Everyone, especially the dictator, is afraid that a son may just know best how to dig up the dad's secret. That's why Silvester, the wild card, has been framed for crime punishable by electrocution. The novel opens with this current event, the miraculous interruption of which we witness instead. And then he escapes almost magically. Thus we are introduced to the current status of the power, a ray beam that, like an expanded takeoff on the wireless telegraphy Dominik developed during World War I, uses all of space as the medium through which its impact travels long distance in an instant. The first time we know for sure that we are seeing the force with us, in action, is when Silvester aims his remote at the plane on the runway and pushes it along while "following like a photographer pursuing an object that he wants to capture on film" (32). As is evident here in plane sight, Silvester, just like an inventor, had neglected such practical considerations as how to aim the ray beam across the long distances open to it if the object, at greater distance, becomes invisible. His friend Erik Truwor works out that missing part. He stumbles on the age-old mechanism of feedback, whereby the energy beamed out returns in the form of an image. His supplemental "television" allows the ray beam to aim and make visible at the same time (99, 101), so that you see what you're looking for within the beam's range (and then you fire) (81–84). Friend number three, Atma from India, has all-natural tele-skills that are more than a match for the hypnotic powers of the dictator's master spy. Dominik often includes for the sake of comparison, or as externalization of the inward turn of technologization, a body trained or drugged to perform the remote-control functions otherwise carried out by men through machine technology.

The other human element that gets mixed in is marriage. As soon as Silvester marries, he and his wife must separate, it's like liftoff, for the duration of the three friends' antiwar and mad-science activities up at the North Pole. Thus the TV channel that Erik grafted onto Silvester's (or his father's) beam holds in place the long distancing of the beloved, the cross or "trans-" that Silvester cannot bear. First he becomes so upset when the videophone can't locate his wife, his life, that he forgets to turn off what is still at the same time a ray gun: the friends and their work are almost destroyed, and another hindrance is added to the already tight schedule they must maintain to keep up with the dictator's war plans. The novel began with the interruption

These four illustrations accompany an entry featuring Freud in the encyclopedia *Welten/Werke/Wunder*, edited by Hans Dominik in 1926. The illustrations are from pp. 434 and 435 and are titled "Thoughts during a normal conversation," "Thoughts while composing a letter," "During a lecture the thoughts of the auditors have free play," and "Some people are fortunate in being able to fall asleep as soon as they go to bed. But with very occupied and especially older people there arises a wild dance of thoughts just as the body begins to find rest."

of Silvester's death by electrocution, at which point, he knows, he survived himself. A certain after-death experience thus enters the circuit and comes on full power when he drops dead from overexposure to the rapid alternation between good and bad news about his wife's whereabouts (195). Erik goes insane. Atma tries counseling him: "You are sick. Silvester's death has shocked your psyche" (202). But Erik is so far gone that all he hears is Atma's reference to the greater power of destiny. He jumps into the "Rapid Flyer" and takes off to battle the destiny he'd like to see that would use *him* as instrument (201–3). He flies so high in the sky that he dies out of sight, out of his mind.

Dominik's next "novel of the future" (this time we're in the twenty-first century) is *The Trace of Ghengis Khan*. United Europe has established vast colonies in Siberia on tracts of land made arable through the 1963 invention (by a German scientist) of "dynotherm." Just sprinkle this substance lightly over your local glacier or ice-topped peak, and all that water will come

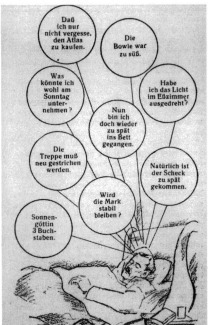

down to adjust deserts. Although the colony is European, for psychological reasons it was decided to break it down into the different segments of a virtual theme park of European cultures. One of the new hubs, Orenburg, is German through and through (it's on a direct flight line to Berlin, with one stopover in Moscow). A local bar is decorated in the "style of old German city hall taverns, as you might still find in the Hanseatic cities on the Baltic Sea. One could have believed oneself transported back into the sixteenth century. Only the teleprinter which stood on a table by the wall and ceaselessly recorded telegrams from all over the world indicated that the world had progressed in the meantime by five hundred years" (35–36).

There are two psy fantasy fulfillments here that take us back to World War I: one, German control of Eastern markets and, two, the replacement of all dependency on oil or coal through techno-power.

During the tour of the colony the German inventor takes with his American friend, they fly over villages that seem American. Yes, but German American, from the Great Lakes region. They joined the original imitation colony because they were feeling at a loss over the black-fire of interracial living. This point of information is the buzzword that sets off the American's old saw about how necessary it is that a clear separation between the races be maintained. But right now—and thus we enter the novel's main multicolored plot—it's the yellow peril that's most pressing down the colony's future. The pan-Mongolian movement is demanding return of the colonial lands. At the same time, the colonists have been asking their neighbors for a peak or glacier of frozen water that they could put to good use dynothermically. The yellows aren't right neighborly.

The novel accepts that at different times, different races hold the top position. And while it is openly admitted that the white race seems, on balance, to be declining, the one contribution they have made to world history, their technological know-how, still keeps them at the head of the race. Yellows and blacks melting-plot together the overthrow of white supremacy worldwide. A big state election is coming up in the United States between white and black candidates. It is expected that if the outcome of this race against time is black victory, the government will look for excuses to void and avoid the finish line. But on the darker side, the race outcome will be a riot they are counting on to keep the United States from entering the war that China will at the same time declare on Europe.

But the Europeans still have two secret defensive weapons: The German inventor of dynotherm has come up with an "anti-toxin" that can contain the volcanic impact of dynotherm that the yellows may choose to inflict on them. (Like psychological warfare and nuclear power, dynotherm is no sooner invented than it has become available to all sides of conflict coming soon.) The inventor has also improved on the original thaw formula: now rather than set new weather patterns in slow motion by starting up a new local chain of being, the new formula cuts right to the lightning and snowstorms that will be heaven sent the yellow army's way. The world race war is quickly contained. American blacks start emigrating to Africa to extend the Liberian experiment into larger regions of the continent. In Asia the Europeans now feel free to start phase two of colonization: following the agrarian pioneers, masses of industrial settlers start moving in. By this time, the end of the novel, the German inventor has been converted to his American friend's KKK principles:

> It was wrong and reckless of our prophets worldwide to promise equal rights. Everywhere on earth the black, the brown, the yellow races demand freedom. Freedom for all the colors of the spectrum.... If we meet them even half way, our race and our existence will be finished. (236)

Yes, the day will come when the whites must fall. If we look back over the centuries of Chinese culture, for example, white hegemony appears to shoot up suddenly like some "volcanic island in an enormous ocean" (236). But in the meantime the dangers the whites face make them stronger, more techno-savvy.

Atlantis, installment number three in Dominik's countdown of the future, is a worldwide web of intrigue and crisis with coordinates at the Panama Canal, the Northern European coastline, and the city of Mineapolis in the United States of Africa. This latter development is a continuity shot of sorts between this one and the earlier future booking: Africa is now an empire under the rule of a former African American who named his big city Mineapolis after his birthplace. But don't listen to what the white race says; watch out for what it does. Race conflict sent American blacks packing for Africa, where, according to the rules of segregation, they formed their own world power. But now tensions over the equal rights issue on African turf between the empire and South Africa (which has Europe's all-out support) must have broken the rules, because it's open season again on black power.

The evil capitalist whose construction companies have been contracted to excavate the Panama Canal for easy passage convinces Congress to let him go ahead and blast it open all the way through all at once. Over the protests of the European Parliament, the deed is done, and Northern Europe is dead in the water no longer warmed by the explosion-diverted Gulf Stream.

The African emperor has commissioned a major dig to tap the inner warmth of the earth for technological application. At the bottom of the shaft, Africa strikes pay dirt: an enormous natural source of carbide opens up (which immediately makes the empire independent of foreign energy resources). But another German converted to the American view goes under cover in Mineapolis as "half-caste" miner to score a terrorist hit for the white race: the explosive charge he sets off turns what was mine, the emperor's, into eternal flames.

Son of Silvester, born to the widow after *The Power of the Three* was all over, has learned to work the remote. With it he "heals the earth" and sets the Gulf Stream back on the old course. The old continent of Atlantis reemerges in the wake of this restoration effort. The new territory is hailed as last resort for all those whose homeland has grown, how shall I say, too cramped by "foreigners" for home style. The whites beat the emperor's race to claim the new land. The sixth continent is "firmly in white hands" (316). The capital city: Neu-Hamburg.

For 1926 Dominik edited an enyclopedia for use in the home entitled *Worlds/Works/Wonders.* The rundown concept, given on the last page of the preface, leads through physiology to make the leap into psychology, the realm or "empire" *(Reich)* of psychic life. Then comes technology with a high beam on the "energy problem which gives our century its particular character." From there a final look into the future: "wonders of the world in our time which surpass the wonders of antiquity by a long shot." In the edited zones, coverage of psychotechnical research refers the readers back to the world war that was the first war for which soldiers passed tests or were assigned special duties based on the test results (404). Under the section title "The Play of Thoughts and Compulsions," Freud, who gets honorably mentioned, meets the hereditary view, which closes the section but leaves an opening for accessorizing or eclecticizing with analysis compatibility. A patient complained that his suicidal ideation isn't in his head; it's in his fingers. This one couldn't be helped and healed: he shot himself. What makes this sort of suicidally ideational compulsion "uncanny" is that it's hereditary. (How had the hand job kept masturbation from crossing the physician's mind?) Thus when even the stray thought of suicide wants to be taken in: resist, with all your willpower. If that doesn't work, try "psychic treatment," which does have a long-playing record of success stories. "It's possible through certain seemingly harmless tricks to wall in these ideas so that the patient under treatment completely forgets them and is thus healed of his affliction" (439). Among the sections that follow suicide, there's an astronomy entry focusing on hypothetical life on Mars (along the equator) or on Venus (at the poles), an entry all about a technologized mining project that would use the earth's inner warmth, and another techno news brief about plans for doubling Manhattan in size by reclaiming land from the sea (the skyscrapers were just the rehearsal for the proposed tip of the iceberg constructions out to sea).

In *The Burning of the Cheops Pyramid* we are introduced to atomic energy: "the most powerful energy source imaginable, which has been for centuries the highest goal of the inventors of all civilized nations" (7). Dominik lets the first discoverer of atomic power be British, but no one in Britain can figure out how to reproduce the discovery after his death. He leaves behind one functional atomic device, which not only resembles "Snow White's coffin" (57) but is even multiply locked up inside his Scottish fortress-estate already world famous for its "security system" (7). The gadget gets stolen and goes to the Mauretanian Empire, a new power on the block resulting from Spain's conquest five years ago by non-Europeans. At the all's fair of world power, the atomic impact of the remote is demonstrated on the Cheops pyramid, which is miraculously restored to its original, smooth, glassy surface (286). Atomic power, like some high-tech face cream, lifts the pyramid worn down over centuries back up, in all its purity, to its original form and complexion. The European community gets the invention back and, thanks to German know-how, reproduces the gadget for energy-saving use. Just drop a little bit of mercury into the new apparatus, and "it's enough for Germany's energy needs for one year'" (287).

The Legacy of the Uranites begins right in the middle of a battle that will conclude the latest in world wars. The Soviet invasion of the rest of the world has been rolling along unstoppably over all resistance. But suddenly there's a news flash: "The Soviet armada has been annihilated" (11). The fighting, which had been up in the air for so long with bombs falling everywhere on the ground, piled up millions for the body count (21). It's forever Gorm who's held up as hated inventor of the new firepower that kept the Soviet invasion rolling forward. Then we meet Gorm, who flashes back to that terrible time when he was the last to know that his invention had been stolen by the Bolsheviks, who used the miracle weapon to overthrow the czar and start the world war of total invasion. (A question or another flashback: is this the equivalent of the psychological-warfare time bomb—his name was Lenin—that the Germans did allow to steal back into Russia?) Although the war has been decided, there's one more leftover battle in South America. In the mode of overkill, the victorious side blasts the Soviets so badly that the earth has been contaminated by the flames of radiation. In the meantime the czar returns (for the second time): it was a second world war that just ended (63). But now the world is united on an eco-trip for the survival of the species. If the radiation contamination isn't contained, the earth will soon no longer be habitable.

We are introduced to the prospects for outer-space travel through an isolated, decontextualized, uncanny news brief. Five dead men have been found in Hyde Park. Among the deep-frozen remains there was a wallet belonging to Professor Jonas Lee. He was the first man to try to fly through outer space several years back. How did the bodies get back to earth, freeze-framed for the long-deferred proper burial? It was Gorm to the rescue. Gorm had been Lee's friend: back then he advised Lee to wait until Gorm had completed work on "electronic propulsion," which was what would be needed for the trip, not the "hydrogen rocket" Lee would have to take if he left right away (81).

A very rich American builds a rocket to dump the toxic wasting of South America onto the moon (experts have been comparing the radiation-contaminated spot to a "cancer" that can only grow fatal without radical intervention) (109). Gorm's rocket designs are circulating, thanks to his American friend since university days, whose only invention is an x-ray camera useful in doing what he does best: stealing Gorm's ideas. Other expert voices warn that whether on earth or on the moon, the spread of the radiation means the end; it's time to look for a new world on Mars or on Venus (145). Then the British helicopter-suspended observatory picks up "image telegrams" that have been beamed from Venus to Earth (179). There are other beings out there, even from another solar system, who have already recently landed on Venus. The aliens send live broadcasts covering their recent graves and two ill survivors, one pointing to a bowl of apples with a dour expression. The audience guesses the charade is a warning label the alien means to stick to the fruit and loom in our minds. The TV is two-way: it offers the first communicative exchange between the visitors to Venus and the Earthlings (205–6). We want to know just how advanced they are in their technology (the interstellar measure of civilization). So we beam up one of our own educational films (perhaps one that Dominik made right after the war) on, say, metallurgy and see what the Uranites send back in exchange. The answer from Venus discloses a binding of gases into ideal construction material, countless miniature machines or "elfin gadgets" that get all the busy and dirty work done (210). No more mass transportation: with barely visible devices, the aliens fly solo (like the Jetsons). But at the end of these broadcasts, we still want to know where the last man is, dead or alive. How could he have buried himself? The surviving and burying other was Gorm again, to the rescue. The completely other or alien race (which, presto-projecto, looks like that noble Aryan race) has always come and gone already, is available only as an object of excavation, at once in the past and in the future (it's evolution timed, like a missing link). Not just the last man's body but the whole legacy of superhuman knowledge have been stowed away by Gorm: humans right now would only destroy themselves with the know-how.

King Laurin's Cloak introduces Arvelin as a kind of Sandman figure who breaks up a couple's union. But then there's a baby, and Arvelin stages a Moses-style arrival for the bundle of boy as though sole survivor of some shipwreck. That's prehistory. Now we're in a war zone between Venezuela and Brazil, a new world power gone to its heads of state. We catch the boy's jump cut to manhood in the war zone within which he takes Venezuela's losing side and serves it well as pilot flying in supplies. Venezuela's hero is Wildrake, whose family came originally from Scotland (the other land of phantoms) back in grandfather's generation, and whose sister is right now strapped to the tracks of distress in a Brazilian prison run by bad official, good official. The latter is a Winterloo, from a branch of the German family, whose head, Karl von Winterloo, is getting ready to go but doesn't have immediate family members to whom to leave his estate. One branch has already started its visitation and vigil: they're "more than half Polish." Part of the Winterloo estate will consist of his invention of a "chemical accumulator" that empowers our current fuels to store twenty times their usual capacity and twenty times the miles (40). In the meantime Arvelin has been working out his own chemical dependency problem: he's trying to devise a chemical "suit of armor" that will protect him against the bad side effects of the cloak of invisibility he has already invented, ready to wear: "The problem would be finally solved if I could bind the poison of the oscillations in another way and could deceive the human eye in larger format" (42).

Back in the Brazilian prison, Winterloo is in conflict between the duty to hate Wildrake and his own conviction that Wildrake was not a war criminal. "Could public opinion force him to submit slavishly to the prejudice born out of the war psychosis of the masses?" (58). Soon this Winterloo is in prison too. Only a miracle can save him. This calls for Arvelin and his cloak. He has given up on the chemical solution and accepts that the poison already inside him will finish him off. So he takes a few more risks with invisibility. To make the most of the energy accumulator that the adopted son of Winterloo has forwarded to the front line of Wildrake's fighting unit, a new fully automatic ship has been designed that flies through the air and goes underwater like a sub (160–62). Wildrake has in the meantime obtained a pirate copy of the Brazilian secret code used for all military communications. Armed with their gadgets and their nonstop intelligence of the enemy's moves, the Wildrakes declare war on the United States of Brazil.

Brazilian military intelligence wears the shades of Enigma, enigmatically in advance of a mistake that's in the curriculum vitae of Nazi German gadget lovers. The conclusion that only the enemy could be so blind is reached from within one's own paranoid blind spot about who's immune. "The possibility that any military objects, in particular the decoder, could fall into foreign hands was so remote, that no one even thought of altering the secret code" (205).

What was first addressed as danger of poisoning, then of the toxicity of the oscillations, now makes a comeback that's all waves or oscillation, but more in the shell-shock mode:

> The amounts of energy which were swinging in his magic coat were only infinitely minimal, and consequently harmless. A tiny source of current could keep on weaving the coat over long periods. But the cloth grows dangerous if cast out too far, to cover or camouflage larger objects. Then there was the danger that the carrier of the source of current would be hit by recursive oscilla-

tions which, as already in earlier centuries with certain high frequency oscillations, could bring forth creeping organic damage.
(249)

At the end all's well, but Arvelin is gone. At future reunions, the freedom
fighters would forever wonder how in fact they had actually won that war.
"Unconsciously, however, there resonated then, in their deepest interiority,
quite quietly the name 'Arvelin.'"

Countdown

By now the countdown is at 1930. *Rubber Latex* is the novel about industrial invention and espionage that's just another day, not a future displacement. The cover for one of the women spies is that she's a widow of an English major who fell in the world war, and therefore she's still young enough to interest the mark (55). At stake are two procedures for making rubber latex that are competing for industrial adoption and priority. Fortuyn proposes electrosynthesis; his competitor, a certain Moran, proposes chemosynthesis. The chemical alternative is just one fallback in the elaborate French espionage network that's all out to steal Fortuyn's procedure. The creation of this other procedure effectively forestalls acceptance of the only real solution, thereby giving the spy ring more time to collar it during the less protected phase of invention. Before the novel ends with Fortuyn's winning out over the spies, we pass through a subplot all about gas poisoning, described as a common affliction of that day. It was gas that turned one woman's husband into a zombie; then Fortuyn, the new object of her affection deficit, gets gassed. She goes into "nervous shock" at the uncanny repetition of an accident that seems to happen to her objects only because it's her recurring theme or problem. But then the poison plot is safely wrapped up in the rubber latex frame of one more electrosynthetic replacement for another natural resource that Germany lacks.

It's still 1930, and the *Command from Out of the Darkness* is upon the Dominik readership. Allgermissen was a mad man. But his ideas weren't so insane. Astenryk is the German scientist who is so close to solving the problem of how to use up coal 100 percent. It's another accumulator that gets the most out of scarcity or near lack. But total use of the coal means that it gets used up completely, without remainder, totally gone:

> "Vanished" is the word that's crucial. Vanished means in this case totally used up without remainder. To put it differently, the problem of the 100% transformation of coal energy into electricity is thereby solved. (13)

Allgermissen's mad science experiments involved taking toxins to influence the brain functions so that "the receptivity or the radiation of the thinking brain gets amplified through one or perhaps through several medicinal preparations" (21). External means of this sort of amplification are developed by Allgermissen's heirs. The resulting amplifier is like a radio speaker, but with the capacity for amplifying all frequencies. "Not just the long radio waves, but even the short and shortest ones, right down to the light waves" (22). Brain waves can be controlled by tape-recorded messages under special amplification. Only steel helmets give cone-of-silence protection to your thoughts.

> Think of the consequences that would follow from further development of this small amplifier into a powerful sender across greater distances, large masses of people...cities...entire peoples, countries....Stop that! Always remember how Allgermissen ended. (25)

Allgermissen's working assumption was that the thinking human brain beams out hertz frequencies. The amplifier he built was able to amplify these thought waves just as radio speakers amplify broadcasting frequencies. And he added to this as afterthought or afterimage the tape-recording device.

Abbot Turi Chan from the Himalayas takes to the all-natural part of Allgermissen's legacy: the thought-wave-bending drugs that let you amplify (50–51). Turi offers himself up as walking amplifier on the side of the yellow race for the war to be waged against the whites (53). Under the influence, Turi's brain works just like the special amplifier: it receives the thought waves of others and sends out waves of its own to exercise control over these others. The yellow air force flies out against Australia. Down under, the whites hear the alarm and turn on their amplifier (which has a 250-kilometer range) and broadcast the command to turn back (157). After it's all over and one of the winners makes a passing reference to the amplifier as a "machine," there's a correction, please: "Don't call it a machine, Mr. Astenryk. After such an achievement you have to call it a mega radar transmitter" (159).

Now (blast off!) it's 1933. Reference books on international science fiction cover Dominik's works but refer only to those published in the twenties and leave the continuity cut off. The German SF movement, we are instructed, picked up again only in the postwar period. The work of reference puts the period to the ellipsis or elision of the substantial German science fiction literature in the twenties, thirties, and forties. Dominik's *Air Race of the Nations* opens in the "Reading House" in New York with the reading of one man's last will and testament. Here's the voice that's over: "My life work concerned especially the development of flight. My final plans, developed over years of work, are now ready for execution. The one who has been called and appointed will realize them after my death" (7). On the first anniversary of his death day, the race is on: once around the

world by plane with one stopover required, one that each national team selected and prepped in the year before. Winner takes all, the fortune and the
plans for building a stratosphere plane (8). During the search for the mid-
point of the round-trip, world opinion mocked as though sympathizing
with "poor Germany" having to find its station in some foreign zone: "That's
what happens when one has lost all one's colonies" (63–64). But then world
opinion turns around to wondering whether a nation without these ap-
pendages isn't the envy of the world. While the colonial powers must
choose diplomatically, Germany can just land anywhere and everywhere
(64).

This novel introduces the Eggerth factory in Germany. During the war
Professor Eggerth had been good laughing stock for his pioneer construction
of an all-metal plane. "And yet this mode of construction began to assert itself generally until around 1940"—now we get the sense that the future is
upon us—"one recalled only dimly that thirty years earlier one once built
planes out of wood, canvas, and other flammable and unlikely materials"
(29–30). The German factory has already launched its own stratosphere
ship, which hovers about and swoops down as extra-special referee of the
plane race. But that makes the "St" ship what everyone's talking about: its
rescue operations are all over the place at once. It's Superman. And it's a
good thing, too. There's Russian and Japanese espionage and sabotage along
for the race. But a good pilot can always "feel it in his subconscious that a
severe threat" hangs over his plane (307). The official German entry in the
race, "The Swallow," finally wins the race, covered, in the last legs, by the
St that must slow down to keep pace in the "nerve wracking tempo of a
hearse" (373).

Dominik's second 1933 salute, *A Star Fell from the Sky*, starts further
along in the series of stratosphere ships (we're up to St 8 now). The newer
models have jet propulsion and automatic steering (44–45). The Eggerth
concern is a conglomerate now together with the former Reading company;
the Eggerth-Reading factories are located in Bay City, U.S.A. While on reconnaissance, St 8 is the sole witness to the cause of worldwide wind-
storms: it was a direct hit near the South Pole of one enormous meteor
(17). There was another time to remember: "In the year before World War
I," a meteorite crashed in eastern Siberia. It became a mining prospect.
This new rock that only the Eggerth-Reading Concern knows about is full
of gold. But a safe way of control releasing this sudden stash must be found
to offset any negative impact on the world market. Europe, which by now
has been torn apart by two world wars, could use a little help back into the
economic running (61–62). That way the world too can get its balancing act

back together again. It's decided to claim the territory around the inland crash for the "German Republic" (71–72). The claim is without contest because it's inside the "no-man's-land" outside the state boundaries, which are on the coast of Antarctica (87). Again the world ironically commiserates: poor Germany has to look for a colony at the South Pole (128). This helps camouflage what the mission is really about (156). By checking out all earthquake registers by radio and TV, they determine the site of the crash within forty-eight hours (80). Once the mine has been set up, the gold production averages $33 million daily (141). Thirty-three is the magic number.

The Steel Secret advertises a new brand of steel, 40 percent more resistant to the melting point or pot. In this novel the reader's entertainment means entering the plain text as slowly, as real time, as the intelligence of the other permits. But then we're out of the false, hysterical geological plans back into the dig. An American company, with the essential help of the German scientist Dr. Wegener, is mining the ocean floor (under pressures that the new steel can withstand) for the ore of the Earth's core. The benefit of underwater work is the freedom from overheating the deeper one digs (170). They drop a pipeline down the water under the sea floor, which is both pressure and earthquake proofed. The steel balls that replace mining carts down the tubes also give extra support. They're equipped with fresh air, electric light, and phones (184). All this excavation and construction is at America's service. Japan has long-term plans for taking the Philippines away from the United States. But their plans and planes require two more years before they will be ready to strike to win (159). In the Pacific the United States has only a one-month window of supplies for waging war. The U.S. military needs at least a year. They need oil supplies on the Philippines, and they need them bombproof (160–61). The pipeline will guarantee just that. But when they hit bottom, they strike magma that glows but doesn't flow, not even under highest gas flame temperatures. "Such fire proof material is of use in technology" (252). Mix the new substance with seawater, and you've got "pure gasoline" (260). Even the waste material of the excavation project turns out to be fuel for sale (253).

It's been stressed that this pioneering work must proceed without the usual safety measures. One safety net is an accident. An engineer falls down the tube, but it's not curtains for him; it's the parachute his jumper blows up as with the sudden backflow of air (284). When his voice is back on the air, up the phone line to his surviving colleagues, it's like "seeing a ghost" (285).

Once the Japanese comprehend the ultimate goal of the pipeline dig—a new unlimited fuel source—it's almost too late: the American position on the Philippines is soon to be invincible (289). Almost: the Japanese decide to strike undeclared while the Americans are not prepared. Give the Japanese a piece of anything, like a sampling of the steel used down the tube, and they figure it out: now they know what kind of bombing can bust the pipeline open wide (289). The Japanese commander rallies the pilots before this rehearsal of Pearl Harbor around recollection of the torpedo strikes against battleships in Port Arthur during the Russo-Japanese War (the primal scene, on the Russo side, of recognition, low-maintenance theorization, and hands-on treatment of war neurotics) (303). But Dr. Wegener can read along through a crack in the Japanese code. Conventional military force is out in abundance. But Wegener decides to do it his way: he stops the attack by opening up the pipeline, which releases a pressure-packed upward mobilization of gas, and then he lights it. The miraculous flamethrower downs the Japanese planes in one blast (307–9). Not even a fighting chance. It's the fantasy of total victory for America thanks to German science. The pipeline is also a brain drain, which is also a connection Dominik gladly keeps open.

In *Atomic Weight 500* an explosion in the lab that's cooking with gas attack scrambles the "nerve apparatus" of the innocent bystanders (297). Sounds like war neurosis, looks like war neurosis. But a new substance comes out with the shock, one that carries an atomic weight above that of radium. Unlike a synthetic product, this substance is brand new; it never before existed on earth (298). But its half-life span is very short (299). The long and the short of it is that natural radium is now superfluous: the Germans don't have it, now they don't want it (346). In the course of rapid-fire work, Dr. Wandel (Dr. "Transformation") turns into an automatic machine at the same time those carrying out his orders are on automatic machine drive (425). The substance that the machinic lab crew is working up will represent a new form of energy self-storage (464). The new intervention will permit controlled release and retraction of the atomic energy (555). Dr. Wandel takes his successes back to Germany (he had to go to the United States to bankroll his research project). Back up out of the drain, he starts building "artificial suns" in which materials are transformed into the "new energy substance" (560). It's the start of a new story and history.

Next Dominik took time out from literature to write a propaganda manual about a new synthetic fiber that Germans were having trouble getting into, owing largely to one consequence of the world war and its mobilization of *Ersatz* substances (he gives it the "medical name": "*Ersatz*-substance Psychosis") (106). But the German wartime simulation industry had made a virtue out of a lack: the nations rich in saltpeter lost a good client in Germany during the war; left to their own resources, the Germans simulated their own functional substitute. Germany's liberation from foreign oil and gasoline commenced with the transformation of brown coal into a useful energy supply (236). For the future, chemistry will be less interested in transforming natural elements into something new in the field of energy and more interested in starting from scratch, simulating from the bottom line on up, as is the case with the latest developments in synthetic fabrics: "direct synthesis of chemically produced connections . . . out of which the molecules of natural silk or wool are built up in test tubes" (246). The book, topic and title, was *Vistra, the White Gold of Germany: The History of an Invention That Moved the World.* Nineteen thirty-six saw the realization of a 1934 plan, which was stage one on the way to the final stage: complete independence from the outside world with new (not natural, but national) fiber cloth and clothing. Synthetic cloth spins right out of the history of modern technological warfare. Only because he had recourse to the new synthetics was Alfred Nobel able to develop the detonative gelatine that his invention of dynamite required. One track of influence passes through photography and cinema (celluloid) while the production of cloth and explosives just kept right on track. World War I mobilization gave rise to an abundance of factories in Germany specializing in explosives production. After the war was over, these same facilities could be made over to house the fabrication of synthetic cloth.

To challenge the war-psychotic resistance to synthetic materials, Dominik busts the boundaries between the natural and the technological:

> The green flora covering our earth is one big enormous chemical factory, which takes in to a great extent and binds the solar energy beaming our way by making out of anorganic substances organic substances. Through events probably of a catastrophic nature great stretches of this prehistorical flora were buried and have been preserved over the ages in the form of coal. Our entire technological-industrial age . . . has based itself on this treasure of coal. But this treasure is by no means infinitely large. The total sum of solar energy bound in it is comparable to the amount of energy the sun still beams down onto the earth in a period of thirty days. (246)

Part of this original edition of Dominik's work of enlightenment, according to the closing note on page 250, was originally the supplement of a little bag containing vistra fibers attached to the book's back cover. In addition to this airsick bag accompanying the flight from nature into the future, the whole orange cover of the book was made out of "pure and unmixed" vistra.

Several brochures designed to sell the new synthetics Vistra and Wollstra to the German public. Reproduced from insert between pp. 212 and 213, *Vistra, Das weisse Gold Deutschlands: Die Geschichte einer weltbewegenden Erfindung*, published by Hans Dominik in 1936.

Life Rays opens with Frankenstein- or Dracula-style drop scenes of breaking and entering into the crypt of mad science: Dr. Eisenlohr won't let anyone penetrate to the laboratory inside his castle. We pan to the doctor at work inside the lab, doubled over the microscope. What he sees is "autonomous movement" (14). "What if it's the primal creation . . . What if the dead

Fashion show highlighting the new German synthetics. Reproduced from *Vistra*, insert between pp. 220 and 221.

matter really was animated by our ray?" (15). The rays they control are comparable to what one could expect to find in outer space; on earth they have first appeared in these laboratory experiments. Rumors fly that Eisenlohr is making counterfeit money up in his castle. He denies or confirms that that's what they thought Daimler was up to when they mistook the pounding of his new machine for the sounds of a printing press (40–41). So that the research team can see the microscopic evidence all together now, the slide is projected onto the big screen. It's a movie starring animated gelatin that digests, doubles, merges, and self-replicates (63–64). These are the "primal cells" (88). Eisenlohr's forward search for the original life substance produces two side effects, one on top of the other. First gold is created in abundance, which put the doctor and one of this assistants at cross-purposes. French espionage together with American capital enters the subplot around the alchemical line of production. Soon it becomes evident that the artificial gold decays rapidly. This diverts attention to side effect number two. Eisenlohr had regularly thrown the gold-dust waste product outside in the fields. Now everyone notices that primordial fecundity has taken over the castle environs. The rapid breakdown or decay of the fake gold is a plant growth promotional. This new fertilizer would permit two harvests per year. The German scientist—only interested in the money because it will keep his

I.G.FARBENINDUSTRIE
AKTIENGESELLSCHAFT
BERLIN S.O. 36

MIT ERFINDUNG
Vistra
TEXTIL-EPOCHE

A Vistra exhibit at an industrial fair. Reproduced from *Vistra*, insert between pp. 220 and 221.

biogenetic research going—agrees to market this byproduct through a new American company, Radiating Powder Co. What lies ahead for the German research team, on the path already established in the cell state of animation, is creation of a life-size replicant, the homunculus (263).

In the *Power of the Heavens* German science is way ahead of what the Americans, for all their extra cash, can buy on their open markets. The American power company that runs a balloonist electricity-gathering station needs the better cables, ray collectors, and cold cathode that the Germans have already developed. The "mouse trap," made in Germany, is just the condenser the Americans need to catch and ground any stray flashes of

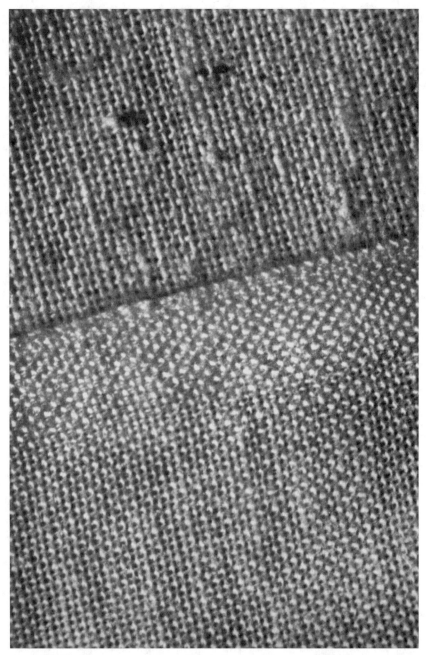

Comparison between the neater weave of Vistra *(below)* and the messier texture of cotton as magnified under a microscope. Reproduced from *Vistra,* insert between pp. 192 and 193.

lightning. According to the Germans, "We control lightning now, like Jupiter, the king of the gods, once did" (176). By making use of the cold cathode, moreover, the German condensers operate without fuel. The novel ends on a peaceful note of cooperation between American and German interests:

> This may represent a first time in thousands of years of technol-
> ogy's history that an invention has appeared that is simply un-
> usable for purposes of war. . . . Just think of the old dream of man-
> kind to swing through the air free as a bird! As soon as it was
> realized, planes were turned into terrible war machines. (300)

Land of Fire and Water concludes the Eggerth series with a reunion all for one new project and goal: finding a stopover point for the new German transoceanic flight lines. (The lost colonies trauma is back again, too.) But the group recalls that during the last exploit, they used some uncharted island for the safe deposit of two snoops for the duration of the mining ex-pedition. But when they finally spot the unmapped isle, it's hardly recog-nizable: it's been volcanically active. An odd glassy piece of volcanic rock attracts attention. Just add water, and it grows, and grows hard. If they could add water right at the molten source of this rock, then the island would expand in size until large enough for the airstrip and even, beyond that, to serve as Germany's sizable colony. Of course, water would just steam away before hitting the lava. But an "ice bomb" dropped into the volcano by plane could make the mix. In the meantime Berlin puts the tiny, inconsequential island on the map as Germany's one colony. The world is rolling in the isles. But then the experiment is on, and the property is a siz-able one. One year later we attend the baptism of the colony's 50,000th cit-izen (189).

In his memoirs, Dominik does more than retell the plot when it comes to his final novel, *Fuel SR*. Perhaps because the writing of the memoirs alter-nated twice with the continuation of the science fiction. It was the summer of 1939, all was well, and no one believed that war could happen.

> There suddenly was no gasoline. Hundreds of cars standing be-
> fore the empty gas stations couldn't proceed for lack of fuel.
> With the last quarter liter of fuel in the tank we made it to the
> next town but by now we also had the impression that something
> was in the air. (285)

On returning to Berlin, Dominik had the idea for his next novel of the future (it was the next item on his wish list). But once the world war starts up in earnest, he decides to write his memoirs instead, his last will and testament.

But then the war is going so well, and the publishing house is pressing him for new material, and so he finishes *Fuel SR* first. And now in the following year, in 1940, he's concluding his memoirs.

Fuel SR opens with Italians dismissing the rumor that the Germans have made it to "production of artificial radioactivity" (7). But then, right on laugh track, something bright crashes down next to them: the weight of the enigmatic object changes each time you turn it around. It's no substance of this earth. Could it be from outer space (10)? We flash back to the source of the explosion-sent object, not in outer space but in Germany. It was the cathode that took off like a rocket. And precisely not like a cannonball, which must give in to gravity one way only, but like a rocket, which "keeps on working like a machine without interruption during its flight" (55). With this cathode tube of theirs, they could fly to the moon, because only one side is radioactive, like the poisoned side of the apple that gave Snow White the look of death or catalepsy (61). The Germans have figured out how to get around, skip, fast-forward beyond the "explosive phase" of radioactivity. They therefore switch from motor to turbine. Through the standoff of equal ray beams, the breakdown of radioactivity can be stopped, turned on, controlled. The next problem to be solved is the storage of the rays.

At Japanese and Italian labs, parallel experiments with atomic energy have catastrophic outcomes. It is decided that the three nations prominent in this new field should pool resources and pull for the safe development of atomic energy. The three nations form an atomic axis. The Americans rush to the moon to land there first, but their return is long overdue: "One was reminded of earlier accidents involving submarines that sank to the bottom of the sea and how one calculated the amount of time before the oxygen ran out" (237). The Italians use the new spaceship technology to create a luxury craft for round-the-world trips. On the maiden voyage, an accident brings the German and Japanese ships to the rescue. After a brief stopover in Germany to quick-fix the Italian craft, all three fly into Rome triumphant.

Hotel Dominik

Rudolf H. Daumann writes his 1937 *Thin as an Eggshell* around the 1983 band of evil who dig into the earth to set off volcanoes and earthquakes at will. A small gang of Germans volunteer for the mission of saving the world. Soon there's a first bombing attempt made on the German leader and the pack, which shows the hand of the enemy's knowledge of their intentions. The bomb goes off in Hotel Dominik.

The mad scientist Dr. Utrusque (whose name could be Pig Latin for Uterus) was instantly suspect to the German hero, Haller, who can give physiognomic and characterological diagnoses in his sleep. The current center stage of Utrusque's mad terrorism and blackmail is Buenos Aires, which is suffering from "anxiety psychosis" (182) over or under the skywriting that advertises apocalypse coming soon (unless!). But Haller starts infrareading and soon locates the techno-source of the finger of God by flying over and filming the city during show time (as always at night). In the lab they develop what was only invisible to the eye. But they arrive at an already split scene. After many more near misses, the novel adds up to, I mean ends up with, Haller's victory.

Paul Eugen Sieg has the password name that goes with the injunction of the group's healing that his two science fiction novels (in 1936 and 1940), outer space or not, are ultimately about. The first is *Detatom,* the proper nomination of the German research facility that gloms onto atom, untranslatably. There's a two-step rhythm between the two novels, and already within the first one, where a first defeat, unfairly inflicted, is the occasion for beginning again: there's Detatom One and then there's Detatom Two— or Too, like the world war that would be coming soon as though on one continuum of effort, comeback, second try. The first plant was protected underground against any attack that would come burrowing out of the trench depths of the lost war. Countless microphones form a web of surveillance picking up every sound around in the dead silence of earth secured against false alarm by poisoning and gassing. The pressure that's on because it's certain that invasion of the plant is in the works triggers in Helo Torwaldt, co-owner and defender of the lab and its research together with best friend Hannes Nord, recollections of frontline experience in the war (20). His girlfriend Ingeborg is visiting him just as the attack is really imminent. The atmosphere of preparedness and defense gives her a first group experience:

In this environment of steel, concrete and uncanny machines . . .
she saw herself suddenly, primordially, as nothing, small, silly,
saw her life . . . as repulsively, selfishly wasted. . . . In terror she
was dragged into a completely different life. Fight down to the
knife. Commitment of strength and personality all the way to
sacrifice of one's own ego. A life of responsibility and work, in
the service of work for the progress of humanity. . . . The proud,
distant Ingeborg had become a woman, one who loved. (35)

But when it's time to get with the group program, she gets a panic attack.
During the crescendo of conversion thoughts, Ingeborg had lost track of
the ten minutes she was supposed to be counting down before pressing the
button somewhere between life and death. Now she's on a roll: lots of self-
criticism and recant for her selfishness that won't let go, let go even in her
conversion from self to groupie. The plant isn't protected against air attack
or parachute landings. But don't feel too bad about the destruction of Detatom One: "The history of war technology proves incontrovertibly that for
every system of defense a new attack weapon will be invented that can
penetrate it" (77).

Now we're in Detatom Two, which is built in the water this time around.
They've built a spaceship that also functions as submarine. The war-technological conditions are quite different now. Helo has developed a substance that's lighter than air but harder than steel, which he has named
after himself: helan. The invention of this new material made the construction of the rocket the next step. The sight of the helan spaceship tends to
bring on attacks of death-driven "we"-ness that overwhelm the group, all
together now:

It was a sight that sent shock waves through the psyche, this
powerful, completely transparent glass torpedo. The two men
inside seemed to be hovering. . . . It was a brief parting, without
many words. The common labor had melded together the men
"under the mountain" into one body. They all knew only too
well that the slightest error in calculation would suffice and the
comrades, the pioneers of a new era, would not come back alive.
The helan ship would be their glass coffin. (124)

Lost in space a clear-as-glass body hovered with the name HD-1,
in hundreds of years still carrying the skeletons of two death defy-
ing pioneers of a new age, mute witnesses of German research
and courage. (144)

But then there's a transferential visitation from the one place where three pasts can overlap: the educational institution. It's Mr. Professor and his three former students (Ingeborg is a scientist now, too). In passing, Helo lets drop that on their last voyage around the moon, the radiotelegraphic equipment worked just fine. Mr. Professor starts sputtering and puffing. Space travel runs on next to no energy: only five kilograms of lead. But don't forget to factor in the atomic breakdown, Mr. Professor. Do you want to see our home movie of our "Trip to the Moon"? When it starts, the really big surprise is that it's even a sound film, too. Now comes the ultimate transference fantasy, one that is realized here in a science fiction novel (and for the Nazi German society outside of laughing comrades and Oedi-pals): Mr. Professor has determined to resign his university position to join the kids on their bigger-than-life projects. Now that that's settled, Helo and Ingeborg can declare themselves to be undyingly in love. But when Inge (the short form has been in order at least since her first group experience) asks to go with Helo to Mars, she has another group thing coming. If Helo says no, it's not because the danger increases or decreases by their double exposure. But he can't forget that she's the radio expert, whose work it will be to get and keep in touch with the spacecraft. Her knowing the drill and her part in the gadget-loving network helps her remember her place (226).

Mars turns out to be a ghost town of monumental ruins. Among the many speculations that cross Helo's mind to explain the colossal extinction of the species there's epidemic disease—or how about "cosmic gas catastrophe" (251). This dead world could become the resource for a brand-new world that would leap into the future out of the work of excavating the secrets of superior but dead beings. That way they (a select group of Germans) could leave the world and its "destructive individualism" far behind (252). It appears that the species on Mars had internalized technology down to the scale of minigadgets: no wires, waves, or transmissions; everything was simply "fully automatic" (264). What's left is a legacy of texts to decipher in the extinct language that's "marsist" (*marsistisch*). Now all that's missing is Inge's voice, Earth to Mars. The connection goes through.

After landing, the helan ship is once more an uncanny item, undead in the water (it's that group, dead thing again): "Dead, without essence, shining in the water, the powerful spaceship, without seam or porthole. Just silver, a huge lifeless torpedo, just hours ago still racing through space at immeasurable speeds, now lying inert under water" (296). At the international press conference, Helo refuses the American offer of big bucks if he addresses their networks first: "My *Volk* comes first!" His first words on the air: "Heil Deutschland" (299). He has decided not to play Prometheus and release the "marsist" knowledge to mankind. He'll be mediator instead, keeping the atomic era on a short control release.

The saga continues with *Southeast of Venus*. Hannes Nord runs station Earth; Helo and Ingeborg rule on Mars. Frank Gunter represents the new generation. In his youth (in the novel before), Helo had been given a unisex twist to his look and behavior, especially when he was being attractive (to Inge). Frank is frankly girlish (or unisex) at first sight: "Thus Frank Gunter's soft expression, the dreamy full lips, the great big light eyes, the long narrow back of the head, and the smoothly combed-back dark blond hair, particularly however the almost womanly, small and delicate hands, could lead one to assume that this was some energy-less easily influenced dreamer" (9). But by the second look, Frank is all pulled together, filled with disdain for the enemy, for life, for low life. Frank is considered all around to be an eccentric, a *Sonderling*, one who, however, when push comes to love of country, is completely reliable. His special curse is that as a hero he gets robbed of his deed or *Tat* over and again because good fortune always intervenes and hands the success right over to him, just like that. He's the new Germany, immune to the dangers of every test, always winning, a little sad, a little pretty. Hannes is called to the phone, makes an about-face turn, and trips over the wire that detonates the pier and the ship. When the smoke clears there's Frank, untouched, holding Hannes, who's knocked out this round, "like a mother cradling her sick child" (32).

Thus Frank is in charge of station Earth when the SOS signals arrive from Mars. The "Mars disease" is back, spreading in epidemic proportions (42). Frank's got a girl, and her name is Frigga, a philologist in "marsist" studies. But she's friggin difficult, independent, and so on. Ingeborg advised him to let Frigga participate in his work, stand by it and him, share the group experience that, as Inge found out on her own hard body, gives love staying power. Frigga joins Frank's perilous shortcutting flight to Mars via dangerous proximity to Venus (where they crash land). On the way she quotes the text of an extinct species: "You stronger ones shall inherit everything!" (110). When it comes time to test that strength beside her man Frank, she has her first group grope response: "Her 'ego' had now turned into a 'we'" (186). The crash separates Frank from the rest on Venus. The planet is crawling with fleshy dinosaurs. Some even look like the torpedo his spaceship resembles (232). At one point he does the boyish swimming-hole-in-the-nude frolicking thing. Then he battles the amorphous mountains of dinosaur meat, which he defeats only to struggle to clear away the masses of dead flesh for hygienic reasons. At the same time, in another part of the planet, Frigga is accidentally knocked out by the tail of the dinosaur she's trying to capture on film. These are completely transparent prenuptial rites of passage connected in this case by the separation of the two. It's more Frank's problems with female flesh that need work. Survival in the round, all around, plus, for the near future, a new research project for development of synthetic radium, and everyone gets over the "nerve shock" (275) of epidemic disease on Mars and stopover in prehistory on Venus.

DOUBLES

Double Amnesia

In a series of works (novels and screenplays), Alfred Döblin joined and separated his psychiatric knowledge, the religious structures attending his sense of the end or the beginning, and an at once literary and mediatic commitment to modernity. His final work, *Hamlet*, is the place to begin rewinding the tapes around the rewounding of trauma that always carved out the inside view of his work in progress. He conceived the testamentary work while in Hollywood exile, and thus while becoming reacquainted with his own originally firsthand experience with shell shock during the First World War, but now in the more distant form of screenplay projects for which he was hired to serve as consultant and author. One of the films he worked on, *Random Harvest*, focuses on a World War I case of shell-shocked amnesia: under its influence, the protagonist nevertheless learns to lead a new life, only to be relieved of that amnesia (and that intervening life) in a traffic accident that cures one amnesia only by introducing another one.

That Hollywood should be the place where World War I experiences of shock were being replayed and rewired for the long-distance relations with the new world war increases in importance, in Döblin's case, by at the same time sharing its proximity with Döblin's own conversion experience. This remarkable conversion to Christianity, then, does not rest only on age-old contexts and contests inside the Judeo-Christian tradition, which would set up Döblin's case as standing in saintly or self-hating rapport with the Nazi persecution from which he too had fled for the cover of Hollywood projections. Instead, inside all the native habits and settings of mediatization and mass psychologization in California, the decision to convert comes to represent that "arrest" of development associated with deferred or perpetuated adolescence.

Already in *Berlin Alexanderplatz* the structure of conversion took over where the psychoanalysis-compatible efforts of the eclectic clinicians had to fail. Conversion thus turns on the tension between the group-bound structures of the military and mass-mediatic psyches and the couplified bonds of analytic therapy. Thus *Hamlet* advertises a kind of family or systems therapy that treats the family unit where it breeds: at the heart of our ongoing technologization and group psychologization. Within the history of psychodynamic therapy, Döblin thus represents another moment of conversion—from the control-released transference within the couplified relations of analysis to the ex-static feedback and reenergizing modalities of group and family systems therapies.

During World War I time, in no time, Döblin wrote *Wallenstein,* a Thirty Years' War epic that's open to all the externals of violence in the trauma zone. Then, in *Berlin Alexanderplatz,* at a major remove of displacement, off with distant reference to the outbreak that desertion represents, the internalizations go down for Weimar. But by the second count, Döblin was writing (in flight from Nazi Germany) another somewhat more real-time epic portion all about the German revolution at the end of World War I. *November 1918* packs inside, in the volume turned up on "Return of the Front Line Troops," an accounting of war neurotics (Maus and Becker are their names) whose visitations by hallucination (in Maus's case) go back to the start of the war, the primal scene of mobilization, but started their repeating now, for the peace. It's like the laugh track that, over time, plays back a dead live audience: Maus knows that all those young men he still sees animated by mobilization, still passing across the city square (upstaged on one side by the movie theater), are dead but back (78). The hallucinated total recall of the opening mobilization was already such a shoot: the pictures Maus sees mutate from photography into the movies. His will to view mastery extends to outer space, and he himself, body and psyche, starts running on empty, like a machine.

> These pictures are first gray and motionless like photographs. Then they get set into motion. And it's as though it were just starting, and is always the same. (37)

> "It's as though a telescope had been pushed in front of me.... The telescope is out of focus. I have turned the knob in order to see the star. But I can't find it. I work the knob and start shaking." (79)

> A sudden downpour of thoughtlessness. Thus he could make his way home, empty, like a machine. (176)

Maus and Becker are helped out through conversion experiences. But their politics are what get awarded the actual diagnosis: "Like the war neurotic always running in spirit to his burial by shell blast and keeps dreaming it up in order to free himself from it, just as he is always again constructing his misfortune, in order to get over it this time, that's how Maus was driven toward Becker" (394).

But by now we can take another direct hit: Döblin's science fiction epic, written right after the war, *Mountains, Oceans, and Giants.* The author's investment carried over to 1932, when he rereleased a much abridged version entitled *Giants: A Book of Adventure.* The 1932 version has a preface for greater access: the book's about the machine that was caged up but then burst out and started being all it could be. And that's the future history now, centuries of it. As far as Döblin can tell, already in 1924, this future is taken out by women who take control worldwide by controlling the distribution of births. "They were well aware what disadvantages their sex suffered on account of pregnancy, birth, nursing. It proved necessary to limit the damage as much as possible, and to make women's reproductive capacity out of a weakness into the strong point" (66). "Giving birth to children was the most terrible weapon aimed at men. Women could be raped but not forced to carry a fetus to term" (67). It used to be that war kept itself and us too going. "Now one could keep mankind moving only through brand new inventions, which brought about the collapse of old industries, and the construction of new ones" (20). The female "organizers" were the techno-avant-gardists of the new machine age that opened up over time a trust in the superiority of their "race" (35). Citizens of the future "surgically" slash the wavelengths on flying machines that "suck" for their power (14). But basically machines are there to observe and record on location, real-time archival and PR powerful (73). These machines advertise what the locals do, what they told each other, how they've changed their dwellings, and, you know, what's happening. Tele-images carry the video portion of the local broadcasts far and wide (20). But corporeal life must be technologized and recycled, too. An inventor in Scotland (land of the phantoms) comes up with an artificial one-size-feeds-all meal named, after him, "Meki meat." In the third or fourth generation of artificial-meat eaters, a male leader emerges who marries a young man, not because either one comes and goes by inversion but because their union would be nonreproductive (125). The reproductive and evolutionary meat of humanity is also worked on in enormous secret laboratories. A welfare state emerges around the artificial food, in which, however, mirror-disguised agents seize citizens invisibly and without further issue, death, or corpse and make them the subjects of the labs (40).

In the centuries of time Döblin gives himself, future rebellions are waged against the machine, originally striking from the periphery right at the machine centers (55). At one point it's the leader who decides to destroy the machinery (it's like the scene in *Metropolis*): "There followed a stunning demolition of the central power stations that had always been so protected, held sacred, and which broke the heart of the city and profoundly shook up millions of citizens, the senate and the people" (108).

A new era of things to do to keep going commences with the big idea to deice Greenland. The result is the release of prehistoric creatures (prehistoric even in our sense) that spray a poison that promotes monstrous overgrowth on contact. Part objects grow way bigger than the whole person. Now there are breast men and legs men in abundance. One individual survives the contact with dead growth by cutting off his arm. He said, about the first contact, that it was the way a woman must feel when she gives birth (412). But then he decided to cut it out. But the experience has changed his blood. The inoculative first defense his survival represents is applied toward creation of monstrous "living towers," large-scale hybrids, also known as "giants," that can stand up against the deiced dragons.

The cities now grow inward like mines (423). The dead are cast up and out, thousands fine for littering the outer rim. Whereas the senate had for centuries made recourse to kidnapping to secure subjects for the artificial food factories and for lab experimentation, now people sell themselves out to the test drive. The fad compares only to the suicide craze that came and went before (431). Through the return of prehistory, the inoculative accident of survival that gave men the secret of "living tower" construction, and through a frenzy of experimentation in the labs, the oldest problem gets solved: now we can breed across animal species. A final female warrior has been transformed into something like a bat (a bird? a plane?) that has the same killer spittle that the Greenland monsters introduced. She bombs London with her saliva salvos, and the city bursts apart at the teeming body parts that turn what lies below her flight into a city of flesh. "That tastes better than Meki" (477). We like to see you smile.

Hunger

An example of such a sequence of events was provided by a
sergeant, an active homosexual, who had been an excellent
fighting soldier. His close comrade and passive partner, a
bisexual, broke their relationship and married; this occasioned
violent quarrels which had no effect but to make the active
invert increasingly unstable and angry. Gradually he grew to
notice that more and more of his men and even strangers in
streets and vehicles were smiling at him in a malicious fashion;
soon he saw a black devil sitting at the foot of his bed every
evening, and finally he passed into a fully-fledged psychosis;
then he was fairly happy for a blue man shared his bed nightly.

—CHARLES ANDERSON, "ON CERTAIN CONSCIOUS AND UNCONSCIOUS
HOMOSEXUAL RESPONSES TO WARFARE"

It's 1932, and Aldous Huxley conveyor-belts us with the future now: reproduction has been replaced by mass production or "hatching" (a term that,
bombs away, is also Margaret Mahler syntonic), child rearing by conditioning (which begins its determinations already in the prehatched phase of development), and "God" by "Ford." Reproduction as an individual's birthright occupies, for the time being, only a disembodied "margin of safety":
while very few fertile ovaries are needed for downing-the-hatching of new
generations, still many more are maintained for safety and for "good
choice" (8). Where there's selection there has to be the insurance coverage
of reserve supplies. Once one model works, the replicational center sticks
with it. The future coming soon is thus being colonized by litters of twins
produced according to the "Bokanovsky Process." Happiness, forget the
right to pursue it, is enforced through likability: "That is the secret of happiness and virtue—liking what you've got to do. All conditioning aims at
that: making people like their unescapable social destiny" (Huxley, 11).

The wild boy, John, who, by accident, was raised by savages on the
reservation that makes it into the future of tourism as theme park, becomes
the last standup crank of resistance (which makes him a major tourist attraction by the end of the book). Before the tour has made the round-trip, the
entry of reading opens up around resistance to the new order. The two resisters, although by birthright part of the in-group, occupy the margin of
the outside: one, Bernard, because he's ugly looking by local Aryan stan-

dards, the other, Helmholtz, because he's too smart and, like wild John, too aware of the "X-ray" power of words (53).

Bernard's boss once visited the savage reservation on a week ending with one missing person, and one traumatized survivor: "'You must have had a terrible shock,' said Bernard, almost enviously" (75). Guided by the other's seeing-eye shock, on his tour of the reservation, Bernard finds the missing woman and the director's accidental son, John. Bernard's reintroduction of Savage John into society makes him the celeb host of a traveling show. In *Brave New World* the sight-seeing tours taken by the order of capitalization on the other's trauma begin and end with the x-ray vision of words internal to the novel's own shock talk. John found among the reservations' artifacts of life copies of Shakespeare, in whose words he recognizes his own Oedipal drama. Words gave him pain, a complex, and a voice to talk its cure. But high or low, the art of language turns on "overcompensations for misery" (170). The happy faces of the future litters of Bokanovsky replicants shine on "the foundation on which everything else is built. They're the gyroscope that stabilizes the rocket plane of state on its unswerving course" (170). This world of mass production, behaviorist conditioning, and feedback may keep on rolling along predictable lines—but only on one condition.

> Our Ford—or Our Freud, as, for some inscrutable reason, he chose to call himself whenever he spoke of psychological matters—Our Freud had been the first to reveal the appalling dangers of family life. (28)

Where mass reproduction switches to the replication and genetic engineering channel, that's where Ford must be transformed into Freud, science fiction into psy fi, and the institutions of resistance (behaviorism and sociology) into the peripheral vision of one greater psychoanalysis. But the family is thus singled out as the last understanding of the future, even one of thought without body, in this Nazi psychoanalytic setting, which includes sexual (or self) difference.

Katherine Burdekin's 1937 *Swastika Night* relocates the lines of opposition drawn into World War II within an unconscious gender escape. Her new world, the result of Nazi victories without end, is completely homoerotic and misogynist up to a point: heterosexual reproduction is still a requirement of the state, which does not give its status of approval to family packaging of the breeding assignment. God's Only Son Hitler wasn't born of woman (sound familiar?), but not even of virgin; he just "exploded" onto the scene (5).

Two "unconscious" developments of resistance are, one, Nazi Hermann's delay in developing a "normal attitude towards women," an arrest that cannot but end in arrest, and, two, the shutdown of women's reproduction of girl babies (11). This refusal to reproduce themselves fulfills the curse of heterosexuality: one man's narcissism is another woman's self-effacement and submission. Back in the prehistory of the "Reduction of Women," modern women struggled for equality only, which was just the final twist-off cap on top of centuries of blind submission to the self-love of men. Not equality but superiority, feminism, is the only match for what has forever not needed to speak its name: menism. Women "are not *themselves.* Nothing can be, unless it knows it is superior to everything else" (107).

A Nazi German family has passed down a secret chronicle containing all that one man back then could remember of all the verbal and historical artifacts that were just then being annihilated. It took this last author in history two years to complete this work of recollection or commemoration. The last of this line, an old knight who lost all three sons in one plane crash, skips generation when he entrusts the legacy to an Englishman, Alfred, who in turn support-groups around this mission with his son Fred and Hermann the German. The three resisters become a people of the book (plus one photo of Hitler the man together with a prehistorical woman, a human) who are forced by yet another mourning occasion to hand over their mission to the state-tolerated Christian underground of family values. In the future that belongs to the resistance (never forget which side won the war), Alfred distrusts and envies his homosexual son ("whole-time homosexuality for Englishmen" was not prohibited in the future) while feeling himself restored by the other, worthy son, Fred, a chip off the old block of *his* self-love.

The symbols and idols that fly in a world of Nazi victory (and crash on the downbeat of mourning) are on the same plane:

> The Holy City, where the Sacred Hangar was, and in it the Sacred Aeroplane towards which all the Swastika churches in Hitlerdom were oriented, so that the Hitler arm was in the direct line with the Aeroplane in Munich, even though thousands of miles lay between the Little Model in the Hitler chapel and the Thing Itself. (6)

It is in an abandoned air-raid shelter, the last-stand crypt of Alfred's resistance, that the threesome builds a second line of defense based on the local legend that the place is haunted: it's a puppet string of zombie apparitions pieced together from the uniformed leftovers of long-dead unburied soldiers.

Scrambling for a reception of the ancient and alien NO SMOKING sign, a name is awarded the ghostly ruler of the bunker (or a ghost is projected to match an untranslatable sign, which always counts as name): King Nosmo (143).

Anthony Burgess's *The Wanting Seed* reports on the psy fi fantasies and headlines of a more recent era: it's the future of "baby boom" and "population bomb" that gets served up on the cold war platter. Again the novel's future setting projects all-out promotionals for homosex as the best replicational sex around. Only a castrato has an outside chance in a world of homosexual competition (28).

> That sort of thing was now encouraged—anything to divert sex from its natural end—and all over the country blared posters put out by the Ministry of Infertility, showing, in ironical nursery colors, an embracing pair of one sex or the other with the legend It's Sapiens to be Homo. The Homosex Institute even ran night-classes. (8)

The narrative of natural ends is colored by Beatrice-Joanna's thoughts (which are the same heir color as Burgess's identification). She has lost her baby boy and is now doing what comes next to natural: she picks up the redemption value everyone gets for the state's use of the dead as fertilizer. Dead or alive, no more than one child is the law. But Beatrice-Joanna is totally into reproductive sex; her instinctual resistance to the steady state (besides her homophobia) is the transgressive desire she nourishes (even as she goes to get her deposit back) for more offspring. The world she lives in no longer organizes itself according to ethnic or racial divisions (war has been outlawed together with the bloodlines of opposition). But if one of the language groups has you tagged, you're in it. Her parting thought smells the blood that will not be ignored:

> Was it, she thought in an instant almost of prophetic power, to be left to her and the few indisputable Anglo-Saxons like her to restore sanity and dignity to the mongrel world? Her race, she seemed to remember, had done it before. (16)

In no time she oversteps her language boundary into the space of race: "The foreign word Urmutter swam up from her unconscious" (36). It's another "race memory" that announces, with Jungian labels showing, the new phase or fashionism coming soon (47).

At any given time, the world is only going through a phase. In the giveaway abbreviation style of the Teen Age, phrases that were Pelagian, Intermediate, and Augustinian are now and forever Pelphase, Interphase,

Gusphase (16). The Pelphase is where we are when the novel begins: it's where the belief in man's perfectibility meets the state's controlling interest. It's always during a mood swing of "disappointment," however, that one phase, say this phase of idealization, collapses onto the Interphase of opposition. What comes between whole phases or objects, a kind of inter-fear, arises with the brutalizing recognition (which hits the authorities first) that man is innately incapable of being good. The shock of violence that follows this recognition must be absorbed in turn by the Gusphase, another phase of stability, brought to us this time around by philosophical pessimism and capitalism. When man turns out not to be as bad as all that, the Pelphase returns, and so on.

With the fall of the Pelphase, which had been "near-vegetarian" and "non-smoking" (33), the repressed isn't near or far; it's just back. When some Christian kid recites for parental approval the meaning of the Savior, he gets stuck on the Son of God's meal service. When the father tries to put his son back on the symbolic track, he finds that he's always the last to know when the rest of the world has gone cannibalistic on him:

> "When He comes again, . . . will he be eaten properly?"
> "What, now, . . . would you be meaning by that strange statement?"
> "Eaten, . . . like Jim Whittle was eaten. . . . Will it be like that Dad?" (98)

With meat eating, close to bone and home, breeding is back, too (for some reason, the "queers," who formerly were in power and uniform, boil up especially nice). War, too, has to make a comeback.

But in a cannibalistic system, war serves the means (and men) of violence control. It's staged with sound and light show effects like in amusement parks and video arcades where, as in the World War II therapeutic settings of inoculation against or desensitization of war shock, a protected reception of catastrophe preparedness is repeated or rehearsed. The difference here is that everyone gets killed (and recycled in cans of cured meat). It's all simulated, *and* it's a live feed. All that's controlled is the amount of mouths to feed and meat supplies to feed them. The military undertaking, on second thought, goes ahead and slaps the grid of selection over the population at large:

> Contraception is cruel and unnatural: everybody has a right to be born. But, similarly, everybody's got to die sooner or later. Our age-groups for call-up will get progressively older—as far, of course, as the healthy and mentally normal sections of the

population are concerned; the trash can go shortly after puberty.
Everybody must die, and history seems to show . . . that the soldier's death is the best death. . . . The War Department is a bit like
prostitution: it cleanses the community. If we didn't exist, a great
deal of nastiness would bubble up in the State. We're the mother-
of-pearl, you see. The ruffians, the perverts, the death-wishers:
you don't want those in the civil community. . . . The final problems of the body politic have been solved. Now we have a free
state—order without organization, which means order without
violence. A safe and spacious community. A clean house full of
happy people. But every house, of course, has to have a drainage
system. We're that. (217–18)

Total or techno- or psychological warfare proved it could recycle the broken-
down civilian psyche as efficient soldierhood. Now (or in the future) the
psycho-pain of war takes a shortcut through the culture or canning industry
of enterdrainment. This forecast presupposes, however, that Everyman in
the future will be neurotic to normal.

At any given time, in one particular state, or sentence by sentence, the
body before us must work out in history, in a metabolism that can only be
externalized over the time it takes to stick to a schedule. The concept that
separates the before and after pictures of this digestive process is "sublimation." Beatrice-Joanna, back in the Pelphase, while contemplating a hit
song about the adorable one being "my meat," mentions it first in those
thoughts of hers that are always nearly the author's: "That, she supposed,
was what was meant by the term sublimation" (70). And when the urge to
eat the one you're with in fact takes control, the Christian Church is brought
back to work its double-crossing of the trans-:

The leaders of the State are suffering from an accession of superstitious fear, that's what it is. They've done no good with their
police, so now it's the priests they call on. There aren't any
churches now, so we have to go up and down our allotted areas,
feeding them all God instead of the law. Oh, it's all very clever. I
suppose sublimation is the big word: don't eat your neighbor,
eat God instead. (112–13)

At this gut level, the hunger that belongs to the future comeback of reproduction turns on identification (and sublimation), not desire. The
hunger, which is sexual but also more than sex, "wants" the meat, not the
man, wants it not the seed. The metahistory of phases runs its commentary
through the tensions going down between replication and reproduction

and out with the externalization of the metabolism that one damaged psyche must build as its own splitting image or apparatus. The damage was done when the mother just couldn't mourn her dead child. Call it the fantasy state of recycling, call it just a phase mankind goes through, it still comes down to the mother, grief stuck, her metabolism opening wide, doubled over (Beatrice-Joanna gives birth to twins, who represent double-or-no replacement at all) with the hunger of wanting it, not the seed, the dead, not the substitute. But underlying the symptomatic phases a perpetual teen keeps going through, we can still discern, by the light of mourning or unmourning, the family as introject and thus as secret or silent partner backing and back with the good future.

Exile on War Neurosis

In some cases, just as the dreams woke the patients, so did
certain patients have to leave the group of patients who were
retelling their combat experiences or leave motion pictures that
showed bombing and shelling. . . . An example of this occurred
when "Mrs. Miniver" was shown near the hospital. Most of the
neuropsychiatric patients had to leave when the "blitz" in the
picture began, and most of them required extra sedation that
night.

—J. L. HENDERSON AND MERRILL MOORE,
"THE PSYCHONEUROSES OF WAR"

Franz Werfel, a conversion groupie like Döblin, but from south of the border,
from Austria, captured his own Californian exile from Nazi Europe in a
science fiction, *Star of the Unborn*. It's all about a certain F. W., who dies
while an exile from Central Europe, is buried in California, is beamed back
up into life (in the future) by his old buddy B. H. (who is on another reincar-
nation), and on the subsequent days tours the California of the future. In
California, gadget rules: a device brings the destination to you on its beam;
no more shell-shocking transport in planes, F. W. reflects with some relief.
But right after F. W. has been introduced by B. H. to the science fiction conditions of his being (dead, summoned, invisible) in California, the newly arrived ghost or alien takes a closer look at his host and recognizes the model
for the synthetic, simulated outfit he is wearing: the same old uniform they
both wore while comrades in arms during World War I (21).

In *L.A. Story* the joke is on the conveyer belt of citation and proper burial that seems to run England right through Southern California. The sub-
text, *Hamlet*, organizes haunting words from the sponsor beaming up on
the digital billboards that go with the traffic flow, the ghost appearance of
Shakespeare's grave in Hollywood, and every auditory hallucination of
that accent, accident of birth, the one that shakes peerage and privilege at
American ears. But the movie gets blocked and displaced around the one
subterranean event that stays there with enigmatic force. We see at the
other end of a line that will never be crossed the Nazi German control center
taking all calls for the restaurant that's so in, an insider's trip, that reservations must be held, on hold, made in advance. The field of calls placed in
installments of unmourning takes down a mega-supply of reservations, reserves, and holds it there: in store for the former, lost wars. No England-to-

California connection without the phantom presence of Nazi Germany down in the displacement center of all bicoastal transfers.

So it is *Hamlet,* the name brand of haunting that Alfred Döblin cosigned with the subtitle *Or the Long Night Comes to an End,* that can fill the bill of Shakespeare's California. In 1945 Döblin commenced his final work while still in Hollywood exile and then concluded it back in Germany the next year. But where was there any return to Germany, except at the one remove or removal of projective displacement, the big one that kept Döblin's transfer attempts still in range of Californian exile? It was ten more years before he could ride in the break of his return by going public, published on the eastern front of another return: Germany, doubled and contained, at a loss for wars. In 1956: first Döblin gets the German repress release. Then he dies.

But along the way, he had to drop from the novel he advertised as "psychoanalytic" the ending that got the protagonist to the monastery and exchange it, in final analysis, for the author's new closure: the bus ride that can now be taken, at the conclusion of the long night, without the transference that finally did get off at this stop. "And thus they drove off into the teeming, noisy city. A new life began." The La Brea bus route circles without end through the fable of how father arrives via amnesia at the pseudonym and imposture of his authorship. At the back of the bus ride that gets or forgets father to make a name for himself there's Edward's first place of treatment in Los Angeles following the war wounding that cut off his leg and, by cutting down the dotted line all the way to earliest relations with the parents, handed him over to psychiatric treatment for war neurosis. For father's birthday, Edward later stages the L.A. story of what's in a name in one acting out that both does the father in by declaring him to be history and, by adding a comedic lube job, aids their identification. It's one of the turning points in a self-analysis the son must undergo beyond his individual treatment for shell shock, now within the group therapy setting of narrative exchange that follows the father's standard, now within the family therapy setting of biographical explosions that mother gets started.

In *Berlin Alexanderplatz* and then again at the other bookend of this is his life, Döblin transferred case work from his other career right to the art of his writing. In his 1929 work, the corridor war replays or plays on between a younger psychoanalysis-influenced but eclectic group of psychiatrists and an older generation that still counts its malingerers before they are patched up with diagnosis of functional or psychogenic disorder. On each side of the generation gap, a different shock of recognition receives the news of psychoanalytic victories. Someone close to Döblin runs the commentary:

New neuropsychiatric soldier-patients at the Eighty-second Field Hospital, Okinawa, at an introductory lecture on 19 May 1945. Reproduced from U.S. Army, *Neuropsychiatry in World War II*, vol. 2, *Overseas Theaters* (Washington, D.C.: Office of the Surgeon General, 1973), 647.

> The younger gentlemen have a special understanding of this con-
> dition: they are tempted to see Franz Biberkopf's affliction as psy-
> chogenic, in other words his paralysis comes from the psyche, it
> is a pathological condition of inhibitions that an analysis would
> be able to clear up, perhaps as regression to the most ancient
> psychic stages, if only—the great big If, the very unfortunate If,
> too bad, this If is really quite disturbing—if only Franz Biberkopf
> would speak and would join them at the consulting table to work
> out with them the liquidation of his conflict. (469)

The newer generation, which also waves through electro-treatment as a possible admixture of prep work for getting the patient to open wide and say it all, still comparison shops the therapeutic approaches that the mass culture of war neurosis first summoned in the new order of their lasting importance.

Although only two in number, explicit references in *Berlin Alexander-platz* to World War I shell shock conditions grow the mold for the novel's displacements of origin and outcome of its story of the protagonist's nervous breakdowns. What may shock Biberkopf is the senior psychiatrist's recall of the pioneer days of treating unhappy troopers to war neurosis—"One knows about high voltage treatment from the war, dear God. It's not permitted, modern torture" (470)—against the backdrop that backs off and falls away with Biberkopf's mention in passing of his own desertion at the Western Front.

Later in Hollywood, Döblin's crossovers from psychiatry to media either screenplayed at the fundamental remove of projection or took novel form in *November 1918: A German Revolution* and again in *Hamlet, or The Long Night Comes to an End*. These mediated case studies from the World War II years reflect or flex a psychiatric assessment that keeps within the hearsay or know-how of an analytic understanding that's always eclectically framed, as already in *Berlin Alexanderplatz*, by direct exposure to the internalization or technologization of trauma going down and out in war neurosis. Working or walking papers issued in Hollywood that gave super saving to the artists and thinkers tagged for extinction back in Germany also lined up Döblin's work as consultant on two major movies, *Mrs. Miniver* and *Random Harvest*.

For *Mrs. Miniver*, Döblin was all set to put the panic back into scenes around the evacuation of Dunkirk. But the first film effort he joined as team player gave the connection between the lines of its propaganda projections and the roses that all identify with, the year's new roses that spell or spill neurosis: "There'll always be roses. It's like no more England." The winner against all odds of the annual rose competition gets blasted in the German air raid that follows close on his acceptance of the award; the new wife, who like the winner of the rose contest skipped classes to prove the democratic way of conferring distinction and breeding rights, gets a mortal hit in the same raid from Germany. This death of the wife, which flies in the face of our nonstop expectation that her flyboy husband will be the one to come and go first, makes another secret deposit to the account that the film's closing projector vault of sky, planes, and hit roof opens wide. Emergency Island's home front has been totaled, and its group psychology, which has risen above class distinctions through the family blending of intermarriage, rises as the match of its total air-war maker.

It was in his capacity as psychiatrist who "was there" back then treating shell-shocked soldiers on the World War I front that Döblin was brought in as the consultant who would know best whatever was possible with the protagonist's projected double bout of amnesia in *Random Harvest*. The plot thickener of amnesia was to be added twice over, with a twist, one by war, the next (in line of displacement) by accident. Döblin cosigned the plot as, divided, it stood, with the protagonist both returning to his pre-war-trauma

Restraint rooms in the neuropsychiatric ward, 251st Station Hospital, Cape Gloucester, New Britain, September 1944. Reproduced from *Neuropsychiatry in World War II*, 2:540.

consciousness and lapsing into a renewal of amnesia that covered this time the two intervening years, in which he had forged ahead a new identity right in the face of forgetting. Döblin's collaboration stopped short, without comment, before the happy ending that kept the story from heading itself off at the impasse. He composed a scene of leave-taking between the double wife and her husband twice removed by the displacement of his amnesia. But the final screen version doesn't get stuck in the groove of the protagonist's war record. Double recall emerges just in time to reintegrate, all together now, the once and future lives of the war neurotic, who recovers himself as happy medium between love and war, transference and trauma.

In the course of this long-term therapy, as in that of the protagonist's treatment in *Hamlet*, the psychiatrist is left handing the individual case over to the self-help regimen going down inside groups, couples, and families. In *Random Harvest* the soldier's accidental release gains the after-the-fact approval of his psychiatrist, who catches up with the patient's new life only to watch over it. He's standing by when the amnesia lifts but shifts its waiting around to remember onto the two- or three-year period of his intervening years of life with the wife, his better half of couplification that the psychiatrist in charge came to cofacilitate as therapeutic. In *Hamlet* the local psychiatrist decides to let his patient go home, which is where the war is. He permits transfer of Edward's shocked state of auto-analysis, the speed race, always and again, between psychotic breakdown and auto-analytic breakthrough, to a family setting of therapy.

On the Second Date

But if you think you'll be able to get out of regular duty by
pretending to be sick, you're mistaken. The sergeants are wise
to every dodge of that nature which the mind of man has been
able to invent through centuries. In fact, if you report sick,
you'll march to the hospital after the call, "Sick, Lame and Lazy,
Outside!" That "lazy" shows you that the Army has the idea
about phony illnesses well up in the front of its mind. And the
Army slang for pretending to be sick is, "Riding the Sick Book."

—PHILIP WYLIE AND WILLIAM MUIR, *THE ARMY WAY*

So, to make him a trustworthy tool of abnormal courage, there
is drill and discipline. That he will not falter like any coward in
the presence of crisis, he is instructed and admonished, paraded
and ordered, taught automatonism—and in such a fashion he
overcomes futurities in his ego: images in time-ahead, imagination itself. Positive imagination would be useful to him in battle,
but, to own it, he must risk its opposite: negative imagining, or
fear. . . . The man in the field . . . must have the future-sense
stamped out of him, or else he will use battle time to think, to
imagine, to dread.

—PHILIP WYLIE, *AN ESSAY ON MORALS*

That a couple of authors wrote *When Worlds Collide* already starts rolling
with the plotline. Two parallel worlds are swinging low; first they'll swing
by so close that little or few will be saved, then, on their second time around,
one comes to knock out planet earth, the other to fly by so that a superselect
few can hop on board in their spaceship. The new world was a planet like
ours that was extinguished not with a bang but with the winter that comes
without a sun. Now that the eccentric course that put it under ice is swinging into orbit around this sun, the conditions for the new life of humanity
will thaw out. (The novel never goes into what about the pileup of corpses
that were also in cryogenic freeze before contact with our sun.)

The leading scientists of the world and other select types have calculated
that two years remain before the world begins ending. The all-American
couple on center stage was on the verge of forsaking all others when the
crisis hit. But now that they look forward to being part of thirty or so survivors of the species in two years time on the other planet, couplification is
no longer an option, because it's not the best value you get for furthering

life, the species, up at their new starting point. Eve lets Tony down off the vow easy. Who will they be up there in the future?

> Individuals paired and set off, each from the others, as here? No; we become bits of biology, bearing within us seeds far more important than our prejudices and loves and hates. We cannot then think of ourselves, only to preserve ourselves while we establish our kind. (Balmer and Wylie, 75)

Tony's projected rival for time-shares of Eve in the bio group where they'd all be coming soon is pilot Randell. Love affairs are already what's happening in camp, as is to be expected when the "flower of young womanhood" and "the best men of all ages" keep meeting like this, "segregated in the wilderness" (253). But after Tony and Randell see action side by side against mob attack (Tony sees Randell three-quarters naked in the close combat), the two former rivals become "blood brothers" (253). Soon Tony assures Eve that he has overcome his jealousy of Randell (like, now they can both take her, but at once). Once mission's accomplished and life on the new planet can begin, we find out again what all must do not just in the future on some remote planet but in every master bedroom.

> We have arrived, not as triumphant individuals spared for ourselves, but as humble representatives of the result of a billion years of evolution transported to a sphere where we may reproduce and recreate the life given us. (325)

While the select few were learning your basic survival skills and building their spaceship (and discovering in the process the how-to of atomic power), the United States was preparing along more familiar lines for the first pass of near-miss catastrophe.

> The machinery which organized millions of men during the war was still more or less available for this much bigger undertaking, from the standpoint of plans and human cogs. (95)

Those preselected plan on creating one new race out of the many diverse (Caucasian) ethnicities represented in the camp. Because the melting pot (an image from a U.S. World War I propaganda play that made a case for the evolutionary virtues of mixing breeds) would model the metabolism of one race under God, the mottoes of the United States are voted in for reuse in the near future. Following catastrophic first contact, bands of survivors form vigilante armies to fight for the little food to go around. They soon know where the select live. "And there is no hate like that of men who have lost their morale, against those who have retained it" (223).

One of the two authorial bodies, Philip Wylie, was proud of the good prophet he'd make if anyone believed him in the here is how of his own journalism. In *When Worlds Collide* Wylie coauthors what the Germans are up to when in 1932 the Americans mobilize for catastrophe along World War I lines: "Germany went fascist; a few communists were killed; and so were a few Jews" (97). (I've got news for you, Wylie.) The Wylie one would, by 1940, give his war support in a manual of "pointers for new soldiers," entitled *The Army Way*. He knew early on that peace wouldn't be given an outside chance, not without the war from hell, world war too, to lighten the weight and wait of American demoralization. This is one of the many forecasts renewing their vows in 1942 in his *Generation of Vipers*. Another one: on his own person, he realized how necessary it was for all the new or old contexts of total war and the peace to come last to last, that we keep up with the Freudian and Jungian brands of analysis.

Wylie's foremost concern or complex was addressed to an American cult of "megaloid momworship" that has mom's foot not up on a pedestal but on the metal, the pedal, at the wheel of the drive (185). This is where what Wylie calls Freud's reading of mother love as "an incestuous perversion of a normal instinct" fell on the open but shut ears of close, giveaway, literalizing attention and resistance: "Unfortunately, Americans, who are the most prissy people on earth, have been unable to benefit from Freud's wisdom because they can prove that they do not, by and large, sleep with their mother. That is their interpretation of Freud" (185). But this is at least as much a case for Jungian psychohistory. Jung was real popular in America, especially with American women, ever since, already during his first visit to the States, he skirted Freud's sex issues often in widely circulating interviews on the anticultural side effects of the U.S. matriarchy. (He also argued that, dialectically speaking, the African Americans were the ones who were really in control.) According to Wylie's update, the American mom is the war in its entirety:

> But mom never meets competition. Like Hitler, she betrays the people who would give her a battle before she brings up her troops. Her whole personal life, so far as outward expression is concerned, is, in consequence, a mopping-up action. Traitors are shot, yellow stars are slapped on those beneath notice, the good-looking men and boys are rounded up and beaten or sucked into pliability, a new slave population continually goes to work at making more munitions for momism, and mom herself sticks up

her head, or maybe the periscope of the woman next door, to find some new region that needs taking over. This technique pervades all she does. (193–94)

In *When Worlds Collide*, Eve flexes her sense of future power coming to her gender through woman's uncouplified position that will be her displacement onto the new planet. She will steer the breeding assignment (266). But when Wylie turns on his *Vipers* in 1942, all he can see is that the American female already only accessorizes with the American male (205). Back inside his own *Generation*, Wylie self-discloses: "I, who grew up as a 'motherless' minister's son and hence was smothered in multimomism for a decade and a half, had an unusual opportunity to observe the phenomenon at zero range" (191). (What does this zero *feel* like, Wylie? Motherless sounds sad to me.)

This undigested biochip off the old blockage of melancholia runs a course of controlled release or avoidance in *When Worlds Collide*. Tony's mother is an early victim of the mob violence that takes advantage of the end-of-the-world sellout to satisfy all one-stop-shopping needs at the local malling. But there was never any question that she would be left behind by her son. At least he was relieved of having to acknowledge or accept his role of accomplice to her eventual murderous exclusion by his own selection for survival as the fittest. That mob violence will also claim many casualties among the camp inmates is too sad, but not so bad. The core group that survives is as many as can fit into the ship before, as last defense, it turns its liftoff flame power against the mob and completely torches the surrounding area. But the mob's war crime against the world's scientific community diminishes in importance, even or especially as occasion for mourning, compared to what's already upon them and what lies ahead. Like the unhappy event of Tony's mother's murder, this setback makes it so much easier for those who will survive. Selection has been kept natural: the gender ratio is now 50:50, and everyone left over will be able to get on board both ships (at this point, they decide to build a second vessel). First it's easy to let millions of people go, then within the group it's suddenly a rescue mission that can leave no one behind. (Of course one of the two rockets, like one of the two planets—like, weren't the two authors even a little superstitious—will never make it.)

The publication date of 1932 makes *When Worlds Collide* just miss the date of the National Socialist takeover of psychoanalysis by one year. The other near-miss date is that projected for *1984*, one year short of the publication of the first concentration of efforts to give up the ghost of the Nazi era of psychoanalysis to consciousness. All they had was a ghost of a chance. All's well that's Orwell (or, since he gave himself the name, all's H. G. Wells that's Orwell). Nineteen eighty-five saw the survival of the Orwell forecast. But in spite of the concert of excavation efforts, 1985 was just another year in which we could not see the other "1984" reference, the one that's already been or is still with us.

1984 begins (and already plots its end) when Winston puts pen to the paper of a diary or journal (which is, as happy-faced medium of teen interiority, always also a suicide note). Dear diary opens with Winston's recollection of his birth year: 1944 or 1945 (10). The world around him is divided up along the trauma lines of the total air war. What was once Britain is now "Airstrip One." War, which is now eternal or internal, is the arrest of World War II developments that keep on replaying both piecemeal, out of context, as accidents or surprise attacks and, on the whole, as the perpetual loop of psychological warfare.

One act of "thought crime" is all it takes. That's why Winston feels he has already hit bottom when he starts his journal. It's only a matter of time before the state apparatus of therapeutic correction openly treats Winston's resistance. In the meantime we become acquainted with Winston's view of the group-psychological manipulations he can't accept.

Doublethink is the language of fetishistic splitting that by 1984 has been set up society-wide as the standard of all (inner and outer) exchanges.

> To know and not to know . . . to hold simultaneously two opinions which cancelled out, knowing them to be contradictory and believing in both of them. . . .
>
> Even to understand the word "doublethink" involved the use of doublethink. (32–33)

The reductionism of language still under way (it's "shrinking") resonates (negative transferentially) with certain interventions we associate with Freud. Thus antonyms will be removed from the language and replaced by "un-" compounds. One party slogan says it all under the cover of blackout: "Orthodoxy is unconsciousness" (47).

Then there's the wild-analytic bout of his heterosexual resistance to the streamlining of society around doubling and fetishism. It's one of those old left-wing rhymes between copulation between the sexes and antifascist revolution. Reich got with the program (and psychoanalysis drumrolled him out for acting out). Early propaganda tensions between Hitler and Stalin were played out between the former's indifference to sex identity and the latter's outing charge that the Nazi state was homosexual. It was this charge that was largely responsible for Nazi Germany's hard line on homosexuality, a line drawn, however, through the split charge that Nazi therapeutic correctness provided. In other words, the Nazi counterstrategy was to mobilize homoeroticism—while, on double take, prohibiting homosexuality absolutely—as the force that was with their new order. According to the future that *1984* brings, both sides were wrong: desexualization running on a low-maintenance grade of gadget love in a stricken world that stopped with World War II is the forecast.

By the end, the world and words of *1984* are coextensive with the endopsychic space of Winston's introjects. Everything was part of the treatment: the shop where he purchased the diary, the upstairs room with a view to freedom where he made love, the circumstances of his volunteering to serve in the resistance under O'Brien's sponsorship, the handbook by Emanuel Goldstein that Winston receives to read up on the resistance view of the current order. Everywhere in this externalized inner space there are dead-air pockets filled with World War II trauma. Goldstein, the former inner party founder who figures society-wide as the traitor behind it all, as internal and eternal public enemy number one, is a reference not only to Trotsky but to all the names in modern history of the Jewish introject. "Emanuel Goldstein" drops on both sides of the ambivalently held, nearly destroyed Jewish object. The inner party, we read in the manual that Goldstein, the head of the resistance, has authored, keeps its steady-state membership always at six million (122). Goldstein's resistance tract compiles isolated pieces of World War II in the psy fi idiom of psychological warfare manuals.

> Cut off from contact with the outer world, and with the past, the citizen . . . is like a man in inter-stellar space, who has no way of knowing which direction is up and which is down. (164)

> With the development of television, and the technical advance which made it possible to receive and transmit simultaneously on the same instrument, private life came to an end. (169)

> Thus history is continuously rewritten. This day-to-day falsification of the past, carried out by the Ministry of Truth, is as necessary to the stability of the regime as the work of repression and espionage carried out by the Ministry of Love. (176)

This manual or manifesto was in fact written by O'Brien. In O'Brien's treatment of Winston, resistance is recognized early and allowed to develop fully, complete with an owner's manual to the transferential movement, until it has reached the limits of its party line introjection. What can be given or induced can also be taken away, healed. Once the resistance is full-blown, O'Brien knows, like the titular asylum psychiatrist at the end of *The Cabinet of Dr. Caligari,* just how to cure him.

The thought that crossed Winston's mind when he opened his resistance diary was that his addressee was O'Brien, a member of the inner party whose path he on occasion crosses down the corridors. In the place where Winston works on the ongoing updates of official history, O'Brien has shown himself already as transferential object. When O'Brien turns out to be the thought-policeman in charge of Winston's case, the two men can agree that they both already knew it would be like this. P-unitive relations with the ambivalently held father must be reestablished inside Winston.

> "Don't worry, Winston; you are in my keeping. For seven years I have watched over you. Now the turning point has come. I shall save you, I shall make you perfect." (201)

> When he spoke his voice was gentle and patient. He had the air of a doctor, a teacher, even a priest, anxious to explain and persuade rather than to punish. (203)

The world of *1984* is not patriarchal; society is ruled by an adoptive organization of "brothers," not by "father-to-son inheritance" (173). The hierarchy O'Brien establishes throughout Winston's treatment uses the father transference for therapeutic purposes only. (Freud too saw "the father" more as therapeutic fiction than as reflection of, or adaptation to, any functional patriarchy out there.) *1984* is one very complete portrait of Nazi psychoanalysis, one that gets its edge of negative transference not so much from the Nazi part as from the main body, the psychoanalysis part.

Manuals

Even though the Germans were more skillful in the marshalling
of weapons and in the purely military side of the struggle, it
availed them little, since their opponents, although blundering
a great deal militarily, employed all devices, especially the
psychological ones, much more effectively.

—JAMES D. ATKINSON, *THE EDGE OF WAR*

Resistance to the psychoanalytic *Roman,* or romance, in technology studies
invests the same contexts of upward mobilization we too have been considering, in which all modernist trends are resituated in relation to their very
own military complexes, but as final reckoning of Freud's science as precisely lost or loser in this reshuffling of contexts or histories. The strategy of
these readings is to go historic or genealogical, but only up to the point of
their up-front phobia about inhabiting the frame of psychoanalysis. The resulting split-level, two-step, reproach styles with gadget-loving acknowledgment of the history of technology while remaining deep down the same old
refraining from any inside viewing of technologization or group psychologization. Even positivism can run under the cover of new-and-improved
brands of cultural studies that try to get psychoanalysis as historicizably
just another turn of resistance to the running continuity of machine history.

The span of this critical attention places these tracts, suggestively or di-
gestively, right up against the 1985 official return of international psychoanalysis to Germany, back for the first time since the Nazi takeover. But it
was also psychoanalysis's date to remember that its self-image as mutually
exclusive with regard to the totalitarian regiment of healing was only manifest fantasy. Nazi research happiness for its part object, part objective mobilized whatever worked for its working part in the total war effort. While
this research agenda found no use for social studies other than as labeling
in propaganda about-facing the other, the use value of psychoanalysis was
a given ever since the success story of Freud's engagement with war neurosis left only psychoanalysis winning the Great War, ultimately a corridor
war between different approaches to psychological interventionism. It was
a victory flashed throughout the peace that everyone was out to win and
by 1941 was won again on all sides of the Second Coming of world war.
This is the other story that the ideologues cited or ticketed earlier have
been near-missing while retelling the opportunism that they do not see is
their own as once upon a time of complicity with terror.

In a 1944 overview of renewed interrelations among psychiatry, psycho-analysis, and the military entitled "Psychiatry and the Army," William Menninger remembers World War I as the first lowering of the boom economy onto psychiatry.

> Until 1917, the practice of psychiatry had occupied a relatively inconspicuous "back room" in the field of medicine. In part, because of the acute need, and in part, because of the brilliant work performed by military psychiatrists at that time, psychiatry, rather suddenly, came into limelight and took a place among its sister specialities of medicine and surgery. The impetus from the present war to the growth and the recognition and the unlimited opportunities of psychiatry will be far greater than that which occurred in 1917 and 1918. (175)

On another downswing, but with tact, Menninger admits that the search for self-help that's along for the choice of psychiatry as one's profession comes on particularly strong in the analytic field. Menninger is exhorting his analytic colleagues to drop their jargonic isolationism and join the group of fellow psychiatrists and physicians whose receptions of psychoanalysis every analyst must watch out for: "One unfortunate immunization makes them impervious to all subsequent attempts at inoculation" (176). Even if the treatment time of analysis remains out of range of the real time or wartime of getting results, still the understanding of psychoanalysis remains universally applicable. Psychiatry has taken the new inroads within the military hierarchy from 1942 onward. But the most recent victory bulletin at the tail end or summa of this rise of a controlling interest that's mutual to be sure between psychiatry and the military, the 1944 release of the latest manual on mental hygiene to all officers, both medical and down the line, owes the direction of its treatment more specifically or explicitly to the "dynamic orientation" (177).

What Menninger on his diplomatic omission gets us to read between or behind the lines is that whatever can be said about the profession at large goes double for the growth of psychoanalysis. With pride of admission, Menninger goes ahead and singles out the psychoanalytically trained psychiatrists active in the service. Two have made it to the top: John M. Murray, chief psychiatrist of the air force, and Roy R. Grinker, in charge of one of the most important treatment centers in the air force (175–76).

Same journal, same volume and year, Murray reports on "Psychiatric Aspects of Aviation Medicine." American know-how had caught up with the Nazi psychological reading lists that the Allied military psychologists

War-neurotic soldier exhibiting fear. He keeps on saying, "Them kamikazes, them bombs."
Reproduced from *Neuropsychiatry in World War II*, 2:661.

back in 1941 could only compile and circulate at the start of playing catch-up with the Nazis. The "feel for flying," for example, that German military psychology had developed by the late thirties into the Nazi state of preparedness along intrapsychic lines at first threw the Allies for a loop until the specialists could throw their own waiting around and take the new emerging state of in-flight techno-merger to the scholarly headlines. Roy Grinker coauthored the earlier U.S. study of flight conditionings that started from the grounded on up but never really made it to automatic pilot. It's Murray alone, according to the contrast he dials up with Grinker, who follows up on the German lead taken by Paul Metz, the flying ace in the whole international roster of the new psychological study of machines, whose work had been given the highlight in the 1941 how-to manual *German Psychological Warfare*. By 1944 Murray can give the facts of half-life in flying, which come down to an unnatural state: "Combat flying is hazardous for all members of the crew. It occasions an almost constant state of tension and preparedness for impending danger" (5). The new pilot series was transforming the split ends that psychoanalysis first found all broken up among the war neurotic's narcissistic supplies into splits truly becoming a cyborgian air head. Trauma conditioning keeps the pilot on automatic; but then, once the same straining program gets the better of his half-life, it drops him from the techno-connection into the flyer neurosis.

> This condition in flying personnel is essentially the result of an abnormal strain being placed on a normal person and arises chiefly as a result of the continuous and long continued repression and suppression of the normal fear reactions present in all types of operational flying. As previously noted in a certain number of flyers, sooner or later, the ability to master this conflict fails and the person breaks out into acute anxiety or symptom formation. (5)

The *Connecticut State Medical Journal* in March 1943 covered "Health Improvement in Design of American Planes." A certain Walter Miles, professor of psychology at Yale University, is quoted on two counts:

> Both seeing and hearing, if accompanied by prolonged attentive effort, especially under conditions of unfavorable plane design, are capable of contributing to pilot and air crew fatigue and loss of efficiency.

> It seems to be true of modern aviation that every time the engineers increase the power and speed of our airplanes, the ears of the pilots take a greater beating. ("Health Improvement," 197)

The article lets airsickness out of the bag as a condition also up for investigation. If you can see where you're going, like the horizon or the ground below, it's not so bad: blind flying is the worst.

At this stage the flight surgeon, one along for every ride, can intervene to keep the pilot up and running. "This is where the Flight Surgeon has his opportunity for service. Through his knowledge and capacity for stimulating trust and confidence, or that phenomenon known technically as transference, the Flight Surgeon can provide much of the necessary strength for restoration" (Murray, 6). The leader-and-the-pack psychology of these surgical interventions pulls up short before a complete breakdown, at which point, as last roundup or line of defense against its centerfold-out spread to the rest of the group, the program must change back to isolation within a longer-term, one-on-one concentration on the transference.

> Once the tolerance of the person has been broken, such simple procedures as these are useless. The man has now entered into a phase of neurosis which is not reversible except by appropriate specialized therapeutic measures which really work out the solutions of his deeper anxious tensions and restore his ego capacity

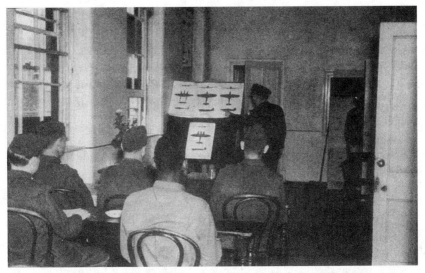

Neuropsychiatric soldier-patients receive training in the subject of air warfare at the Thirty-sixth Station Hospital, Exeter, England, in 1943. Reproduced from *Neuropsychiatry in World War II*, 2:200.

to tolerate these. This man should be removed from the group. He is an infectious focus for lowering morale and precipitating unhappy reactions in others. (6–7)

The wide-open spacing of eclectic opportunism—between the individual or the couple and the group or family pack—throughout the research laboratory of total war represents a final markdown in the sellout of Freud's influence. But even though peacetime, piecemeal analysis identifies with a staying power to change that leaves out all the prosthetic shortcuts that for the time being do get around jump cuts of separation and loss, during World War I psychoanalysis opened up its own eclecticized concession for the treatment of the epidemic portions of war neurosis. In his 1949 review of the war years of eclectic analytic therapy, J. G. Watkins sets up psychoanalysis as the model that "did develop the basic ideas on which modern psychiatric treatment rests" (15). But the timer had to be reset to afford quicker therapy for more reasonable success rates. Watkins spots for the war egos that are doing sets of building, lifting, waiting around, and, in shorts, putting through the direct techno-connection. Bottom line is the firing line: "Predisposition cocks the mechanism and stress pulls the trigger" (16). The intake and exchange of Pentothal treatment, "called 'walkie-talkie' by the soldiers" (9), join the crowding in the inroads to the unconscious that must be blazed with such items from the military instrumentarium as "certain submarine methods, certain diving-bell techniques by which we can penetrate a little further down into the unconscious personality" (14). The soldier who acknowledges that he's neurotic gets "some insurance against recurrence of the symptoms" (37). But the talking cure exceeds the insurance policy and war economy of analogy that make the difference between us and them. The U.S. soldier breaks through the "first line" that techno-analogy gives the therapeutic process by fessing up to neurosis (23), "while the helpless patient, like the slave laborer in Nazi Germany, must say and do that which continues his own enslavement" (24).

Already in 1942 Lawrence S. Kubie could outline a reorganization of the growing psychiatric service that no longer had to exclude the implications of or for psychoanalysis but only water them down for easier following and swallowing:

> In the selection of . . . staff a thorough training in psychoanalytic theory and technique is essential. This is not in order that every patient should be subject to psychoanalytic study or treatment. On the contrary, it is obvious that the general hospital must be used as a proving ground for shorter methods of achieving the insight and relief which at present are attainable mainly through analysis. However, because such methods derive from analysis, and because the analytical technique affords a unique opportunity for the intensive study of the neuroses, a background of thorough and mature analytical experience is an essential element in the equipment of psychiatrists who would seek short-cuts to practicable, limited therapeutic goals. ("The Organization of a Psychiatric Service," 258)

But Kubie drops to his footnotes to identify the resisters of analytic understanding in a lineup with their counterparts or look-alikes rounded up from the greater history of science:

> To the naturalist the student of evolution seemed an extravagant theoretician. The anatomist made the same accusation against the early physiologist. And again the psychiatrist makes this charge against the analyst. . . . Nevertheless, in the course of time the anatomist himself became a physiologist, the naturalist a student of evolution; and the psychiatrist is becoming an analyst. (258 n. 3)

In 1943 Kubie issues a "Manual of Emergency Treatment for Acute War Neurosis" that recognizes the advances of eclectic mix-ups from scratch-and-sniff preventive deconditioning (which weeds out at "the neurotic roots" [593]) to the entertainment business of occupational therapy (during which playtime the patient is *listened to* and thus given back his interest in the reality principle [586, 590]) for just what they are—reterritorializations of and through psychoanalysis. It was largely up against large numbers of traumatic amnesiacs in World War I that a "fusion of methods" (combining hypnosis, psychoanalysis, and the hypnogogic reverie) proved necessary (594): "These various procedures for the exploration of unconscious processes are at present the chief weapon on which psychiatrists rely in their treatment of the acute war neuroses" (595). The method of hypnogogic reverie, which wakes up out of sleep therapy, gets more than its share of overdetermined attention in the Kubie manual. Kubie is fascinated by the prospect of the transition from waking to sleep (or back again) opening up a first site of neuroticization (584): sleep patterns must be controlled to keep the transition instantaneous (585). At first sight, a common thread of relaxation is what keeps the patients from unraveling any further. But if we look again, this time within the bigger picture of Kubie's research interests, there's that "trans-" again, that "across" that we must all bear in fantasies of being both genders.

The changes going down at the home front must pay the prize, the Kubie doll, the "unattainable goal" of remixing the interpersonality of the two sexes along the unisex intrapsychic axis, access, excess. "The Drive to Become Both Sexes" began as a conference paper entitled, in 1932, "Transvestism in a Teen-Age Girl" (198). Now it's 1954, and "this process of postponement must come to an end: I must grapple with the process of putting it into final shape as best I can" (198). "No matter how much it may expose me to misunderstanding and misinterpretation, I will have to carry it through to its own logical conclusion" (200). Watching pornographic films, "and especially perhaps of intercourse among groups of men and women of mixed races," has made it clear to Kubie that "the goal of a great deal of these frantic struggles in sexual intercourse is neither orgasm nor the begetting of children, but rather a process of magical bodily change" (198).

> Pornographic literature represents the endless, sad search for something unattainable, often repellent. It also carries the implication of a frustrated orgy, of a whole group of men and women struggling nakedly together in a frenzy of futility as they attempt to achieve an impossible alchemy of change in which all differences will be transmuted into one likeness, multiple sexes into one sex. No matter what kind of physiological ecstasy is achieved, the end is spiritual disaster. (218)

> When the unconscious goal of sex is the unattainable one to change sides, intercourse ends in frustration. And if this unattainable goal also represents a desire to go in two divergent direc-

tions at the same time, it results in a deeper inner schism in the personality—a schism which can be represented by insatiable compulsions and obsessions and by the superimposed construction of opposing phobias. Everything becomes split, and it is on this splitting among conscious and unconscious purposes, and preconscious struggles to achieve these purposes, that psychotic disorganization is based. (199–200)

Kubie reads fetishism or gadget love "in reverse," for the reversals of the trans- phantasm suffered, in particular, on the homosexual person and, on the other hand, the same hands, on the masturbating body.

> In fact, the major, soul-scarring penalty that is paid by the homosexual is not the degree of social disapprobation or persecution or legal unfairness and injustice to which he exposes himself through the unattainability of his own unconscious goals. It is this which tumbles him into depression and rage. (199)

> Masturbation often embodies the quintessence of the fantasy of serving oneself in the capacity of being both sexes for oneself, which probably explains in part the tenacity both of the compulsive, insatiable component in masturbation and of the guilt that attaches to it. (233)

Kubie's discovery of this new drive (to become both sexes) doubles as his version of the double bind (219), which he takes out on a double date. He makes out with Freud's improvement.

> This is an important addition to the earlier concept of intrapsychic conflicts as always arising between id processes and superego processes, but it is not irreconcilable with them. They are supplementary and in no sense mutually exclusive. (248)

Kubie was Bateson's analytic colleague in the cybernetic group that modeled postwar family systems therapy. Bateson at one point suggested, in the course of elaborating the double bind, that the introduction into a telephone exchange of the regular misdial that would systematically confuse numbers for letters (and names) would be technically schizophrenic. How to teach a telephone exchange to make this error? The double bind idea gets raised with this question. One brother died in World War I; another brother shot himself soon thereafter. The 1946 meetings on feedback mechanisms (Kubie regularly attended the Bateson group meetings right from the start) opened with investigations of the Iatmal culture, in which the ceremony of transvestism serves as a homeostatic mechanism whenever divisive hostilities were on the rise. This cultural model points to how adequate theorization in the social sciences might proceed to the head of the class. Bateson's wish to replace libido with information sets a cryptanalytic development in motion. One suggestion: social history, the analytic session, and the transference should be declassified as espionage, confession, and conversion (Heims, 131).

Efficiency Pack

In 1944, following the reopening of analytic concessions made to the eclecticism of auxiliary techniques only useful in the short term or attention span of mass war conditions, Menninger points out the inside view of the mass psychic apparatus afforded through the small world after all of psychosis.

> The whole world is being shaken in an "acute psychosis"; and it is an opportunity, in fact, a responsibility, to study this psychopathology, to attempt to understand it, and, primarily, to make heroic efforts towards immediate therapy and plans for future reconstruction.... This war will probably cause a reorientation in methods of quick evaluation of the person.... Never before has there been so extensive an opportunity to observe how the personality functions under stress.... Never before has there been such rich opportunities for studying therapy.... This opportunity not only exists within the Army, but is already widely available in civilian life. The great limitation of psychiatry has been the fact that it could not reach the masses despite the fact that the masses needed help. Of all the highly individualized treatments, psychoanalysis has probably the widest applicability and the greatest availability. How can its principles be applied to a group? Not only is the knowledge needed for use within the Army, but it should be provided for the increasing need in civilian life. ("Psychiatry and the Army," 178–79)

Menninger advertises the large-scale experimental opportunities available in wartime that were already not to be missed down the new inroads that had come to an analytic understanding. The process of selection, as old as World War I, was evolving technology-compatible reformulations of postwar states of being in groups. Military psychological selection followed the endopsychic conditions and criteria of living in the war machine down the borderline shared with the latest intrapsychic openings. Retraining or "retaining" centers for revival of the fittest psychological casualties, for example, were set to synchronize selection with the conditions of spontaneous admission.

> One very successful project was undertaken in the establishment of some experimental retaining units within replacement training camps, composed of a battalion of trainees who were psychoneurotic patients taken from hospitals. (177)

In wartime, selection is a nonstop evolutionary process of adaptation. The no-man's-land or border zone between psychosis and neurosis that Freud first opened up for theorization in his 1918 analysis of war neurosis was pressing, on new location, for the newly revised criteria of selection:

> Many can be eliminated with positive assurance. Others are on the borderline where rejection or acceptance depends on the attitude of the examiner. Even with adequate study, some of those thought able to "make the grade" within the Army prove unsuitable on trial. Those who may make excellent soldiers despite their neurosis or neurotic "acting-out" are sources of the greatest perplexity. A number who have developed into psychoneurotic "casuals" have been decorated for bravery in action. (178)

What winds down one soldier shows the way, down the streamlines of eclectic therapeutic adjustments, to winding up the "efficient soldier," a new genre of research subject or study that first passed through a certain Major Needles and on to psychoanalyst Eissler. In his pro and contra coverage of U.S. overreliance on selection, which needles Eissler into taking much stronger reaction, William Needles describes modes of self-help adopted by neurotics in the armed services to make it through for as long as they did before breaking down. From self-medication with alcohol (680) to the more direct or immediate impulse toward self-destruction (677), behavior that presents the problem in civilian practice serves the neurotic in a military setting to keep up, for a time, with the war effort. When makeshift cognitive auto-therapy self-helps one neurotic out of his troubles and keeps him running on what the psychiatric literature he has consulted calls normal, it is still a simulation of health, which is still neurotic. The soldier act could only last as long as the one-time limited offer of willpower.

Eissler follows the case chart of one soldier whose analysis-compatible, insight-oriented progress was a measure undermining his usefulness for his part in the war machine:

> Each success brought this patient closer to doom, and the first step of wholesome reorientation would have been for him to permit himself to suffer defeat. On the other hand, his career illustrates impressively how psychopathology may lead to the attainment of socially constructive and desirable goals, even over long periods of time. ("The Efficient Soldier," 74)

A therapy of reassurance and superficial appeasement of anxiety supported the upward displacement both his psychopathology and his career could follow, but with one difference, one substitution, please.

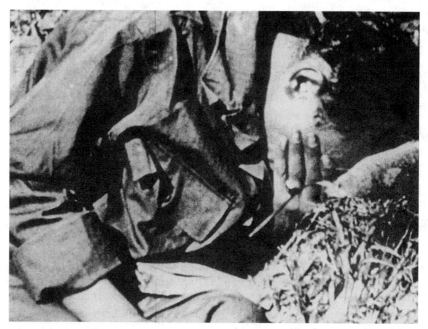

War-neurotic soldier-patient cowering in fear of attack. Reproduced from *Neuropsychiatry in World War II,* 2:655.

> He informed me that he felt terrified during flights because he labored under the compulsion to do the very opposite of what he should do in view of what the instruments on the panel board indicated. Such obsessions gripped him when he cruised alone through the vastness of space. Yet it turned out that he did not feel alone in such circumstances. He felt in contact with me.... Flying became a kind of gamble of whether he could be stronger than God, or a sort of test whether God would help him. (77)

The efficient soldier described a new norm of functioning in sync with the techno-merger falling between the borderlines that otherwise kept out psychosis, that extratransferential visitation. It was the opening of a new outer space of oscillation between the diagnostic extremes on the psychopathology continuum. As Eissler concludes his case of an efficient soldier whose war shock was doubled and contained by eclectic, electric shock therapy, his resulting "functioning as an automaton" tows the lines of the new ideal's assembly: "Although not yet deprived of the capacity to evolve a delusion or produce anxiety, he lost the capacity to react to his individual, internal, microcosm and thus came closer to what quite possibly may become the ideal of modern man, namely, a machinelike structure dependable in the management of certain sectors of reality" (78–79). Recycling of psychological casualties of war back to frontline service is the military-psychological installation in the group of the inoculative speed race between psychosis and the saving power of self-help.

> From their cases, perhaps, something can be learned about what it may be possible to do in an emergency, in rendering resistant to the disorganizing impact of prolonged combat experience soldiers who cannot, because of shortness of time, be prepared for warfare by effecting adequate structural personality changes. It would, it seems, be a matter of properly directed magic, a technique which can be learned only from the sick who has seemingly recovered by the upsurge of pseudo ego strength. (85)

John Frosch recommends that we skip a step and proceed directly to the psychiatric institutions and scout about for war economy talent. What's the difference between occupational therapy and work in defense plants? For this kind of low-maintenance recycling, Frosch highly recommends borderline or military psychoses, neuroses, reactive depressions, alcoholism. Mental hospitals and selective service boards should cooperate, not so much to grant them "a blanket deferment, as to facilitate a closer individual evaluation of each case, so that they can be used to the best purpose in our wartime economy" (321).

In the October 1943 issue of *Psychosomatic Medicine*, Henry Brosin gave a few recommendations for "The Unfit: How to Use Them." In addition to special units in which the cases weren't acute but cute, and not casualties but members of the "casual detachment" (later turned into "Enlisted Men's Replacement Pool"), Brosin has therapeutic advice for us. Face the facts. This is a whole new class of citizens with their own special interests.

> This vast population, whom we now regard as our patients, are also potential voters, lobbyists, strikers, malcontents, absentees, members of potent political organizations, who will demand some type of relief for their problems. In this sense, by sheer mass, they will be our masters for they will compel social changes whether we approve them or not. (346)

Kurt Goldstein puts the war-compatible "psychos" (as psychoneurotics were called, for short, in the service) in an aside that lets them pass if they don't tell.

> On the contrary, many men known to be neurotics in civilian life situations behaved especially well in dangerous situations.... In general one could say that certain individuals are more threatened by the inner conflicts related to civilian life than to experiences in war.... For them the military situation represents an escape mechanism. These men sometimes show outstanding performances. (382)

During World War I, Kurt Goldstein was in charge of the treatment of brain-injured soldiers. Among the future psychotherapists who passed through Goldstein's hospital (Fritz Perls was one of them) there was Frieda Fromm-Reichmann (introduced by Edith Weigert, in the preface to *Psychoanalysis and Psychotherapy*, as "a born psychotherapist" [v]). Her first position after graduating in medicine in 1914 was as a member of Goldstein's staff. The reactions of the brain-injured prepared not only Fromm-Reichmann for a growing understanding of psychotic states. Her next apprenticeship, during the early 1920s, was with J. H. Schultz, whose sanitarium was well known for the yoga-inspired relaxation therapies Schultz marketed under the name "autogenic training." This is the same Schultz, of course, who later advanced to a position as leading man in the institution of eclecticization and reunification of the psychotherapies in Nazi Berlin. One could say that Schultz stayed behind—or just stayed. Like Goldstein, Fromm-Reichmann couldn't choose to stay: she was Jewish. Between Schultz and her flight from Nazi persecution of the Jews, she first discovered Freud—and she was taken aback by his understanding of transference phenomena to the point of starting over again with renewed focus on the doctor-patient relationship. Her guide at this time of introduction to Freud was Georg Groddeck, who contributed the *es* word—the "it" or id word—to Freud's second-system lexicon. But contact with Freud didn't stop Fromm-Reichmann's drive to accessorize or eclecticize with all the theories of greater psychoanalysis. Following her job displacement in the United States, she attached herself, in her usual mode of hero worship, to Harry Stack Sullivan.

During World War II, Fromm-Reichmann formulated precepts and techniques for her own version of psychoanalytic psychotherapy that specialized in treating psychotic patients. In her 1946 essay, "Remarks on the Philosophy of Mental Disorder," she looks back across a summary review of the positions she had come to occupy:

> Serious mental disturbance—psychosis—can potentially be treated successfully by a collaborative effort between the mentally disturbed person and the psychiatrist as participant ob-

server, with modified psychoanalysis—dynamically oriented in-
tensive psychotherapy—even after many years' duration. . . .
    The emotionally and mentally disturbed reactions which . . .
hospitalized . . . patients showed are different in degree only, and
not in kind, from the emotional and mental experiences and
modes of expression of so-called healthy people. (*Psychoanalysis
and Psychotherapy*, 4–5)

The only difference between mental experiences lies in the role of sleep.
Sleep therapy is beneficial for psychotic patients, but it is counterproductive
to interpret their dreams. In their dreams, the healthy are psychotic; the
dreams of psychotics are just more of the same disjunction with interpersonal realities that already dominates their waking state.

    In her review of the conclusions she has come to in working with psy-
chotics, Fromm-Reichmann covers their assets. We all have a great deal to
learn from psychotics. Psychiatrists, for example, can learn from their psychotic patients the special conditions of establishing contact with even the
most extreme cases. The psychotic too can benefit from his "previous liabil-
ities in terms of his pathogenic history, the expression of his subsequent
mental disorder—that is, symptomatology—or his inner response to either
of them" by converting them into "assets" (5). Taking her inspiration from
Nietzsche, Fromm-Reichmann argues that whereas many of your normal
to neurotic types don't have a mind to lose, with psychotics there can be no
question that what was lost was once there and is there to be found. "It is
no overstatement to say that the mentally sick, who allegedly have lost their
minds in their interpersonal struggles, may be useful to the mentally healthy
in really finding their minds, which are all too frequently lost, as it were, in
the distortions, the dissociations, the hypocritical adaptations, and all the
painful hide-and-seeks which modern culture forces upon the mind of man"
(24). With the war behind her, Fromm-Reichmann's sense of what the future
holds for psychotic patients turns on artistic expression. Her star case is
that of a catatonic psychotic who was a poet but didn't know it until after
years of psychotherapy with Fromm-Reichmann. But the background to
many of the techniques she borrowed in her quest for the artist symptomatizing to get out of the psychotic involved treating war neurotics with the
aim of restoring them, from the inside out, to war steadiness. In 1942, in
her article "Insight into Psychotic Mechanisms and Emergency Psychotherapy," for example, Fromm-Reichmann openly draws from the success stories
of new therapeutic techniques practiced on the war-traumatized confirma-
tion for her own approach to working with patients. The civilians who suffered air attacks were first in rate of success: "In all psychiatric air-raid

Occupational therapy for psychiatric soldier-patients at 112th Station Hospital (a program run by the American Red Cross), 16 August 1944. Reproduced from *Neuropsychiatry in World War II*, 2:447.

casualties in which the method of immediate thorough discussion of the accident and the victim's emotional reactions to it, with subsequent sedation, could be accomplished, complete cure was obtained" (56–57). While in military psychotherapy similar experiences were gathered, the treatment of civilians was more effective. This underscores Fromm-Reichmann's sense of "the therapeutic significance of the personal relationship" between doctor and patient as equal partners, a significance she observed hands on in her work with psychotics. That in the military setting the treating physician or psychotherapist is an officer, and the patient most likely a noncommissioned soldier, prevents the establishment of the therapeutic *inter*relationship. "Successful psychotherapy can be done only on the basis of a successful patient-physician interrelationship" (62). She concludes this article by setting her fundamental tenet on the conflict of the world war.

> In addition to its therapeutic value, there is another reason why non-authoritarian psychiatric guidance on the basis of a valid doctor-patient relationship is of paramount significance in our days. To some patients the individual experience of that type of relationship may serve as illustration and symbol of the gen-

eral idea for which combatant and non-combatant victims are supposed and are willing to suffer and to fight, real human inter-relationships in the spirit of freedom and democracy versus totalitarian submission and versus authoritarian leadership. (62)

GI Joey

Bruno Bettelheim's case study of Joey, the so-called mechanical boy, follows in the footnotes of Margaret Mahler and Victor Tausk. At one point Bettelheim makes a theoretical or therapeutic controversy out of overuse and under-understanding of "regression." The upbeat point he makes about regression as always a simulation that's at the same time a progressive breakthrough in relations with others, from early childhood through adolescence, is therapeutically correct. However, the theoretical frame he grants Joey represents, compared, say, to Tausk and Mahler, a literal regression. The anti-Oedipals, Deleuze and Guattari, have their field day with Bettelheim as though on one field with psychoanalysis. By turning the mechanical boy into the antihero of their schizo-nomadic affirmations, however, they just miss the same point of resistance that makes Bettelheim so smarmy and lets them fly so high on themselves.

Born to a completely shut-down mother (his value-free representation of her role in his life is as "incubator"), Joey's only lifeline of defense before entering the Bettelheim school of success stories had been to go autistic. In the course of his schooltime, Joey gets rehumanized, in part through whatever returns or regressions to infant care were still available to someone who had utterly—udderly—missed the first dyadic chance you get with mother. If already in infancy only machines gave Joey shelter, the motive force for the boy was the sheer terror that originates with the "over-all experience that his mother did not hold him securely riveted to this world by her attachment" (*The Empty Fortress*, 263). Pretreatment Joey was instead riveted down to the delusional and acted-out technologization of his gastrointestinal system. From start to finish, he was a techno-tube padded with battery cells, electrical wires, more tubes, the works.

The Bettelheim school goes for whatever "regressions" can be promoted along this highly protected and projected rerouting of the boy's metabolizations. Free-form excretion and voluntary eating, in both cases without the whole tubular apparatus he was given to bring to toilet and to table, were offered as the first step, give and take, toward Joey's "humanization." Here's the first sentence, the sentence Joey was under, of the section entitled "A Curb on Tubes": "It was around eating that we first interfered with the acting out of Joey's preventions, perhaps because we dimly felt that problems of intake at that time were less central to him" (255). In exchange for the absence of any pressure to eat, for example, Joey accepts a reduced lower-tech representation of the full-scale apparatus that essentially powered his ingestion, but only, it seemed, by also preventing his sheer ability to eat by the burden of proof Joey required especially at table that he was so techno.

And then Joey seems to take in a few classical memories or constructions (the corrective of "simulation" that Bettelheim would add to the limited notion of regression comes to mind). A primal scene gets reconstructed; the screening device of the venetian blinds that linked up and shut down Joey's range or rage of vision gets conjoined with the castratively threatening rotation of the blades of a fan belonging to the first model of little Joey's gadget love. When we have Joey's words for this so-called primal scene, it all sounds way off the mark that Bettelheim feels he has scored: "I got scared and thought it was a ghost who did all those horror things" (261). All we really know is that little Joey thought he once caught a glimpse of the ghost lying between his parents, the ghost that already had Joey in his parents' possession.

What Bettelheim and company may consider only as the discrete influence on the mother's condition at the time of Joey's birth could fit another layout of Joey's techno-encryptment: "Each parent had entered marriage on the rebound, in the wake of a frustrated love affair. In the mother's case, she had loved a man who had only recently died in air combat (World War II). Each parent had suffered deeply from strong emotional attachment to a friend they had lost" (239). Joey's parents had married—the father was another pilot, and Bettelheim's description of his premarital affair makes it likely that his own loss, perhaps the same loss, was in the register of buddy love—and reproduced, as a desperate acting out of substitution or efficient mourning that only issued, through Joey, in the creation of a monster or robot in place of the work of mourning that the mother could not undertake. Joey took in with mother's ice milk the unlaid ghost of someone doubly missing (the missing airman takes off from uncharted, unmournable zones of loss).

Bettelheim dates Joey's machine identification to age one, to the impact on him of the gift of a fan. Somehow he knew this was it; he would need to understand it inside and out. Joey's sexual research took the form of gadget-loving attention to the detail of ghosts between his parents. He was very soon able to take it apart and put it together again quite effortlessly or, perhaps, automatically. That the fan blades at the same time recall propellers is self-evident. Bettelheim links the association to little Joey's trips to the airport to see his pilot father off or to welcome his return. Takeoffs and landings are peak reasons for fear of crashing. By age four, Joey would gyrate his hands like a propeller; by extension he showed interest only in objects that could be recycled as propeller or fan blades. Bettelheim's humanizing interpretation: this early investment reflected Joey's recognition that the plane was most definitely a source of emotional responding on the part of his parents, which he, somehow, for his part, just couldn't get them to expend on him. It's an interpretation or translation that gives up the ghost.

Joey would break his machine routine only for his so-called explosions, during which he would throw and break tubes or lightbulbs while crying out, "Crash! Crash!" But even on this plane that's either full or empty—"Joey's eating had no purpose except to power elimination" (285)—Joey is the figure of survival even of every crash landing. For the first two years at the school, Joey "would do no reading ... unless he could skip the word 'father' when it occurred on the page" (252). This is just one of those things he won't introduce into his GI complex. Joey admits leaves and ashes (the before and after pictures of one burning) into the field of his self-representation: let's not overlook but indeed overhear in these burning leaves both the "leave-taking" and the "leaves" periodically granted those in the military, which by his mother's earlier leave had already burned and crashed. If "post," the curse that can be a legacy of sorts, out of sorts, across generations, can sound like "box" to Bettelheim, then the "crib" in the "cribbage" Joey took to playing could sound like "crypt." Among his neologisms, "bond-nap" and "ashtie" can be heard to refer to the mother's safe depositing and tube tying of her unmetabolizable loss deep inside her baby boom.

As with any new techno-gadget, it's not so much its invention or existence that makes the difference; it's the reception that must be created. Joey thus extends his tubular experience to include technologization of his counselors:

> These imaginary electrical connections he had to establish before he could eat, because only the current ran his ingestive apparatus. He performed the ritual with such skill that one had to look twice to be sure there was neither wire nor outlet nor plug. His pantomime was so skilled, and his concentration so contagious, that those who watched him seemed to suspend their own existence and become observers of another reality. (235)

> Just as none of us wishes to come between nursing mother and child, is hesitant to break into their life sustaining circle, so children and staff took spontaneous care not to step on Joey's imaginary wires lest they interrupt the current and stop his being. (236)

> It was as if in watching him and emotionally trying to join him in his mechanical world we lost some of our humanity ourselves. (236–37)

In contrast to the interplanetary first contact Joey offered—"he told us he was living on Mars, sometimes Jupiter, but always on another planet than we" (256)—Bettelheim proposes a new world order of "feelings." In Bettelheim's theory-phobic discourse, "feelings" function as a desperate short stop or stopover, a plug for, or libidinization of, what we all already had given up on. But Joey has Bettelheim fooled. "Recalling his 'Radiant TV' float of the previous year, he decided to do something entirely different. He made a float for his favorite teddy bear and had him carry a big sign that read: 'Feelings are more important than anything under the sun'" (327). What's allegedly entirely different bears the stamp above all of group approval. Joey adds to his technologization another turn of internalization in the form of group psychologization.

When Joey returns on a visit three years after his release from the Bettelheim school, the young man remembers little of the techno-details; in place of recollection or self-understanding, he treats Bettelheim to the echo chamber concert version of "Feelings."

> I think a great deal of it had to do with the fact that I was afraid to tell any person how I felt. (330)

> As I remember it, I had a feeling, a long time ago, that I would find out that somebody wouldn't like me. (330)

> Another very important factor is . . . I was really becoming able to tell people more freely how I felt . . . like when I first start having the feeling, instead of waiting until long after. (331)

Now, if young man Joey loves his parents so, why back then was he such a pain?

> Well, I . . . what it was is, feeling two ways at the same time. . . . I felt so angry that I had to have some way to let go of it. . . . Because I kept so many of my feelings to myself. (338)

New early memories with new dates are what Joey now recalls via his mother's memory and hearsay. He does recall a certain double occupancy, however, one that he instantly interpersonalizes for the benefit of his feel-good doctor (even Bettelheim has a sense that Joey wanted to make a "good impression" [339]). Bettelheim asks Joey about his earlier urge to be enclosed in moving vehicles. Joey dates this development back to the time he started coming closer to people: "I'd have fantasies about a car or anything that moved on wheels that was enclosed and I'd have a fantasy that I was in it myself. Well, I'd always picture that somebody else was in it with me" (333).

He is currently studying electronics and brings with him on this visit a gadget he has been able to build in a more functional, less allegorical, less psychotic mode: "It was a rectifier and its function was to change alternating current into direct current. And he showed us again and again how this device he had constructed himself changed the eternal back-and-forth of the alternating current into a direct continuous flow" (339). Bettelheim sees this as the symbol for Joey's exchange of those staticky mixed feelings for a "straightforward direct encounter" with life (339). But it is the gadget of double occupancy that he had originally and always fed with a continuous lifeline of current. The technology of encrypting the missing pilot that he largely pulled out of his rectum, he now carries in the rectifier. The inefficient protection of autism or outer space has been exchanged for the more friendly and thus more efficient mode of unambivalence: he respects his mom and dad. The charge he now gets out of or into his family (battery) pack doesn't overload him: it's his friend.

The group password, "feelings," gets him liking to be liked by those he likes and would like to be like. And they are all gadget lovers, too, just like him. And like them, perhaps to varying degrees, he's the rectifier of an other's disowned loss in some current mode of undeath and identification. In the shelter of analysis, with Bettelheim standing to the side, outside, Joey grows a playback function. There's more to psychoanalysis than what fits into the alternative affirmations of the Deleuzers.

Family Program

A new air field of psychiatry, an incorporation formed with the whole of modern medicine, was opening up. In his 1943 article "How the Flying Fighters' Doctor Is Made," Eugen Reinartz presents the parallel universals of psychiatry and artificial flight:

> As difficulties appear, they naturally fall into the medical field and the practice of medicine has been most closely linked with aviation since its inception. One cannot, therefore, discuss the one without telling the story of the other, at least in part. This is produced by the very intimate relationship between certain basic principles of aviation medicine, the fact that the pilot plays such an important role, and the success in the design, operation, and piloting of aircraft. (820)

C. Charles Burlingame gives his flight surgeon's–eye view of these changing planes of psychiatry. "We have seen how quickly our great airplane manu-facturers have allowed for fluidity in design for their ships. There is every indication that a similar fluidity and purposefulness is needed now in the field of psychiatry" (478).

But recycling retro-libidinizes what was already given up on and brings it back into the holding pattern. One therapy regrouping that recycled what the Nazis had abandoned still comes family size. Reinartz gives the lead in retro-packaging of the therapy format to the flight surgeon, who, at least in name, was created in 1918 as act of commemoration of the first medical offi-cer to be killed in a plane crash. What flyboys need is a family doctor:

> The Flight Surgeon is always on the "flying line" before the take-off on a mission, discussing with each pilot casually some matter of little moment all the while sizing up the pilot and air crew members whom he knows intimately, to determine whether there is any deviation from the individual's known normal state. (827)

In charge of selection and maintenance, the flight surgeon must pick and choose from the backyard pool of candidates according to what at first sight appear to be radically defamiliarized criteria of merger with the flying machine. A gadget lover or "compensated introvert" is ideal to take to the skies. At the same time as his narcissism is flight compatible, certain neu-rotic side effects must bring him way down in the compression and accel-eration contexts of air power: "The symptoms of disease encountered in flying personnel are the same as one finds in civil life and yet they may

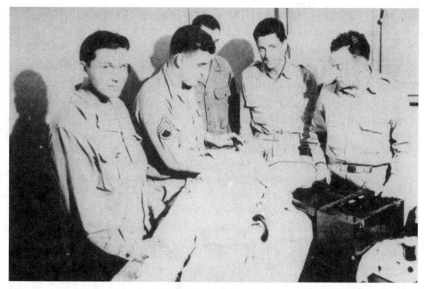

The electroshock treatment team at Twelfth General Hospital. Reproduced from *Neuropsychiatry in World War II*, 2:151.

well be compatible with terrestrial existence while their development in aviators would be incompatible with flying" (820). That's why the so-called aeroneurosis must be mastered down to its preflight conditions. Human error or folly had to be excised from the control panel.

Gadget goes air show, the competition down the runway between deneuroticization of overattachments to the gravity of earthbound or, on the ultimate upswing, even fuel-bound technologies and the breakdown swing of psycho flight up and away from all object libido—into an ego all set to implode. If the major's in the air force, the minor is in psychosis. "The hazards involved in aviation have always made it a fertile field for the development of minor psychoses" (826).

Abram Kardiner's 1947 *War Stress and Neurotic Illness* (the second edition, revised in collaboration with Herbert Spiegel, of his 1941 *The Traumatic Neuroses of War*) rejoined the pilot studies of war neurosis in getting right in the interface of machines. But also first discovered in the specific case of air war, there are two major downers for the soldier that redefine the flight conditions of narcissism: destruction of the beloved gadget and the death of your "buddy." When Roy Grinker and John P. Spiegel move out of the restricted circulation of their war effort research, *War Neuroses in North Africa: The Tunisian Campaign*, to publish the 1945 book version, *Men under Stress*, gadget-loving details of unconscious machine identification have been reunited for the end of the war with family membership. "The men and their plane become identified with each other with an intensity that in civil life is found only within the family circle" (24). They repeat the family comparison and then warm up to the brotherhood line, the cut loss that the circle of family and friends must recuperate:

> In truth, they are brothers-in-arms in more than a figurative sense. They actually feel toward each other as if they were brothers. It is a very common thing to hear a flier say of his buddy, "He reminds me of my brother" or "I felt closer to him than to my own brother." (25)

The therapeutic frame must support the group relation on this other plane.

First the flight surgeon "evokes definite transference attitudes in the flier" (157). But this lead transference must not fall for nurturing conditions too often reproduced in psychotherapy. "Too much gratification from a parental transference" is a real danger, "resulting in spoiling for future army duty" (374). Second, "thoughts of home, home, home" organize his ambivalence up and down the mood swings. It's the idealized place to be, a reunion of Oedi-pals: "For a time at least, there is an attempt to envisage their fathers without the role of authority, fantasying them as equals or pals" (185). But what's in an ideal if not fear of retribution. "Leaving the crew... creates a sense of guilt; the thought of those who die and can never go home intensifies this feeling. It is this feeling of guilt that is the basis for considering the last mission to be so dangerous. It is the projection on fate of the accusing finger of the flier's own ego-ideal, which cannot tolerate his desertion of his dead and living comrades. All these emotional reactions, stimulated by the anticipation of returning home, probably decrease efficiency and make the fliers more vulnerable to disaster on their last mission, which superstition has it is the most dangerous—'the jinx mission'" (183–84).

According to Murray's 1943 summary of psychiatric procedures in the Army Air Force, the initial interview "deals especially with family and childhood, and a very detailed personal history" (21). Problem number one, Murray has found, is posed by "flyers who deny any trace of neurosis in order to qualify" (23). When flying stress or fatigue occurs, it's no surprise: "This condition in flying personnel arises chiefly as a result of the continuous and long continued repression and suppression of the normal fear reactions present in all types of operational flying" (23). Just like a child from the parents, so "the patient borrows strength by identification with the therapist" (23).

In the November 1945 issue of the *Bulletin of the U.S. Army Medical Department*, Stanley Olinick and Maurice Friend's "Indirect Group Therapy of Psychoneurotic Soldiers" provides the measure of expansionism that's been psychiatry's war-given pleasure (after having been cooped up exclusively inside psycho wards) but, when it comes to the focus for each treatment, has a more economy model in mind, compatible with the same interpersonal-relations approach to which the authors ascribe psychiatry's spread, one that comes family size:

> Psychoneurotic symptomatology is one manifestation of warped interpersonal relations. These difficulties in living are conditioned in the adult by experiences remote in time but currently active in blocking the basic human drive toward security and satisfaction. In this program, so far as was possible within military society, security and satisfaction of needs were opened to the men in return for sustained, directive effort on their parts. The result was a process of acculturation and socialization not essentially different from that undergone by children in family and school groups. (Olinick and Friend, 151)

George Gardner and Harvey Spencer observed "Reactions of Children with Fathers and Brothers in the Armed Forces," which were in sync within one ongoing family relation or system of relations. In the United States, without the extra distractions of air attack, for example, the war is brought home with loss of a family member through enlistment: "The voluntary or enforced loss of a family member is the severest test so far set for American children in this conflict" (36). One boy's depression following an older brother's enlistment in the air corps found a first clearing and then took an upswing: he showed the psychiatrist letters he had received from his brother and declared "his intention of becoming a flier when he grows up," up and away (38). But anxiety increases around the sound of planes or of the air-raid sirens were registered in one boy after the enlistment of his foster father. The increased chances for the foster father's death that the boy hears in the only sounds of war available causes the death wisher to fear the retribution of his own bombing. Superego says: "You wanted a bombed father, go ahead and be the bombed father." It would be too perfect if "getting bombed" was what the foster father did whenever he had already gone out.

Gardner and Spencer discern a new guideline for separating the more treatable kids from the dead-set delinquents that follows the reader of the war effort with gadget-loving detail:

There is a striking lack of information among the delinquents about the war fronts, war events, and the important persons involved. There is lacking also that information about planes, ships, tanks and other military equipment that the non-delinquents and the clinic group have so well in hand and display at every opportunity. (43)

Louis Lurie and Florence Rosenthal report on the techno-war adjustments of problem boys just in time for the current "alarming increase in the incidence of juvenile delinquency" (400). One boy with a record makes an altitude adjustment. The authors are "tempted to speculate" that not all psychopathic or psychoneurotic individuals should be excluded from military service as breakdown material. The war is an adjustment resource: "Evidently social maladjustment or neuropsychiatric disorders are not always necessarily incompatible with normal adjustment to military life" (404). Although burdened by a morbid fear of death—of the dead—"following the death of a younger sister to whom he was greatly attached," and generally insecurized by early home experiences, the homeboy follows his discharge with enlistment in the National Guard in 1938. At this time he was so into his uniform that he wore it all the time, even on the occasions that the uniformity was not permissible. But then war broke out, and he exchanged his therapeutic holding pattern to reach for the sky:

He enlisted in the Air Corps the day following the attack on Pearl Harbor.... In spite of his instability and neurotic personality, knowledge of which at the induction center would have excluded him from military service, the boy had adjusted splendidly as an aviator. (403)

Jean Arsenian observes "Young Children in an Insecure Situation." (The net results of the interest in security, which moved from insurance coverage to the sheltering of containment, get around to this day under "safety.") "There is no need to remark the importance of the concept of security in contemporary psychology." It was almost as popular back then as the concept of adjustment (225).

Because black-outs have become a recurrent phenomenon on one coast and authorities contemplate the possibility of future large-scale evacuations of children from coastal areas, the assemblage of methods for immunizing the insecurity of children in unstructured environments has particular urgency. (248)

The main method for granting immunity is the familiar one of including or introjecting a part of the family:

> The most certain provision that can be made for the security of young children faced with unstructured environments appears to be the presence of a familiar adult whose protective power is known. Even a familiar *object* may lessen in some degree the insecurity of children in strange situations. (248–49)

Sandor Lorand argues that object constancy is needed if you're going to fight out of conviction. The case Lorand is presenting is of neurotic rebellion against the (transferential) threat the army's discipline posed for him.

> He distrusted Army life ... just as he was suspicious of the ideals which his parents represented to him in early years. This distrust of early ideals, and the inability to identify with them had an important bearing on his character. It left him unable to form strong or permanent object relationships and he was therefore unable to develop strong convictions about anything. Patriotism and patriotic ideals were exposed to the same scrutiny that his parents' ideals had been, once upon a time. Thus, when confronted with a task that demanded conviction—accepting military ideals and the need to fight—he was unable to go through with it. (188)

In her analysis of "The Fear of Explosion" in children, mothers, and soldiers, Mildred Burgum sets the cracks in the shelter of constancy on the self's start from a scratch fixing to burst wide open:

> Essentially the fear of bombs exploding seemed to be a projection of the more basic fear of the explosion of the physical self ... and the panic they all experienced during the air raids was an expression of their fear of their own rage. (349)

That covers the little boys and future soldiers. But according to Burgum, the mother, too, is ready to explode. One mother brings a fully formed, repeated or rehearsed, insight to session:

> "Albert is my bomb," she remarked, and added, "we will best be able to fight the war outside when we have won the war within ourselves." (353)

Mother diverts attention here from the secret bomb shelter where she and Albert tick, tick away. The child's fear of bombing, a dread of separation from the mother's war economy, does double duty: he is both the little boy and the foreign body or bomb dropping on him, inside him. He's doubly

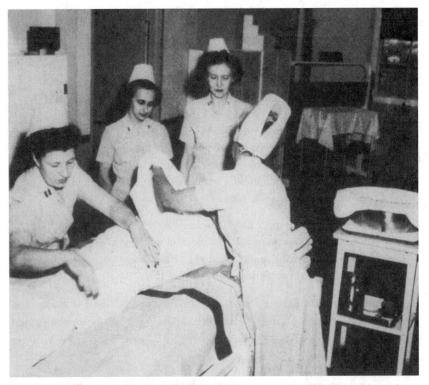

Demonstration of application of a restraining pack used for neuropsychiatric soldier-patients at the Medical Field Service School, Brooke Army Medical Center, Fort Sam Houston, Texas. Reproduced from U.S. Army, *Neuropsychiatry in World War II*, vol. 1, *Zone of Interior* (Washington, D.C.: Office of the Surgeon General, 1966), 639.

ticked off. With the proviso that a melancholic delegation informs Albert's impossible desire to be bombproof of what mother already deposited inside him, Burgum's conclusion still stands: "Perhaps the type of individual I have described should, in a more general sense, also be considered as candidate for neurotic war reactions" (357).

Edward Strecker's focus on the mom behind every war neurotic takes it from a family system that runs on or averages out substitution as the healthy alternative to the pathogenic couple or dyad. It's the system that's modeled on the military unit that also doesn't break down under the distress of loss. "During three years of work as consultant to the Secretary of War and to the Surgeons General of the Army, Army Air Forces, and Navy, I have seen the results of both 'moms' and 'mothers'" (13–14). The dyad opens wide to network with such surrogate moms as alcoholism, homosexuality, schizophrenia, National Socialism, and U.S. isolationism. The isolationist movement may have been stopped short with the takeoff of the first "robot bombs" and thus of the future prospect of robot plane wars carrying atomic bombs and directed by TV (116), but the most lethal weapon around is the letter a mom writes to her son in the service.

> In my tours through the various camps and bases during the war, I saw hundreds of lonely youngsters trying desperately to make the grade, attempting to acclimate themselves psychologically to military life, who were completely broken by a typical mom letter which filled their minds with worries about home and particularly about mom. The final result in a large percentage of case studies was a discharge for "psychoneurosis." (34–35)

> In the armed services I have seen men not able to perform their duties, or perhaps going through the motions robot-like, haunted and harassed by memory pictures of an "ailing" mom who "needs" them as her letters amply testify. (59)

The specialness of the mom and all her sons makes for fused relations that can't get out and circulate or substitute. There's no family system where mom's method rules. There's only a lowering of the "boon" of emancipation onto the sad sack of a son.

> Our war experiences—the alarming number of so-called "psychoneurotic" young Americans—point to and emphasize this threat to our survival. No one could view this huge test tube of man power, tried and found wanting, without realizing that an extremely important factor was the inability or unwillingness of the American mom and her surrogates to grant the boon of emotional emancipation during childhood. Already we have incurred a large penalty. The threat to our security must not be allowed to go farther. . . . Mom is a surface fissure warning us of deeper defects. (219)

Family Outing

J. L. Henderson and Merrill Moore are of two minds about how war neurosis happens. One mind is really open to the spectacular exception of the buddy's death:

> The killing of a "buddy" is of great importance. It appears that every serviceman goes into war with the philosophy, "It can't happen to me." This belief is severely shaken when a man with whom he has so strongly identified himself is killed. In a sense it is "me" being killed, and so the death is intolerable. (355)

A general comment about treatment that follows the death that tear jerks us around inside a buddy movie is really the only time that the two authors invoke analytic therapy, but on a fee basis of one remove or removal from the immediate scene through intellectualization or, as projected on the patient, personality disorder.

> Because these psychoneuroses had their origin in distortions of personality development, we believe that the only lasting therapy is of the individual type in which an alteration of the personality structure is effected. (355)

The disorder Henderson and Moore are minding recontextualizes the pop-psychological struggles against momsterism or enmeshment within family systems. A soldier's mental disorderly conduct begins in the home:

> It seems that the man who has developed a so-called "war neurosis" was predetermined before he entered the Service. It might even be said that war neuroses are "made in America" and only come to light or are labeled in combat. (354)

The home life could be broken externally or caught in the vicious spin cycle of early interpersonality problems:

> Those patients who came from homes that were broken by separation, divorce or death, or distorted by neurotic parents, were found to have personalities insufficiently developed to deal rapidly or adequately with the problems of life, particularly with the problems of war. (349)

> This vicious emotional cycle in the family set up was repeatedly described, and in nearly every case a mutually dependent neurotic relation existed between mother and child. (354)

In 1945 Henry Fox trains his focus on a family of relationships as the context for emotional problems in the soldier boys. A soldier falls ill in and of the group; the primal model of every social group is the family, a system inevitably larger than the mother and child reunion: "Since almost all the patients were young men, their emotional attitudes are usually an immediate outgrowth of their family relationships. The problems of adolescence are often incompletely solved, and the pattern of resentment and dependence is usually an expression of delayed maturity" (132). By 1947 John P. Spiegel can open his research and treatment update, "Neurosis," as follows (the war): "The past year has seen a great decrease in the amount of attention paid to the neuroses of war, whereas the neurotic difficulties of adjustment to the postwar period are just being studied" (394). In the meantime the traditional concept of neurosis can be officially listed as war casualty. The old concept died in application to the neuroses of war. The shorthand of theory was thrown to the second wind given the long hand of therapy recording itself in a descriptive diagnostic system filled with "practical information regarding type and degree of illness—a fingernail sketch of the real status of the patient" (395). In contrast, then, to "the old idea of specific disease entities," "a new concept has arisen which holds neuroses to represent failures of adjustment to specific situations based on the past history of the individual" (394). According to William C. Menninger's 1945 address "Modern Concepts of War Neuroses," what was a war service exclusive has become postwar a public service announcement that tunes or turns the American family into the receiving area of neurosis, both as condition and as concept.

> As a conservative estimate, there are at least a million more people in this country tonight than there were three years ago, who have heard of, have dealt with, or are personally concerned with that medical entity called psychoneurosis.... We in medicine are confronted with the fact that the membership of the military and their families at home have become increasingly educated on this subject, for better or worse, during the last three years. (227)

In his "Character and the Traumatic Syndrome," Harold Kelman joins the end-of-the-war family-sizing of relief, which the soldiers and their family members can expect when the wartime leave of the senses comes home. Everyone will need to readjust come peacetime: "The increase of the number of juvenile delinquents is but one expression of this problem, both in England and the United States" (121). In 1943 the Harlem riots already spooked Kelman with the prospect of group-level release (without letup or relief) of aggression: "Almost any adverse incident could have ultimately set off these riots" (129). Such narcissism is hard to take and even harder to treat. Only when narcissism got mixed up early on with object relations does it have the kind of record that suggests that it will heal. But outright narcissists, among whom he counts traumatic neurotics, are hard nuts to track. In war neurosis, however, the fixation is on the trauma, meaning the "effects of the trauma have made a permanent alteration in adaptation but not an arrest in development which was Freud's concept of fixation" (126).

Kelman decides therefore to slip on Karen Horney's science of character analysis, which, less "mechanistic, evolutionary and descriptive of a dynamic process" than Freud's thoughts on the subject, is a better fit (128). Horney had been horning in on analysis for some time already. Part of the original prewar neopsychoanalysis movement with Schultz-Hencke by her side, her reception in Berlin was still going strong during the Nazi period. She went to Berlin to lecture as late as 1936. Like Schultz-Hencke, she thought she wanted it all perfectly clear. The "defenses" that the public took offense to can now follow or flow as "character trends" that allow Horney-follower Kelman to take the setting of the cure, the timer of the disorder's etiology and prognosis, two ways at once:

> Everyone has his breaking point. No one is completely or perfectly adjusted. (135–36)

> Actually all emotional problems are chronic. Only because of their internal configuration and the external pressure do they become evident, as though of recent origin or of long standing. (143)

The solution that the war neurotic selects (now, at breaking point, and, on the chronicity axis, already forever) entails "the drive . . . to maintain the illusion of the idealized image, save face and blame others for the failure" (138). That sets a trend that in the two world wars proved that the neurotically maladjusted type can make the top grade as soldier boy (144).

Meyer Maskin and Leonard Altman examine "Military Psychodynamics: Psychological Factors in the Transition from Civilian to Soldier." Selection doesn't answer all the questions: "Some neurotics adapt splendidly to military life" (263). But for the majority, it's true: neurotics don't benefit from (because they crave too much) the communion or community service.

> It is clinically incontestable that considerable numbers of psychoneurotics maintain themselves adequately and usefully in civilian life. . . . If unmolested, these persons do not usually request

medical attention and remain part and parcel of the great sub-
clinical psychiatric demi-monde. However, if their arrangements
are disturbed, as, for example, by entry into military service, casualties ensue. (263)

The balancing acts of family life are upended by the plain texts of "Sub-
mission-Dominance" and "Obsessive-Repetition" (264). In the category of
"Socio-Sexual Frustration," the couple of authors point to a "problem in
the army" that is "nuclear." "For the soldier, the letter from home is an un-
mitigated necessity" (264). The American family, which was always more
about the future now of peer groups outside the immediate family than
about the extension of the family across generations, suddenly acquires a
history, a history of loss, which gives the American teen in the army now a
first taste and task of mourning:

> For the American the future has always been important. Sud-
> denly, in the army, the past becomes important. . . .
>   The depression which occurs occasionally upon induction
> is characterized by a feeling of emptiness and loss and is dynam-
> ically analogous to the bereavement felt on the loss of a loved
> object. (265)

The indiscretions bred by frustration are all along for the narcissistic regression that empties out of the missing family pack (the "past" of family and
friends back home gets majorly idealized, the authors stress, which of course
is a way of getting back at them for letting him go). In the midst of all the
nonadult outlets of camp sexuality from the "hyperaesthetic sexual attitude"
evident at any "post theater" and renewed "emphasis on secondary eroge-
nous zones" to "masturbation, promiscuity and homosexuality" there comes
the mention of adultery prospects, which like all these alternatives pack a
mega-charge of guilt and reversal of charges. The one contemplating adultery makes the paranoid jump from his own guilt "to anxiety concerning
the sexual behavior of the wife at home" (265). As every couch potato
knows, evenings of *un*adulterated pleasure in front of maternal symbols
(feeding-time props like TV or VCR) are the standing, standard offer of
family life. The rest is "restlessness, boredom, depression, alcoholism and
aggressive behavior" (265–66). "There is no mother surrogate in the army"
(266). But the American family set up here as terminal or object is in transition now, an in-between phase that the military life of World War II has
fast-forwarded into the great divide between the old family values and
new ones, with a healthier system on its way. "War is cultural revolution.
Inevitably remarkable metamorphosis in value occurs" (266). Thus while

traumatic neurosis, conceived as "breakdown" in a soldier's "security techniques," happened because it recurred psychogenically under "sufficient tension and danger," the analysis and breakdown of war gives both sides of the history: "If war is destructive, it possesses no less power for construction and therapeusis" (267). The old "provincialism" of hometown America (267) was on one continuum with an army that was essentially "a culture complex without women" and thus foregrounded conflicts and anxieties about homosexuality often even in the commission, but big time in the projective and "panic reactions" (266). All this comes down to the closing section, "Feminine Emancipation." "The introduction of women into the armed forces of the Allied Nations has facilitated the development of feminine social parity.... Increased cultural emancipation serving, as it does, to enhance assertiveness, security and personality growth, must inevitably reduce the incidence of feminine neurosis." The authors borrow from the idiom of Victorian decline (Stoker got to gnaw it up close in his typeface) when they face "the new woman" before whom many men will "cringe."

> However, the renascence of women will ultimately beget a new, freer, collaborative and democratic relationship between men and women. In this improved relationship will be found considerable prophylaxis against neurotogenic factors arising out of familial discord. (269)

The 1949 hand-me-down handbook *Bulletin of the U.S. Army Medical Department* 9, supplemental number, shows that the family, if left unreadjusted to the changes programmed into soldiers, can only undermine morale (then as now) as though some prewar, pretechnological, prehistoric object of nostalgia. In other words, not only must a sense of unity bind the soldiers to their organization and nation, but the home too must be shock inoculated, made friendly and efficient, not the kind of object relation that one could lose or return to. "Lacking both a sense of responsibility with regard to war objectives and the security that comes from identification with a company or regiment, the more dependent soldier in times of stress can turn only to home as a source of security. Nostalgia is, therefore, not merely the result of a drive for secondary gain, but, even more, an integral manifestation of the neurosis itself" (131–32). The war has shown that family life and group psychology (and technology) must coexist and yet cannot if they keep coming at each other from different time zones or planets. What no longer fits inside the old pocket of resistance wears and tears pathogenically within family relations. But if there is no such thing as pure accident—for example, in the choices that make up the idiom of radar—

Studying a training chart in Texas. "Rough riding without the rim!"—the rim, that is, of cooperation that rounds out the patient-centered complex or concept of treatment. Reproduced from *Neuropsychiatry in World War II*, 1:638.

then it becomes possible, even necessary, in the technological settings of modern war and peace, to home in on one's targets or objectives.

The Allies were tuning the therapeutic apparatus (that was already in place for guiding not only soldiers but civilians through the air pressures of total war) to the final station of the crossing of conflict: the homecoming. In his war-timely essay on family problems, James Bossard highlights self-help as the legacy of Freud (65). But the self-analysis Bossard has in mind concerns the family's evaluation of wartime developments that fast-forwarded peacetime changes going down in the institutions of marriage and family to the home front of survival of the species. For the first part of the twentieth century, the American family has been off and running through war to science fiction, the low-maintenance plan colonizing perversion, group psychology, and psychosis all the way to where no one had been emboldened to go before: "It might have been spoken of in biological parlance as an active mutant" (65).

The release of pressure on the young to marry through the new libidinal upsurge of war weddings that rush to make the deadline uses war conditioning to promote a rising ratio of bad marriages now breeding their own psychological damages. "This pressure operates—at the induction center, in the platoon, on the ship, in the ground crew, the girls' sorority, the crowd, the clique—everywhere there is the contagion of example" (67). But with this one exception of a mismatch that catches on, epidemic proportions are otherwise assigned in these studies only to the most severe cases of war neurosis, which must be quarantined in analytic therapy. The exception that proves a rule of couplification is taken to the limp wrist that the partner in a bad marriage and the symptomatizing soldier have to hand each other. Same-sex ties both undermine long-distance marriages and promote the latest fad of marrying quickly and badly.

> There may be homosexual developments, as past experience reveals. Sublimating forms of activity may be accepted. Finally, affectional relationships may be developed with other men with or without sexual exchange, and with or without subsequent feelings of guilt. There is ample evidence from this and previous wars that all these reactions occur, and again it is important to remember that the longer the separation continues, the longer the new affectional lines have a chance to crystallize. (68)

Ever since its analytic discovery or recovery during World War I, the bottom line of narcissistic wounding that the cracked cases of war neurosis opened up has been interpersonalized by just about everyone but Freud as the homosexual problem. This interpersonalization of the flaw in the psychic appointment of war-neurotic soldiers gave a rise to the nomination or name-calling of the homosexual tendency as the weakest link in an evolutionary chain of command. In Britain, group therapies developed during World War II for managing symptomatizing soldiers and, one heartbeat later, for treating problem adolescents and children who had been evacuated to group settings from their homes, homes on the target range of air war, could immediately be recycled postwar for treating homosexuals. In the United States, family therapy values ruled the metaphors that got mixed in the war labs to diagnose the constitutional possibilities of breakdown. Before the big jump cut to post–World War II homophobia there was, during the war, that option of or opening for internal recycling of homosexual components via the new no-man zones of Freud's theorizing of narcissism, perversion, psychosis, group psychology, you name it, back inside the libido pool of applicants of choice for the efficient soldier position of techno-merger.

There was, for example, female trouble with the wartime separations between front line and home front by the one it takes to know one, Edith Weigert, in her 1943 article for *Psychiatry*. The push you have received, women of America, toward independence seems proportionate to the shove back into Victorianism that the Axis has commanded just for the sexual difference. For the Allied side, this means elimination of "some of the traditional differences by which the behaviour of the sexes is characterized" (375). Separation without difference equals the regrouping of women around themselves and around their self-hatred. In other words: "War separates families, and creates opportunities for transient extramarital or homosexual relations" (375). That's a rich "or" Weigert is mining. She demonstrates the attention a term can get when she sizes up "penis envy" for the sick sense that jump-cuts out at you, right in your type-face. The standard definition doesn't apply to her three cases of women for whom the war emergence of more masculine self-assertions was couched in the need for analysis. But the term has force of its own, burrowing beneath the labels that don't fit to find its one bitch of a meaning:

> Since psychoanalytic terms have become quite popular, patients offer the concept of penis envy frequently as explanation for their problems. In one of his last papers Freud called penis envy the "bedrock" of resistance against therapy.
>
> It is also my experience that neurotic women use this concept as a stronghold of resistance against any readjustment, as a biological rationalization for their lack of self respect and for a vindictive hatred against the male. It implies the tendency to consider feminine insecurity as fundamentally irreparable. Nothing can be done about an anatomical deficiency, and the therapist is helpless as long as the patient upholds the view that the penis is the basic requirement for human self respect. But such a phallocentric prejudice, which has some similarity with the postulation of a master race, does not sufficiently explain the tendency of self defeat in neurotic women. (377–78)

Thus Weigert (a name that means in German "declines" or "refuses") rereads Freud's resistance address, penis envy, as the label showing neurotic resistance on the part of women who submit to the missing part. But the new Allied family declines resistance labels of separation just as it refuses the appeal of Nazi regression. In other words, the new parity or couplification between the sexes transfers peer pressures from the group to the family setting.

In "A Variety of Furlough Psychosis" Fox explores what he calls "biographical explosions" or, by any other name, psychotic breaks that fall between the cracks of separation and give psychiatry an outside chance to observe what's going down.

> To anyone particularly interested in the dynamics of human behaviour, the Army scene provides experiments in biography simplified by a most instructive reduction in the number of variables.... The response to authority is often sharply outlined in personal relation to non-commissioned and to commissioned officers; and the degree of emotional dependence on home ties becomes very evident when there is a physical separation of many thousands of miles lasting from several months to several years." (207)

Those are the breaks psychiatry gets to read the identificatory label on the back of the projection: "In all four examples the psychotic content included allusions to homosexuality, which with alcoholism and paranoid trends forms a familiar triad" (208). The peer pressurization was, in a word, "dynamite." There is a homosexual undertow in the wave of a future given in the emergency breaks of psychosis that requires the setting up of breakers against what's current in group psychology. The gang bang conditions of soldiers on leave of their senses arouses a certain, unquestionable "homosexual satisfaction derived from the awareness that the other man is sharing a sexual opportunity" (209). But the candidate for homosexuality or war neurosis can, for all the same reasons, enter himself as group-of-one, as gadget lover, in the beating pageant of techno-prowess. One man's break is another man's success story. The placeholder for the breakup of one of the soldiers studied by Fox was the soldier's alcohol abuse, which held in place his nonstop communion with his mother, while holding him back from self-realization of his ambitions up the hierarchy of flight. "It seems likely that in his case the urge to be a flyer represented primarily a need for identifying himself with the speed and power of his plane" (209). Soon the streamlining or straightening out that's along for air force can go without saying.

In Bossard's study of war marriages, too, the other new addition that can be made (as though only in the gap of separation or as fallout of the failure allowed to grow within the deregularization of heterosexuality in wartime) is the gadget-loving attention to the detail, the military unit or unity of every soldier-husband for himself marching to the upbeat of transmutation. The family pack to which he marches back must also make this cutting in of change.

> War time training has wrought miracles, not only in the physical appearance but also in the social personality of the trainees. Perhaps nowhere can this be seen more clearly than in the picked personnel that goes into military aviation.... Underlying all of these efforts, both in democratic and totalitarian countries, there is the conscious purpose of the reconstruction of the personality; for purposes of this analysis, it is evident that all members of families involved will not share equally in these processes. To the extent, then, that the personality of one member of the family is reconstructed, and others are not, family disorganization must inevitably result. ("Family Problems in Wartime," 70–71)

Therapy Values

With the absence of a leg to stand on, Edward attends the reopening of the spot he was already in with his parents. But the dropped bomb of absence also cuts off the leg of a journey around world conflict that was phallically propped up by his friend Jonny, who, innocently standing by, died in the blast that took the legs and brought back the legacy of their original absence. The first close call of transference that Edward accepts is to Jonny, whose dead body lies at the opening of the narcissistic precincts that crack under the hard shell of shock. After the first shot of truth serum, Edward leaks the secret of the dead seaman.

> It was clear: he concerned himself a great deal with the deceased, he identified himself in part with Jonny, this gay brother, in whom he saw everything that he loved.... That is why he attached himself to him, followed him into the realm of the dead, played the dead part. (Döblin, *Hamlet*, 24)

Like game, when it's up, Edward played dead at impact, but the shock values stayed on and took him down with his friendship. It's like a replay of the primal onset of the silent treatment Franz Biberkopf gives himself after the multiple loss through betrayal of a friendship that's homoerotic. The betrayal gets doubled back onto the invasiveness of too much loyalty by half, by the better half that it just takes two men never to consummate.

When Edward first comes out of the shocked silence that's been following the bomb dropped on him, he's all hands on deck, all over the withheld fear blasting from the past, living for the one moment of impact. When he's taken below, out of earshot of the other soldiers who are in recovery all set to hit the deck, he asks the first of the questions that fill his Oedipal research-and-destroy program: he wants to know the who and where of what he is. Then he quickly slides across this first patch of bottomless questioning back into the vegetable state of total amnesia he's bringing home. Edward's silence and his restarting to speak in questions are at the thought-disordered end of the psychopathology continuum. As he rattles past deathlike silence into speech, it's as though the apparatus, like an engine, were misfiring, near missing. But he keeps on plugging into the questioning that's the only outlet he knows to spite the nothingness that's in his face. "An enigmatic sphinx was lodged inside him and moved his lips, but didn't let him formulate the right sentences" (32).

Soon the questioning gets on the circling La Brea bus of the father's sentencing. Locked onto a transference beam, that of p-unitive relations with father, the discourse fine-tunes to questions of war guilt. "Ever since Edward has improved his father is no longer the same as before. When Edward was bedridden, immobile, all was for the best at home and as usual. Now the boy is shaking up the family" (370–71). Another veteran comments on the overkill of serving in two wars: "Stupid family stories. We made it through the war only to be dragged again through this morass" (305). But the mother of all the wars points out that Edward's questioning gives them all back a peace that's only of their own minds: "This is where Edward grew up and became the way he is" (344). Or again: "We don't need any expeditions to foreign lands in order to wage this war. We don't even need to go to the movies to follow it: we can find it all comfortably where it belongs in the home" (411).

The father began the narrative round with a story that picked up a cure-all morale for the masses taken from his own narcissism: imposture for all. If we're all becoming more phantomlike, as Edward concludes from the narrative of the father's name, then where's the other whose loss comes first, or, in other words, whose death wish is it anyway? Edward, for his dead part, senses his own proximity to the ghosts of the war dead (167). "I returned from the war—not just with this stupid torn-off leg but rather—without me. My psyche was also stolen. I know father's story about Lord Crenshaw who doesn't find his self. He doesn't find his real self, he searches, but in the meantime he does after all have one. I have none. Just a vacuum and always terrible anxiety, and then dreams, in which I am attacked" (155).

Oedipus literalized as Edward's implant or techno-chip on his shoulder lines up with the rapid turnover between analogy and illness that war first mobilized for the inside review of psychoanalysis. Psychic apparatus and flight into illness were two or three things Freud knew about the psyche that he watched grow through literalization into a mass or measure as big as any norm. Next, analysis of war neurosis opened up the narcissistic resources of libido filling up the emergency tanks of psychotic war economies. The psycho who had last been seen occupying, together with his broken-down see-through apparatus, the conceptual boundary of psychoanalysis could now be nominated in the roll call of war neurosis as the new Everyman—every man, that is, for himself. Literalization shares its edginess with the breakdown articulation of a schizophrenic thought or speech disorder. In 1919 Freud announced that schizophrenia could be one more extratransferential or narcissistic disorder that discoveries now going down around the war neurotic and with regard to the bigger than the facts-of-life resources of narcissism and ego libido would be bringing within range of understanding and treatment. New therapy settings were developed for the mass condition of shell shock that in fact quickly found extension to treatment of severe regression at large. First there were the saturation interpretations of the transference by Klein and her object-relations followers. Then the followers discovered the group-therapeutic auto-healing mechanism, the ready-made that gave follow-up treatment. On another World War II transmission, the balancing acts of feedback and homeostasis could now be discerned throughout all the family packaging that even or especially schizophrenics cannot leave behind. Both schizophrenics and their families were taken for what they were: interlocking parts of a nonautomobilic machine or system of self-regulation that operated in the place or displacement of the interior reaches (and retches) of loss management. That the family to schizophrenic continuum could be seen as systemic rather than as fuel driven became the free gift—the saving power or safety zone— that was issued through analytic attention to psychotic membership in the package dealings of family life.

Between the impostor father's screen memories and the son's actual but unconscious stay, the L.A. address is shared only by Döblin, whose own busman's holiday in Hollywood issued the Hamletian case of the soldier whose war neurosis belongs in the home. At the end of his consultancy for the Hollywood movies, in which the downswings of war neurosis alternated with, were the alternator for, the upward mobilizations of psychological warfare, Döblin underwent conversion in California. The memory of transference tickets for the La Brea bus screens the metabolization of losses through conversion, through the converter driving us into the teeming mass psychology of adolescence and driving apart the individual relations of therapeutic correctness into new regroupings of therapy in groups, families, and couples. The psychodramatic consequences of the American conversion craze that, beginning in the late eighteenth century, brought us the birth or rebirth of adolescence are still in therapy.

The amnesia genre that's been so cyberspecial in such movies as *Total Recall* and *Johnny Mnemonic* first hit the screens of projection in the follow-up treatments of shell shock dating back to World War I, the first media war. The soldiers returned from the caesura of some blast or wound as though edited and projected for the quaking sensurround of symptomatic jump cuts and freeze-frames that leave them hanging in the lurch. What fills up with aftershocks of a memory image drawing blanks in its own time zone sends displacements and symptom formations to all the forward fronts and about-faces that miss the moment.

The forget-together of trauma marked the spot we were in with the new technologies and with the concurrent regrouping of conflict and resolution that began with splitting the research subject of war into egoic doubles at internal or eternal war with themselves. But trauma could only render missing what was already due to absence or separation. Trauma is always at the same time early trauma, the kernel or colonel of one continuum and column of wounding that begins and ends with the routing of the damn spot of early loss. It's the exhaust, the backfire, of the unknown loss that, along for the development drive, requires the stockpiling of symptoms around the missing or remote center of control, command, communications.

Hitchcock's *Spellbound*, his 1945 contribution to the amnesia genre (which tracks back to the German and Austrian intake of war neurosis backing the *Caligari* projection), stirs the beginnings of trauma analysis with what's already transgression against the transference. Drawing up its symptoms in a perspective it shares with the genealogy of total or media wars, the amnesia genre often sets a spell with transference transgression. In its explicit dealings with "psychoanalysis," *Spellbound* works out the tension between interpretive shorthand and the metabolization of transference in terms of a transgression that's also a race between analytic breakthrough that's been working on the transference all along mourning and psychotic breakdown of boundaries.

To set the spell, interpretation restores the Oedipal identity of the amnesiac. But only his transference affair to remember with colleague, lover, and analyst in one gives the command to heal: "I can't remember except that I love you." Because it's the analyst who is the one with a bad case of ct's, the analyst of the analyst, back home from the army hospital, gets called in to contain the leak. Jokes at his own polymorphous expense lube the transferential connection to the grandparent, the trans-parental figure and primal father. First joke interprets the protagonist's resistance: "Apparently the mind is never too ill to make jokes about psychoanalysis." Second joke issues the invitation to send in your primal submissions now to a transference without conditions: "Any husband of Constance is a husband of mine, so to speak." With transference love or transference transgression in good supply for the speed race that alternates between the breaks you get and the ones you're left embodying and that settles down the lines flagged and redrawn by after-the-fact father transferences, the amnesiac's self-parking that throws away the key in early childhood trauma gets validated: it was a brother's accidental death that had all along been deduced and deducted from the dolorous sense the survivor picked up from his own unconscious commissions of murder. The currency of the double crisis of amnesia is all up front about its origin in plane wreck. The crash landing of this second amnesia destabilized what was forgetomatic about the first amnesia, right down to its defensive emergency. His wrecked nerves shut down the one current memory of accident that, together with his more primal recollection, ran from the one commentary of his guilty assumption that all the murders were his to commit to memory.

In *True Lies* the morale that's given is that the family is the super savior of world crisis. But behind the lies or lines, we know it took the world or world wars to save the family. The family unit or unity is flown in by air power across the new frontier or borderline of psy fi. There are three psy fi relations fostered across the airwaves: the solo bond between pilot and plane, the total group resolve and reservation that, bottom line, follows the bouncing bombs, and then the family setting that fits in with the assemblage of coworkers around and in planes or any of the other gadget foci of total or media war, including, within the civilian attention span, the establishment of TV (which, at one outer limit, in the Nazi German TV rooms [*Fernsehräume*], could be expanded along group-psychological lines to a maximum occupancy of three hundred viewers). Even before VCR, the return of the big screen of projection to TV formatting in small groups and family packs had to occur on planes.

What fits the plane, the planning in small format, is the family unity with the internalized machine. It was time to cut our losses and share the splits with our machines. This is where the amnesia genre fits right in and sets its spell. Just in time for World War I, the term "blackout" started getting around as a theatrical special effect or Oedipal side effect that could give a scene primal clearance. (The *OED* gives it a first date of 1913.) By 1934 the term covered both failure of electric lights and temporary loss of memory. Next year blackouts in the home meant obscuring all light at night during the open season of air raids. By 1940 the blackout trajectory took to the skies, where the term now signaled loss of bearings through temporary blindness—the all blackness in front of the eyes that the Germans first called "curtains"—that spins off with the physical derangement produced by a sudden sharp turn or acceleration that the craft is the first to undergo or go for. In his *Military Psychology,* in the chapter that gives the breakdown and analysis of machine psychologies ("Adaptation of Skills to Military Needs"), Meier lists the "black out" or cerebral anoxia, which had most recently been associated with dive-bombing, as one of the side effects coproduced by "artificial aids" and trained skills that must operate so routinely as to appear automatic (111).

Within psychoanalysis, now and again as the owner's manual of our ongoing technologization, amnesia has an early start covering the primal scenes of one-on-one trauma secreted within the family, spilling but absorbing the shocks to family integrity in the identifications of the patient. Once fantasy is admitted, infantile amnesia becomes the fact of life that sets up screens for every consumer's protection. (Ever since we've been hanging with the see-saw, present-past, of witness projection between the repressed memory and the memory of a repression.) The convergence of the two blackouts, within traumatic amnesia, a conditioning that might follow techno-accidents, as in a train wreck or as in war, really gets mentioned only once by Freud, as passing analogy with the missing piece for which fetishism performs a double take of substitution. Freud's take on fetishism in his 1929 essay is given with the flight pattern of oscillation he extends to the psychic organization of two sons who both know and don't know, in either case, that their fathers are dead. It's the place of breakdowns that turn around into adjustment, low maintenance, and all the other standards of war technologization. Even the fetish, the gadget, takes us outside the reproductive packaging of families only to balance the act and give all feedback back to the family system.

Family therapy, formulated by the 1950s as the approach that still during the 1990s was the treatment of choice within the U.S. establishment of eclectic psychotherapy, grew directly out of the trial runs of World War II. In theory, family systems therapy is based on the computer-compatible communications model of mental life that took off first in the corpus of Gregory Bateson, where it followed, in the shadow of the first takeoff of rockets, the dotted line of nonstop decoding of a random secreting or scrambling of commands that repeated or rehearsed the invention of automatic math or computing. Bateson's further mixing of the metaphor—for example, of feedback—through communication studies all the way to a new theory and therapy of psychology in groupings was never far removed from its model, the original soldier cyborg, first standing to the attention of research in the broken-down and thus opened-up state of war neurosis, and then in restarted upwardly mobile form as the gadget lover of total war merging across the airwaves with his machine. Bateson therefore counts his Pacific Rim propaganda work during World War II as already doubly bound to trigger schizo short circuits in the enemy psyches:

> We had a small radio station in Chittagong which broadcast to the Japanese-occupied territories of Southeast Asia. We professed to be a Japanese official station and our policy was very simply

> to read the enemy propaganda every day and to rebroadcast it
> with thirty percent exaggeration. (*A Sacred Unity,* 207)

In 1944 Bateson was seeing double or nothing when he invoked Freud's reading of an aggrandized state in *Totem and Taboo:* "Perhaps some advance in culture, like the use of a new weapon, had given them the feeling of superiority" (*A Sacred Unity,* 16). Bateson follows Freud's reference to Atkinson's *Primal Law* and discovers a missing link: "Freud does not comment on the parallel between pubescence and the 'new weapon'" (16 n. 6). But it's Bateson who pulls up short before the "primal law" of the precursor and doesn't follow Freud into his post–World War I system, where his theorization of group or adolescent psychology is ready and waiting. At this point of not following, Bateson is bound twice over to his own cyber-take on doubling, his discovery of the prosthetic range of gadget love and its group internalizations, and his opening of a psychic or psychotic apparatus that, running on automatic, for the cover of outer space, does compute.

Helm Stierlin is the analysis-compatible family therapist for postwar Germany. His notion of delegation maps a multigenerational trajectory of melancholia that, for example, in the rewiring he undertakes of Rudolph Binion's deep read of Hitler, his mother, and his dead siblings, folds group-psychological prospects out of the individual case of his family. Student of Karl Jaspers, Mitscherlich, and Viktor von Weizsäcker, Stierlin followed the beat where Harry Stack Sullivan patrolled psychotics. His following and understanding of Sullivan's work established first contact with the families of schizophrenics. By 1968 Stierlin had determined that not only the mother but even and especially the whole family was so important to the work with schizophrenic patients. He thus joined the lineup of family systems theorists from Bateson on up or down.

> Family therapy implies a system rather than an individual (or at
> best a dyadic) approach, that observable transactions often have
> primacy over inferable intrapsychic processes, and that therapeu-
> tic activism may be more effective than a passive furtherance of
> insight. (*Psychoanalysis and Family Therapy,* 13)

Family systems therapy advertised "a new language that . . . was scientifically more up to date than that of psychoanalysis. To a large extent, this was the language of cybernetics" (13). The more timely a language, however, the faster it's dated and disposable.

What attracted Stierlin was the "focus . . . on those mostly unconscious and/or unnoticed mechanisms which in psychoanalysis show up in intrapsychic conflicts and defenses, and which in family theory recur in family myths, processes of delegation, 'invisible loyalties,' the trading of dissociations, mutual enslavements through shame and guilt, and many more. To me, these dynamics imply yet also transcend a psychoanalytic point of view" (14). What's thus bigger than psychoanalysis can also do a few overlaps with "existentialism" (in particular its popularization as model of self-help or acceptance of one's own death) and with a focus on object relations.

> These comments point to a seeming affinity and complementarity between the schizophrenic condition and existentialism. (43)

> The inner objects determine our relational course like a gyroscope, a steering device which minimizes the distracting impact of weather conditions. Therefore I shall refer to their *gyroscopic function*. (132)

Out of these synthetic texts on the periphery of an aggrandized, family-size psychoanalysis emerges Stierlin's conclusion to his Hitler study, namely, that he has all along been assessing not Hitler versus non- or anti-Hitler but the bad family therapist compared to a really good one (*Adolf Hitler*, 130–31).

The postwar family gets reorganized, Jetsons style, around the newness of the shock of war. As Bossard concludes: "The resiliency of the family— this is its answer to the wars of the past. The family has survived many wars" (72).

Because the Nazi military-psychological complex promoted techno-fantasies of race or species unbounded by couple or family values, the Allied psychological war strategy took up the struggle for what was thus endangered: family and couple, procreation and love. To admit a victory celebration on the basis of greater technological know-how without at the same time filing for victim status could only mean or equal for the Allies being Nazi too. What survives or bounces back for more is the ghost we thought the family had given up but which the family now becomes—packs off and control releases to all our remote cornerings by long distance and the unconscious. The Nazi mobilization of the transitional objection that reproduction still makes to techno-replication was antifamily in the divisions it made and sent to the techno-future between the couple and the group. The Allied psy war counteroffensive defended the target values of the family. The Nazi techno-operation was paranoid in its one-way understanding of the other's psychic makeup and in the accompanying blindness to constitutional weak spots in one's own psychic functioning, which was not seen, however, only to the extent that they could be seen through all the

A WAC psychiatric social worker in Texas interviews a neuropsychiatric soldier-patient. Reproduced from *Neuropsychiatry in World War II*, 1:614.

way to total healing. The Allied psyche kept its victim status, its own internal losing streak, right on the front line of winning. Although it has been said that the Nazis lost only because they didn't know when to stop winning, the Allies, in turn, seemed able to win just like a victim. The victim or what family systems therapy refers to as identified patient survives World War II as the stand-in for the family packaging of loss mismanagement, the stand-up diversion at family dysfunctions. In the course or crisis of World War II, the total fantasies of conflict left the face-off squarely between the individual in therapy (in other words, the transferential couple) and the group (the leader and the pack identification that's mutual over time). Plane flight and TV viewing reset group psychology on the family pack format. The family was thus technologized and doubled as favorite haunt for all the balancing acts of techno-tension going down between the couple and the group, between reproduction and replication.

EPILOGUE ON FIRE

Leave a Message, but Don't Forget to Breathe

"Kick mommy," the loving husband and father-to-be suggests. "Kick, kick, kick." Mother abuse? No, it's just another day at Prenatal University, where parents talk to their unborn children in the hope of helping them be smarter, happier newborns. In 1979 Rene Van de Carr, a California-based gynecologist and obsetrician, founded his Prenatal University on the idea that we can build better babies if we start before they're born.... PU matriculation begins in the fifth month of pregnancy. The curriculum calls on mom and dad to repeat simple verbs like "pat" and "rub" while they're patting and rubbing. (Mothers-to-be with soft voices use "pregaphones" to address their midriffs; fathers just bend over mom's belly and speak.)

—*NEWSWEEK*

A mile above the Pacific Ocean, the light plane's engine popped and failed and Rodger LaRue plummeted toward what he felt was certain death—so he grabbed the cellular phone and called his mother. "Tell dad I love him," LaRue said. "I love you, too, mom." ... LaRue thought of his mother, telling her over the phone that the engine had failed and they were going to go into the ocean. He said he asked his mother if she wanted to stay with him until the end. She said it would be too painful, and the two hung up.

—JULIE M. ZEIDNER, *LOS ANGELES DAILY NEWS*

The No Smoking sign lit up first in the West. On the descent into Los Angeles, we still watch the swimming pools catch the rays of the setting sun. Down in the uncanny hideaway below that's, lo and behold, precisely where we were to join the forget-together at what's hip we find, on our decline into the west, a pooling of resources for having fun (yet)—that goes down and out to the body count. Every backyard has one: a body of water (bodies are, at the bulk rate, basically water) artificially contained and pumped up, through, and away with the nonstop recycling efforts that keep what's in effect dead just a heartbeat away from decay. The regimen of dialysis—the workout of pool cleaning—is administered by the local cute teenager.

Poolside is the favorite haunt of adolescence: it's where the need for a job is flexed in the first place, but given only a headstart away from the other short-term goals of the Teen Age: from learning how to have fun (the group-sizing of libido) to how to pump up into the body of the group while scheduling the date within the Elysian force fields of high ambivalence between the couple (the basic unit of mourning) and the group (which never mourns).

The reflecting pool in the atrium is the only simulacrum at the Getty Museum that's out of all proportion with the original imitation villa (and thus very much in sync with the giveaway alterations and reductions that go into the representation of the everyday in amusement parks or mortuary palaces). It had to be made shallow rather than dug deep because according to California law, any public space surrounding sink-or-swim bodies of water requires a lifeguard in attendance.

No smoking poolside. According to local custom, it is unthinkable, as it was even during the first phases of transition, of phasing out, to smoke by the pool. The active or reactive lungs of lap swimmers would be passively smoking too deeply. The same fact or fantasy of counterproductivity runs like a laugh track alongside runners in the smog. Remember, when dealing with the natives, that Californian friendliness is a new-and-improved mode of efficiency, of preparedness in groups (right in the face—the happy face—of catastrophe).

During the period of transition to smoke freedom, phones were stuck in the seat backs in front of you. Yes, it recalled the phone services extended around 1900 to the dead, who were thus given protection and projection, an outside chance in the event of live burial. Inside those crypts or booths, one could still change into a survivor body. In the family setting of bodies in rows plugged into tubes of audiovisuals, the phone call is reserved for the final journal entry, the last will and testament, the suicide note. If you get voice mail, then the jet lag of postal messages still applies (if a vestigial answering machine is the other's placeholder, then screen or scream memories still admit, death wish style, the earshot of the other). If the transmission is a live one, it's as much a merger as a murder that's going through down the hotline that groups support around the catastrophe one signs up for with every leave-taking or takeoff. There's the psy fi fantasy out there, somewhere over the transference where science fiction meets psychosis, that the wound of takeoff can be converted in a flash into the wonder, the miracle, of merger with the machine in flight (and thus with the first trajectory of our technologization that can skip or skip around the gravity, the grave of earth and body). But the postop conditions of in-flight phone service can't make it out of the family packaging. Up in the air, not even the back-of-the-busing segregation of smokers could protect one's personal space from invasion and contamination.

The Teen Age

With the advent of codependency, everyone started qualifying for support group psychology within an extended-family setting tuning in primal scenes of addiction or abuse. Substance or child abuse fills in the blanks and takes aim, in group, at the childhood that can only be found missing.

The cure-all administered in AA groups gets at the heart of the problem and keeps it there: inside a free association that's compatible both with the mass at large (what Christianity and techno-group formation have and hold in communion) and, case by case, with psychosis. The group therapy format takes its mainline compatibility with these modern masses or measures of adaptation—but always at an inoculative distance or dosage. The group rates of interchange and charge between these two extremes of anonymity give the addict (who is us) shelter, coverage, or recovery. If we take it as interpersonally as it was given, the AA group grope response to habit formation—today one of the largest "religions" on earth—was the inspiration, the dictation taken down from Jung, whose short attention to psychoanalysis spanned one conversion experience that, as always, gave itself away totally in the channel switch to the next conversion. The step program Jung got with could be found already exorcising such dangers to health and wholeness as drinking and smoking ever since the American craze of conversion or, at the very latest, since the turn-of-the-century psychological study of this crowd phenomenon. The same delegation that addressed smoking first and, now, last as the ultimate teen habit, haunt, and rebellion without a pause was the one that met Freud and Jung when they visited psychoanalysis on America.

But Jung's program, the one we're still getting free with AA group membership, was the already late arrival of a mass craze of conversion that had its history taken by turn-of-the-century psychologists specializing in the makeup of crowds, groups, masses. When Freud (according to Jung, according to Lacan) looked forward to his American tour as spreading the "plague" of psychoanalysis to open-headed consumers, he was still cosigning his science with Gustave Le Bon's epidemic version of crowd psychology, which, though on one date with the release of Bram Stoker's *Dracula*, another premier owner's manual to the new group psychology of gadget love, was still too stuck on the vampire's spread of his own essence to see how it was all already so superseded, new and improved, in the group effort mobilized to hunt down the bloodsucking dad, I mean, dead. The invitation to the vampire that was issued by American host Stanley Hall was accompanied by a local reading assignment, Hall's own two-volume study entitled, simply but subtly, *Adolescence:* the host study even already cited Freud. American hands-on examination of local histories of conversion had thus added one twist that could only take European crowd psychologists by surprise: what Freud too would later consider as group psychology served up with this twist was already personalized by American host Stanley Hall as the "adolescent psychology of conversion." But today's all-out drive to contain smoking as the ultimate habit, haunt, and rebellion of our Teen Age is not a displaced delegation of conversion psychology; rather, it is, according to the material Hall presented, just what first went up in smoke according to the original conversion rate of exchange in groups. On the sidelines of the teen passion of conversion there were, already back then, forty-year-old smokers support-grouped around the break that only groups can give addiction or identification at more inoculative levels of administration in timed release.

Middle Ages Crisis

> The harmoniously trained human body is today rightfully the
> one that all of us demand, and it no longer goes without saying
> that the man over forty should become a cumbersome product
> of deliberate fattening up.
>
> —J. H. SCHULTZ, *PSYCHIC HEALTH MAINTENANCE*

According to Hall's discovery or recovery of adolescence, the buff body of the group pumps up ultimately to pass a test of willpower. It was just a test that his own midlife criticism was able to pass on as will or testament. In 1901, at the local YMCA, Hall addressed one of the premier or pioneer groups of teens and midlife types to start working out this delegation.

> Remember that nowadays at forty, most men are either invalids
> or philosophers—invalids if they have done their work wrongly
> or are burned out with vice, individual or hereditary, and philoso-
> phers if they had the rare insight to learn to know themselves so
> as to keep completely well.... Try these things yourselves faith-
> fully, and you will begin to feel within you this new gospel of
> the body, the light of which is now being shed abroad in the
> world as never before. ("Christianity and Physical Culture,"
> 377–78)

Try to reconstruct your adolescence—forget childhood, the kiss of death after forty, and no longer the kept promise of eighteenth-century agendas of development that first came together under *Bildung*, the original body-building plan for drawing from the newly opened accounts of childhood credit and loss. If the unconscious that Freud discovered has a history, it would have to be coextensive with the era that begins as printing-press culture and extends into our time zone of live transmissions. Ever since the advent of the printing medium, early childhood was conceivable as the preprogram of desires and tendencies that one must by young adulthood begin to match in the choice of one's line of work. That's the way it goes in all those German novels of *Bildung*, or "development." At the psychoanalytic bookend of the genre, Erik Erikson therefore counsels that finding employment is probably the major task of adolescence (Erikson, 302). While this advice is right on insofar as it qualifies the popular view that in adolescence it's one's sexuality alone that's at the top of the agenda of things to do or figure out, it is at the same time misleading with regard to where development, in the linear view, is going. The job placement of the teen is part of a group membership drive. The real job, namely, the work of identification one enters within a series of one-on-one matches (from the promise one keeps from childhood to the vow one exchanges within the couple), comes, down the line, around the specter or crisis of middle age. And that means that adolescence, while it's happening, can only maintain mega-ambivalent relations with the couple (both the parental one that's off-limits and the future one that the teenager is scheduled someday to join in matrimony). In the couple, in the future, we'll be working on the transference and all that mourning gets in the way. The teen group-of-one traffic-jams with or gags on all the intact and undisclosed identifications or incorporations—*the* mother, *the* father—that catch him where and when he breeds. Twisting, shouting, breaking up make up the special blend that control releases invasive ancestral samenesses on the inoculative assembly line of all-around likability, of mutual admiration or identification in groups. If the promissory investments of childhood were designed to yield interest only by middle age, then adolescence, as the interruption or limit concept of adult developments, represents, even if allowances are made, only small or, more likely, no change. And that's the attraction. The mourning that gets generated between child and adult is skipped via the teen and midlife continuum of crisis that at one end acts out identification and at the other recovers or redistributes it with a longer fuse for the longer haul of a second chance or comeback. The teen group member flips through the many channels open to a short attention span. That's why the couple is the ambivalently focused outside of the adolescent group. If the self-other relation of childhood (to which the adult couple returns via the detour, interruption, or boundary of adolescence) is the stage of all development, then one could characterize adolescence as the vampiric place of nonchange.

But teen vampirism and unmourning can be work, too. "We are coming to know the age of adolescence from the early teens into the early twenties, and we find that one of its chief features, when normal, is muscle growth" (Hall, "Christianity and Physical Culture," 375). Indeed: "By weight the adult human body is nearly one-half muscle" (375). This better half gives the measure of one of two capacities: either waiting around inside or working out of a stuck metabolism. "The muscles are the only organs of the will and are likely to share its strength or weakness" (375). "Rational muscle culture," the only way to go, "is the gospel...so reinforced by all the new knowledge we are now so rapidly gaining of man's body and soul" (375). What's gaining on us with all the speed of the adolescent growth spurtings that are our midlife focus is the insight that the new cute teenager depends, like every bulimic and vampire, on an externalized metabolism for "circulation or irrigation of the tissues with blood": "Youth must be intense; must tingle and glow; have excitement; stretch lungs, blood vessels, muscles to their greatest capacity by warming up and getting second breath for both mind and body" (376). But the second breath or wind you catch rewinds around the double genealogy at once of technical media and occult mediums.

Don't forget, Hall instructs between reps, that the second chance youth must get in middle age is just a second breath away. There's that ghostly ring to second breath that's exchanged whenever it's time for seconds, like second sight or second coming. But the seconding expressed, expired here in the context of midlife recovery of adolescence refers, beyond the one-on-one relations of haunting, to the budding other side of the long-term diagnostic tension or decision between reproduction, as the norm or way to come and go, and phantasms of self-replication that have historically fallen by the wayside, faraway inside psychosis. By now the sides taken up by, one, the childhood or parenthood of individual development and, two, the adolescent-to-midlife attention-getting span of group psychology or technologization have shifted along an evolutionary scale: now reproduction is what we still depend on, but only for the time being, to restock the pool of applicants for techno-evolutionary lab experiments that are promoting relations of replication for the survival of the species. But the dependence that is still there is at the same time on the couple formation that exchanges a good mourning, the coupling, still along retro lines of reproduction, through which the other's missing body gets placed at our disposal service for future incorporation or replacement. Ever since the eighteenth century, the onset of the era of inside-out machine relations, the egos, and I mean us, have been picking up the superegoic takeout order to live on through future generations by going to the register of the psychotic sublime and checking out all together now at the same time. The suicidal bottom line was the fine print where the egoic techno-fantasy found a way to break contract with the superego—by putting the contract out on the ego itself (and on its machinic other or double). Mass suicide doubled as a kind of negative theology of replication. Science fictions or fantasies of replication and doubling keep catching up with life's old-fashioned breeding assignment. The short egoic attention span has been extended now into five-year plans that will lead ultimately to the realization of immortality now. Nonsmoking to this day, as the front line of midlife recoveries of adolescence, is another haunt deep down inside the fine print of the superegoic contract where we do overlaps between a techno-hope and the living end.

When Hall tries to divert us with the German connection, which the Americans have left so far behind that what connects us is more of a cut, *we* make the jump cut into the future terminal of these tracks, the emergence of psychological or media warfare (the first application and final frontier of Freud's group psychology). The youth, the energy, that's otherwise wasted in and on youth has to be rewired, already *during* adolescence, to the new youth-to-midlife regimen of working out and techno-externalization of our metabolism in groups.

The precursor German system of physical training bears the curse of uniformity, command, and one-sided patriotism. The so-called alternative of the American gospel—which differs from the German gymnast cult of the body only in the pedigree of onset, as one phase to another one, of the development of the group body—is more openly mass psychological, plugging equally into the modern mass and the communion of Christianity: "We are soldiers of Christ, strengthening our muscles not against a foreign foe, but against sin within and without us" (377).

Freud would bring this general or generic branding of the American body into focus as the secret psychological weapon that won the Great War. Woodrow Wilson and the Fourteen Points followed a plan as old as Christianity and as new as modern mass conditions. (The Germans were stuck on a countertransferential order or command that totally neglected the balancing act down the ranks of love and identification.) Christianity is what's new and improved in the American mass culture of mutual identification (as Freud notes at the close of section 5 in *Civilization and Its Discontents*). The immediate outcome took the form of winning the war to end all wars; in the longer run of content or discontent, it's Jonestown that's being passed down and around.

The YMCA chain operation of building bodies that Hall commemorated and transmitted in 1901 had started up and spread in the United States in the wakes of the Civil War, the first techno-war. For the time being or the time to come, the fit with technology must be physically forced. Only the hard body can shoulder the pressures of being part of machines going under or beyond natural boundaries. But there is a Dasein rhyme that gives the introductory offer of the new postnatural techno-maternal body an exquisitely funereal setting. The Civil War also introduced embalming practice on the dead, originally to keep the casualties of war just the picture of death until they could be buried back home.

Jung Frankenstein

To this day, the leading presupposition of adult-development theories—that there are phases of development that are at least equal to, but at last independent of, childhood development—still props itself up as inspired by Jung's 1933 *Modern Man in Search of a Soul* (in particular chapter 5, "The Stages of Life"). What underlies both so-called linear and dialectical theories of adult development is Jung's early displacement of Freud's emphasis on childhood (as the preprogram of all development) onto the more important process of growing up teenage going on adulthood (during which development happens not because it recurs but because it occurs here and for the first time). Jung's declaration of independence from Freud's overuse or abuse of early childhood appeared same time, same station of the double cross, as Jung's first pronouncements as international leader of the new Nazi psychotherapy that reunified the eclecticism of therapies that had, originally, split psychoanalysis. But Jung didn't want to fix those split ends of the new science. That he was just the same, even or especially as the mascot of one German psychotherapy for all, coming into contact with psychoanalysis really pushed his buttons. He could only keep the dial on denial:

> The most precious secret of the Germanic peoples—their creative and intuitive depth of soul—has been explained as a morass of banal infantilism, while my own warning voice has for decades been suspected of anti-Semitism. This suspicion emanated from Freud. He did not understand the Germanic psyche. (Jung, "The Meaning of Psychology for Modern Man," 166)

By 1933 Aryan, as opposed to Jewish, psychology had found its place in the son. Freud was convinced by this time that anti-Semitism was the same thing as resistance to psychoanalysis. All Freud needed to do was listen to the inquiring mind of his number one resister: "In my opinion it has been a grave error in medical psychology up till now to apply Jewish categories indiscriminately to Germanic and Slavic Christendom" (166). The Jews, then, have been keeping us from working out the Middle Ages crisis, the one that National Socialist "energy" (another teenage unconcept) has finally released from "infantilism" and given over to growth. It's okay for the Jews to roll with the negative impact of the unconscious raised to conscious power, but projected onto their so-called neurotic other—namely, the Aryan race—they risk losing the race at the finish line they must draw in the showdown between the unconscious and their one theory of the unconscious. Jung elaborates:

> It is in general less dangerous for the Jew to put a negative value on his unconscious. The "Aryan" unconscious on the other hand, contains explosive forces and seeds of a future yet to be born, and these may not be devalued as nursery romanticism without psychic danger. (165)

But as hard as either side might try to separate the Jung from the late Freud, for example, even the most far-out eclecticizations of the intrapsychic model, which are more often than not interpersonalizations of that model and thus technically valid as far as they go, still belong to the system of Freud's influence, the institution that can, by now, go by the name of "greater psychoanalysis." Jung's diversification of the development portfolio to junior highlight teens and adults is symptomatically in sync with Freud's own explorations of group psychology, perversion, and borderline conditions as modes of functioning that are compatible with, or internal to, a techno-aggrandized state of psychosis that can no longer be bracketed out as limit concept beyond all transference and legibility. When Freud interpreted anti-Semitism first for the resistance and then for the transference, he guaranteed that there could be no brand of acting out, Jung or age old, that didn't at the same time perform a piece of the theory.

Thus in the 1933 study that still leads the way to adult development theories, Jung issues his one condition: to make it out of adolescence (that is, out of the perpetuation of adolescence), and into the next big phase of change, the loss of parental guidance is a requirement. Thus the many subtle changes emerging from the unconscious can be delayed in their appearance, Jung adds, "by the fact that a person's parents are still alive. It is then as if the period of youth were unduly continued" (Jung, "The Stages of Life," in *Modern Man in Search of a Soul*, 105). This rare admission by Jung of the range of the death wish gets him back to Freud (whose back is up to the hilt of the young one's get-better wishes). Childhood has been edited out, and Freud's got to go. He's the father the perpetually teen Jung wants dead, but only in the name of the significant change of adulthood, which is the dimension of development that he marks as his own discovery. That's why Jung introduces religion on the season finale. When it's getting late, to develop means, after the fact, to have been looking forward to a goal. The belief in the afterlife, for example, helps us out of a morbid experience during the closing phasings-out of life. Old age and childhood, all together now, are therefore "the stages of life without any conscious problems" (144). At least Freud didn't experience any pain.

Last Word

Kurt Lewin gave us a future peace of his mind. There are two things (really just one) to keep in mind if we are not again to lose the peace to the Germans:

> One can safely guess that Nazism is deeply rooted, particularly in the youth on whom the future depends. (555)

> If a sufficiently deep and permanent change is to be accomplished, the individual will have to be approached in his capacity as a member of groups. It is as a member of a group that the individual is most pliable. (565)

Gregor Ziemer joins the rundown of "Fascist Youth":

> We can punish the leaders in Nazi Germany and in Japan. But what will we do with the youth which they perverted? . . .
> Germany will be our real laboratory. (584)

But when Lewin closes his account with an evocation of Moses's sense of timing as model for what the postwar Germans will need to defer, he implies some connection between the Nazi Germans and the Jewish slaves of Egypt in spite of the radical difference that, no matter how choice teens may be, the Nazi ones are not chosen. Lewin, who doesn't acknowledge transference or the unconscious in his fieldwork, genuinely believes that one can skip a generation (without at the same time murdering and incorporating it, for example).

> Moses led Israel through the desert for forty years, until the generation that had lived as slaves might die, and the rest learn to live as free people. Perhaps there are still no faster or better methods for the permanent cultural reeducation of a nation. (566)

From Freud's point of view, Lewin's lineup isn't inadmissible; it's just sloppy. Freud in fact is even more relative (but also relational) when it comes to good and evil. According to Freud, we are all party to not-seeing. However, even that which was murderously resisted and not-seen can continue. When the interruption of this continuity subsides, that, too, is our party.

In *Moses and Monotheism*, Freud stressed that the staying power of Moses' legacy had to reassert itself after years without end of murderous rejection and total forgetting. He addressed this overcoming of the gap in the legacy's transmission—to the extent that it was, as per usual, part of the gaping whole of repression—via the model of traumatic neurosis, specifically the way in which the traumatic neurotic symptoms manifest themselves more often after a delay than right on impact with the traumatic event. "On reflection, it must strike us that, in spite of the fundamental difference between the two cases—the problem of traumatic neurosis and that of Jewish monotheism—there is nevertheless one point of agreement: namely, in the characteristic that might be described as 'latency'" (*SE*, 23: 67–68). In this flight manifest of the history of the Jews (during Exodus *and* World War II), the latent part is Freud's identification with Moses, and the future of his science with the survival prowess of monotheism. That Freud signs in here with traumatic neurosis is a late acknowledgment of the import of his World War I engagement with this exceptional case of neurosis (exception to the rule also because the traces tied in childhood in this case can appear elusive) and the starring role of psychoanalysis in the story of the war neurosis epidemic to which he could hitch his thought and the spread of his influence. Freud's first comparison stop in presenting the force that is with the event or advent that, though pushed down and out for the time to come, nevertheless returns intact—continuity shot—without going the disfiguring route of return of the repressed is the delayed but unstoppable recognition of Darwin's rightness and greatness. "During the whole time of the struggle the subject with which it was concerned was never forgotten. We are scarcely surprised that the whole course of events took a considerable length of time; and we probably do not sufficiently appreciate that what we are concerned with is a process in group psychology" (*SE*, 23:67).

Then Freud shifts to the individual formatting of the same sort of example. In the mental life of an individual, a person learns something brand new that he knows is true but at first "shocks a few convictions that are precious to him" (67). He hesitates but then acknowledges what is true as well as how difficult it was for him to accept it (and why). This is a resistance-free moment. Freud's third example, the technical one, is introduced as having "even less in common with our problem" (67). But in traumatic neurosis, despite the delay, the symptomatization remains directly recognizable as responding to the specific traumatic incident in the past or recent past. Therefore repression cannot account for the delay in response.

Via the analogy, Freud argues that in the case of monotheism, repression was reserved for the fate of Moses, whereas disavowal covered the missing fact of Moses' foreign status. But that concerns the written record, which increasingly contradicts the oral transmission, which—and this oral force of the truth of trauma enters analysis via the in-session transference—Freud links to the staying power of monotheism as tradition. "What had been omitted or changed in the written record might very well have been preserved intact in tradition" (68). On their own, oral transmissions can disappear into the gap between generations, leaving only the written record, which is all the show. But tradition can in turn transfer itself to written recording (as was happening just then under Freud's pen). "The phenomenon of latency in the history of the Jewish religion, with which we are dealing, may be explained, then, by the circumstance that the facts and ideas which were intentionally disavowed by what may be called the official historians were in fact never lost" (69). The transmission or tradition (or transference) grows stronger to the point of exercising "a decisive influence on the thoughts and actions of the people" (69). With this "remarkable fact" or "unfamiliar idea," we find ourselves once again "in the field of group psychology, where we do not feel at home" (70).

Freud's next example again reflects the pull of the recent past, which, according to Adorno, is always the most primal past, the past lost to catastrophe that therefore cannot arrive or continue but can only come back, ghostly surprise attack (Taylor, 112). Freud raises (like a ghost) the question of the origin of the legend materials mediated to us through Greek high culture. The discovery of a more ancient Mycenaean civilization on Crete—which Freud once before analogized with the discovery by his women followers of the pre-Oedipal phase, an extension of his science that was precisely not directed against him—gives Freud grounds for this raising to consciousness. "The answer would have had to be that this people had probably experienced in their prehistory a period of external brilliance and cultural efflorescence which had perished in a historical catastrophe and of which an obscure tradition survived in these legends" (70).

For the next section, entitled "The Analogy," Freud checks out of religion and group psychology and into psychopathology, the psychology of individuals. Here Freud advances the role of trauma in every neurosis, with the proviso that one remain clear just how one defines the word "traumatic." The effects of trauma are either positive or negative. The tendency of trauma to set itself in operation again in the neurotic is positive to the extent that repetition is on the way to recollection, (re)experience, and substitution via analogous relations. What's so negative is when "nothing of the forgotten traumas shall be remembered and nothing repeated" (76). All these trauma effects "have a compulsive quality: that is to say that they have great psychical intensity and at the same time exhibit a far-reaching independence of the organization of the other mental processes" (those concerned with the demands of the outside world) (76). These pathological phenomena, in their opposition to external reality or to its psychical representatives can become "a State within a State, an inaccessible party, with which cooperation is impossible, but which may succeed in overcoming what is known as the normal party and forcing it into its service. If this happens, it implies a domination by an internal psychical reality over the reality of the external world and the path to psychosis lies open" (76). The trauma model of neurosis, which follows Freud's turn to traumatic neurosis to mine an analogy for the persistence of monotheism (as of psychoanalysis), even or especially when it looks like it has gone away, cuts just enough slack to get around the scrambling deviousness of repression and return of the repressed—or to hang oneself up on the psychotic pathway.

Primal Time

Erwin Reiss sets the coordinates for beaming up the genealogy of television—the one we've been "not seeing." In 1979 a peep show, a retrograde technology, was left standing at the attention of Berliners right where in 1939 a so-called TV room *(Fernsehstube)* had attracted the local press of fans. Adorno was right on, it's always the recent history we repress even as it just happens that flashes back discontinuously, catastrophically, as primal. That we continue to "not see" this primal time of the popular medium may amount to one of our bigger symptoms. Yearning, which in German is always shadowed by a sense of addiction to seeing, was hitting high points, somewhere over the two waves of the future: air power and TV power. On 22 March 1935, a Nazi official could review a history of media that was looking forward to total TV. Whereas in 1933 radio was mobilized to give Hitler's voice live coverage and transmission to the nth degree, now, in 1935, the highest mission is to "plant the Führer's image ineradicably in all German hearts":

> The community life of National Socialism will receive its highest and most noble form in the future through the participation of our highest and most noble sense organ, the eye. . . . It is the magnificent assignment of the National Socialist TV service to call upon a people to see in the true sense of the word. (in Reiss, 34)

But a double movement was under way: TV's technical developments were driven fast forward while its home set installment plan for individual or family consumption was held back and then withdrawn. In 1937 there were maybe seventy-five home sets in private use (in contrast to the over 8 million radio sets in the Reich that networked the largest reception in Europe). TV development was a case (perhaps the first case) of the sending side being the focus of rapid developments that remained out of sync with slow-step developments on the reception or consumer side.

Network TV development was seen first in the military complex frontforwarded for the war effort, but then it got dropped or wasted by the same effort it took to keep its cabling system expanding or contracting with *Blitz* speeds. But cable networking pulled up short before its safer live transmission could be implemented. Radio broadcasting across airwaves, the live transmission densely crisscrossing the heartbeats of German population centers, either guided bombers on nighttime missions or had to be shut down after sunset, the programming time for psychological

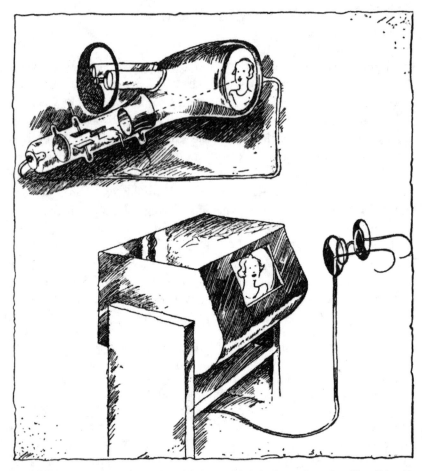

How 3-D TV programming and reception might be possible in the future. Reproduced from Eduard Rhein, *Wunder der Wellen: Rundfunk und Fernsehen dargestellt für jedermann* (1935), 291.

air defense. The cable network, by contrast, could not be used by the air force that was with the enemy. But its use, even or especially in the long run, required stable boundaries and containment on one's own side. Thus when Hitler sent Franco a TV set, the cabling prospects for a military intercom system ran up against the shifting fronts of the Spanish Civil War. When it came to technology, the Nazis were near missers who didn't have rhythm. Their on-again, off-again investments in the future of cable cut short exploration of ultrashortwave technologies, which were so decisively implemented by the Allies, always with just the right element of surprise. The segregation of airwave transmissions during the waiting period for cable service also held back TV's expansionism as mass medium. While the

Nazi command was seeing far into the future when they watched their live coverage of V-2 experiments on their 1942 sets, the Allies were winning the war in the shortwave. (But the Nazis lost, right?) At the same time, the Nazis were pressing TV into the service of teleguiding unmanned vehicles and onward toward the future remote control of the flying and firing of fleets of bombers. By spring 1945 TV-guided air attacks could be aimed at bridges spanning the Oder in the all-out effort to stop the advance of Soviet troops in the tracks of their automobilic technologies. Nice try! Near miss.

Wonders Never Cease

In 1935 Eduard Rhein's *Wonders of the Waves: Radio and Television Presented for Everyman* appeared in a popular ("entertaining") science book series that already counted books on artificial flight, physics, machines, chemistry, geology, biology, and the motor. (The book is one of Reiss's archival digs, in particular for documenting the Nazi German cult of Nipkow, adopted "father" of television.) By the second chapter, we are listening in on a boy's daily lessons in media technology given by his boss. He starts out naive. Thus he gets all confused by mention of hertz; he thinks it means heart because that is what it sounds like in German *(Herz)*; but no, it means the number of oscillations per second (32). The boy's naïveté is countered by examples of experiments conducted on the sense of hearing. A tiny hole drilled into the cochlea of a half-deaf dog proved one point (39). "One has 'tortured' humans with very loud deep and high tones and thereby established that average tone can be amplified 1,000 times before it becomes painful" (44). He shows the boy with some more scary examples that electric waves are everywhere, some just more visible than the others. Even a lit match produces sufficient electric waves to send music and language as wireless transmission (48).

> Consider this: the sun rays ionize our air from above. Imagine it like this, as though a man one floor up was slowly letting gas into my office through a hole in the ceiling. What would happen? First a thin layer of gas would collect just under the ceiling, for coal gas is lighter than air. The lower border of this layer would sink down more and more the longer the man upstairs carried out the "gassing" *[Vergasung]*. (60–61)

The most important part of the lesson on wireless technology is its tubular configuration (72). Only a short time ago, hardly anyone knew about these wonder tubes:

> Only a few engineers and a few radio operators...had learned during the Great War to watch over this miracle shape of technology like a priceless treasure: a few grams of glass, the tiniest bit of metal, put together according to a simple scheme, the whole shape then pumped airless.... The girl for everything!...Just as electricity opens up continually new regions, so the tubes conquer in their unparalleled march of victory one area of technology after another. (73)

An illustration of the transitional mode of television, grafted onto rapid film development, which the coverage of the Berlin Olympics still largely employed: first filmed, quickly developed, then transmitted as TV, nearly live. Reproduced from *Wunder der Wellen, 263.*

The most important tube is the one that amplifies: "It is the magic ring in the hand of the engineer" (74).

> We must be clear from the start on one thing: that the amplification effect of the tubes can to some extent be compared to the magnification effect of a projection apparatus. The magic lantern does not make a big picture out of a little one, but rather with the help of a strong light source and a lens permits us to see the small picture big. Just so the amplifier tubes: they don't make a strong current out of a weak one, rather they create only the possibility, with the help of a powerful source of current, ... of enlarging small variations in current such that we "see big" the audio image, that is, we hear it louder. (90)

Now add to the amplifier tube a storage battery, a so-called condenser: "It functions like a great big storeroom and jumps in helpfully during short pauses in the transmission of current" (80). That is a cross section in miniature. Now for the big picture of broadcasting. The song of a nightingale travels from the south of Germany all the way to Berlin.

> And before it arrives in Berlin it has already gone through 100 million times amplification, has been chased at monstrous velocity through spools and tubes and wires, over resistances and

condensers, and carried through airless spaces by electrons. And just the same: clear and pure and uncompromised the electric miracle messenger carries it to the Sender.... And the entire magic of that small natural voice from the Bavarian woods is still within this oscillating stream. (86)

On the next page, our educator in techno-magic spins further the relay of recordings and retransmissions. The listener to the broadcast in East Prussia records it on a record and sends it to Munich, where it is again broadcast on the air; someone in England tunes in, "magically records it on the narrow tape of audio film," and then listens to it again through the speakers. "Technically all that would be quite possible, and even then the love song of the little troubadour would still be audible and absolutely recognizable. That is the great miracle [Wunder]: the unbelievable precision with which the amplifying tube magnifies the image of a voice, and transmits the finest and smallest detail" (87). In sum, we have learned about the three "building blocks of the tubes": the two poles and then "nothingness. The airless vacuum, where those mysterious processes invisibly unfold, which transforms the modest human product made of metal and glass into a magician of technology" (88).

There are limits, however, for example in the form of a noise that is an effect of rises in temperature, which would thus cease with the nonexistence of the sun: "But then we too wouldn't be alive!" (95). There's another secret troublemaker caused by the way the electricity atoms form the electron current of the tubes. These atoms don't strike uniformly or simultaneously: "Tiny variations of the electron current are therefore unavoidable.—That causes noise disturbances which already at high degrees of amplification make themselves powerfully audible. You see—there are 'miracles' [Wunder], which are not exactly pleasant" (95–96). And the instructor quickly switches to the topic for next session. Won't that be fun! "Wunderbar" says the boy. But he gets in a quick question: back to the nightingale, just how does the sound emerge in the larynx? "Is there something in there too that vibrates?" Techno-teacher: "You bet!—In the larynx the vocal cords vibrate.... The air current is 'cut up' into separate parts during the oscillation of the cords; thus arise convulsions of the air, air waves" (96).

The next topic: selectivity (Trennschärfe). How is the "miracle" achieved as we turn the dial (98)? The human ear can't do it; depending on the distances, various sound sources will come in loud or unclear all at once, a veritable "wave salad." In broadcasting, however, "one has the power to cut out every channel from the chaos of waves with knife-sharp exactness." To this end, one uses the phenomenon of resonance. To tune in one specific broadcast, "one must bring the receiver and the wave into 'resonance'" (100). In this setting we learn that no tinkering will do away with at least some degree of attenuation, "for nothing in this world is without loss" (108). One has to accept the "cutting off of the high tones" (112); the word that makes the cut, *Beschneidung*, also means "circumcision." "It is clear that for these reasons one searched—and is still searching—world wide for a tuning device that would cut off the neighboring waves with the sharpness of a razor but would just the same let the chosen station come through in its full breadth. One has found a very nice solution of this task: the tape filter. It gets its name from its ability in fact to let all 9,000 hertz of the carrier wave uniformly through like a tape, without cutting off the high tones and yet shaves away completely the neighboring waves" (112). It's a complicated procedure and very costly right now in the making, but this solution is coming through soon. Then our guide to media technologization prospects pulls out another comfort that is already in place. "But there is a rather comfortable—in its simplicity even elegant—means to reduce the attenuation even of a poor oscillatory circuit during reception, indeed to bring it in fact down to zero. This method of de-attenuation is feedback [*Rückkopplung*]" (114). "If through feedback one can turn back a portion of these amplified oscillations to the tuner, then through this extra force one can again equalize the losses which the arriving wave suffers in the tuner and even in the receiving antenna connected to it" (115). But temperature changes can still influence the waves, muddle them. But once again there is already a solution in place:

> Through the "glass heart" [*das gläserne Herz*]. One of the most wonderful formations of our engineers: Somewhere—quite unnoticeable and hidden—it sits in the great body of the sender. And only a few engineers know that this miracle work of precision determines the second-by-second pulse of the giant. In the case of Berlin, for example, 841,000 hertz. (118)

The glass heart keeps the "body" temperature uniform on the inside. Its renaming by the Americans has stuck, but one has to hand it to them that they were the first to understand how to use the German invention in radio. It is called the superheterodyne receiver or, for short, the superhet: it creates out of two waves a third or new wave (123). The Theremin musical instrument (which supplies the sound effects of so many horror and sci fi movies) is constructed on the basis of this wave procreation.

Then there's ultrashort wave, six to ten meters in wavelength; as far as could be determined to date, these waves are not at all influenced by atmospheric disturbances. But then there are other disturbing factors, brand-new ones that are sparked, for example, by the ignition charges of passing cars and planes. The boy wonders if one couldn't just keep on shortening the waves until the cessation of disturbances was achieved. But then, our instructor includes in the speculation, there might just as well appear new and as yet unknown factors of disturbance. He wants to make an example with light rays—but the boy loses it in amazement: What does light have to do with sound? It's all waves, my son, light too. What's the difference between visible or invisible, really? Light waves could under the right techno-conditions carry music or language. Ultrared rays already prove this wave character of light (146).

Engineers today are running a magic world. But technicians also need to follow an upbeat belief. "You are going to see a thousand wonders still, as a new, bigger miracle of technology ripens to completion: television!" (151). The didactic broadcast couple gets lost now in a crowd of voices. Imagine the Wireless Exhibition in the year 2000. The Seventy-seventh Great German Wireless Exhibition. Mechanical voices, cars and planes everywhere, endless subway trains, masses of visitors. But another voice comes on: "Foolishness! In 2000 there won't be a Wireless Exhibition anymore, just as there probably won't be theaters or cinemas. In the year 2000 the world will look somewhat different!" (152). The next science fantasy is just a keystroke away.

> "The television is coming on!"
> "For me?"
> "Blue light in the channel selector.... That is your identification color, isn't it?"
> "So, what is it?"
> "77th Great German Wireless Show!"
> "That's right. I tuned it in 6 days ago." (154)

But still there are boring plenary lectures and words of welcome. The viewer switches to Philadelphia and a cooking show. Then to Bangkok. Maybe there's a movie on worth watching. Even in this future, the TV user will have reason to wish he had been born 100 years later. Now *Sehnsucht* comes on strong, a yearning for the past, a past in which one could still look forward to the wonders that were coming soon. Because the wish to be born later can also give way to a sense that one has been born too late. We're back in 1924, the year of the first Wireless Exhibition. We can't really see the future, but we can see the past. We discover that we have been standing on a preamble to a full-on new section of the book entitled "The Steel

Voice." The didactic couple has disappeared. But a dynamic of teaching continues. Perhaps we readers are the unnamed charges. The book starts up again from scratch with the record on the gramophone. We're back with problems of disposal of waste and loss. "Loudspeakers are better heaters than they are generators of sound" (186). The *Sehnsucht* for a secret sharer in living, loving, and suffering (in German they're the three Ls) will be stilled when "sounds from wherever—invisible and untouchable—waft your way. When a small voice sings for you and speaks. Only a steel voice. A bit of cardboard—some metal. Just a loudspeaker" (191). Soon talk about record grooves gives way to the "singing tape" (196). "Let us cut a small piece away from any old sound film. We see the image and next to it a narrow tape ... the audio strip. ... At least as mysterious as the oddly winding curves of the record" (196). "One has often and seriously attempted to create a new 'gramophone' on the basis of sound film" (199). The singing tape, while available in the labs, has not yet been introduced into the market. It's just too expensive, complicated, sensitive. "Anyway, the idea is good, and maybe the film-gramophone will happen just the same" (199). On the next page we read a forecast, down to the magnetic details, of the tape that would in fact be Nazi Germany's postwar legacy to Hollywood and the world, the tape called in 1935, in this book of wonders, "the singing tape" (200). This tape packs a conserving moment, a span of retention. Neither the live transmission nor the conserving aspect will lose anything. The conserved sound simply gets reanimated. Nineteen thirty-five is then given as the date of the introduction of magnetic audiotape that marks an improvement over the waves (203). Records and sound films now have rivals, at least within the institution of broadcasting. An imaginary figure asks, Why can't one just forbid feedback? The answer: "This whistling of the feedback is right now the highest virtue of the medium."

That the protagonist in the movie *Contact* (Arroway is her name) becomes an astronautics expert—and ultimately an astronaut—is shown to grow out of childhood years of death cult radio service together with her instructive dad across long distances traversing the mother's missingness. The film's title also refers, it turns out, to the aliens' first contact with us through the first major electronic output on earth, the live coverage of the 1936 Berlin games. Between the lines of the television transmission received up and above and returned to earth, the aliens have encoded plans for building the rocket that will take a representative of earthlings (this would be Arroway) way away to an outer space encounter with aliens first contacted by the medium, not the message, of Nazi Germany. Once there, contact has been mediated and personalized. Arroway finds herself inside a fantastic familiar sensurround of reunion with her long-dead dad on the beach. Between these lines that they give her (taken from her own science fantasy), the aliens transmit their message. Arroway has it all on tape. But when she's back, the tapes play back white noise, static, like the sound between radio stations, like the snow between TV channels. But all this noise, which fills the tapes the full real time Arroway claimed for her round-trip and not just for the moments the witnesses on earth were sure they had seen the mission abort, backfire, and knock Arroway unconscious, doubles as ghostly placeholder for the missing encounter, for contact with the missing.

After 1945 the magnetic tape made in Nazi Germany stole the audio show (immediately getting into pictures made in Hollywood, for example). At the same time, a relay of figures displaced by the events of World War II discovered what would be known as the Voice Phenomenon. Friedrich Jürgenson was the first to overhear in the noise of the tapes he left outside to record birdsong on their own ghostly attempts to make contact. His preferred medium source for noise to tape and decipher was soon the radio static that is out there without the identification of station. After rewinding and playing back their tapes, over and over again, operators of the Voice Phenomenon found they had opened up lines of communication in the first place with their own recently deceased friends and family (with mother always at the front of the line), but in close second place (and repeatedly) with the leading men of World War II, including notably Churchill, Hitler, Goebbels, and Jung.

If video and audio tape technology holds the place of live or undead transmissions which becomes especially apparent—a parent—when the record speaks for itself, then it is also the case that this evidence of the senses or extra-senses is inadmissible *as* evidence. Simulation and tampering can cut in—in the splitting of a second—right where ghostly voices get their break. Every transmission, tradition, or transference still coming down to us to this day passes through a phase of continuity and co-occupancy with National Socialism while at the same time admitting saving relations with psychoanalysis, the science of techno-mediation, doubling, and haunting.

But in 1935 Rhein introduces singing tape together with the whistling of its feedback on the upbeat as part and portrait of the future coming soon. As we too will soon see, even this wondrous future must admit by the end, in the transference, or rather in its transgression inside Oedipedagogical precincts, a psychic (or psychotic) (after)life.

We get the vision of an autopilot trip to New York. The ship climbs high like a rocket—to the stratosphere (205). It's time to go to the concert. There's a tentative plug for techno music, the kind produced by the *Elektron-*

ium. Our unnamed guide doesn't want to take a stand in the controversy over electrical musical instruments replacing those of our fathers. The latter, however, "are today dead. Souvenirs of long-ago submerged times" (206). The few who can still command the old techniques are asked to step up to the microphone. It's time to record it for memorial playback.

We're back in front of the tube. A gypsy violinist is on live transmission. One viewer finds the sound quite OK, but the instrument so awkward. The other viewer is transported: "Artist and instrument—he senses this clearly in this moment—are struggling now with passion, with ecstasy, to touch the chilling down heart of humanity" (206). Then the *Elektronium* is introduced. The announcer says the instrument will now reproduce the sounds of the violin you just heard. "But it isn't music. It is cold and dead." The elegant man at the controls starts to fine-tune the sound. After a few adjustments, the sound lives. The announcer: "We now know with which 'technical' effects the master violinists of the past produced, perhaps half unconsciously, their heart-breaking influence on the masses" (207). In the year 2000, one Nazi German raves on to the other one: "Oh just listen, listen! Get high on surrogates! Your children will prefer the Stradivari imitation to the real Stradivari" (208).

After this interlude we're up against the next section that was deferred by sound developments: "The Magic Mirror." We are introduced to this seeing-eye "brother of the 'blind' radio" (211). We're off and running now on electron rays. It's just like with the miracle of human vision. The eye doesn't see: it transmits the information to the brain, which raises it to consciousness. To this end, the visual information is broken down into dots (212). "It is as though the cells were made to oscillate through light contact. Much as the piano string vibrates with the stroke of the key" (216). The eye is slow. That is the secret to the success of motion pictures. Television goes one step further by joining vision in breaking down the visual information (218).

A German, Paul Nipkow, invented television. Fifty years ago! At a time when even the telephone was considered by the vast majority a superfluous plaything (219). He turns to the mosaic to solve the problem of transmission of an image. Isn't the mosaic in fact the law of our own vision? (220–21). The electric cell would see the whole image. Back to our problem. But then show it the image to be transmitted point by point, "just as the reading eye must grasp letter by letter" (223). But this pointillism must be performed mechanically. Nipkow conceives the round disc that covers the image to be transmitted except for what can be seen through a few holes. But what is the man in tele-city going to do with all these dots? He must store them in

The TV process attributed to Nipkow is demonstrated as the imaginary transmission of the *Mona Lisa:* an "electric eye" sees—takes in and takes apart—the image point by point, line by line. Reproduced from *Wunder der Wellen,* 223.

The complete picture of the *Mona Lisa*'s transmission according to Paul Nipkow's basic idea of TV. The painting is being read in "Here-village" and received in "Distant-" or "Tele-city." Reproduced from *Wunder der Wellen*, 227.

his memory and reassemble them after the last one has been transmitted. The slowness of the eye helps us out. If all the dots were shown in a split second, then none of the points of light would have time to be lost to the eye. "Memory and new perception flow into one another, forming bright points into a bright image" (228). All you need is two discs, one in here-city, the other in tele-city, and they just need to turn in synchrony. That's TV. Unfortunately the technology was not yet ready for this invention way back then, Christmas Eve 1883. What worked on paper had to wait another fifty years: 1933, the year of wonders.

There was no reliable light source that could keep up with the speed of the turning discs and maintain precision. The available lightbulbs were just too slow. In the meantime, film conquered the world. Then radio followed. Then the two were joined in sound film (232). In this same time, TV research was stuck on the mechanically driven parts. What was needed was something "like the amplifier tubes that worked without inertia and purely electrically" (233). Then one remembered that there was already just such a device that could be summoned to the rescue: the Braun tubes. They had been developed originally (also in the late nineteenth century) as highly sensitive instruments for measuring and registering data in research labs. By conveying "the miracle of invisible rays" that could be guided magnetically, these tubes picked up where the Nipkow discs were left behind in their mechanical tracks (238). These rays carrying the negative charge of electricity were electron rays, which could be guided and diverted. "A moving point of light, electrically guided here and there...Paul Nipkow—your idea has found a marvelous helper" (241).

For the time being, television is still dependent on between-film processing (264). But an American invention will soon get us past this vestigial

Another demo, this time with the proper name of the German inventor of television. First the mosaic is "transferred" by telephone. The next illustration shows the receiver at the other end of the line following the instructions "Line 13, number 9, a black stone." Reproduced from *Wunder der Wellen*, 220–21.

mediation. Dr. Zworykin developed his iconoscope on the basis of a notion of energy storage. It takes TV out of its sound film dependency and puts it in the home, in every home (266). The rise in the number of lines of visual information to be transmitted will soon overwhelm the mechanical "TV-eye." "The iconoscope with its five to ten million 'see-cells' has far greater reserves" (274). But now it is once again time for the Germans to be sent to

the front of the line: "Waves which were considered unusable just a few years ago have been conquered for television. Thanks to the diligence of German scientists" (275). The liveness of light waves, their on-off relationship to light (otherwise it would be day all day along), was turned around by Schröter to TV's advantage. Because long distance is not an option for light, one can reuse the same ultrashort waves an indeterminate number of times. "This reduces the danger that there would one day arise similar unfortunate conditions as was the case with radio waves" (276). In any event, "it would not have been possible to transmit the required number of points of light on longer waves" (278). The rapidity of TV impulses required special cable, and the first TV cable was laid in Berlin in 1934 (279).

We close our lessons with "A Glimpse into the Future." The TV image can be improved. It still emerges as though out of rings of smoke. And what about color? "What our grandparents could hardly hope to dream has been accomplished: submarine, airplane, radio, television" (297). Now these accomplishments need only to be perfected.

> Still slumbering in the oscillating wave are unguessed possibilities. Will it be possible one day to transmit power wirelessly, will the plane shooting past like lightning be able to seize its fuel through two thin short antenna wires? Will the speeding ship crossing the ocean be supplied with energy wirelessly from its home harbor? . . . Can electromagnetic waves build bridges one day to distant planets? (298)

The ultimate stopover of this perfectibility drive in future tense waves all the gadget-loving details through the psyche, which was therefore all along the endopsychic address of the book's dictation, taken down with schoolboy passion, of postmachinic inventions. In 2033 the professor announces his latest discovery to the packed lecture hall:

> Many of you know that for more than twenty years I have studied the anatomy of the psychoses. . . . I presupposed, in deliberate contradistinction to modern science, that all thought processes are manifestations of electrical frequencies. Where disturbances disrupt the development of thought, there had to be, according to my theory, disturbances of the normal frequency causing them. . . . I concluded furthermore: we have all experienced how a thought is simply suddenly wiped away. . . . As long as one presupposes that all thinking comes down to electromagnetic processes of frequency one can explain this momentary shutdown of the brain as the consequence of an external electrical disturbance. . . . Every brain "vibrates" in a different frequency. And for that reason we are not able to guess the thoughts of our fellow beings. Only very few people can somewhat alter their brain waves and thus tune in the thoughts of others. I tried to establish the "brain wave" of a six-year-old child. This wave was then— just as at the radio station—"modulated" with a particularly

simple melody. We transmitted this to the sleeping child.... When the child awoke there was a dream to tell. About a lovely melody.... And the child sang this never before heard melody!... This is the school of the future. One learns in one's sleep. And everyone learns—if he wants to or not. (300–302)

After one hundred years the Third Reich waves through wonders no longer Jewish at "heart." The hertz unit of frequency referred to the German Jewish scientist Heinrich Hertz, who discovered and formulated it. But official efforts to rename the unit in Nazi Germany kept on bouncing off the popular radio wave name. Like the Freud names, "hertz" had to be retained alongside all the Aryan synonyms within what was still, even on TV, a "mosaic" pattern. Brain modulation, then, skips the mosaic law of transference, and writing can transmit without reading. Wanting to or not wanting to need never again be raised—as question or as ghost. In other words, this science fantasy at the limit registers as full the level of psychoanalysis saturation in the 1935 world of wonder.

TV Services

In 1935 Göring, not Goebbels, was put in charge of the TV service, called, in its potentiality or totality, *Fernsehwesen* (which might be translated "TV essence" or "TV creature"). The führer's memo handing the authority over TV in the first place to the head of air transportation ("in consideration of the special importance of TV service for flight security and national air defense"), to be exercised in conjunction with the minister of the postal service, gave rise to a conflict between Göring and Goebbels, which prompted Hitler's addendum that same year. The entertainment value or channel of the new medium, which was handed over to the minister of popular enlightenment and propaganda, would be run in cooperation with the separate but equal channel, still in the hands of Göring's remote control, of air defense and flight security.

Soon the Third Reich started rerunning Paul Nipkow as father of television. (Nipkow's contribution in fact reduplicated the invention of a spiral technique that was already outmoded by an even earlier English discovery of pointillist breakdowns of the image into lines that could beam onto special screens that were also already in place, this time via a French invention that preceded Nipkow's patent and parental guidance.) Nipkow's 1883 preview of TV recombined the wrong preexisting component parts: in short, he was stuck on mechanical TV, which by 1935 had most definitely given way in theory and in practice to electronic TV. But the outmoded, ventriloquized, recycled loser, perfect placeholder of the missing father, was the ideal group mascot of an anti-Oedipal team effort. According to the fantasy of Nipkow's creation, it was his "yearning" to be with his family over the holidays that got him started. If he couldn't be with them, then if only, at least, he could see them "across rooftops and separating night" (in Reiss, 62). At last one could.

In 1937 a certain Ohnesorge, who was head of postal and telecommunications services in Nazi Germany, was without worry when he reported the completed installation of television-phone service between Berlin and Leipzig at the front of the many new lines in the planning. Keeping in touch will go where no language barrier has gone before: "[The TV image] speaks to everyone in the same language, is understood everywhere and works its effect somehow on all without any racial or educational difference. In one respect it surpasses even the mother tongue" (322).

The culture of live transmission marks the outer-limit concept of the photographic and cinematic media of haunting or transference. It marks the spot the psychotic used to be in, but out of which, by 1926, the fetishist gets himself: the fetishist gets around the requirements of mourning without getting stuck on melancholia. Freud reserves for fetishism what can be confirmed for TV: it covers wavelengths of oscillation between neurosis and psychosis.

Videophone service throughout the Reich was under development right up to the opening of the world war. This represented at the same time, by no default of its own, a postal investment in television. Videophone service was thus self-addressed via the post office of the other: the rights of privacy, confidentiality, or "postal secrecy" (*Postgeheimnis*) reintroduced the openness of transmissions across airwaves as a problem. Cable TV arose over this old postal issue. The cable network between cities expanded alongside the building of the *Autobahn* until, between Berlin and Nuremberg and Munich, the largest TV cabling system in the world could let roll. But there was next to no demand for the videophone service, and the public booths, nicknamed "coffins," were taken away after four more years were up. The High Command of the German army took and remade the network of so-called coffins, the supermen booths of the short-lived videophone service, as a military exclusive.

A really big state funeral was accorded Nipkow in 1940 (he was the first "humanist" to receive such an honor). The parting shot was broadcast live across the small private network and the larger chain of "TV rooms" open to the public. The Berlin Olympics in 1936 had already established a precedent for the live transmission of events. The intermediary stage of rapid film development, a vestigial organization belonging to mechanical or cinematic TV, could be skipped during the games. By 1936 TV was hailed as employing no mechanical moving parts whatsoever: the image was taken in, analyzed, and transmitted purely electrically. At that time Nipkow could be interviewed live outdoors rather than in the enclosed, encrypted studio space or darkroom that had framed earlier transmission attempts. In 1937 the transitional piece that could now be left out was analogized with the place of the LP in the course of audio technology (Reiss, 80). Also in 1937 there was another analogy, one that came from on high, between television and flying: in both instances, according to the Nazi official's line, we access the same unlimitedness that makes possible the conquest of the world (Reiss, 84). The yearning that TV captures is to overcome the limitations of the sensorium; that's why TV should be coupled first with artificial flight in the ongoing merger with automatic functioning. Computerization, which stilled the first hunger pangs of feedback that got the V-1 and V-2 rockets off the ground and flying on course, reintroduced into fantasies of autopilot the place held by man in the merger that's going through.

By 1937 the evolutionary program of the TV image, from uncanny smearing to the clearing in which one could at least (at last!) identify and identify with what was transmitted dead or live, was already up for documentation or review. It had indeed been a process of beaming up into another dimension intimated (in the context of crossover into the third one) within Masaccio's paintings, for example, where the torment, say, of the crucifixion shows us the transition we're undergoing, near missing the merger that's going through. TV torpedoes were on the drawing pads waiting to be launched alongside three-channel precision bombing by plane. At safe distances, the plane could launch the missile, which would keep on target through TV tracking of, and feedback from, the missile's flight course. With the aid of a follow-up surveillance bomb, the fact and effect of impact could be reported back for past and future reference. By spring 1943 the TV gadgetry for guided missiles was being serially produced (for use on planes and in tanks).

Already in 1938 the following rundown of points in support of TV cable networking in wartime became part of the files of the ministry for postal service (on 29 April). Not only is TV a fast and secret message service between discrete points in the military chain of commandants, but augmented by the hard copy of photography, the clear images even of long texts are as quickly gone from the channel of transmission, thereby throwing off the following of espionage, from encoding to decoding (and back again).

Following the recentering of the cable network for the contexts and stations of the war effort from 1939 onward, the TV rooms that were still open (and by 1939 they admitted as many as three hundred people per show, now that the screen image was viewable from the side, too) informed audiences about the progress of the war with station breaks for entertainment and instruction (including the first exercise classes on TV). The infotainment values of TV reception were soon monopolized for the ideological healing of the war wounded (there were special shows for the wounded and also by the wounded for the wounded) and for steeling the nerves of munitions workers. While TV was being fine-tuned increasingly for its restricted use in military communications and control, public broadcasting was reserved until 1942 for the gadget lovers of war just in off the street and thereafter exclusively for the war wounded and the Hitler youths.

The authorities were frustrated by the TV room audiences who appeared stuck on a residual cinematic desire for amusement (instead of the rapt, therapeutic contemplation of the technical developments of television that was the how-to of Nazi guidance) that inevitably admitted the stow-away threat of contamination. Nazi TV guides or leaders monitored the audiences watching in the TV rooms. While the audience was being checked out, TV camera technology was able, by 1938, to go candid: TV could now film outdoors on location and seek out for human-interest broadcasts "suitable sacrifices," as the professional jargon goes, on the streets of Berlin or, out in the country, among the Hitler Youth volunteers who were also the targeted viewers of most broadcasts. Audience surveillance always gets syndicated as audience participation in their own viewing, their own being viewed. In 1938 the candid TV began loading search bulletins for special broadcast down the tube. A raincoat found at the scene of one murder was shown in detail to produce witnesses and give the immediate audience not so much a scare as a time-share in surveillance. Gadget-loving attention to the military details of self-observation was thus not the only request from the audience served up in the TV rooms, open since 1938 until midnight. The streamlining of TV in the course or service of healing in groups along the lines of mutual surveillance or identification was, however, also always in danger of disruption by the specters of untreatability still emanating from the postal or cinematic past. The following report, submitted and filed away on 11 February 1937, fills in, with a well-armed bulletin, the blanks in the stare, in the air, of the surveillance:

> According to earlier observations it appears as though in part it's always the same people who show up regularly in the TV rooms, people who are less interested in being informed about the latest state of television than in finding there a cheap place of amusement and source of warmth. Thus it was observed in one TV room among other things that a certain Jewish tradesman with his dirty sack attended not only one show but both broadcasts. In this way however other citizens are denied access to the TV rooms or their stay there is compromised. (in Reiss, 85)

A Couple More Drags

Nazi psychotherapy had come under the protective, projective wings of the air ministry not only because Göring's cousin, who was also a Luftwaffe officer, was in charge of the Berlin psychotherapy institute. The technicians and clinicians saw the future of air war, and it prescribed, one, psychotherapeutic lubing of the pilot's merger with the automatic functioning of his flying machine and, two, group therapy down in the air-raid shelters to give psychological preparation and protection where air defense would inevitably leave off giving flak to the enemy. The plane, the bomb shelter, the group therapy session, the TV room: these are the interchangeable articulations of one new techno-space.

This airspace of surveillance can't make it out of a certain family packaging of live reception; in size it cannot exceed an extended or reunion family format in which all of us in attendance really are in this together again. But it's a space that cannot hold the monumental breakdown, the before *and* the after, of discrete identifications; it's where all-out healing allows everyone to blend in. Except those passing specters of untreatability and contamination. In Berlin it was the uncanniness, the homelessness of a leftover Jew in front of the new group tube; California in-flight it's the smoke screen of a formerly projective arrangement of risk that can now only contaminate the personal space of the group's sharing and caring.

In other words or worlds, the "TV" in rooms and bars stands for "transvestism." The audience at the "TV" show can either flip between or segregate two channels: one, improv nightmare, shows the cuts and sutures of a projective pastime stretch-marking the body of the queen dragging on a cigarette; two, perfect imposture, has everyone fooled by what's the difference between a woman onstage and this man. From California in-flight to New York City on TV, it's the smoke of crossing over from the projective repast that fills and pollutes the airwaves of live transmission.

What was once the drag of mourning loses the "trans-," the cross it bore, to a ghostless, smoke-free channeling beyond the death wish (or pleasure principle). But in the office of accident—of the other—TV almost killed Hitler before his time was up (the time that was set aside for his suicide). Right after Hitler had walked through the TV room at the big annual techno-exhibit in Berlin in 1939, the set imploded. It was another near miss articulating the National Socialist share in one big psy fi fantasy.

In the Wolf Man case, Freud looks into the compulsion to breathe out in the face of evil-eye types (cripples and the like) (*SE*, 17:66–67). Freud charges his heavy breather with having transformed what was, in the beginning, a benign identification with father (the kind belied by caricatures, for example, which are always drawn against father to give a jumpy-jerky lube to the identification) into a malignant identificatory blockage filled with terror of contamination. But it's still ambivalent, it still has hidden mascot and jerk-off status, because the anonymous call of breathing puts the one with the hangup somewhere near his father's place at the time of the primal scene. Repression, finally, turns heavy breathing into the expiration of spirit or life turning into the death wish rebound of evil spirits or demons. Fear of breathing in contaminants that are mixed on the downside of ambivalence joins vegetarianism and teetotalism as the hit brands (they were Hitler's!) of refuse, refusal, re-fusing of all relations with the dad. Once when Freud invited Jung to down spirits with him, the dutiful disciple, who was a nondrinker, started babbling on about recently disinterred mummies. Freud fainted dead away, in the drop scene of identification with a missing brother. In the stations of identification crossed by Freud and Jung, father was nowhere to be found. It was a murderous peer relationship consummated over an undead brother. It was the split-level family relation that always reactivated within every instance of Freud's most fateful form of misappropriation or mispronunciation: friendship.

The residual caricature assignation underlying Wolf Man's heavy breathing promises transference compatibility. (Freud lists Wolf Man's empathy bonding with the Jews around the cut of circumcision as one of the ingredients of this father-bound, rebounding ambivalence.) Until the end of World War I, Hitler too was a regular jerk. In his unit he was everyone's bro, mutually identifiable as one of them, but with an application in for mass mascot. "Despite his lectures on the evils of smoking and drinking, 'Adi' was generally liked because of his reliability in a crisis" (Toland, 65). Hitler's father, an abuser whose job security and family values depended on the maintenance of good boundaries between Austria and Germany, was annexed and nixed as part of the package deal of his son's mergers and murders. *Anschluss!* (Gesundheit!)

The trauma of World War I shell shock was the last withdrawal that broke the bank of paternal guilt currency. Toward the close of the war, Hitler was blinded by gas attack; shortly after he recovered his eyesight, Germany's surrender gave him a blinding flashback. He had the hallucinatory vision of Mother Germany, who was also calling him, reversing the charges, putting him in charge of restoring all losses to her undead body. Within the year that followed, every thought crossing his mind completed itself in the new system of his anti-Semitism (Toland, 70).

Up in Smoke

Three cigarettes on one strike of a match, and you're out: that's the black-out etiquette that began in the trenches of World War I. In the corner of every group-sizing and lab-spacing of human subjects promoted by the total wars (beginning with the American Civil War), we can follow the bouncing butt of the by now triumphant no-smoking campaign that has been waged most effectively or symptomatically in the air, across the airwaves of our home set, our family-formatted receptions. Looking down the double barrel of Nazi German investments in air power and TV, we find ourselves again in the claustrophobic space of not smoking. But by now in California, we are not smoking in exchange for stakes that are life or death in strict adherence to the deferral or installment plan Freud developed by the end of World War I as his thesis of the death drive.

Dragging on cigarettes once belonged to an era of the other, where health and fatal illness were at fixed-front face-off rather than, as now, in interface. In the era of smoking, channels could still be crossed in a show of resistance. It *was* mythic thinking that originally led the jogger to run for his life, to run in exchange for more life. Now everyone has or will have a deadline (from, say, adolescence on), a terminal case that *can* be deferred in its outcome by running for recovery.

With AIDS, the psy fi passion play of replication versus reproduction beams up across the one body that's to die for. AIDS strikes down the body's own self-replicating resources of antibody building while spinning off cancer (the disease of replication's nonmetabolization that's paced nonstop in all the wrong places) as side effect. Between cancer and AIDS, we're arriving or surviving at the living end, free of smoke and spirits. The live transmissions of drugs, techno-media, and AIDS have by now gone beyond the point of return: the body's projective wiring is over and out. Never before was Freud's death drive thesis more right on. The death drive, the life insurance policy of groups, exchanges the horror movie and death wish static of so-called natural death for the preparations already going down in all of us, together with our inner and outer machines, for our live or life's transmission up to death. There's a fantasy of immortality along for this drive.

The *Titanic* Conference, held the year following the unthinkable event of the ship's passing into nothingness, did not go down with the sinking feeling that the invincibility or immortality fantasies brought to us by technology were false advertising. Instead it was determined that if the wireless networks were always on live transmission, the SOS signals back then would have summoned rescue efforts in time for the saving. Now a technology-compatible law, a form of insurance, could be issued: all radios on deck must remain on at all times. That was just the beginning. Ever since, we've been staying tuned. AIDS is the millennial sign or symptom of global live transmission. The myths at its origin put through the most fantastic connections. The first diseased transmitter was an airplane steward; the first "case" was that of a Norwegian sailor and his family.

The end is now a given, right from the start, a diagnosis or verdict that's cureless but open to the deferral strategies of recovery. Soon we'll be too busy living with our deadlines to comparison shop mourning and melancholia for our dead others. But while there are still those among us who, for the time being, must die, near missing some new low-maintenance drug or any of our other techno-prospects for immortality now, and while we in this same interim period of still surviving the other continue to catch ourselves in the draw between mourning and melancholia, we cannot but sign off, if only for now: No Smoking and No Substitutions, Please.

References

Adler, Alfred. *Cooperation between the Sexes: Writings on Women, Love and Marriage, Sexuality and Its Disorders.* Ed. and trans. H. L. Ansbacher and R. R. Ansbacher. Garden City: Anchor Books, 1978.

Adorno, Theodor W. "Freudian Theory and the Pattern of Fascist Propaganda." In *Gesammelte Schriften.* Ed. Rolf Tiedemann. Frankfurt a/M: Suhrkamp Verlag, 1972 [1951]. 8: 408–33.

———. *Minima Moralia: Reflexionen aus dem beschädigten Leben.* Frankfurt a/M: Suhrkamp Verlag, 1971.

———. "Zum Verhältnis von Soziologie und Psychologie" [On the Relationship between Sociology and Psychology]. In *Gesammelte Schriften* 8. Ed. Rolf Tiedemann. Frankfurt a/M: Suhrkamp Verlag, 1972 [1955]. 8: 42–92.

Alexander, Franz, and Gerhard J. Piers. "Psychoanalysis." In *Progress in Neurology and Psychiatry,* ed. E. A. Spiegel. Vol. 2. New York: Grune and Stratton, 1947.

Alexander, Franz G., and Sheldon T. Selesnick. *The History of Psychiatry: An Evaluation of Psychiatric Thought and Practice from Prehistoric Times to the Present.* New York: Harper and Row, 1966.

Anderson, Charles. "On Certain Conscious and Unconscious Homosexual Responses to Warfare." *Yearbook of Psychoanalysis* 1 (1945 [1944]): 215–36.

Angell, James Rowland. "Radio and National Morale." *American Journal of Sociology* 47, no. 3 (November 1941): 352–59.

Appel, John W. "Current Trends in Military Neuropsychiatry." *American Journal of Psychiatry* 101 (July 1944): 12–19.

Arato, Andrew, and Eike Gebhardt, eds. *The Essential Frankfurt School Reader.* New York: Continuum, 1985.

Arsenian, Jean. "Young Children in an Insecure Situation." *Journal of Abnormal and Social Psychology* 38, no. 2 (April 1943): 225–49.

Atkinson, James David. *The Edge of War.* Chicago: H. Regnery, 1960.

Balmer, Edwin, and Philip Wylie. *When Worlds Collide.* 1932; Philadelphia: Lippincott, 1950.

Bateson, Gregory, ed. *Perceval's Narrative: A Patient's Account of His Psychosis, 1830–1832.* Stanford: Stanford University Press, 1961.

———. *A Sacred Unity: Further Steps to an Ecology of Mind.* Ed. Rodney E. Donaldson. New York: Harper Collins, 1991.

———. Section of Psychology (18 January 1943). *Transactions of the New York Academy of Sciences,* ser. 2, vol. 5, no. 1 (November 1943): 72–78.

———. *Steps to an Ecology of Mind.* San Francisco: Chandler, 1972.

Beck, Walter. "Zum Panik Problem." *Soldatentum* (1937): 296–306.

Benjamin, Walter. "Das Kunstwerk im Zeitalter seiner technischen Reproduzierbarkert" [The Work of Art in the Age of Mechanical Reproduction]. *Gesammelte Schriften* 1, no. 2 (1980 [1936]): 435–508.

———. "Über einige Motive bei Baudelaire" [On Some Motifs in Baudelaire]. *Gesammelte Schriften* 1, no. 2 (1980 [1939]): 605–53.

———. "Was ist das epische Theater?" [What Is Epic Theater?]. *Gesammelte Schriften* 2, no. 2 (1980): 532–39.

Bettelheim, Bruno. *The Empty Fortress: Infantile Autism and the Birth of the Self.* New York: Free Press, 1967.

Bjerre, Andreas. *The Psychology of Murder: A Study in Criminal Psychology.* Trans. E. Classen. London: Longmans, Green, 1927.

Bjerre, Poul. *Psychosynthese.* Stuttgart: Hippokrates Verlag, 1971.

———. *The Remaking of Marriage: A Contribution to the Psychology of Sex Relationship.* Trans. T. H. Winslow. New York: Macmillan, 1931.

———. "Spökerier." Stockholm: Centrum, 1947.

———. *Das Träumen als Heilungsweg der Seele: Systematische Diagnose und Therapie für die ärztliche Praxis.* Zurich and Leipzig: Rascher Verlag, 1936.

———. *Unruhe, Zwang, Angst.* Munich: Kindler, 1968.

Bossard, James H. S. "Family Problems in Wartime." *Psychiatry* 7, no. 1 (February 1944): 65–72.

Brady, Robert A. *The Spirit and Structure of German Fascism.* London: Victor Gollancz, 1937.

Brauchle, Alfred. "Seelische Beeinflussung in der Gemeinschaft." *Münchener medizinische Wochenschrift* 87 (1940): 317–20.

Braun, Wernher von, et al. *Conquest of the Moon.* New York: Viking Press, 1953.

Braun, Wernher von, and Willy Ley. *The Exploration of Mars.* New York: Viking Press, 1956.

Brecht, Karen, et al., eds. *"Here life goes on in a most peculiar way . . ." Psychoanalysis before and after 1933.* Trans. Christine Trollope. Hamburg: Kellner Verlag, 1985.

Bresler, J. "Geisteskrankheit als Kampf" [Mental Illness as Combat]. *Psychiatrisch-Neurologische Wochenschrift* 46 (1940): 466–69.

———. "Gibt es nationale Psychotherapie?" [Does National Psychotherapy Exist?]. *Psychiatrisch-Neurologische Wochenschrift* 2 (1940): 12–14.

Brill, A. A. "Various Schools of Psychotherapy." *Connecticut State Medical Journal* 7, no. 8 (August 1943): 530–36.

Brosin, Henry W. "The Unfit: How to Use Them." *Psychosomatic Medicine* 5, 4 (October 1943): 342–63.

Burdekin, Katherine. *Swastika Night.* 1937; London: Lawrence and Wishart, 1985.

Burgess, Anthony. *The Wanting Seed.* 1962; New York: Ballantine, 1970.

Burgum, Mildred. "The Fear of Explosion." *American Journal of Orthopsychiatry* 14, no. 2 (April 1944): 349–57.

Burlingame, C. Charles. "A Psychiatrist Looks at War and Peace." *Connecticut State Medical Journal* 7, no. 7 (July 1943): 476–81.

Butler, Samuel. *Erewhon.* 1872; New York: Limited Editions Club, 1934.

Caidin, Martin. *Ghosts of the Air—True Stories of Aerial Hauntings.* New York: Bantam, 1991.

Canning, Peter. "Here Comes the Sun." *Qui Parle* 2, no. 1 (1988): 70–76.

Culpin, Millais. "Mode of Onset of the Neuroses in War." In *The Neuroses in War,* ed. Emanuel Miller. New York: Macmillan, 1940.

Daly, C. D. "A Psychological Analysis of Military Morale." *Army Quarterly* 32 (1936): 59–75.

Daumann, R. H. *Dünn wie eine Eierschale* [Thin as an Eggshell]. Berlin: Schützen-Verlag, 1937.

Deleuze, Gilles, and Félix Guattari. *Anti-Oedipus: Capitalism and Schizophrenia*. Trans. Robert Hurley et al. Minneapolis: University of Minnesota Press, 1983.

Derrida, Jacques. "No Apocalypse, Not Now (Full Speed Ahead, Seven Missiles, Seven Missives)." Trans. Catherine Porter and Philip Lewis. *Diacritics* (summer 1984): 20–31.

———. "Fors: The Anglish Words of Nicholas Abraham and Maria Torok." Trans. Barbara Johnson. Foreword to *The Wolfman's Magic Word*, by Nicholas Abraham and Maria Torok, trans. Nicholas Rand. 1976; Minneapolis: University of Minnesota Press, 1986.

Döblin, Alfred. *Berge Meere und Giganten* [Mountains, Oceans, and Giants]. 1924; Olten and Freiburg: Walter-Verlag, 1977.

———. *Berlin Alexanderplatz: Die Geschichte von Franz Biberkopf.* 1929; Olten/Freiburg im Breisgau: Walter-Verlag, 1961.

———. *Drama, Hörspiel, Film.* Olten: Walter-Verlag, 1983.

———. *Giganten: Ein Abenteuerbuch* [Giants: A Book of Adventure]. Berlin: S. Fischer, 1932.

———. *Hamlet: Oder die lange Nacht nimmt ein Ende* [Hamlet, or The Long Night Comes to an End]. 1956; Olten/Freiburg im Breisgau: Walter-Verlag, 1966.

———. *November 1918.* 4 vols. 1939; Munich: Deutscher Taschenbuch Verlag, 1978.

———. *Wallenstein.* 1920; Olten/Freiburg im Breisgau: Walter-Verlag, 1965.

Dominik, Hans. *Atlantis.* Leipzig: Ernst Keils Nachfolger (August Scherl), 1925.

———. *Atomgewicht 500* [Atomic Weight 500]. In *König Laurins Mantel; Atomgewicht 500.* 1935; Munich: Universitas, 1980.

———. *Der Befehl aus dem Dunkel* [Command from Out of the Darkness]. 1932; Munich: Wilhelm Heyne, 1973.

———. *Der Brand der Cheops Pyramide* [The Burning of the Cheops Pyramid]. Berlin: Verlag Scherl, 1927.

———. *Das Erbe der Uraniden* [Legacy of the Uranites]. 1935; Berlin: Verlag Scherl, 1943.

———. *Himmelskraft* [Power of the Heavens]. Berlin: Verlag Scherl, 1937.

———. *John Workmann, Der Zeitungsboy* [John Workmann, the Newsboy]. 1909; Leipzig: Koehler and Amelang, 1925.

———. *Kautschuk* [Rubber Latex]. 1930; Berlin: Verlag Scherl, 1942.

———. *König Laurins Mantel* [King Laurin's Cloak]. In *König Laurins Mantel; Atomgewicht 500.* 1928; Munich: Universitas, 1980.

———. *Land aus Feuer und Wasser: Ein klassischer utopisher Roman* [Land of Fire and Water: A Classical Utopian Novel]. 1939; Munich: W. Heyne, 1982.

———. *Lebensstrahlen* [Life Rays]. Berlin: Verlag Scherl, 1938.

———. *Die Macht der Drei: Ein Roman aus dem Jahre 1955* [The Power of Three: A Novel of the Year 1955]. Leipzig: Scherl, [1922].

———. *Vom Schraubstock zum Schreibtisch* [From Bench Vise to Writing Desk]. Berlin: Verlag Scherl, 1942.

———. *Die Spur des Dschingis-Khan: Ein Roman aus dem einundzwanzigsten Jahrhundert* [The Trace of Ghengis Khan: A Novel of the Twenty-first Century]. Leipzig: E. Keils Nachfolger (A. Scherl), 1923.

———. *Das stählerne Geheimnis* [The Steel Secret]. Berlin: Verlag Scherl, 1934.

———. *Ein Stern fiel vom Himmel* [A Star Fell from the Sky]. Leipzig: Koehler and Amelang, 1934.

———. *Treibstoff SR* [Fuel SR]. Berlin: Verlag Scherl, 1940.

———. *Vistra, Das weisse Gold Deutschlands: Die Geschichte einer weltbewegenden Erfindung* [Vistra, the White Gold of Germany: The History of an Invention That Moved the World]. Leipzig: Koehler and Amelang, 1936.

———. *Der Wettflug der Nationen* [The Air Race of the Nations]. Leipzig: Koehler and Amelang, 1933.

———, ed. *Welten/Werke/Wunder: Ein Buch des Wissens für das deutsche Haus* [Worlds/Works/Wonders]. Berlin: Universitas, 1926.

Drayer, Calvin S., and Stephen W. Ranson. "Combat Psychiatry." *Bulletin of the U.S. Army Medical Department* 4, no. 1 (July 1945): 91–96.

Eichacker, Reinhold. *Panik.* Munich: Universal Verlag, 1924.

Eissler, K. R. "The Efficient Soldier." *Psychoanalytic Study of Society* 1 (1960): 39–97.

———. *Freud as an Expert Witness: The Discussion of War Neuroses between Freud and Wagner-Jauregg.* Madison, Conn.: International Universities Press, 1986.

———. *Goethe: A Psychoanalytic Study, 1775–1786.* Vol. 1. Detroit: Wayne State University Press, 1963.

Endres, Franz Carl. "Vom nächsten Krieg." *Archiv für Sozialwissenschaft und Sozialpolitik* 59 (1928): 48–74.

Epp, Karl. "Paniken und ihre Vermeidung." *Militärwissenschaftliche Mitteilungen* 10 and 11 (1937): 783–99, 876–84.

Erikson, Erik Homburger. *Childhood and Society.* New York: W. W. Norton, 1950.

Ewers, Hanns Heinz. *Horst Wessel: Ein deutsches Schicksal.* Stuttgart and Berlin: J. G. Cotta'sche Buchhandlung Nachfolger, 1932.

Farago, Ladislas, ed. *German Psychological Warfare: Survey and Bibliography.* New York: Committee for National Morale, 1941.

Farrell, Malcolm J., and John W. Appel. "Current Trends in Military Neuropsychiatry." *The American Journal of Psychiatry* 101 (1944): 12–19.

Fenichel, Otto. *Rundbriefe.* 23 January 1941–15 March 1943. Bancroft Library. University of California–Berkeley. Collection number 88/2z.

Fox, Henry. "Neurotic Resentment and Dependence Overseas." *Bulletin of the U.S. Army Medical Department* 4, no. 5 (November 1945): 131–38.

———. "A Variety of Furlough Psychosis." *Psychiatry* 7, no. 3 (August 1944): 207–13.

Freud, Sigmund. "Der Humor." In *Studienausgabe,* ed. Alexander Mitscherlich, Angels Richards, and James Strachey. Vol. 4. 1927; Frankfurt a/M: Fischer Verlag, 1970.

———. *The Standard Edition of the Complete Psychological Works.* Ed. James Stachey. London: Hogarth Press, 1953–1974. Cited in the text as *SE.*

Fritzsching, Leonhard. "Der seelische Zustand von Soldaten vor der Gefangennahme." *Soldatentum* (1939): 221–36.

Fromm-Reichmann, Frieda. *Psychoanalysis and Psychotherapy: Selected Papers.* Ed. Dexter M. Bullard. Chicago: University of Chicago Press, 1959.

Frosch, John. "The Psychiatric Patient in a Wartime Community." *American Journal of Orthopsychiatry* 14, no. 2 (April 1944): 321–24.

Gardner, George E., and Harvey Spencer. "Reactions of Children with Fathers and Brothers in the Armed Forces." *American Journal of Orthopsychiatry* 14, no. 1 (January 1944): 36–43.

Gillespie, R. D. *Psychological Effects of War on Citizen and Soldier.* New York: W. W. Norton, 1942.

Goebbels, Joseph. *Michael: Ein deutsches Schicksal in Tagebuchblättern.* Munich: Zentralverlag der NSDAP, Franz Eher Nachf, 1929.

Goethe, Johann Wolfgang von. *Briefe aus der Schweiz.* In *Goethes Werke,* vol. 19. 1796; Weimar: Hermann Böhlau, 1894.

———. *Dichtung und Wahrheit* [Poetry and Truth]. In *Goethes Werke,* vols. 9–10. 1811–1814; Hamburg: Christian Wegner Verlag, 1955–1959.

———. *Die Leiden des jungen Werther* [The Sorrows of Young Werther]. In *Goethes Werke,* vol. 6. 1774; Hamburg: Christian Wegner Verlag, 1951.

———. *Römische Elegien* [Roman Elegies]. In *Goethes Werke,* vol. 1. 1790; Hamburg: Christian Wegner Verlag, 1948.

———. *Der Triumph der Empfindsamkeit* [The Triumph of Sentimentality]. In *Goethes Werke,* vol. 17. 1777; Weimar: Hermann Böhlau, 1894.

Goette, A. *Über den Ursprung des Todes.* Hamburg, 1883.

Goldenberg, E. "Das Wissen vom Gegner." *Soldatentum* (1938): 259–63.

Goldstein, Kurt. "On So-Called War Neuroses." *Psychoanalytic Medicine* (1943): 376–83.

Grinker, Roy R., and John P. Spiegel. *Men under Stress.* Philadelphia: Blakiston, 1945.

———. *War Neuroses in North Africa: The Tunisian Campaign (January–May 1943).* Air Surgeon Army Air Forces. New York: Josiah Macy, 1943.

Hale, Nathan G., Jr. *The Rise and Crisis of Psychoanalysis in the United States: Freud and the Americans, 1917–1985.* Vol. 2, *Freud in America.* New York: Oxford University Press, 1995.

Hall, Stanley. *Adolescence: Its Psychology.* 1904; New York: Appleton, 1924.

———. "Christianity and Physical Culture." *Pedagogical Seminar* 9 (September 1902).

———. "Practical Relations between Psychology and the War." *Journal of Applied Psychology* 1 (1917).

Harbou, Thea von. *The Rocket to the Moon.* Trans. Baroness von Hutten. New York: Worldwide Publishing, 1930. [*Frau im Mond,* 1930.]

Hattingberg, Hans von. "Ehekrisen ärztlich gesehen." *Deutsche medizinische Wochenschrift* 66 (1940): 909–12.

———. "Zur Entwicklung der analytischen Bewegung (Freud, Adler, Jung)." *Deutsche Medizinische Wochenschrift* 59 (1933): 328–33.

"Health Improvement in Design of American Planes." *Connecticut State Medical Journal* 7, no. 3 (March 1943): 197–98.

Heims, Steven Joshua. *The Cybernetics Group*. Cambridge: MIT, 1991.

Henderson, J. L., and Merrill Moore. "The Psychoneuroses of War." *Military Surgeon* 95 (November 1944): 349–56.

Hesse, Kurt. *Der Feldherr Psychologos: Ein Suchen nach dem Führer der deutschen Zukunft*. Berlin: E. S. Mittler and Sohn, 1922.

Heyer, G. R. "Aus der Psychotherapeutischen Praxis: Eine Folge von Briefen." The forty-three letters cited in the present volume of *Nazi Psychoanalysis* originally appeared in the journal *Hippokrates*, vols. 12–38, between 21 March 1940 and 15 September 1943.

Hoffmann, E. T. A. "Der Sandmann" [The Sandman]. *Nachtstücke*. In *Poetische Werke*. 1817; Berlin: Walter de Gruyter & Co., 1957.

Hohman, Leslie B. "Rehabilitation of Veterans." In *Progress in Neurology and Psychiatry*, ed. E. A. Spiegel. Vol. 2. New York: Grune and Stratton, 1947.

Huxley, Aldous. *Brave New World*. 1932; New York: Harper and Row, 1960.

Jacobson, Edith. *Depression: Comparative Studies of Normal, Neurotic, and Psychotic Conditions*. New York: International Universities Press, 1971.

———. "Observations on the Psychological Effect of Imprisonment on Female Political Prisoners." In *Searchlights on Delinquency*, ed. K. R. Eissler. New York: International Universities Press, 1949.

———. *The Self and the Object World*. New York: International Universities Press, 1964.

Jaensch, E. R. "Die Psychologie und die Wandlungen des deutschen Idealismus." In *Gefühl und Wille*, ed. Otto Klemm. Jena: Verlag von Gustav Fischer, 1937.

Jung, C. G. "After the Catastrophe." In *Civilization in Transition*. Trans. R. F. C. Hull. 1945; New York: Pantheon, 1964.

———. *Flying Saucers: A Modern Myth of Things Seen in the Skies*. Trans. R. F. Hull. 1958; Princeton: Princeton University Press, 1978.

———. "The Meaning of Psychology for Modern Man." *Civilization in Transition* (1933): 134–56.

———. "The Stages of Life." In *Modern Man in Search of a Soul*, trans. Cary F. Baynes. New York: Harcourt Brace Jovanovich, 1933.

———. "The State of Psychotherapy Today." *Civilization in Transition* (1934): 157–73. ["Zur gegenwärtigen Lage der Psychotherapie." *Zentralblatt für Psychotherapie* 7 (1934): 1–16.]

———. "Wotan." *Civilization in Transition* (1936): 179–93.

Jünger, Ernst. *Copse 125: A Chronicle from the Trench Warfare of 1918*. London: Chatto and Windus, 1930. Translation of *Das Wäldchen 125* (1926).

Kardiner, Abram. *The Traumatic Neuroses of War*. New York: Paul B. Hoeber, 1941.

Kardiner, Abram, and Herbert Spiegel. *War Stress and Neurotic Illness*. New York: Paul B. Hoeber, 1947. [Revised edition of *The Traumatic Neuroses of War*.]

Kellermann, Bernhard. *Der Tunnel*. Berlin: S. Fischer, 1913.

Kelman, Harold. "Character and the Traumatic Syndrome." *Journal of Nervous and Mental Disease* 102 (1945): 121–53.

Kennedy, Foster. "Nervous Conditions following Accident with Special Reference to Head Injury." *The Practitioners Library of Medicine and Surgery* 9 (1936): 439–74.

Kittler, Friedrich. *Grammophon—Film—Typewriter.* Berlin: Brinkmann and Bose, 1986.

Kittler, Wolf. "Stay Tuned—to Immaculate Conceptions." To appear in *On the Genealogy of Media,* ed. Laurence Rickels.

Kracauer, Siegfried. *From Caligari to Hitler: A Psychological History of German Film.* Princeton: Princeton University Press, 1947.

———. *Propaganda and the Nazi War Film.* New York: Museum of Modern Art Film Library, 1942.

Krauskopf, Alfred A. "Tiefenpsychologische Beiträge zur Rassenseelenforschung." *Rasse* 5 (1939): 362–68.

Kris, Ernst. *Psychoanalytic Explorations in Art.* New York: Schocken, 1974.

Kubie, Lawrence S. "The Drive to Become Both Sexes." In *Symbol and Neurosis: Selected Papers of Lawrence S. Kubie,* ed. Herbert J. Schlesinger. New York: International Universities Press, 1978.

———. "Manual of Emergency Treatment for Acute War Neuroses." *War Medicine* 4 (1943): 582–98.

———. "The Organization of a Psychiatric Service for a General Hospital." *Psychosomatic Medicine* 4, no. 3 (July 1942): 252–72.

Künkel, Fritz. "Seelenheilkunde." *Süddeutsche Monatshefte* 33 (1936): 294–300.

Kupper, William H. "Observations on the Use of a Phonograph Record of Battle Sounds Employed in Conjunction with Pentothal in the Treatment of Fourteen Cases of Severe Conversion Hysteria Caused by Combat." *Journal of Nervous and Mental Disease* 105 (1947): 56–60.

Lasswitz, Kurd. *Two Planets.* Trans. Hans H. Rudnick. Carbondale: Southern Illinois University, 1971. A translation of the 1969 edition, abridged by Erich Lasswitz.

———. *Auf zwei Planeten.* 1897; Leipzig: Verlag von B. Elischer Nachfolger, 1908.

Lewin, Kurt. "The Special Case of Germany." *Public Opinion Quarterly* (winter 1943): 555–66.

Lindner, Robert. *The Fifty-Minute Hour: A Collection of True Psychoanalytic Tales.* 1954; New York: Bantam, 1966.

Lorand, Sandor. "Psychoanalytic Investigation of Reaction to the War Crisis of Candidates for Induction." In *Clinical Studies in Psychoanalysis.* New York: International Universities Press, 1950.

Lurie, Louis, and Florence Rosenthal. "Military Adjustment of Former Problem Boys." *American Journal of Orthopsychiatry* 14, no. 3 (July 1944): 400–405.

Lyotard, Jean-François. "Can Thought Go On without a Body?" In *The Inhuman: Reflections on Time,* trans. Geoffrey Bennington and Rachel Bowlby. Stanford: Stanford University Press, 1991.

Maskin, Meyer H., and Leon L. Altman. "Military Psychoanalysis: Psychological Factors in the Transition from Civilian to Soldier." *Psychiatry* 6, no. 3 (August 1943): 263–69.

Meier, Norman C. *Military Psychology.* New York: Harper, 1943.

Meier-Welcker, ———. "Gedanken über Gehorsam." *Soldatentum* (1938): 68–73.

Menninger, William C. "Modern Concepts of War Neuroses." *Yearbook of Psychoanalysis* 3 (1947): 227–42.

———. "Psychiatry and the Army." *Psychiatry* 7, no. 2 (May 1944): 175–81.

Metz, Paul. "Die Eignung zum Flugzeugführer als Anlagenproblem." *Zeitschrift für Psychologie* 143 (1938): 12–14.

———. "Funktionale und charakterologische Fragen der Fliegereignung." *Zeitschrift für angewandte Psychologie*, supplement, 72 (1936): 153–72.

———. "Die Orientierung beim Fliegen." In *Gefühl und Wille*, ed. Otto Klemm. Jena: Verlag von Gustav Fischer, 1937.

———. "Die Prüfung der Fl.-Orientierungsfähigkeit." *Soldatentum* (1935): 302–10.

Mohr, Fritz. "Aus der Praxis der Psychotherapie." *Medizinische Klinik* 42 (1917): 1116–19.

———. "Die Behandlung der Kriegsneurosen." *Therapeutische Monatshefte* 30 (1916): 131–40.

———. "Einige Betrachtungen über Wesen, Entstehung und Behandlung der Homosexualität." *Zentralblatt für Psychotherapie* 15, nos. 1–2 (1944): 1–20.

———. "Friedrich Nietzsche als Tiefenpsychologe und Künder eines neuen Arzttums." *Leibniz, Carus und Nietzsche als Vorläufer unserer Tiefenpsychologie*. Special issue edited by Rudolf Bilz. *Zentralblatt für Psychotherapie* (1941): 47–66.

———. "Grundsätzliches zur Kriegsneurosenfrage." *Medizinische Klinik* 121 (1916): 89–93.

———. "Das Leib-Seele-Problem (vom Standpunkt des Psychotherapeuten aus)" [The Body-Soul Problem (from the Point of View of the Psychotherapist)]. *Münchener Medizinische Wochenschrift* 86 (1939): 61–64.

———. "Zur Entstehung, Vorhersage und Behandlung nervöser und depressiver Zustandsbilder bei Kreigsteilnehmern." *Medizinische Klinik. Wochenschrift für praktische Ärzte* 22 (1915): 607–10.

Mowrer, O. H. "Educational Considerations in Making and Keeping the Peace." *Journal of Abnormal and Social Psychology* 38, no. 2 (April 1943): 174–82.

Müller, Ronald. *Beate Uhse: Vom Mut einer Frau*. Schwedt: Kiro Verlag, 1994.

Murphy, Gardner. "Psychology in the Making of Peace." *Journal of Abnormal and Social Psychology* 38, no. 2 (April 1943): 132–40.

Murray, John M. "Psychiatric Aspects of Aviation Medicine." *Psychiatry* 7, no. 1 (February 1944): 1–7.

Needles, William. "The Successful Neurotic Soldier." *Bulletin of the U.S. Army Medical Department* 4, no. 6 (1945): 673–82.

Oberth, Hermann. "My Contributions to Astronautics." In *First Steps toward Space*. AAS History Series, vol. 6. San Diego, Calif.: American Astronautical Society, 1985.

Oelrich, Winkler von. "Zum Panik-Problem." *Soldatentum* (1937): 291–96.

Ohnesorge, ———. "Das Fernsehen—Möglichkeiten und Erreichtes." *Welt-Rundfunk: Ständige Beilage zur Zeitschrift für Geopolitik* 4, no. 2 (1937): 321–23.

Olinick, Stanley L., and Maurice R. Friend. "Indirect Group Therapy of Psychoneurotic Soldiers." *Bulletin of the U.S. Army Medical Department* 4, no. 5 (1945): 147–53.

Orwell, George. *1984*. 1949; New York and London: Signet Classic, 1992.

Peil, Hellmut. "Über die Hysterie: Ein Beitrag zur Krise der Medizin." *Volksgesundheitswacht* 2 (1935): 4–7.

"Pennsylvania Psychiatrist Talks on Shell Shock." *Connecticut State Medical Journal* 7, no. 4 (April 1943): 274.

Pérignon, L. "Die psychologischen Grundlagen der Selbstschutzausbildung." *Soldatentum* 6 (1939): 299–305.

Pini, Udo. *Leibeskult und Liebeskitsch. Erotik im Dritten Reich.* Munich: Klinkhardt and Biermann, 1992.

Pynchon, Thomas. *Gravity's Rainbow.* New York: Viking Press, 1973.

Rado, Sandor. "Pathodynamics and Treatment of Traumatic War Neurosis (Traumatophobia)." *Psychoanalysis of Behavior: Collected Papers.* New York/London: Grune & Stratton, 1956 [1942].

Rathenau, Walther. "Die Resurrection Co." In *Gesammelte Schriften.* 1898; Berlin: S. Fischer, 1918.

Reinartz, Eugen G. "How the Flying Fighters' Doctor Is Made." *Connecticut State Medical Journal* 7, no. 12 (December 1943): 820–27.

Reiss, Erwin. *"Wir senden Frohsinn." Fernsehen unterm Faschismus.* Berlin: Elefanten Press Verlag, 1979.

Reitsch, Hanna. *Flying Is My Life.* Trans. Lawrence Wilson. New York: G. P. Putnam's Sons, 1954.

Rentschler, Eric. *The Ministry of Illusion: Nazi Cinema and Its Afterlife.* Cambridge: Harvard University Press, 1996.

Rhein, Eduard. *Wunder der Wellen: Rundfunk und Fernsehen dargestellt für Jedermann* [Wonder of the Waves: Radio and Television Presented for Everyman]. Berlin: Im Deutschen Verlag, 1935.

Ronell, Avital. *The Telephone Book: Technology—Schizophrenia—Electric Speech.* Lincoln: University of Nebraska Press, 1989.

Sachs, Hanns. "The Delay of the Machine Age." Trans. Margaret J. Powers. *Psychoanalytic Quarterly* 11, nos. 3–4 (1933): 404–24.

Schäffner, Wolfgang. "Der Krieg ein Trauma. Zur Psychoanalyse der Kriegsneurose in Alfred Döblins *Hamlet*." In *HardWar/SoftWar: Krieg und Medien 1914 bis 1945,* ed. Martin Stingelin and Wolfgang Scherer. Munich: Wilhelm Fink Verlag, 1991.

———. "Norm und Abweichung: Zur Poetologie psychiatrischen Wissens bei Alfred Döblin." Ph.D. diss., Munich: Ludwig-Maximilians-Universität.

Schenzinger, Karl. *Der Hitlerjunge Quex.* 1932; Berlin: Zeitgeschichte-Verlag, 1941.

Schmuck, L. "Wehrerziehung, Wehrmannschaft, Erbe der Front." *Soldatentum* (1939): 247–51.

Schöffler, Herbert. "Die Leiden des jungen Werther." In *Deutscher Geist im 18. Jahrhundert.* 1938; Göttingen: Vandenhoek and Ruprecht, 1956.

Schreber, Daniel Paul. *Memoirs of My Nervous Illness.* Ed and trans. Ida Macalpine and Richard A. Hunter. Cambridge: Harvard University Press, 1988.

Schultz, J. H. *Neurose, Lebensnot, Ärztliche Pflicht* [Neurosis, Life Crisis, Medical Duty]. Leipzig: Georg Thieme, 1936.

———. *Die seelische Gesunderhaltung* [Psychic Health Maintenance]. Berlin: E. S. Mittler and Sohn, 1942.

Shelley, Mary. *Frankenstein, or The Modern Prometheus*. 1818; New York: Signet Classic, 1965. Translation of third revised edition of 1831.

Sieg, Paul Eugen. *Detatom*. 1936; Berlin: Verlag Scherl, 1944.

———. *Südöstlich Venus* [Southeast of Venus]. Berlin: Verlag Scherl, 1940.

Simmel, Ernst. "Zweites Korreferat." *Zur Psychoanalyse der Kriegsneurosen* (1919): 42–60.

Soldan, George. *Der Mensch und die Schlacht der Zukunft* [Man and the Battle of the Future]. Oldenburg i. O.: Gerhard Stalling, 1925.

Spiegel, Herbert. "Psychiatric Observations in the Tunisian Campaign." *American Journal of Orthopsychiatry* 14, no. 3 (July 1944): 381–85.

Spielrein, Sabina. *Die Destruktion als Ursache des Werdens*. 1912; Tübingen: Edition Diskord, 1986.

Stierlin, Helm. *Adolf Hitler: A Family Perspective*. New York: Psychohistory Press, 1976.

———. *Psychoanalysis and Family Therapy: Selected Papers*. New York: Jason Aronson, 1977.

Stoker, Bram. *Dracula*. Westminster: Constable, 1897.

Strecker, Edward A. *Their Mothers' Sons: The Psychiatrist Examines an American Problem*. Philadelphia: J. B. Lippincott, 1946.

Sutton, D. G. "Psychology in Aviation." *United States Naval Medical Bulletin* 28 (1938): 5–13.

Szasz, Thomas Stephen. *The Therapeutic State: Psychiatry in the Mirror of Current Events*. Buffalo, N.Y.: Prometheus Books, 1984.

Taeschner, Titus. *Der Mars greift ein* [Mars Intervenes]. Leipzig: Wilhelm Goldmann Verlag, 1934.

Taiminen, Tero, Tuuli Salmenpera, and Klaus Lehtinen. "A Suicide Epidemic in a Psychiatric Hospital." *Suicide and Life-Threatening Behavior* 22, no. 3 (1992): 350–63.

Tausk, Victor. "Über die Entstehung des 'Beeinflussungsapparates' in der Schizophrenie." In *Gesammelte psychoanalytische und literarische Schriften*, ed. Hans-Joachim Metzger, 245–86. 1918; Vienna/Berlin: Medusa Verlag, 1983.

Taylor, Ronald, ed. *Aesthetics and Politics*. London: NLB, 1977.

Theweleit, Klaus. *Male Fantasies*. Vol. 1. Trans. Stephen Conway. Minneapolis: University of Minnesota Press, 1987.

Toland, John. *Adolf Hitler*. Garden City, N.Y.: Doubleday, 1976.

Tolman, Edward. "Identification and the Post-war World." *Journal of Abnormal and Social Psychology* 38, no. 2 (April 1943): 141–48.

U.S. Army. "Combat Psychiatry: Experiences in the North African and Mediterranean Theaters of Operation, American Ground Forces, World War II." *Bulletin of the U.S. Army Medical Department* 9, supplemental number (November 1949).

U.S. Army. *Neuropsychiatry in World War II*. Vol. 1, *Zone of Interior*. Washington, D.C.: Office of the Surgeon General, 1966.

U.S. Army. *Neuropsychiatry in World War II*. Vol. 2, *Overseas Theaters*. Washington, D.C.: Office of the Surgeon General, 1973.

U.S. Army. "Psychiatric Nomenclature." *Bulletin of the U.S. Army Medical Department* 4, no. 2 (August 1945): 134.

Villiers de L'Isle-Adam, Auguste. *L'Ève future*. 1886; Paris: Fasquelle, 1928.

Wagner, Gerhard. "Neue Deutsche Heilkunde" [New German Knowledge of Healing]. *Deutsches Ärzteblatt* 16 (18 April 1936): 419–21.

Watkins, J. G. *Hypnotherapy of War Neuroses*. New York: Ronald Press, 1949.

Weber, Samuel. "Introduction to the 1988 Edition." In *Memoirs of My Nervous Illness*, by Daniel Paul Schreber, ed. and trans. Ida Macalpine and Richard A. Hunter. Cambridge: Harvard University Press, 1988.

Weigert, Edith Vowinckel. "Women in Wartime: Disabilities and 'Masculine' Defense Reactions." *Psychiatry* 6, no. 4 (1943): 375–79.

Wells, H. G. *Experiment in Autobiography: Discoveries and Conclusions of a Very Ordinary Brain (since 1866)*. New York: Macmillan, 1934.

———. *The Time Machine*. 1895; Garden City, N.Y.: Dolphin/Doubleday, 1961.

———. *The War in the Air, and Particularly How Mr. Bert Smallways Fared While It Lasted*. London: G. Bell and Sons, 1908.

———. *War of the Worlds*. 1897; Garden City, N.Y.: Dolphin/Doubleday, 1961.

Werfel, Franz. *Star of the Unborn*. Trans. Gustave O. Arlt. New York: Viking Press, 1946.

Whitehorn, John. "Changing Concepts of Psychoneurosis in Relation to Military Psychiatry." *Research Publications Association for Research in Nervous and Mental Diseases* 25 (1946): 1–10.

Winter, Frank H. "Camera Rockets and Space Photography Concepts before World War II." In *History of Rocketry and Astronautics*. AAS History Series, vol. 8. San Diego, Calif.: American Astronautical Society, 1989.

Wuth, Otto. "Über den Selbstmord bei Soldaten" [On Suicide by Soldiers]. *Soldatentum* (1936): 84–90.

Wylie, Philip. *An Essay on Morals*. New York: Holt, Rinehart and Winston, 1951.

———. *Generation of Vipers*. New York: Farrar and Rinehart, 1942.

Wylie, Philip, and William W. Muir. *The Army Way: A Thousand Pointers for New Soldiers Collected from Officers and Men of the U.S. Army*. New York: Farrar and Rinehart, 1940.

Ziemer, Gregor. *Education for Death: The Making of the Nazi*. New York: Oxford University Press, 1941.

Zilboorg, Gregory. "Present Trends in Psychoanalytic Theory and Practice." *Yearbook of Psychoanalysis* 1 (1945): 79–84.

Filmography

Algol. Dir. Hans Werckmeister. Deutsche Lichtbildgesellschaft, 1920.

Casablanca. Dir. Michael Curtiz. Warner Bros., 1943.

Contact. Dir. Robert Zemeckis. Warner Bros., 1997.

Dr. Mabuse, der Spieler [Dr. Mabuse: The Gambler]. Dir. Fritz Lang. Uco-Film, 1922.

FP 1 antwortet nicht [FP 1 Does Not Answer]. Dir. Erich Pommer. Ufa, 1932.

Frau im Mond [Woman on the Moon]. Dir. Fritz Lang. Ufa, 1929.

Geheimnisse einer Seele [Secrets of a Soul]. Dir. G. W. Pabst. Neumann-Filmproduktion, 1926.

Germanin: Die Geschichte einer kolonialen Tat. Dir. M. W. Kimmich. Ufa, 1943.

Gold. Dir. Karl Hartl. Ufa, 1934.

Hitlerjunge Quex [Hitler Youth Quex]. Dir. Hans Steinhoff. Ufa, 1933.

Johnny Mnemonic. Dir. Robert Longo. Columbia Tristar, 1995.

Das Kabinett des Dr. Caligari [The Cabinet of Dr. Caligari]. Dir. Robert Wiene. Decla-Bioscope, 1919.

L.A. Story. Dir. Mick Jackson. TriStar Pictures, 1991.

Metropolis. Dir. Fritz Lang. Ufa, 1926.

Mrs. Miniver. Dir. William Wyler. MGM, 1942.

Münchhausen [The Adventures of Baron Münchhausen]. Dir. Josef Von Baky. Ufa, 1943.

Paracelsus. Dir. G. W. Pabst. Bavaria Filmkunst, 1943.

Random Harvest. Dir. Mervyn LeRoy. MGM, 1942.

Sieg in Westen. [Victory in the West]. Dir. Svend Noldan. Ufa, 1941.

Spellbound. Dir. Alfred Hitchcock. Selznick International Pictures, 1945.

Stukas. Dir. Karl Ritter. UFA, 1941.

Die Tausend Augen des Dr. Mabuse [The Thousand Eyes of Dr. Mabuse]. Dir. Fritz Lang. CCC Filmkunst, 1960.

Das Testament des Dr. Mabuse [The Testament of Dr. Mabuse]. Dir. Fritz Lang. Ufa, 1932.

Things to Come. Dir. William Cameron Menzies. London/United Artists, 1936.

The Time Machine. Dir. George Pal. MGM, 1960.

Total Recall. Paul Verhoeven. Carolco, 1990.

True Lies. Dir. James Cameron. Lightstorm, 1994.

Der Tunnel [Transatlantic Tunnel]. Dir. Kurt Bernhardt. Vandor Film, 1933.

Wunder des Fliegens [Miracle of Flight]. Dir. Heinz Paul. Reichsminister der Luftfahrt, General der Flieger, Hermann Göring, 1935.

Index

Laurence A. Rickels is professor of German and comparative literature at the University of California–Santa Barbara, and adjunct professor in the art studio and film studies departments. He is the author of *The Vampire Lectures* (Minnesota, 1999), *The Case of California* (Minnesota, 2001), and *Aberrations of Mourning*, and the editor of *Acting Out in Groups* (Minnesota, 1999). He is a therapist as well as a theorist and has appeared on the Web in this double capacity as Dr. Truth. He has also completed a series of "vampire screen texts."

Benjamin Bennett is the Kenan Professor of German at the University of Virginia. He is the author of many books, including *Theater as Problem: Modern Drama and Its Place in Literature* and *Beyond Theory: Eighteenth-Century German Literature and the Poetics of Irony*.